# VAMPIRE KNIGHT: MEMORIES
## Vol. 1
Shojo Beat Manga Edition

**STORY AND ART BY**
MATSURI HINO

**Adaptation**/Nancy Thistlethwaite
**Translation**/Tetsuichiro Miyaki
**Touch-Up Art & Lettering**/Inori Fukuda Trant
**Graphic Design**/Alice Lewis
**Editor**/Nancy Thistlethwaite

Vampire Knight memories by Matsuri Hino © Matsuri Hino 2016
All rights reserved. First published in Japan in 2016 by HAKUSENSHA,
Inc., Tokyo. English language translation rights arranged with
HAKUSENSHA, Inc., Tokyo.

Printed in the U.S.A.

Published by VIZ Media, LLC
P.O. Box 77010
San Francisco, CA 94107

10 9 8 7 6 5 4 3 2 1
First printing, August 2017

Matsuri Hino burst onto the manga scene with her title
*Kono Yume ga Sametara* (When This Dream Is Over), which
was published in *LaLa DX* magazine. Hino was a manga artist
a mere nine months after she decided to become one.

With the success of her popular series *Captive Hearts*,
*MeruPuri* and *Vampire Knight*, Hino is a major player in the
world of shojo manga.

Hino enjoys creative activities and has commented that
she would have been either an architect or an apprentice to
traditional Japanese craftsmasters if she had not become a
manga artist.

Shojo Beat

VAMPIRE
KNIGHT
MEMORIES

VOLUME
1

STORY & ART BY
Matsuri Hino

# The Story of VAMPIRE KNIGHT

## Previously...

Yuki Cross, Zero Kiryu and Kaname Kuran attended the prestigious Cross Academy, which divided students into either the Day Class for humans or the Night Class for vampires. The academy sought to advance coexistence between humans and vampires. Yuki and Zero loved each other, but Yuki had to part ways with him when it was revealed that she was the pureblood vampire princess of the Kuran family. Kaname decided on his own to turn Yuki back into a human. He gave his pureblood vampire heart that would become the new Ancestor Metal, a substance used in the weapons of vampire hunters to kill vampires. Most vampires were eliminated, but the remaining few chose to peacefully coexist with humans. Kaname slept in a coffin of ice created by Aido... And after a thousand years, Yuki gave her heart to bring Kaname back from his sleep. What happened during those years of Kaname's slumber will now be revealed...

## CHARACTERS

### YUKI CROSS

The adopted daughter of the headmaster of Cross Academy. She is a pureblood vampire and the princess of the noble Kuran family. She has always adored Kaname, even when she did not have her memory.

## KANAME KURAN

A pureblood vampire and the progenitor of the Kurans. He is Yuki's fiancé and was raised as her sibling. He knows Yuki's true identity and cares for her...

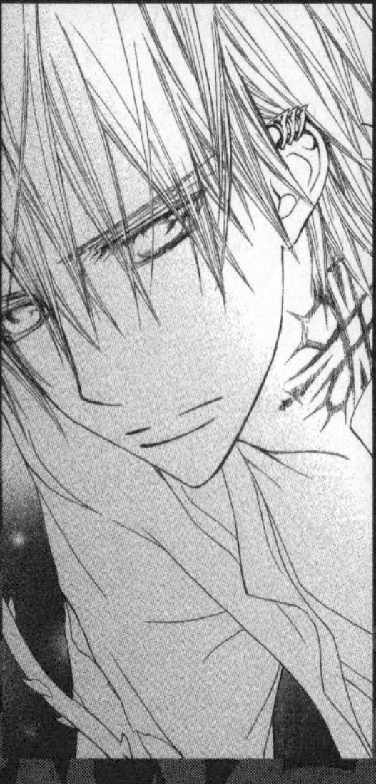

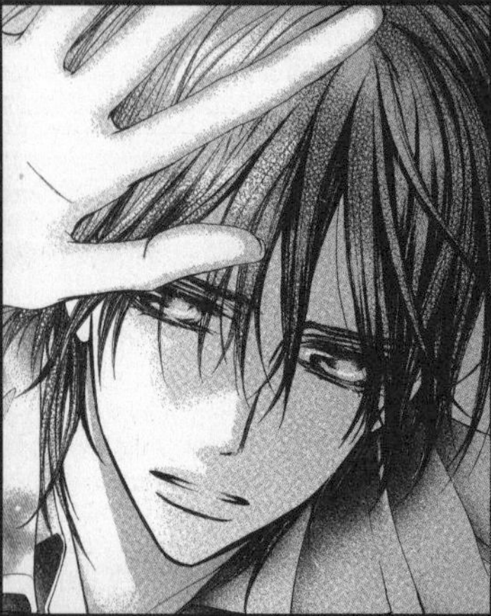

## ZERO KIRYU

He was born into a family of vampire hunters and later was turned into a vampire. His parents were killed by a pureblood. He has agonized over his feelings for Yuki and his role as a vampire hunter.

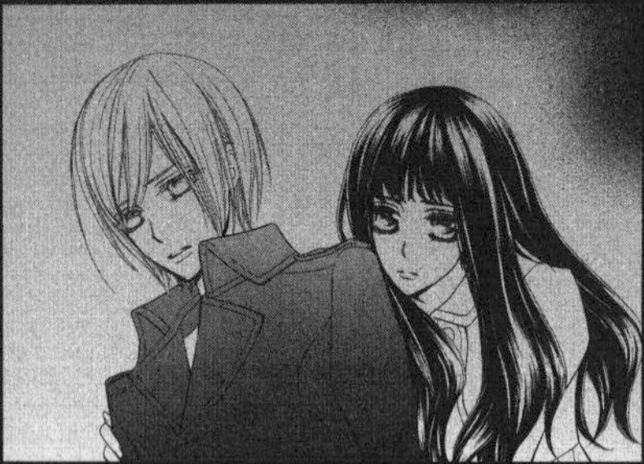

## REN AND AI

Yuki's children

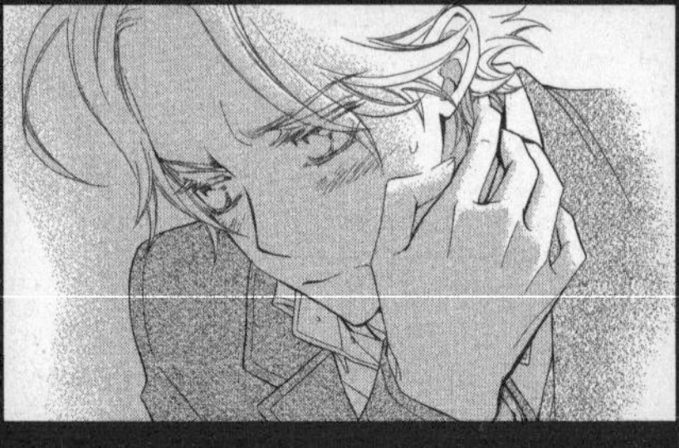

## HANABUSA AIDO

He was an upperclassman in the Night Class. He is working to create a medicine that will turn vampires into humans...

# VAMPIRE KNIGHT
## MEMORIES

## CONTENTS

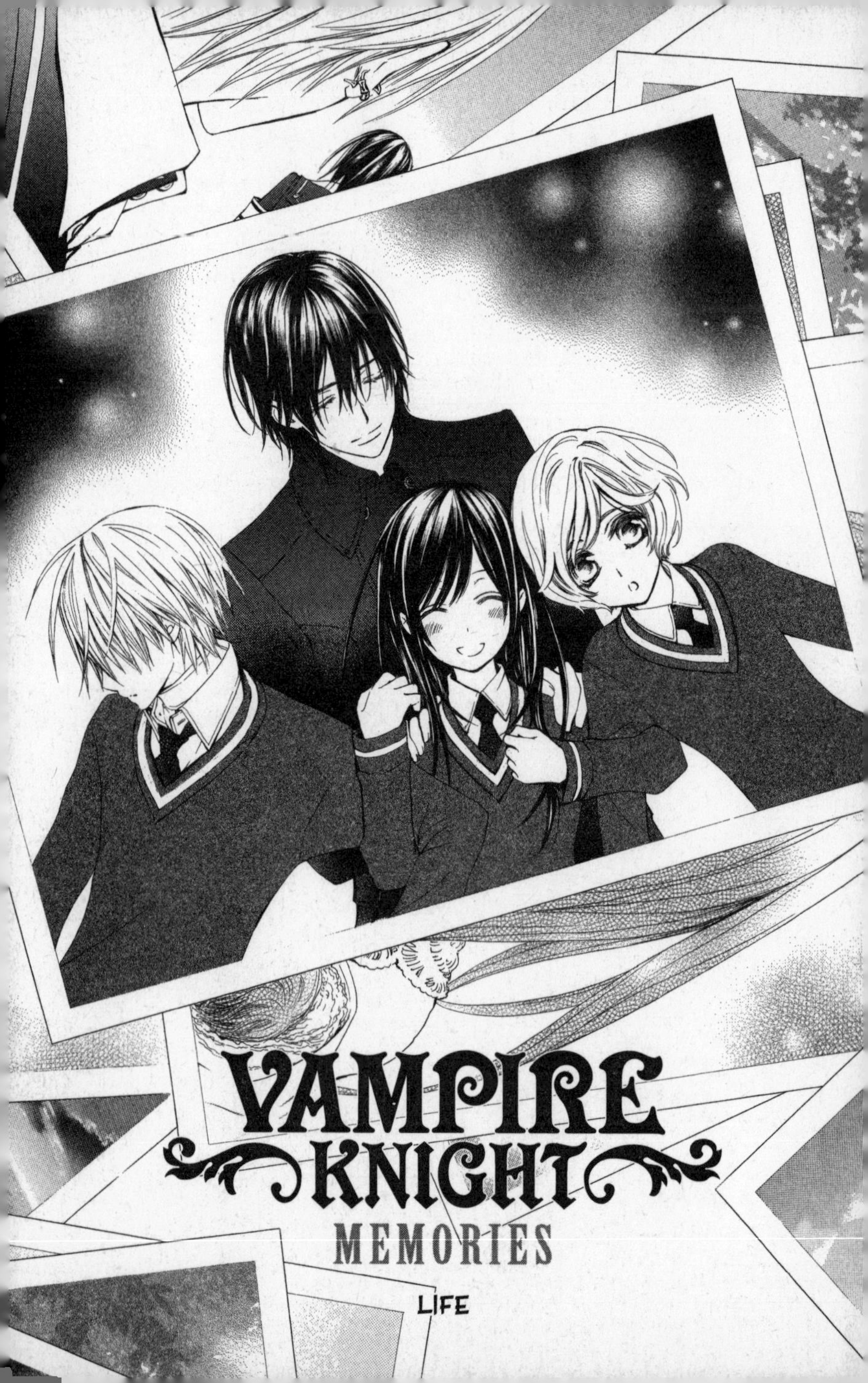

# VAMPIRE KNIGHT
## MEMORIES

LIFE

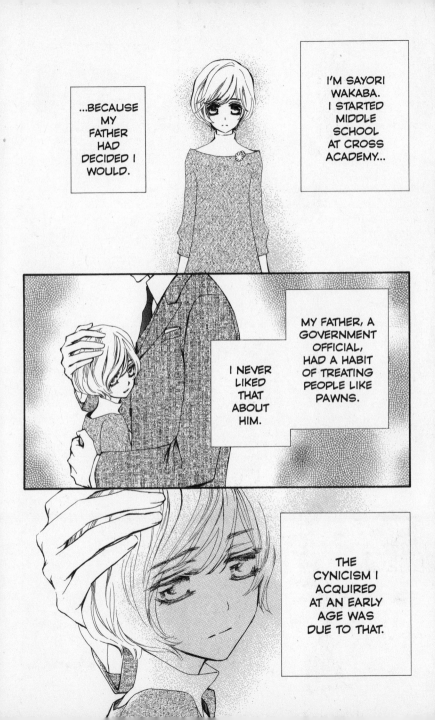

I'M SAYORI WAKABA. I STARTED MIDDLE SCHOOL AT CROSS ACADEMY...

...BECAUSE MY FATHER HAD DECIDED I WOULD.

MY FATHER, A GOVERNMENT OFFICIAL, HAD A HABIT OF TREATING PEOPLE LIKE PAWNS.

I NEVER LIKED THAT ABOUT HIM.

THE CYNICISM I ACQUIRED AT AN EARLY AGE WAS DUE TO THAT.

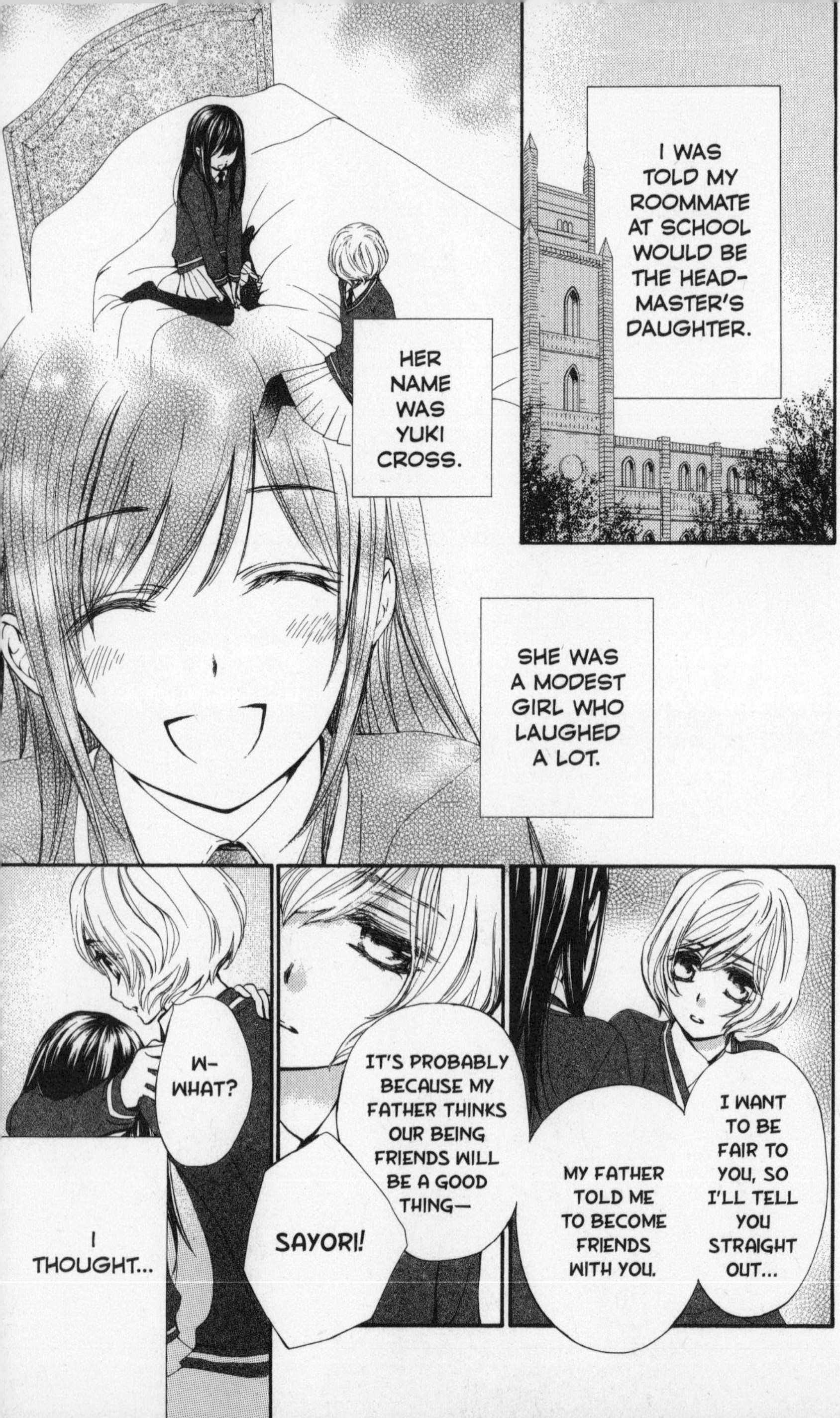
I WAS TOLD MY ROOMMATE AT SCHOOL WOULD BE THE HEAD-MASTER'S DAUGHTER.
HER NAME WAS YUKI CROSS.
SHE WAS A MODEST GIRL WHO LAUGHED A LOT.
I WANT TO BE FAIR TO YOU, SO I'LL TELL YOU STRAIGHT OUT...
MY FATHER TOLD ME TO BECOME FRIENDS WITH YOU.
IT'S PROBABLY BECAUSE MY FATHER THINKS OUR BEING FRIENDS WILL BE A GOOD THING—
SAYORI!
W-WHAT?
I THOUGHT...

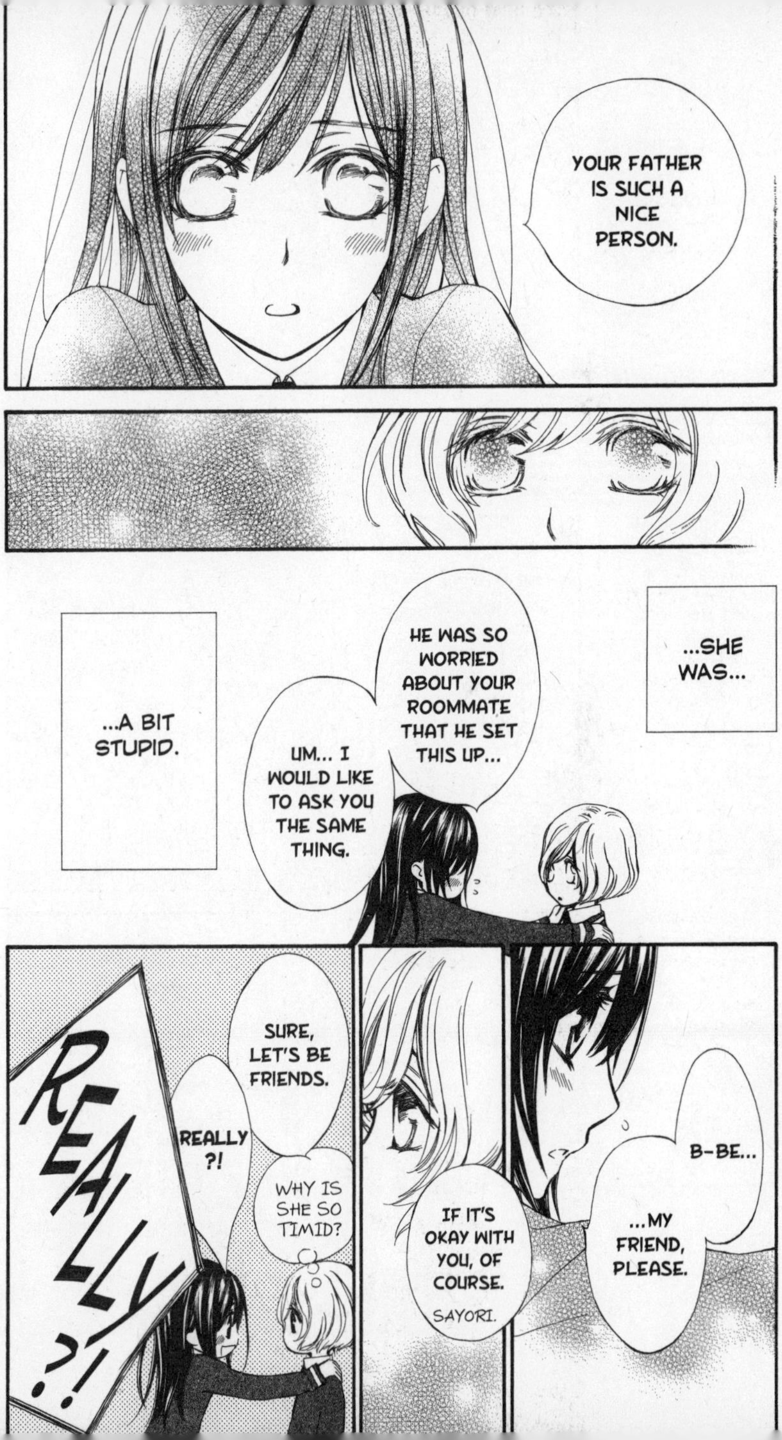
YOUR FATHER IS SUCH A NICE PERSON.
...SHE WAS...
HE WAS SO WORRIED ABOUT YOUR ROOMMATE THAT HE SET THIS UP...
UM... I WOULD LIKE TO ASK YOU THE SAME THING.
...A BIT STUPID.
B-BE...
...MY FRIEND, PLEASE.
IF IT'S OKAY WITH YOU, OF COURSE.
SAYORI.
SURE, LET'S BE FRIENDS.
REALLY?!
WHY IS SHE SO TIMID?
REALLY?!

## -1-

Vampire Knight: Memories Volume 1

Thank you very much for picking up this volume.

This is a compilation of stories that were published in *LaLa Fantasy* and *LaLa DX* at various times.

Even though these are one-shots, thanks to your support I was able to continue them. (And I'm indebted to Hakusensha...)

And now these special chapters will continue in *LaLa DX* as the new series *Vampire Knight: Memories*...!

*Vampire Knight* was made into a theatrical play in 2015, and this new series was yet another big surprise for me.

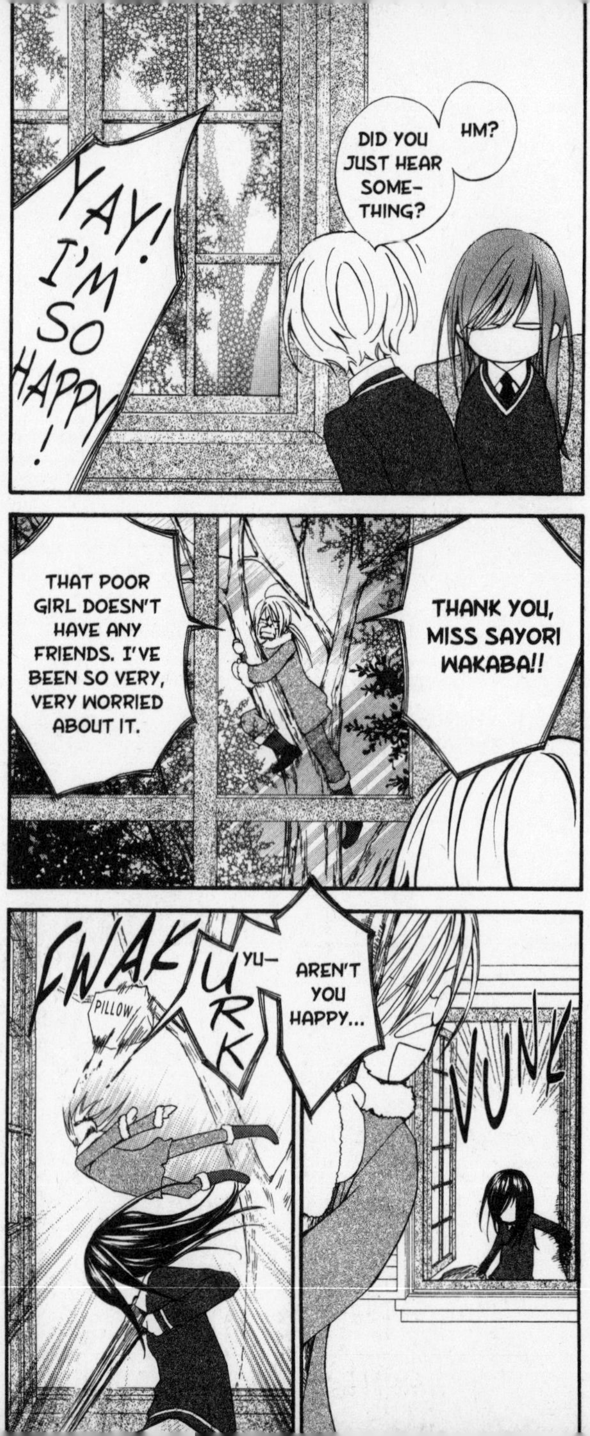
HM?
DID YOU JUST HEAR SOME-THING?
YAY! I'M SO HAPPY!
THANK YOU, MISS SAYORI WAKABA!!
THAT POOR GIRL DOESN'T HAVE ANY FRIENDS. I'VE BEEN SO VERY, VERY WORRIED ABOUT IT.
AREN'T YOU HAPPY...
YU—
URK
FWAK
PILLOW
VUNK

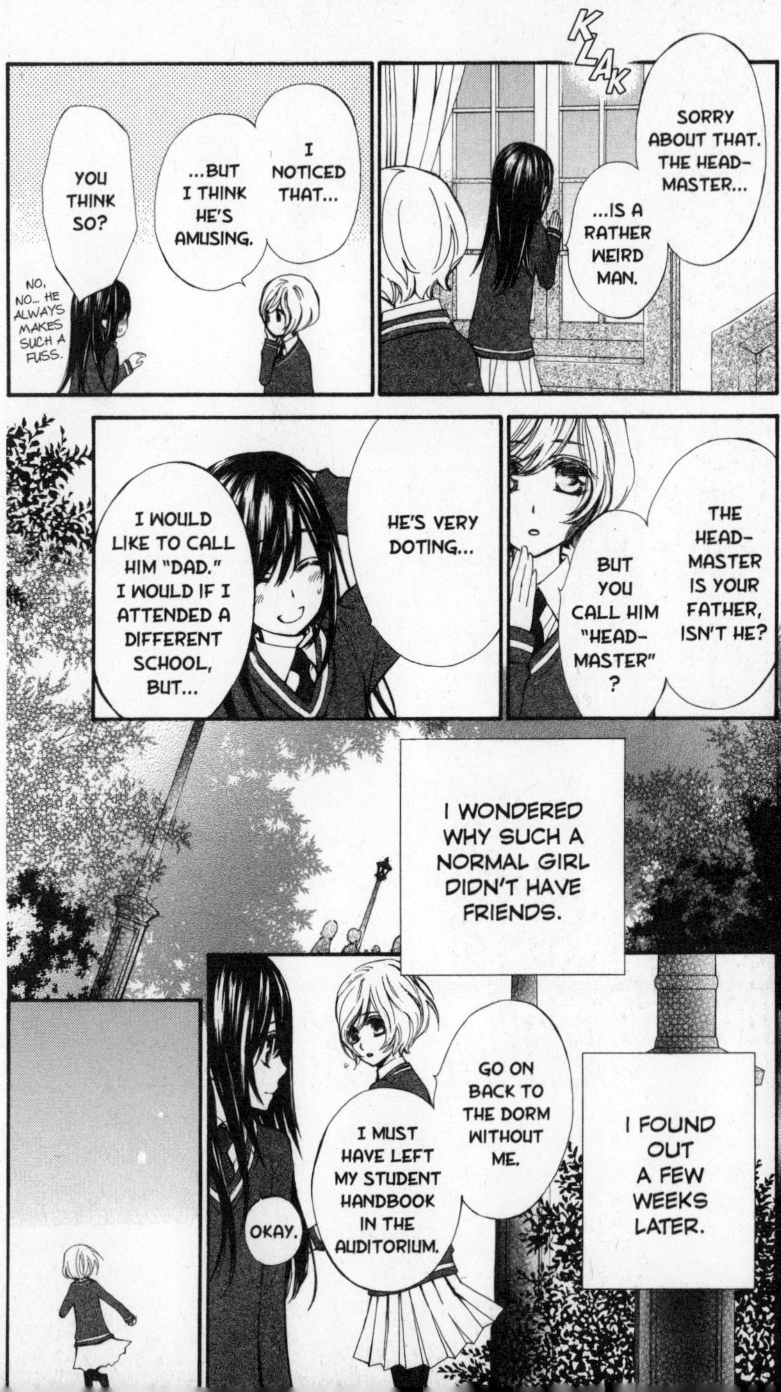
KLAK
SORRY ABOUT THAT. THE HEAD-MASTER...
...IS A RATHER WEIRD MAN.
I NOTICED THAT...
...BUT I THINK HE'S AMUSING.
YOU THINK SO?
NO, NO... HE ALWAYS MAKES SUCH A FUSS.
THE HEAD-MASTER IS YOUR FATHER, ISN'T HE?
BUT YOU CALL HIM "HEAD-MASTER"?
HE'S VERY DOTING...
I WOULD LIKE TO CALL HIM "DAD." I WOULD IF I ATTENDED A DIFFERENT SCHOOL, BUT...
I WONDERED WHY SUCH A NORMAL GIRL DIDN'T HAVE FRIENDS.
I FOUND OUT A FEW WEEKS LATER.
GO ON BACK TO THE DORM WITHOUT ME.
I MUST HAVE LEFT MY STUDENT HANDBOOK IN THE AUDITORIUM.
OKAY.

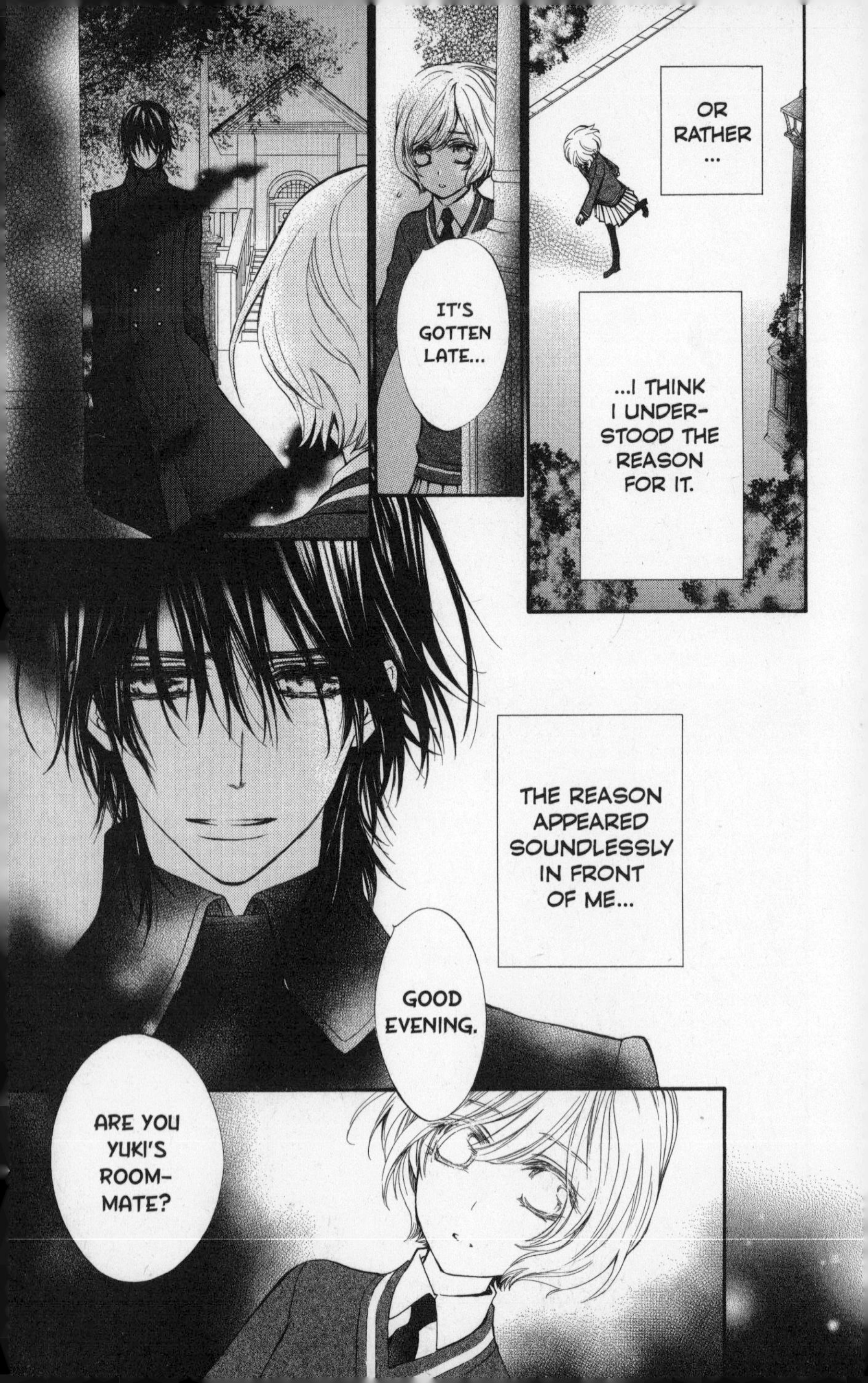
OR RATHER ...
...I THINK I UNDERSTOOD THE REASON FOR IT.
IT'S GOTTEN LATE...
THE REASON APPEARED SOUNDLESSLY IN FRONT OF ME...
GOOD EVENING.
ARE YOU YUKI'S ROOMMATE?

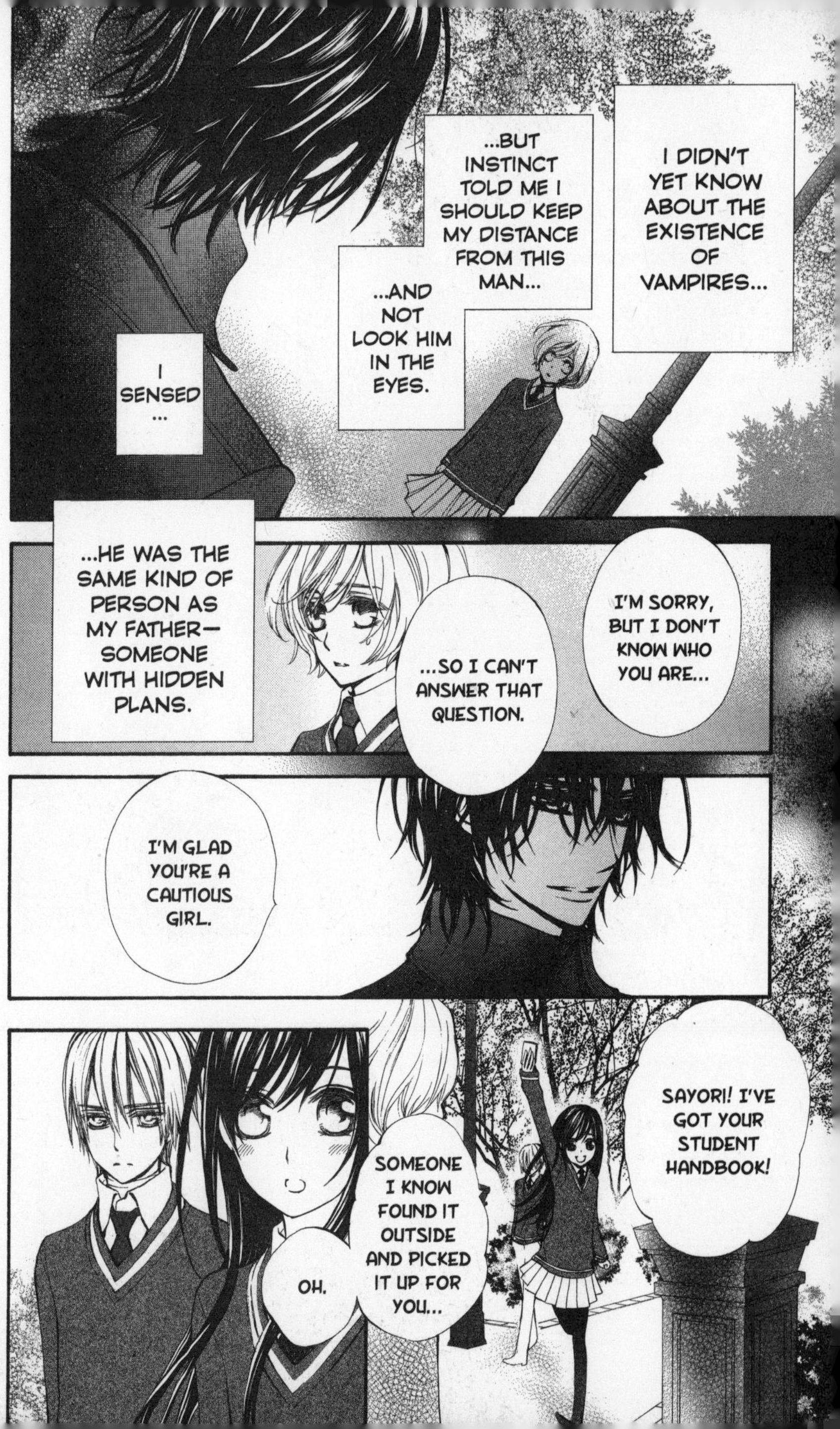
I DIDN'T YET KNOW ABOUT THE EXISTENCE OF VAMPIRES...
...BUT INSTINCT TOLD ME I SHOULD KEEP MY DISTANCE FROM THIS MAN...
...AND NOT LOOK HIM IN THE EYES.
I SENSED...
I'M SORRY, BUT I DON'T KNOW WHO YOU ARE...
...SO I CAN'T ANSWER THAT QUESTION.
...HE WAS THE SAME KIND OF PERSON AS MY FATHER—SOMEONE WITH HIDDEN PLANS.
I'M GLAD YOU'RE A CAUTIOUS GIRL.
SAYORI! I'VE GOT YOUR STUDENT HANDBOOK!
SOMEONE I KNOW FOUND IT OUTSIDE AND PICKED IT UP FOR YOU...
OH.

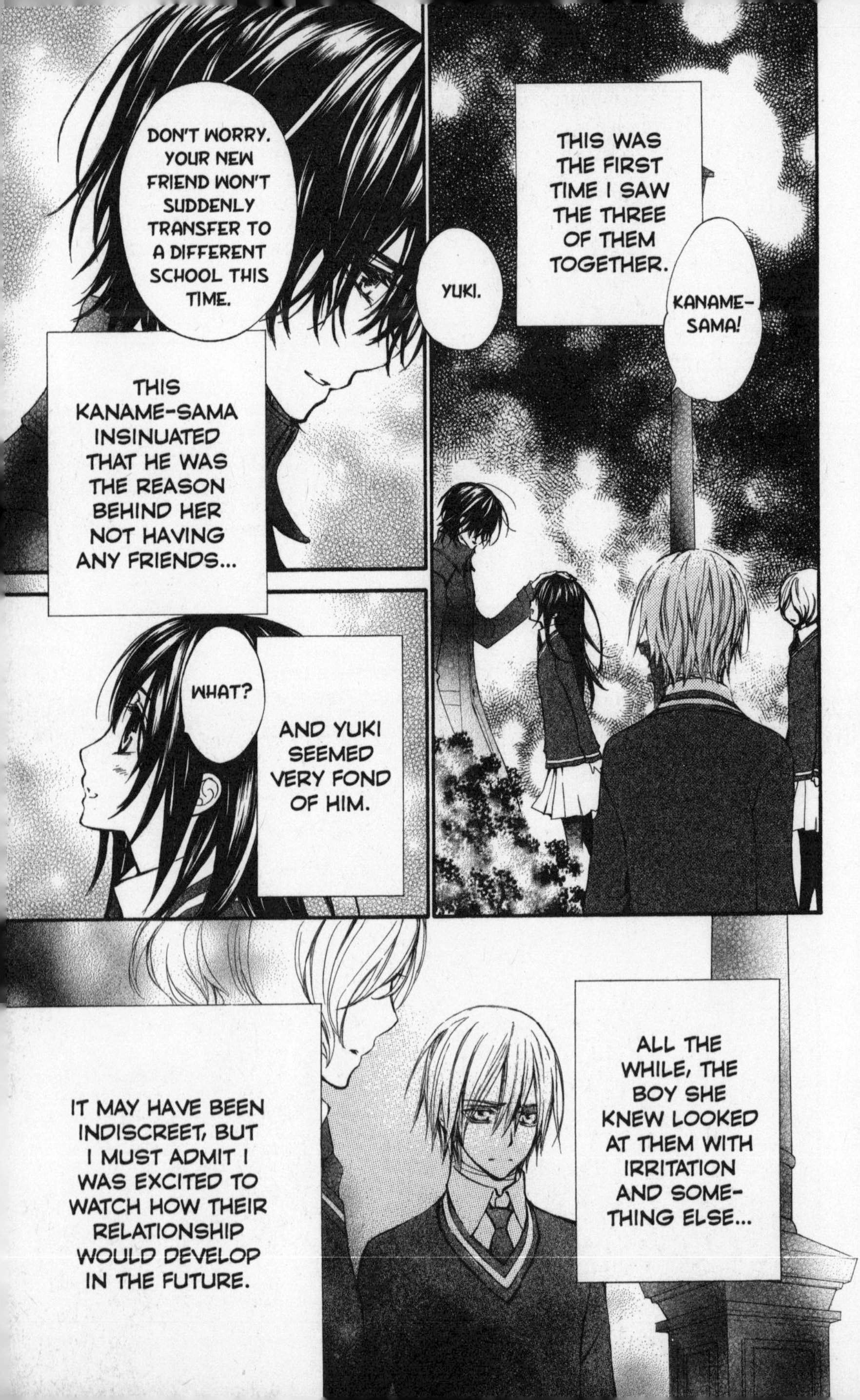
THIS WAS THE FIRST TIME I SAW THE THREE OF THEM TOGETHER.
KANAME-SAMA!
YUKI.
DON'T WORRY. YOUR NEW FRIEND WON'T SUDDENLY TRANSFER TO A DIFFERENT SCHOOL THIS TIME.
THIS KANAME-SAMA INSINUATED THAT HE WAS THE REASON BEHIND HER NOT HAVING ANY FRIENDS...
WHAT?
AND YUKI SEEMED VERY FOND OF HIM.
ALL THE WHILE, THE BOY SHE KNEW LOOKED AT THEM WITH IRRITATION AND SOME-THING ELSE...
IT MAY HAVE BEEN INDISCREET, BUT I MUST ADMIT I WAS EXCITED TO WATCH HOW THEIR RELATIONSHIP WOULD DEVELOP IN THE FUTURE.

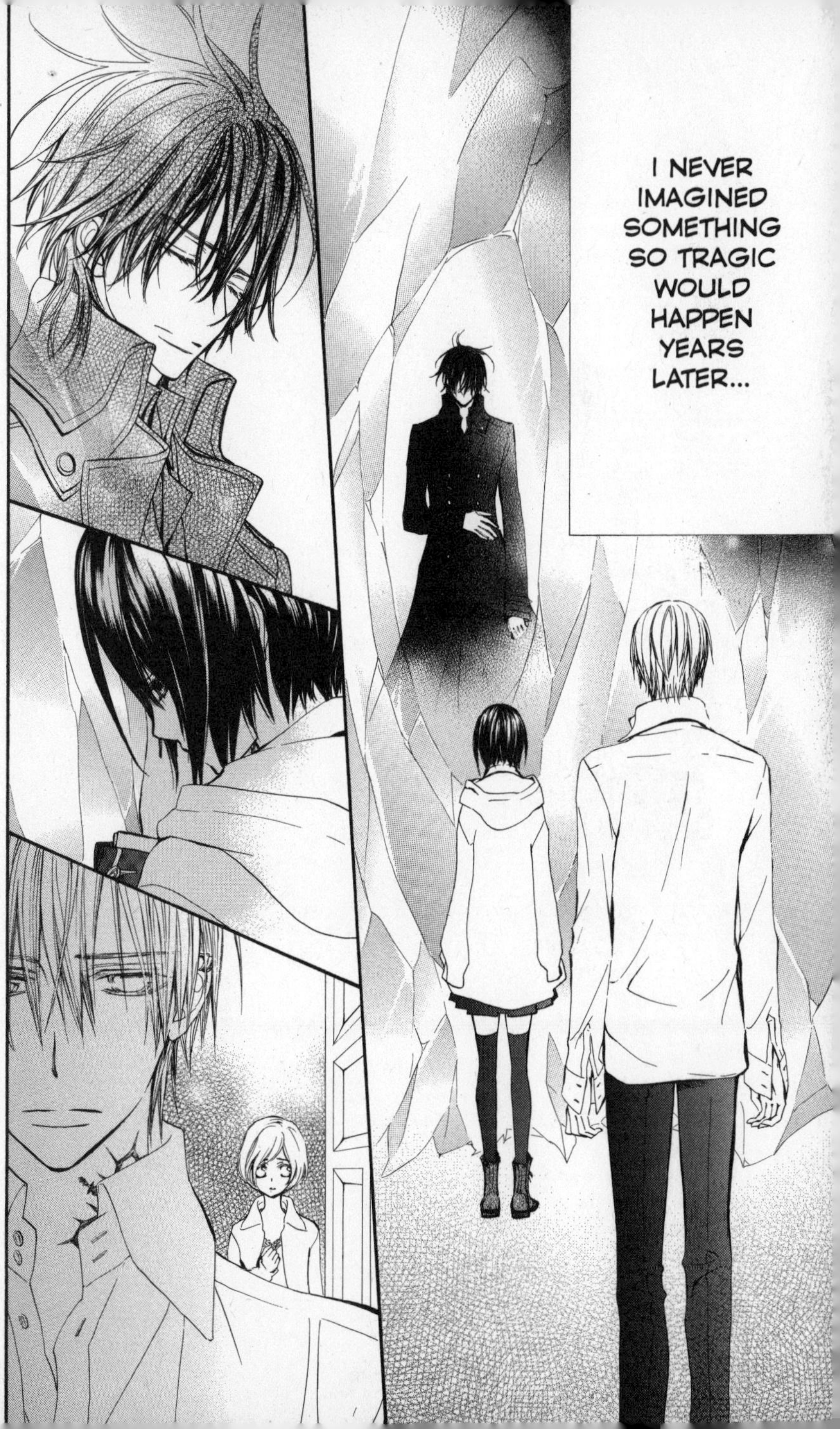
I NEVER IMAGINED SOMETHING SO TRAGIC WOULD HAPPEN YEARS LATER...

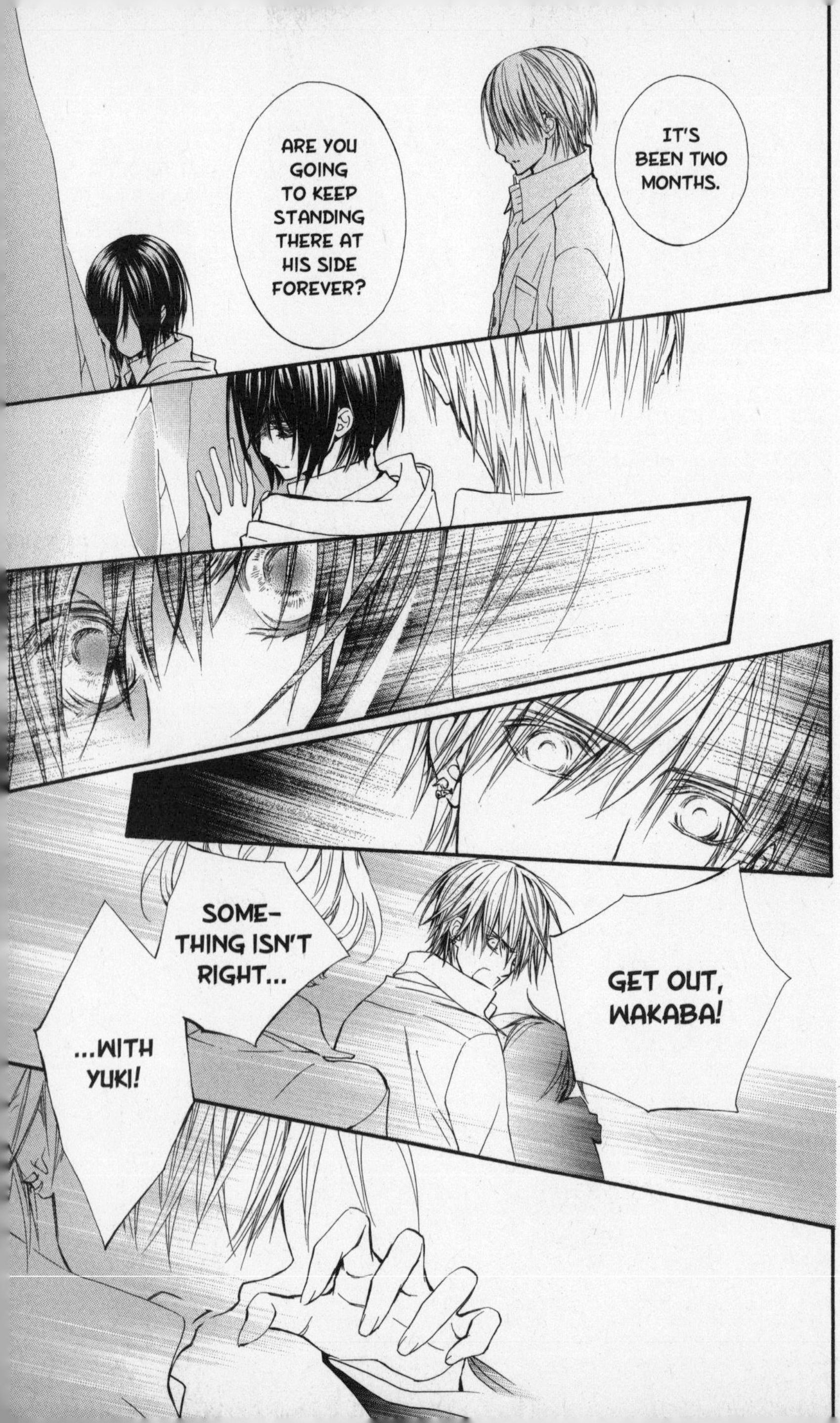
IT'S BEEN TWO MONTHS.
ARE YOU GOING TO KEEP STANDING THERE AT HIS SIDE FOREVER?
GET OUT, WAKABA!
SOME-THING ISN'T RIGHT...
...WITH YUKI!

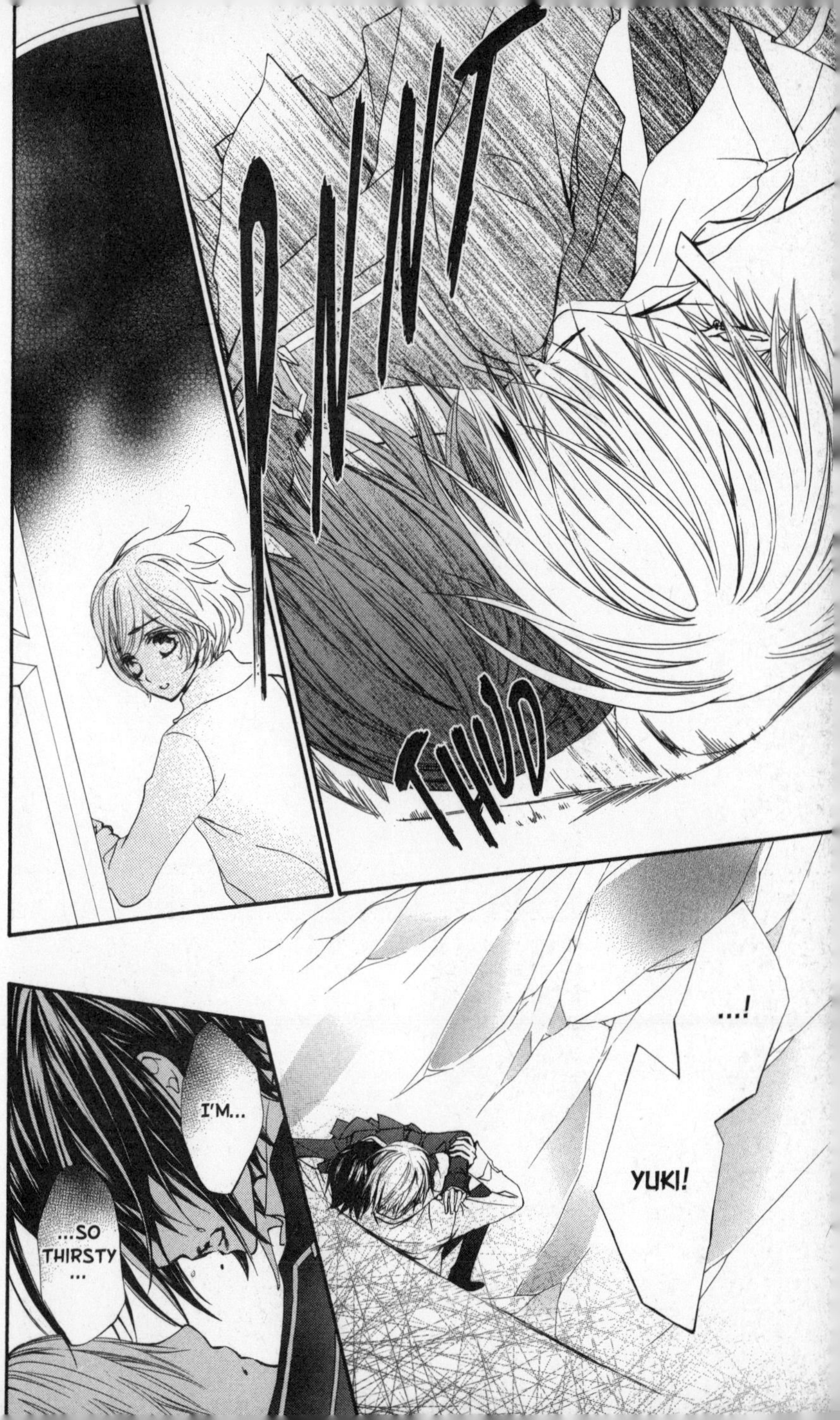

THUD
...!
YUKI!
I'M...
...SO THIRSTY...

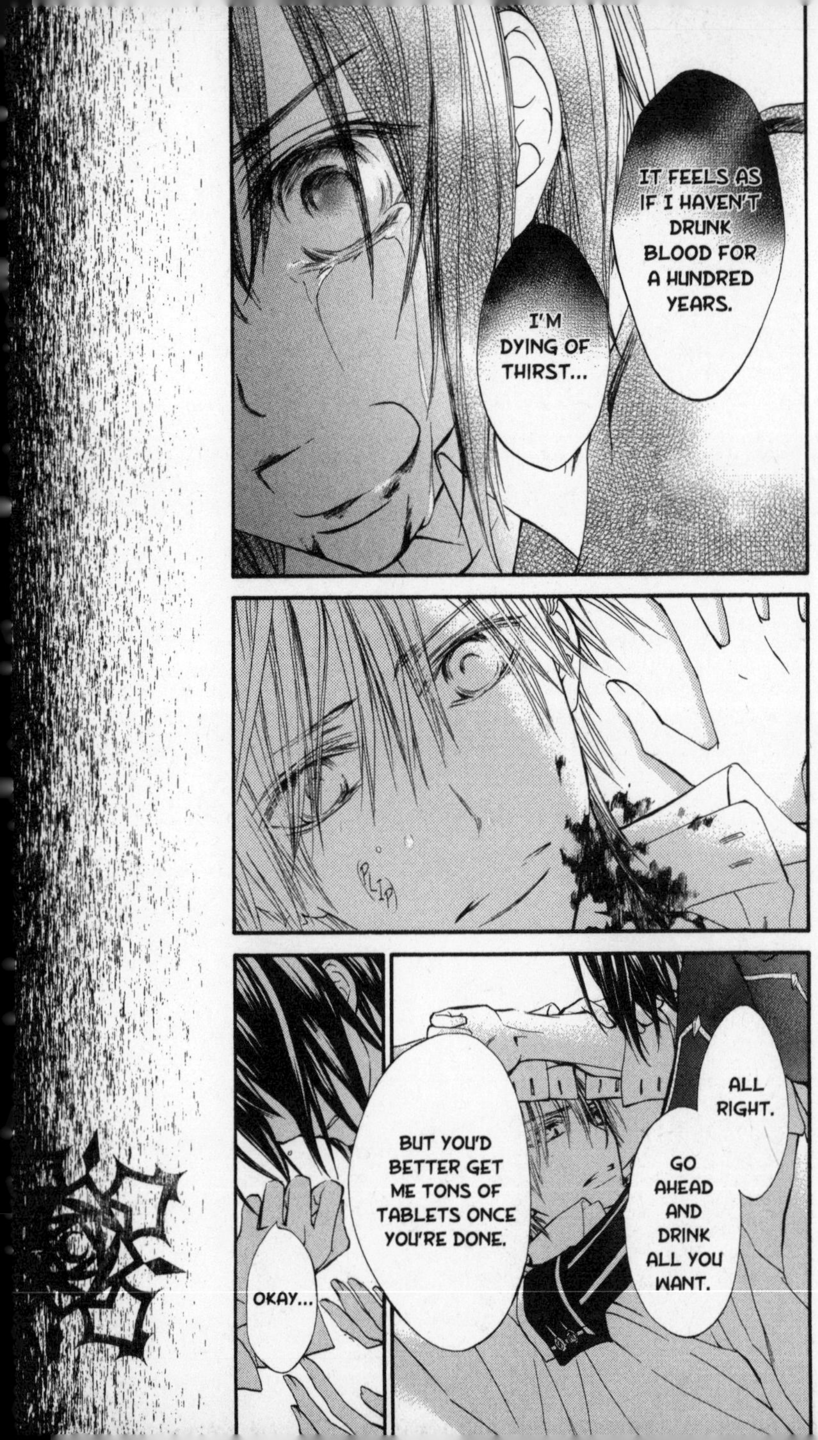
IT FEELS AS IF I HAVEN'T DRUNK BLOOD FOR A HUNDRED YEARS.
I'M DYING OF THIRST...
PLIP
ALL RIGHT.
GO AHEAD AND DRINK ALL YOU WANT.
BUT YOU'D BETTER GET ME TONS OF TABLETS ONCE YOU'RE DONE.
OKAY...

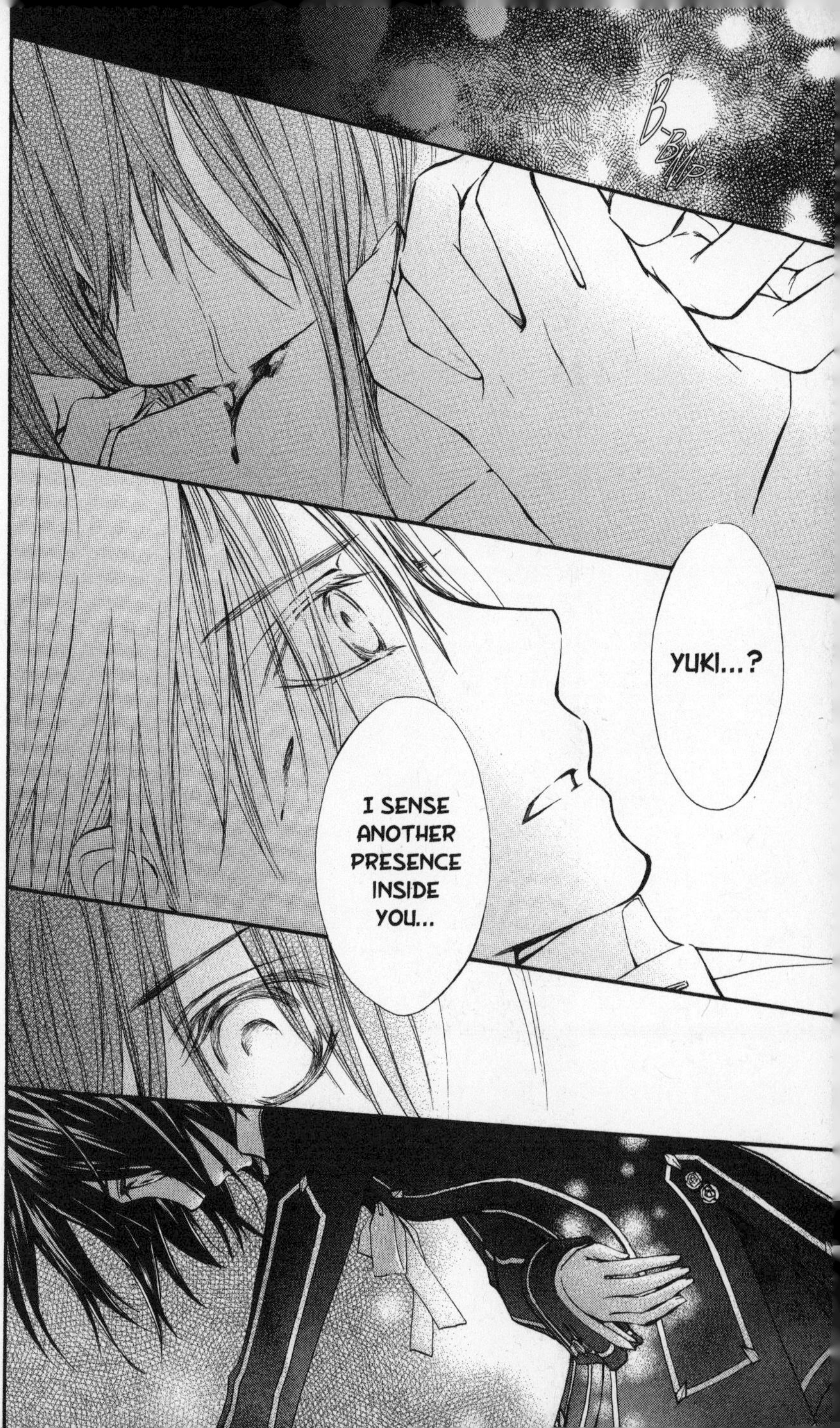
B-BMP
YUKI...?
I SENSE ANOTHER PRESENCE INSIDE YOU...

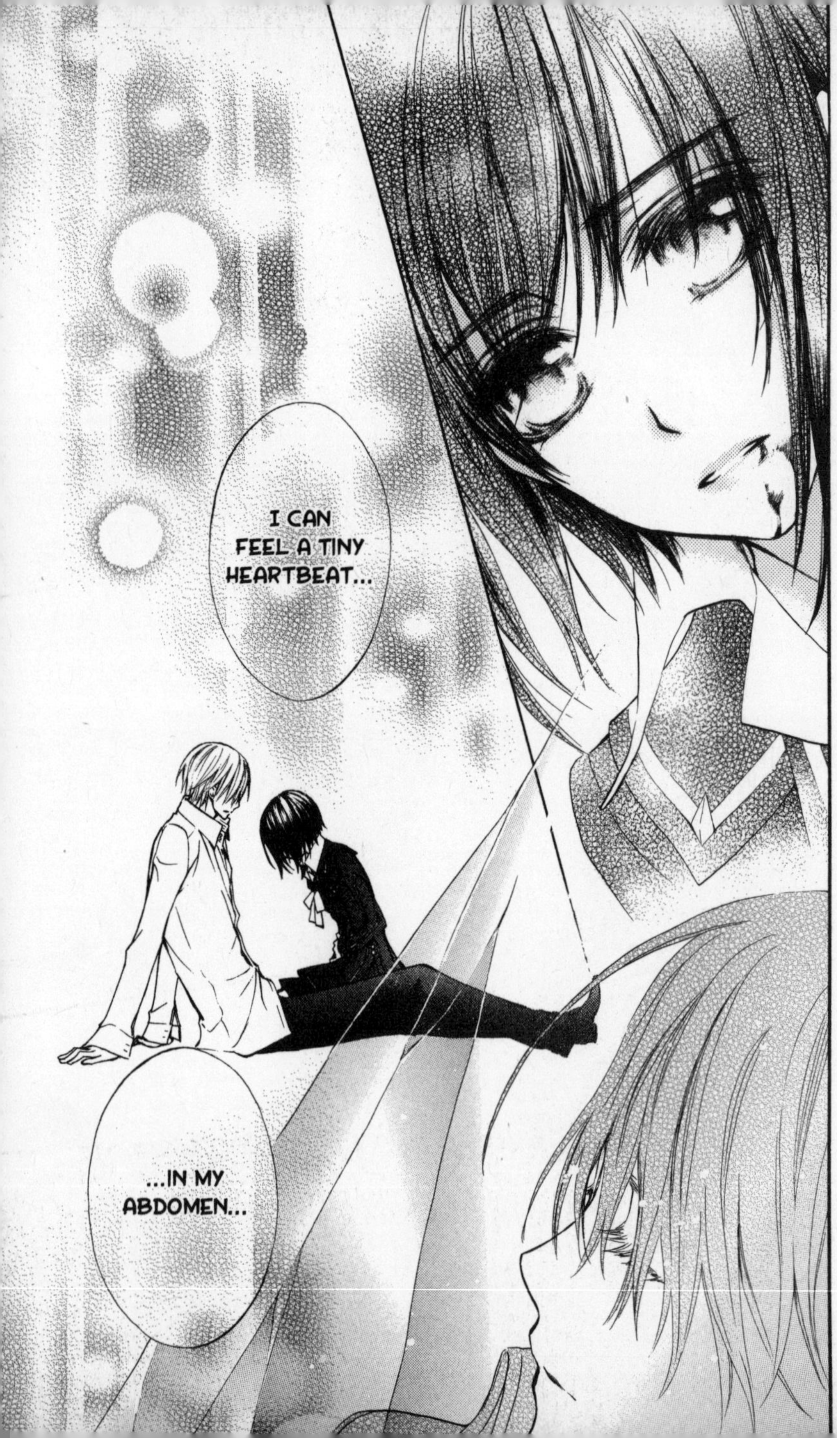
I CAN FEEL A TINY HEARTBEAT...
...IN MY ABDOMEN...

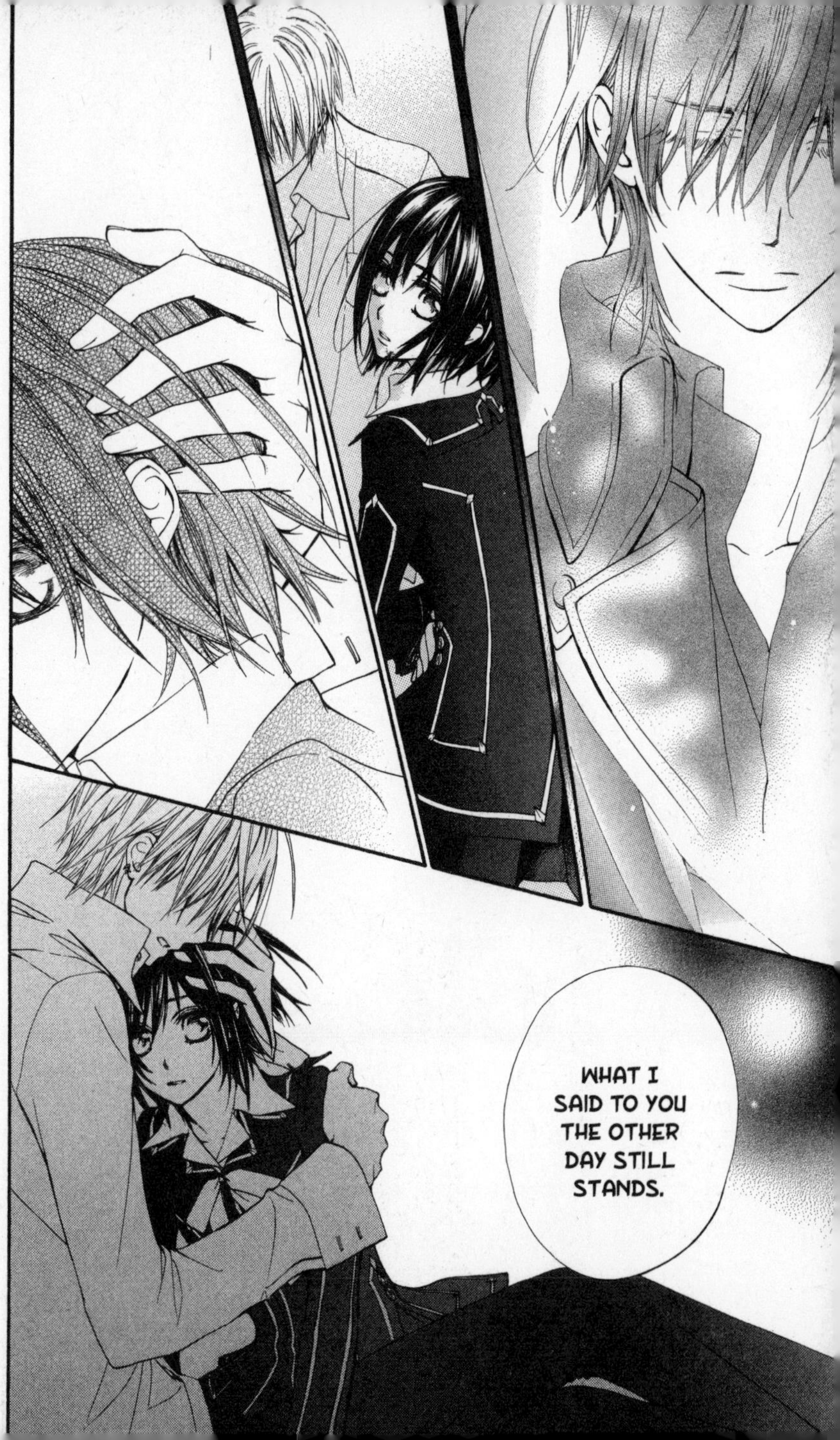
WHAT I SAID TO YOU THE OTHER DAY STILL STANDS.

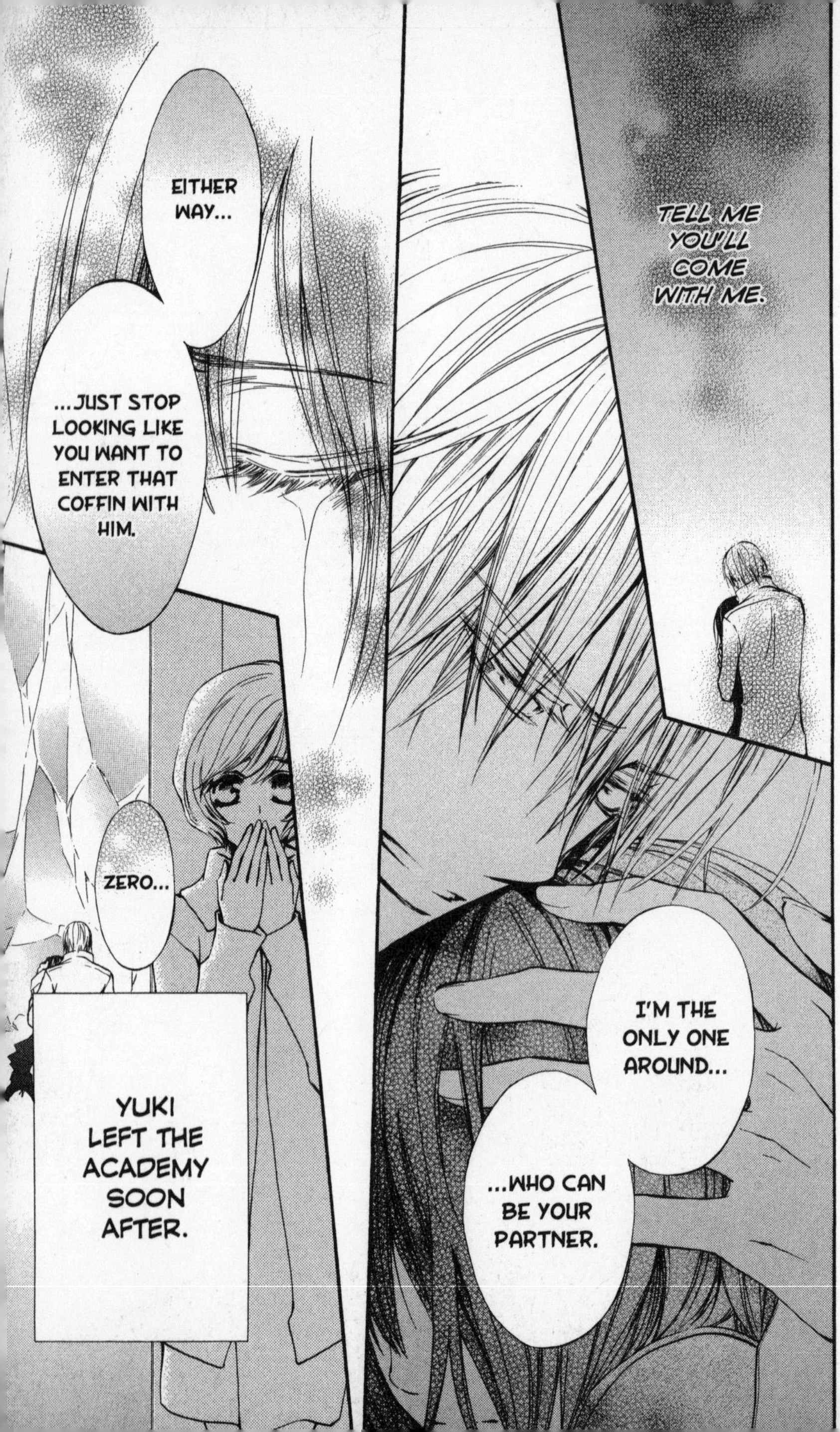
TELL ME YOU'LL COME WITH ME.
I'M THE ONLY ONE AROUND...
...WHO CAN BE YOUR PARTNER.
EITHER WAY...
...JUST STOP LOOKING LIKE YOU WANT TO ENTER THAT COFFIN WITH HIM.
ZERO...
YUKI LEFT THE ACADEMY SOON AFTER.

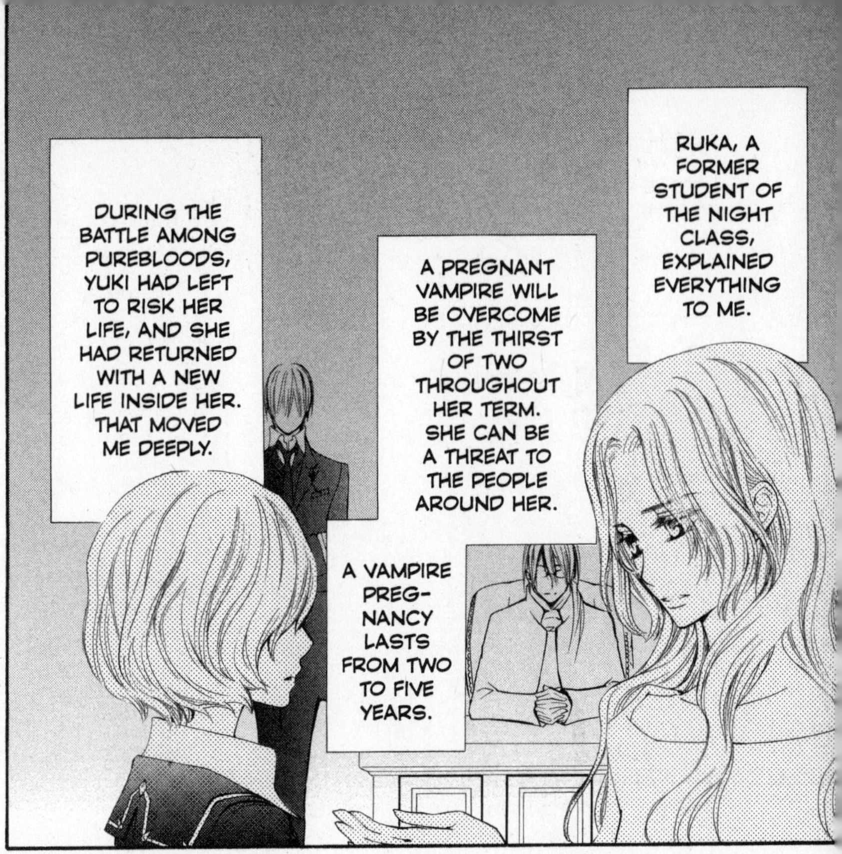
RUKA, A FORMER STUDENT OF THE NIGHT CLASS, EXPLAINED EVERYTHING TO ME.
A PREGNANT VAMPIRE WILL BE OVERCOME BY THE THIRST OF TWO THROUGHOUT HER TERM. SHE CAN BE A THREAT TO THE PEOPLE AROUND HER.
DURING THE BATTLE AMONG PUREBLOODS, YUKI HAD LEFT TO RISK HER LIFE, AND SHE HAD RETURNED WITH A NEW LIFE INSIDE HER. THAT MOVED ME DEEPLY.
A VAMPIRE PREG-NANCY LASTS FROM TWO TO FIVE YEARS.

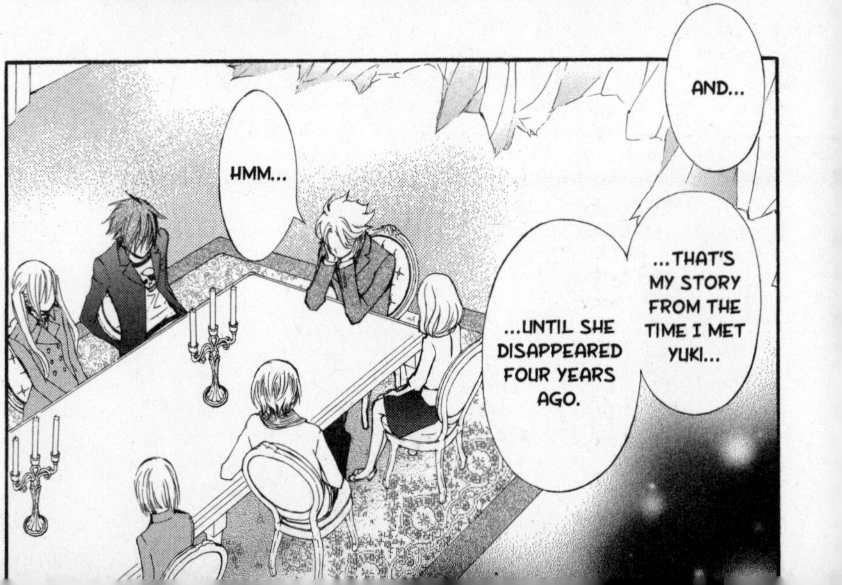
AND...
...THAT'S MY STORY FROM THE TIME I MET YUKI...
...UNTIL SHE DISAPPEARED FOUR YEARS AGO.
HMM...

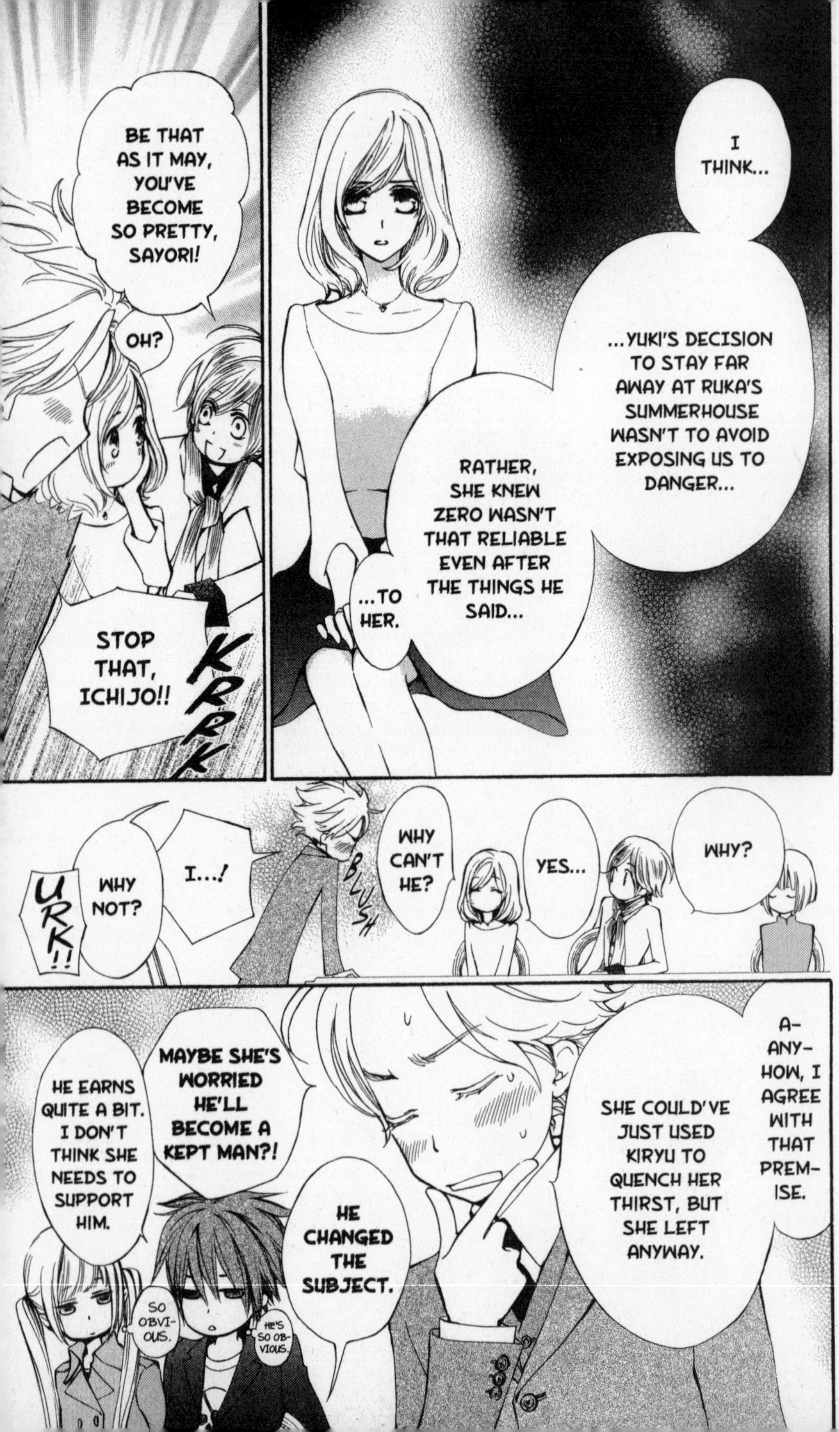
I THINK...
...YUKI'S DECISION TO STAY FAR AWAY AT RUKA'S SUMMERHOUSE WASN'T TO AVOID EXPOSING US TO DANGER...
RATHER, SHE KNEW ZERO WASN'T THAT RELIABLE EVEN AFTER THE THINGS HE SAID...
...TO HER.
BE THAT AS IT MAY, YOU'VE BECOME SO PRETTY, SAYORI!
OH?
KRRK
STOP THAT, ICHIJO!!
WHY?
YES...
WHY CAN'T HE?
BLUSH
I...!
WHY NOT?
URK!!
A- ANYHOW, I AGREE WITH THAT PREMISE.
SHE COULD'VE JUST USED KIRYU TO QUENCH HER THIRST, BUT SHE LEFT ANYWAY.
HE CHANGED THE SUBJECT.
MAYBE SHE'S WORRIED HE'LL BECOME A KEPT MAN?!
HE EARNS QUITE A BIT. I DON'T THINK SHE NEEDS TO SUPPORT HIM.
HE'S SO OBVIOUS.
SO OBVIOUS.

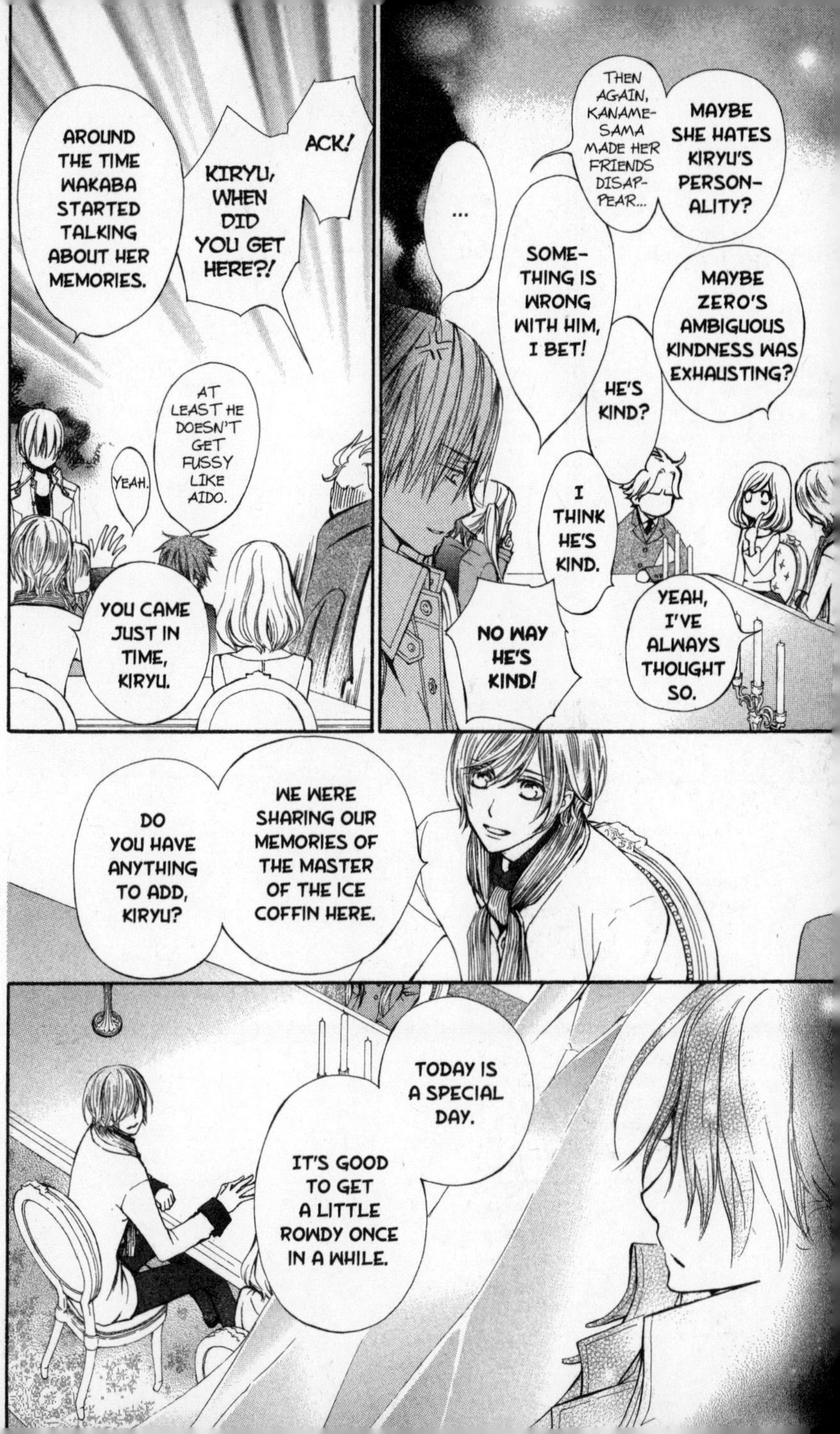
MAYBE SHE HATES KIRYU'S PERSONALITY?
THEN AGAIN, KANAME-SAMA MADE HER FRIENDS DISAPPEAR...
...
MAYBE ZERO'S AMBIGUOUS KINDNESS WAS EXHAUSTING?
SOMETHING IS WRONG WITH HIM, I BET!
HE'S KIND?
I THINK HE'S KIND.
YEAH, I'VE ALWAYS THOUGHT SO.
NO WAY HE'S KIND!
ACK!
KIRYU, WHEN DID YOU GET HERE?!
AROUND THE TIME WAKABA STARTED TALKING ABOUT HER MEMORIES.
AT LEAST HE DOESN'T GET FUSSY LIKE AIDO.
YEAH.
YOU CAME JUST IN TIME, KIRYU.
WE WERE SHARING OUR MEMORIES OF THE MASTER OF THE ICE COFFIN HERE.
DO YOU HAVE ANYTHING TO ADD, KIRYU?
TODAY IS A SPECIAL DAY.
IT'S GOOD TO GET A LITTLE ROWDY ONCE IN A WHILE.

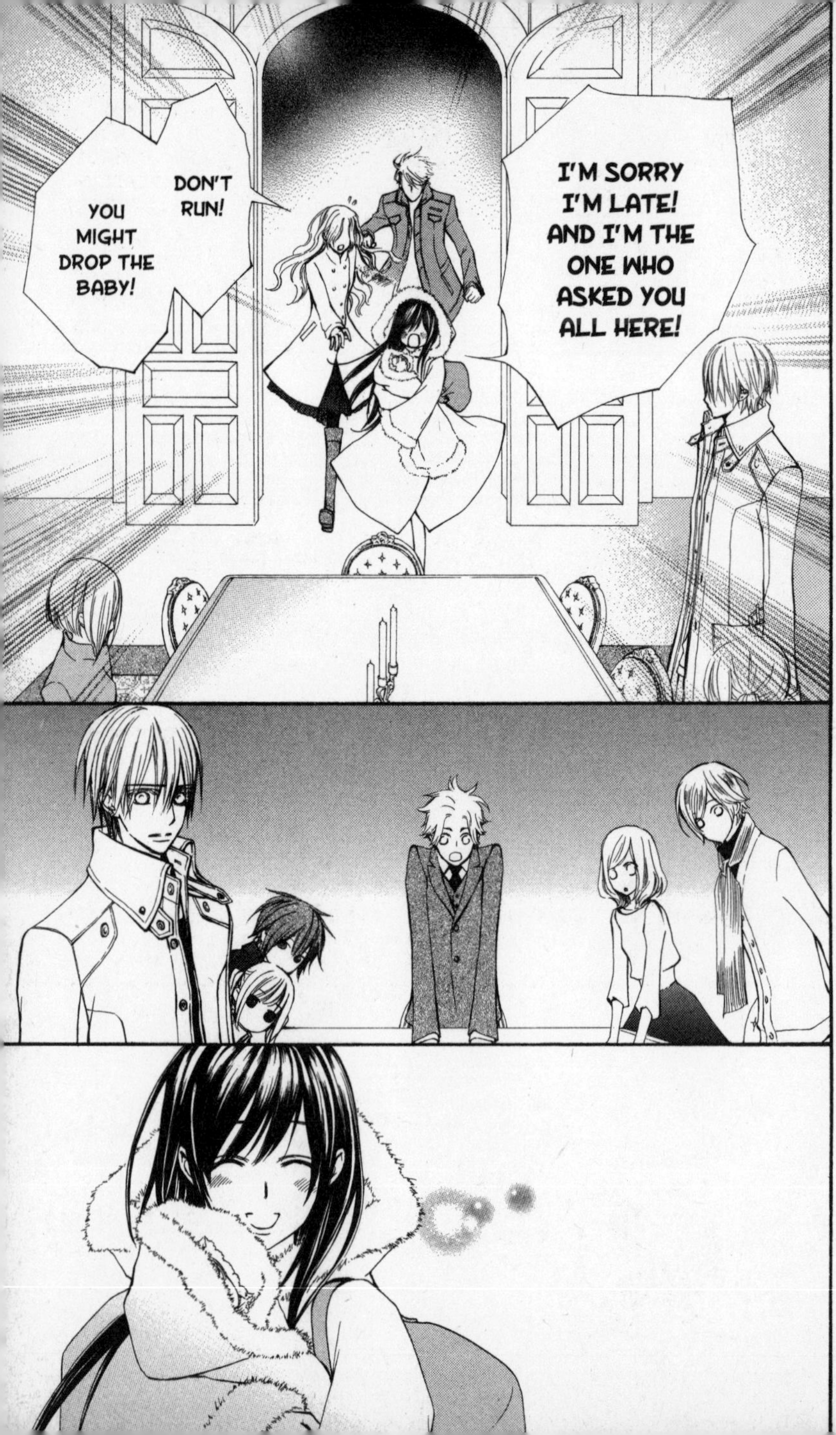
I'M SORRY I'M LATE! AND I'M THE ONE WHO ASKED YOU ALL HERE!
DON'T RUN!
YOU MIGHT DROP THE BABY!

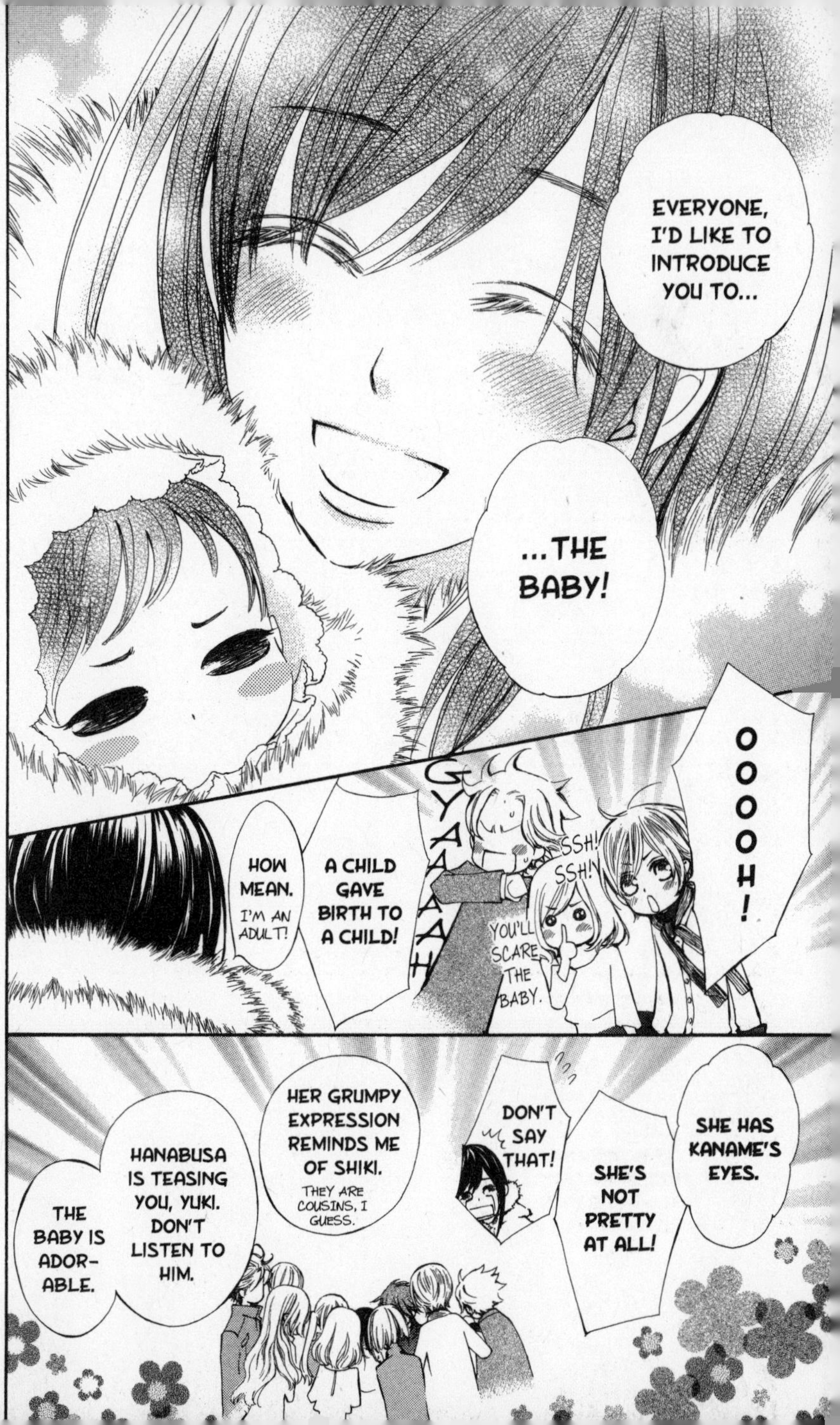
EVERYONE, I'D LIKE TO INTRODUCE YOU TO...
...THE BABY!
OOOOOH!
SSH! SSH!
YOU'LL SCARE THE BABY.
GYAAAAAH
A CHILD GAVE BIRTH TO A CHILD!
HOW MEAN.
I'M AN ADULT!
SHE HAS KANAME'S EYES.
SHE'S NOT PRETTY AT ALL!
DON'T SAY THAT!
HER GRUMPY EXPRESSION REMINDS ME OF SHIKI.
THEY ARE COUSINS, I GUESS.
HANABUSA IS TEASING YOU, YUKI. DON'T LISTEN TO HIM.
THE BABY IS ADOR-ABLE.

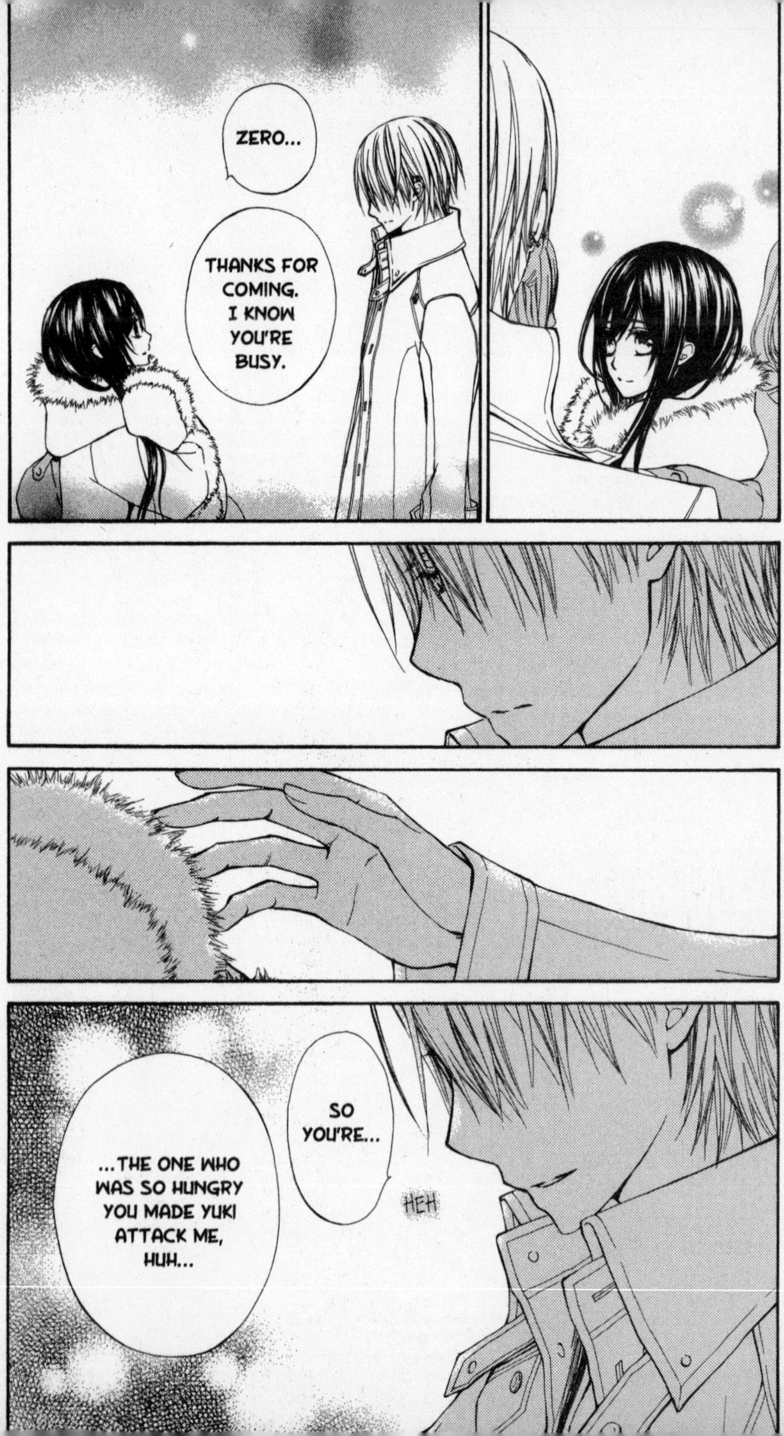
ZERO...
THANKS FOR COMING. I KNOW YOU'RE BUSY.
SO YOU'RE...
HEH
...THE ONE WHO WAS SO HUNGRY YOU MADE YUKI ATTACK ME, HUH...

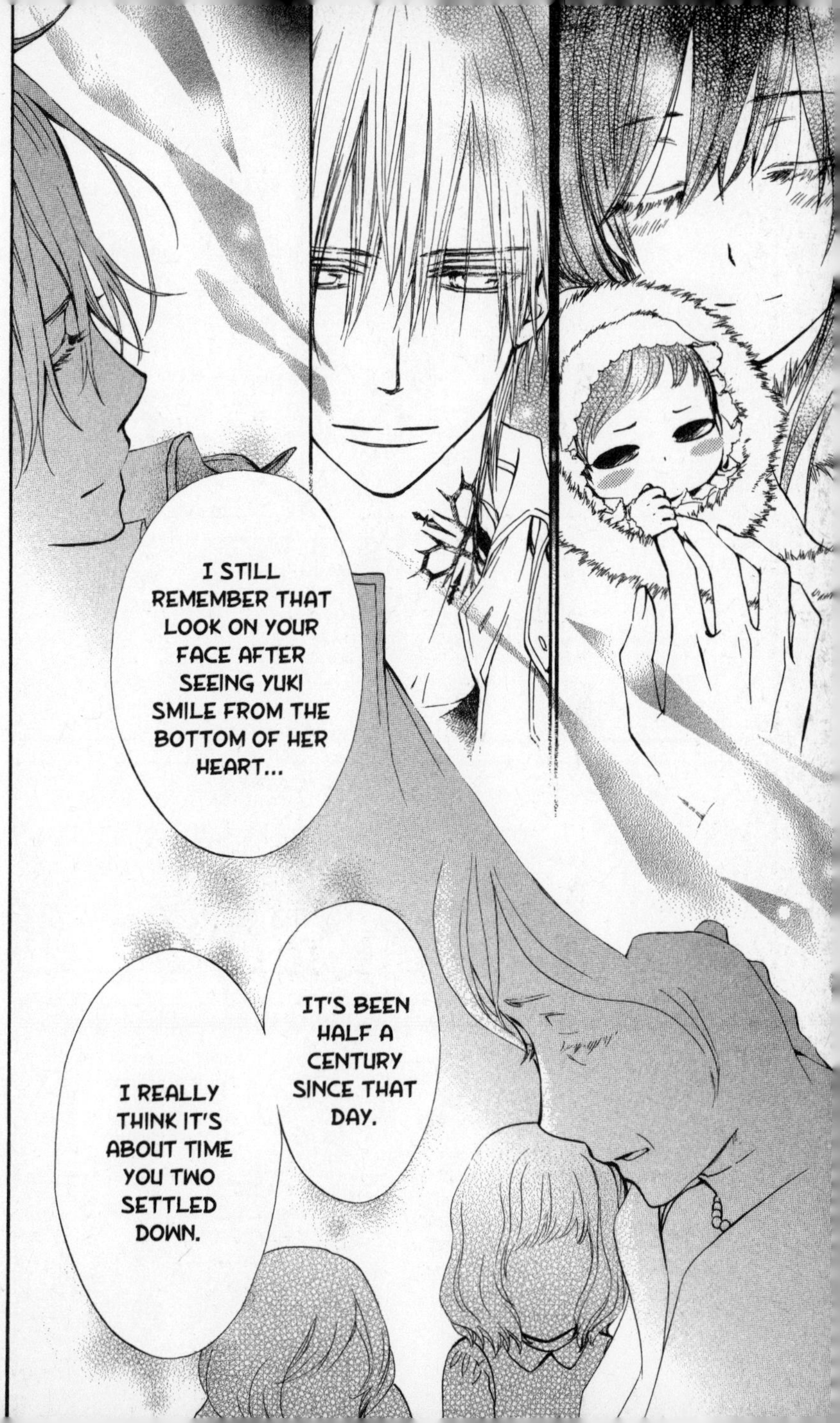
I STILL REMEMBER THAT LOOK ON YOUR FACE AFTER SEEING YUKI SMILE FROM THE BOTTOM OF HER HEART...
IT'S BEEN HALF A CENTURY SINCE THAT DAY.
I REALLY THINK IT'S ABOUT TIME YOU TWO SETTLED DOWN.

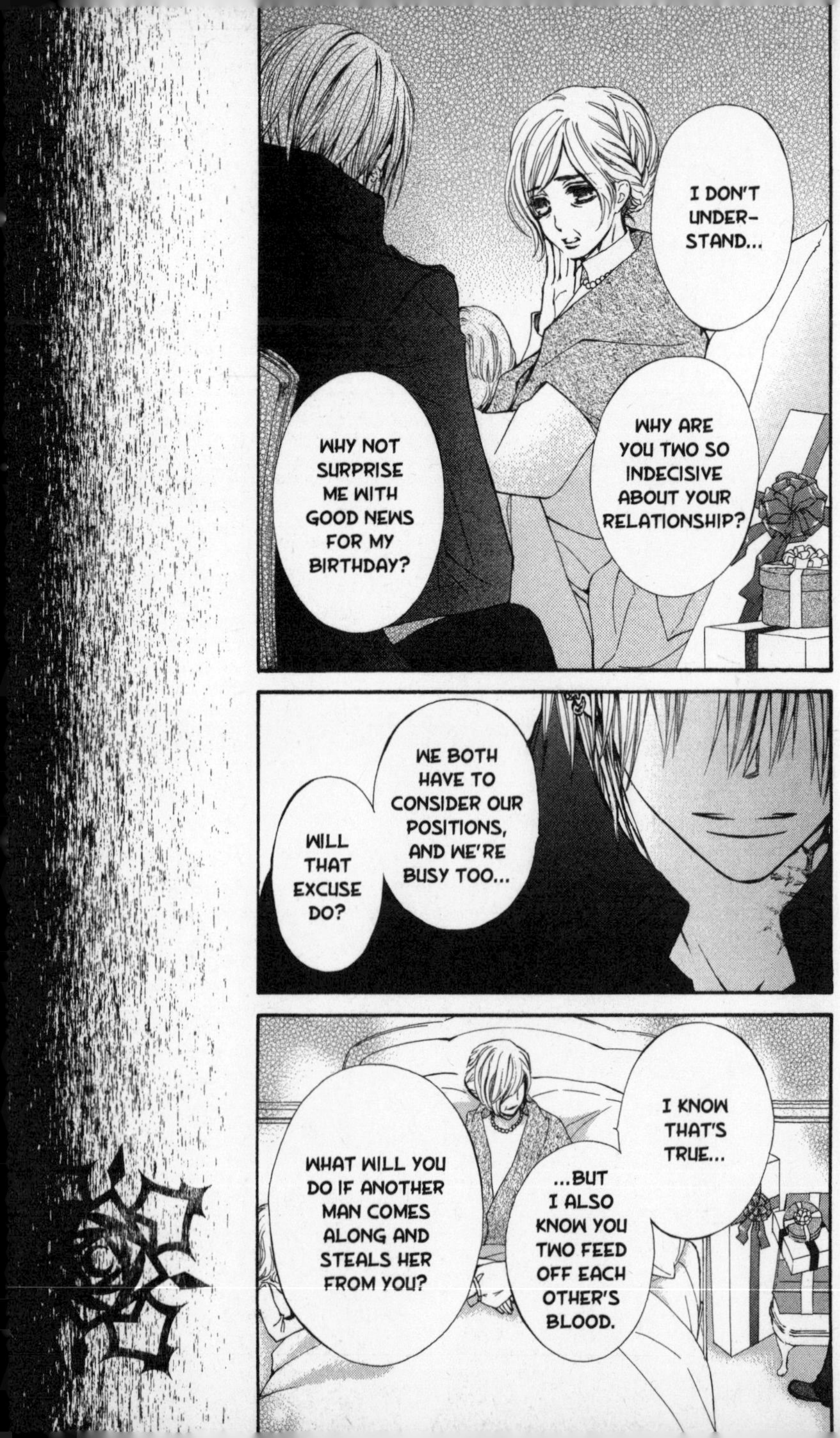
I DON'T UNDER-STAND...
WHY ARE YOU TWO SO INDECISIVE ABOUT YOUR RELATIONSHIP?
WHY NOT SURPRISE ME WITH GOOD NEWS FOR MY BIRTHDAY?
WE BOTH HAVE TO CONSIDER OUR POSITIONS, AND WE'RE BUSY TOO...
WILL THAT EXCUSE DO?
I KNOW THAT'S TRUE...
...BUT I ALSO KNOW YOU TWO FEED OFF EACH OTHER'S BLOOD.
WHAT WILL YOU DO IF ANOTHER MAN COMES ALONG AND STEALS HER FROM YOU?

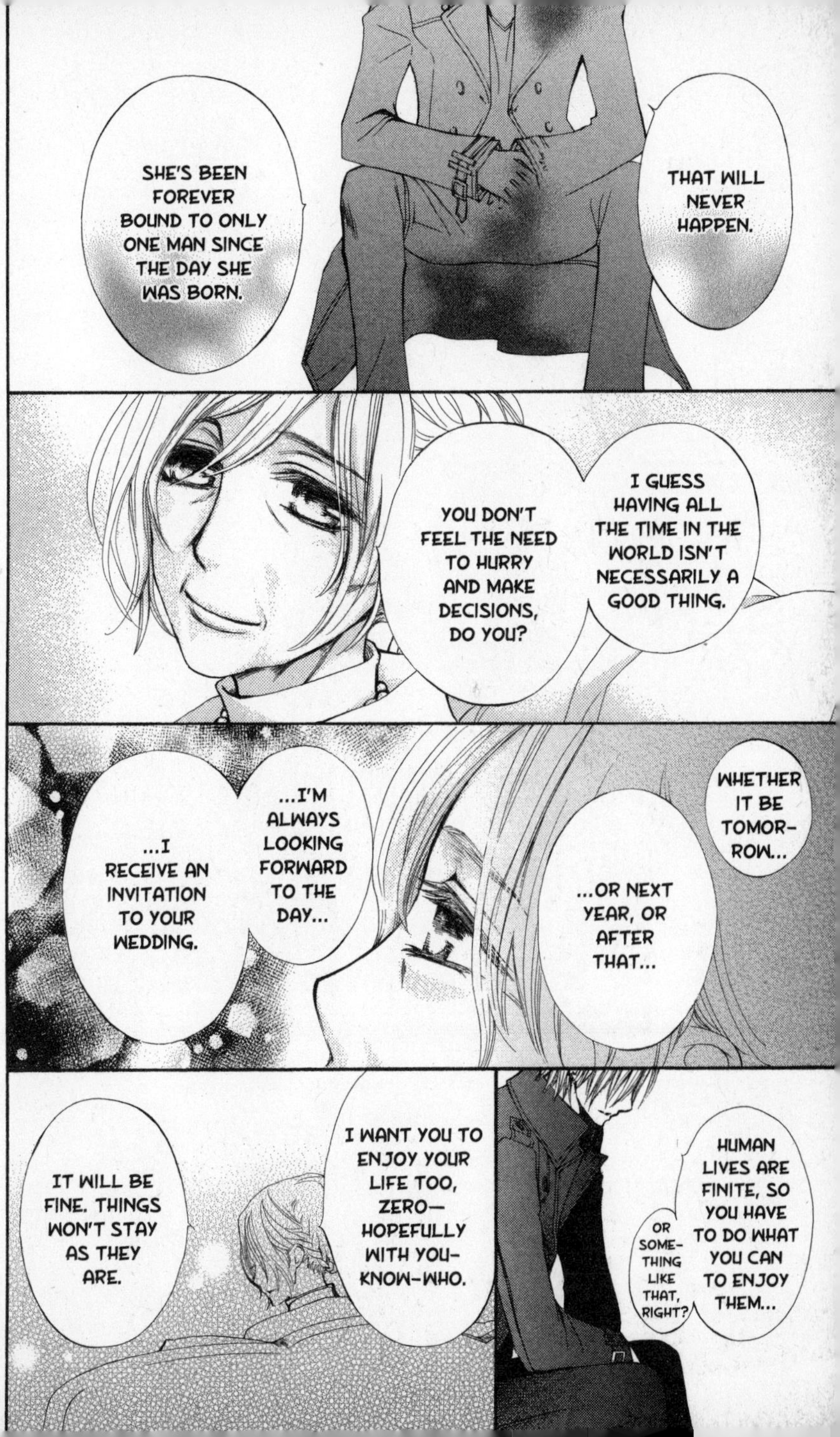
THAT WILL NEVER HAPPEN.
SHE'S BEEN FOREVER BOUND TO ONLY ONE MAN SINCE THE DAY SHE WAS BORN.
I GUESS HAVING ALL THE TIME IN THE WORLD ISN'T NECESSARILY A GOOD THING.
YOU DON'T FEEL THE NEED TO HURRY AND MAKE DECISIONS, DO YOU?
WHETHER IT BE TOMOR-ROW...
...OR NEXT YEAR, OR AFTER THAT...
...I'M ALWAYS LOOKING FORWARD TO THE DAY...
...I RECEIVE AN INVITATION TO YOUR WEDDING.
HUMAN LIVES ARE FINITE, SO YOU HAVE TO DO WHAT YOU CAN TO ENJOY THEM...
OR SOME-THING LIKE THAT, RIGHT?
I WANT YOU TO ENJOY YOUR LIFE TOO, ZERO— HOPEFULLY WITH YOU-KNOW-WHO.
IT WILL BE FINE. THINGS WON'T STAY AS THEY ARE.

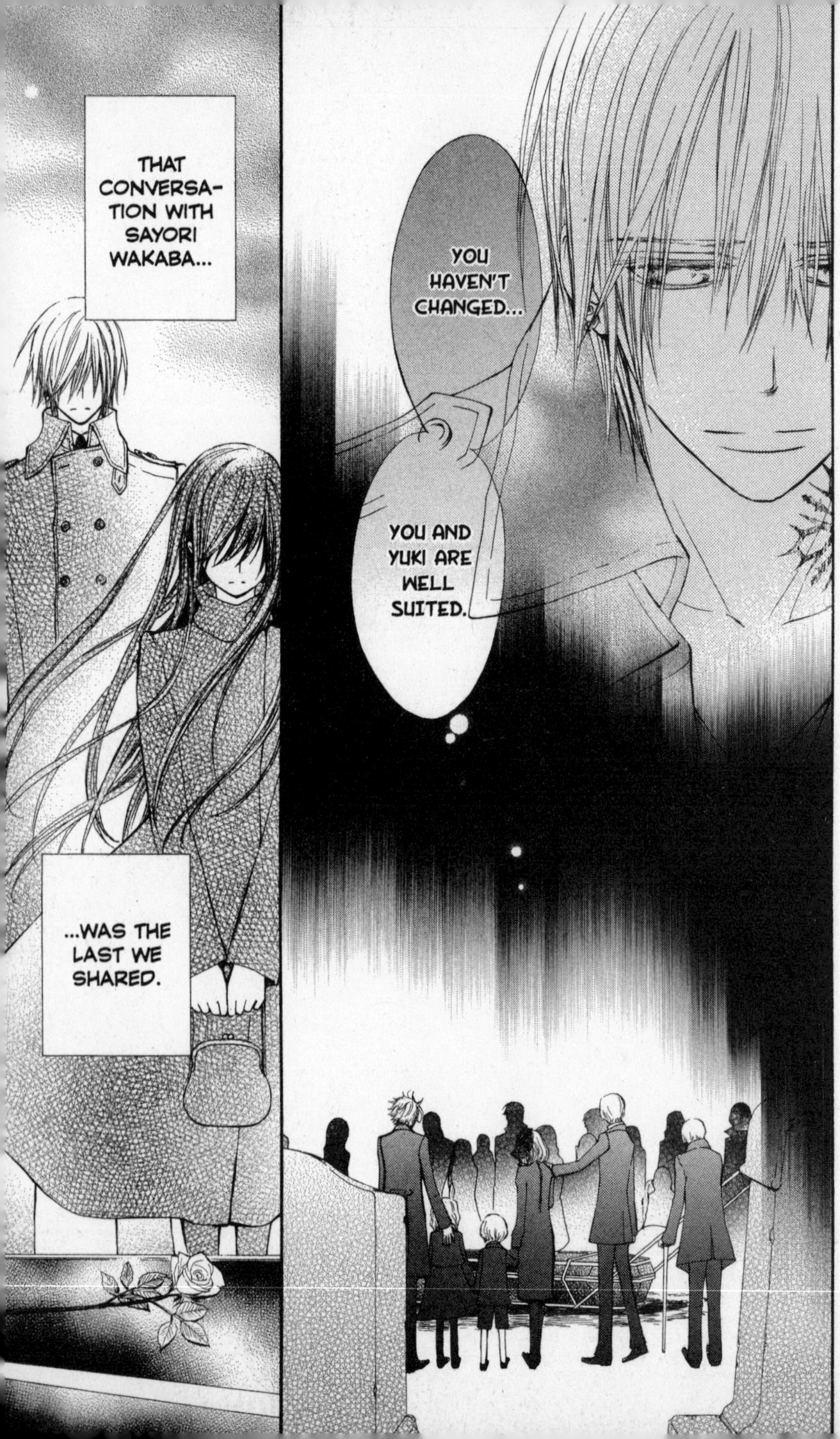
YOU HAVEN'T CHANGED...
YOU AND YUKI ARE WELL SUITED.
THAT CONVERSA-TION WITH SAYORI WAKABA...
...WAS THE LAST WE SHARED.

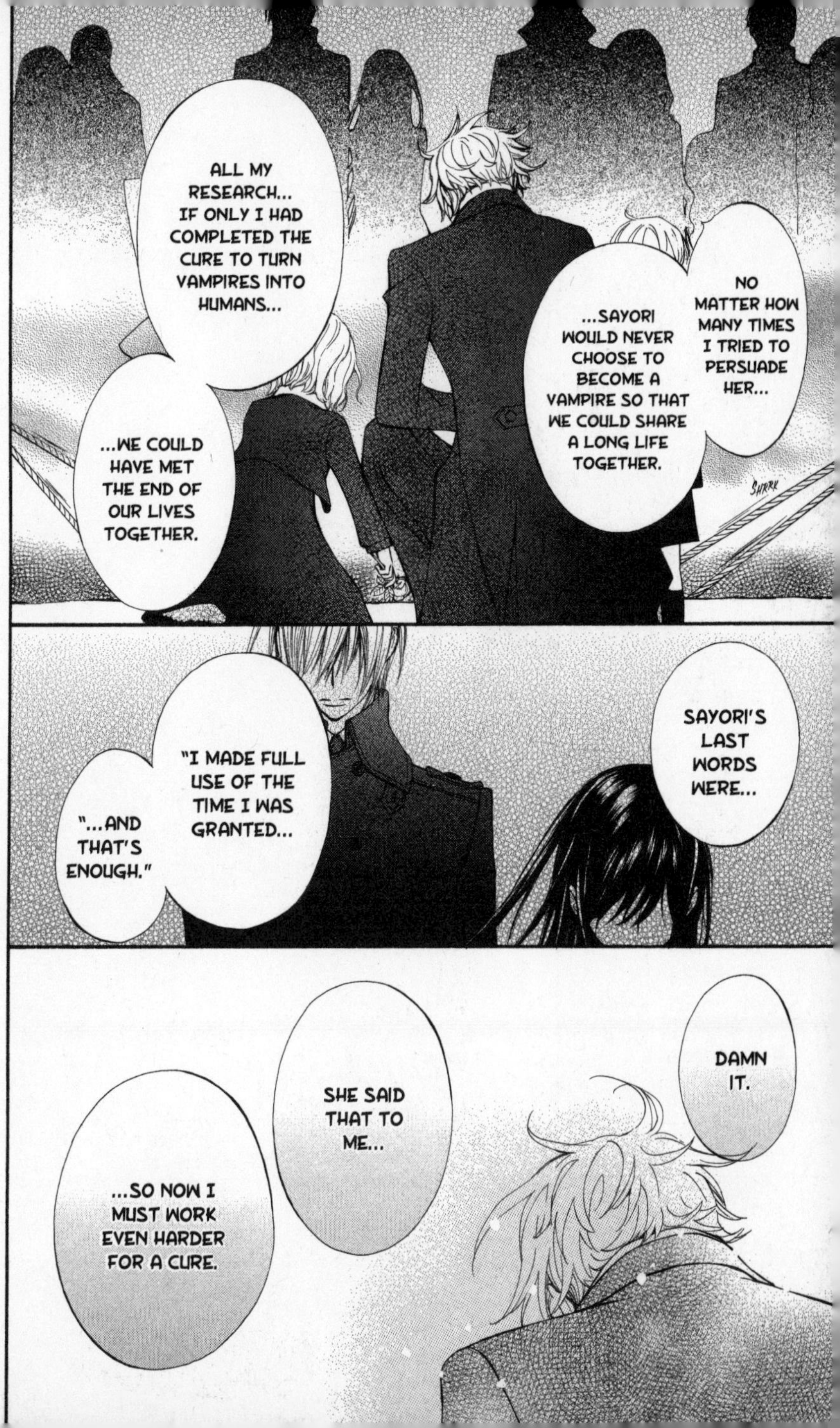
NO MATTER HOW MANY TIMES I TRIED TO PERSUADE HER...
...SAYORI WOULD NEVER CHOOSE TO BECOME A VAMPIRE SO THAT WE COULD SHARE A LONG LIFE TOGETHER.
SHRRK
ALL MY RESEARCH... IF ONLY I HAD COMPLETED THE CURE TO TURN VAMPIRES INTO HUMANS...
...WE COULD HAVE MET THE END OF OUR LIVES TOGETHER.
SAYORI'S LAST WORDS WERE...
"I MADE FULL USE OF THE TIME I WAS GRANTED...
"...AND THAT'S ENOUGH."
DAMN IT.
SHE SAID THAT TO ME...
...SO NOW I MUST WORK EVEN HARDER FOR A CURE.

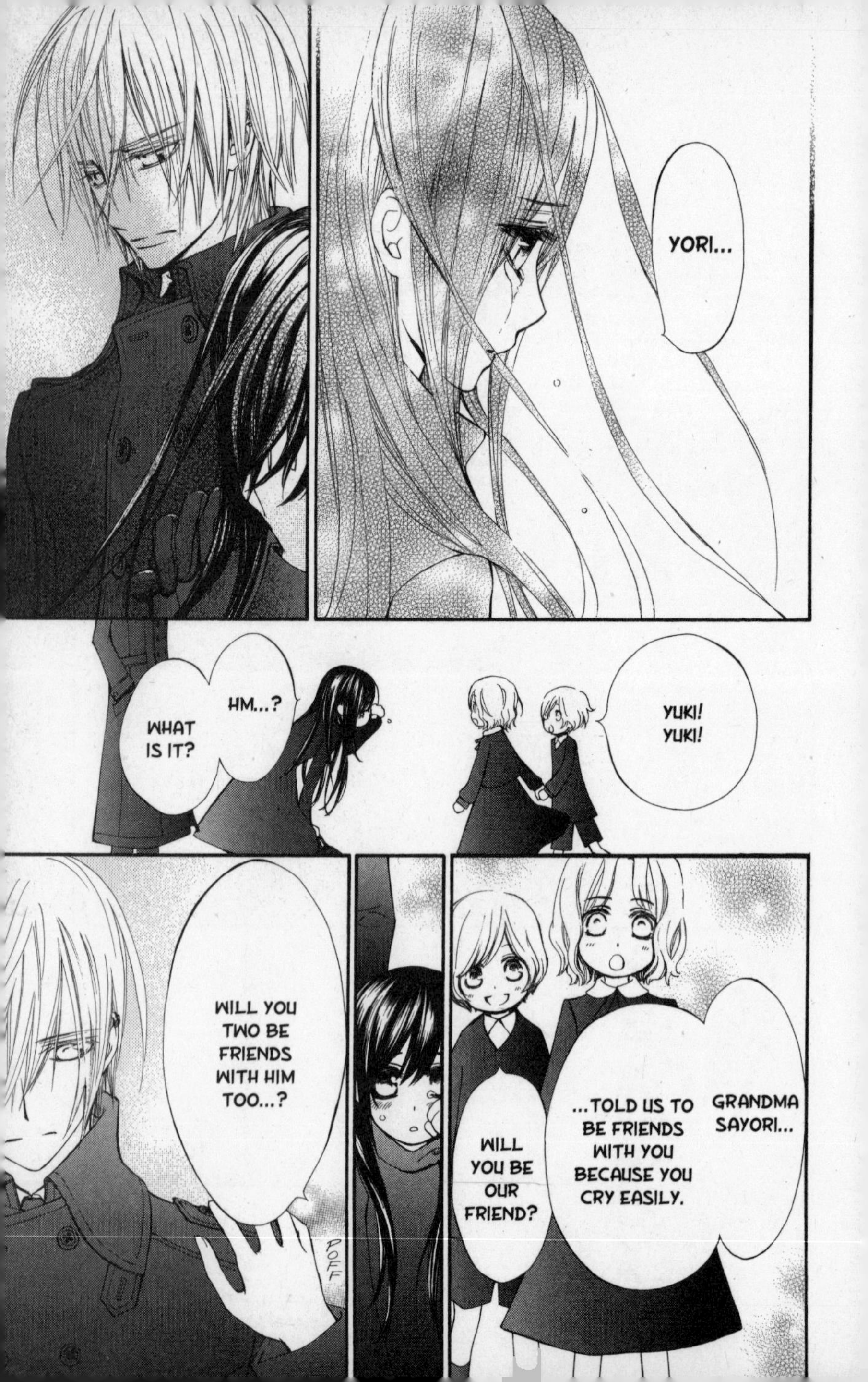
YORI...
YUKI! YUKI!
HM...?
WHAT IS IT?
GRANDMA SAYORI...
...TOLD US TO BE FRIENDS WITH YOU BECAUSE YOU CRY EASILY.
WILL YOU BE OUR FRIEND?
WILL YOU TWO BE FRIENDS WITH HIM TOO...?
POFF

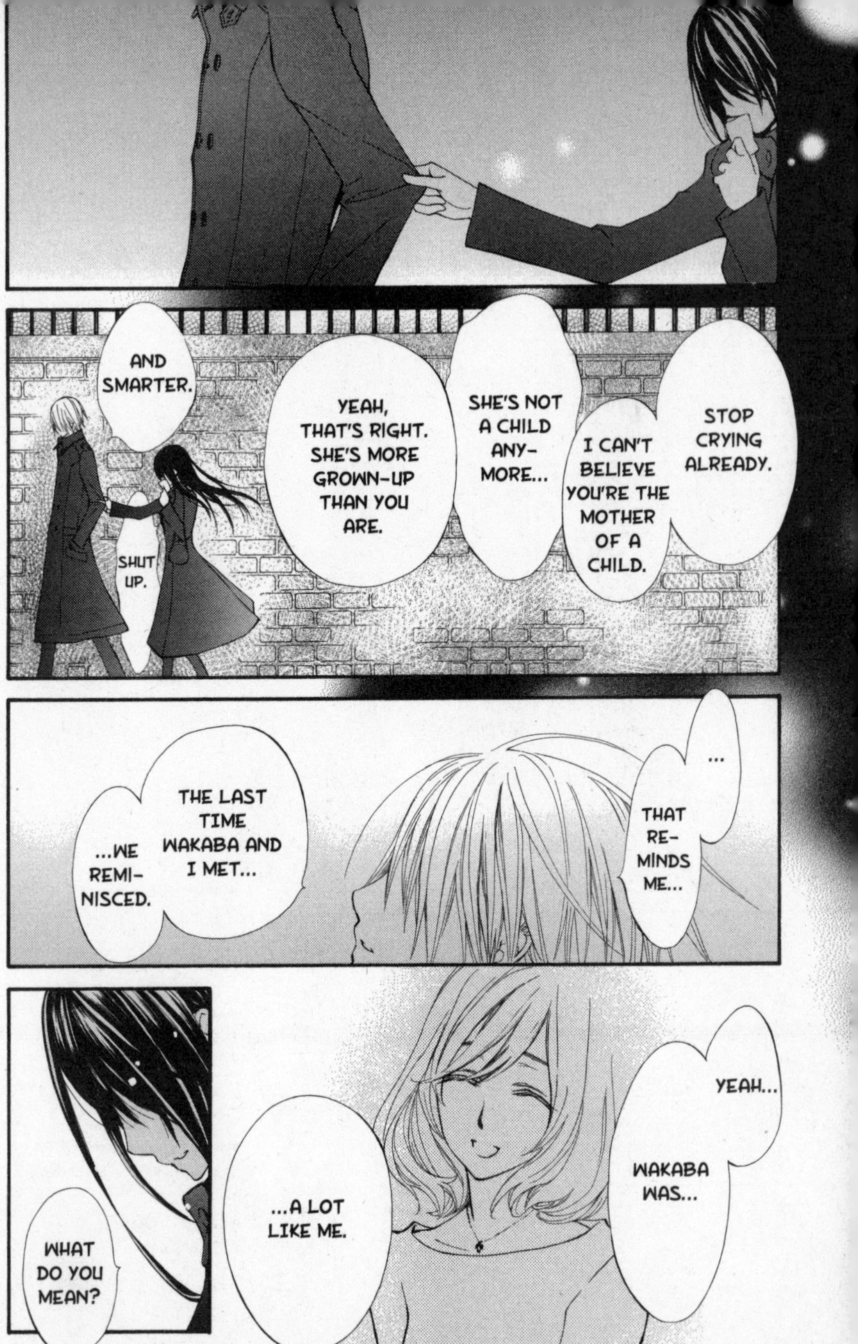
STOP CRYING ALREADY.
I CAN'T BELIEVE YOU'RE THE MOTHER OF A CHILD.
SHE'S NOT A CHILD ANY-MORE...
YEAH, THAT'S RIGHT. SHE'S MORE GROWN-UP THAN YOU ARE.
AND SMARTER.
SHUT UP.
...
THAT RE-MINDS ME...
THE LAST TIME WAKABA AND I MET...
...WE REMI-NISCED.
YEAH...
WAKABA WAS...
...A LOT LIKE ME.
WHAT DO YOU MEAN?

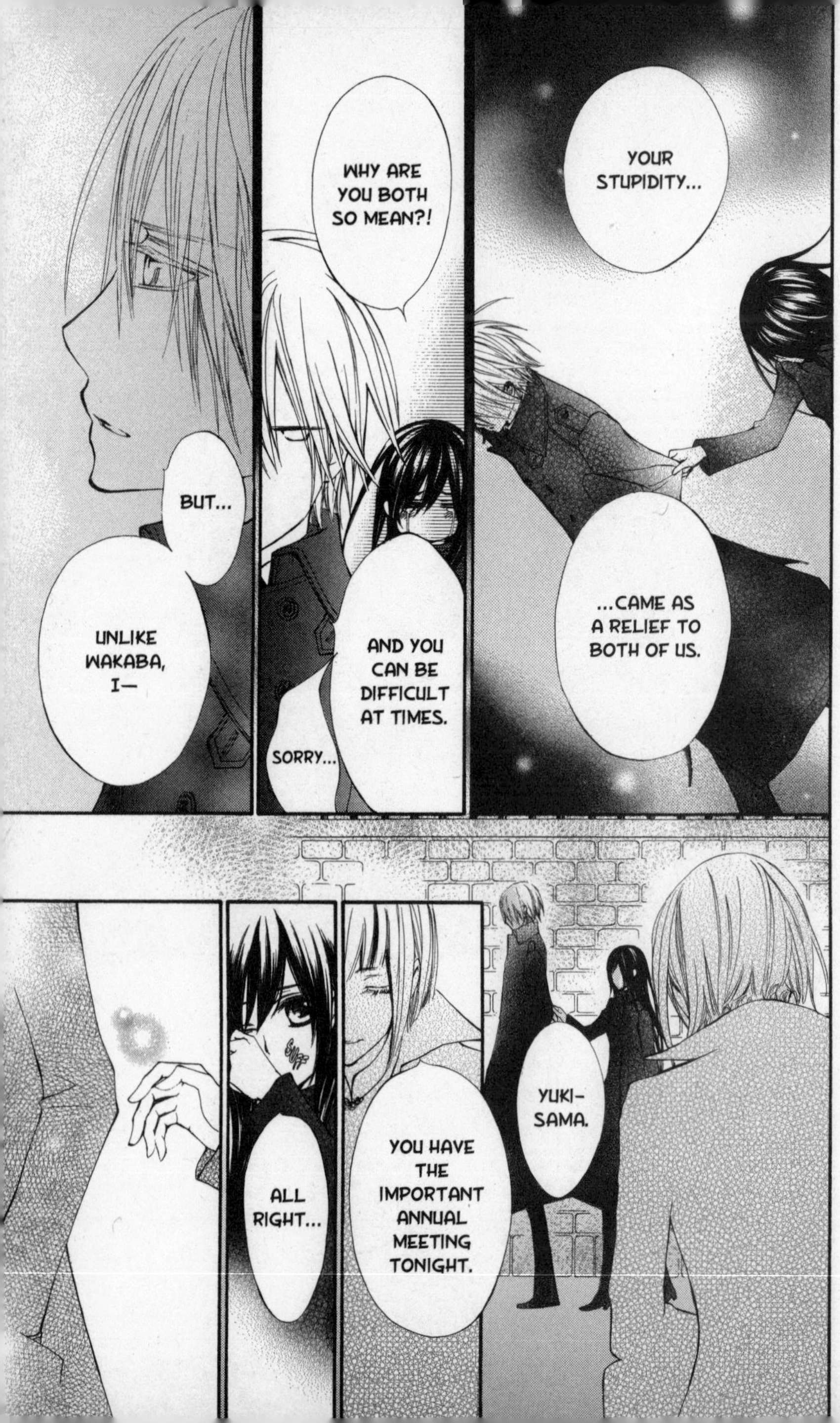
YOUR STUPIDITY...
...CAME AS A RELIEF TO BOTH OF US.
WHY ARE YOU BOTH SO MEAN?!
AND YOU CAN BE DIFFICULT AT TIMES.
SORRY...
BUT...
UNLIKE WAKABA, I—
YUKI-SAMA.
YOU HAVE THE IMPORTANT ANNUAL MEETING TONIGHT.
ALL RIGHT...

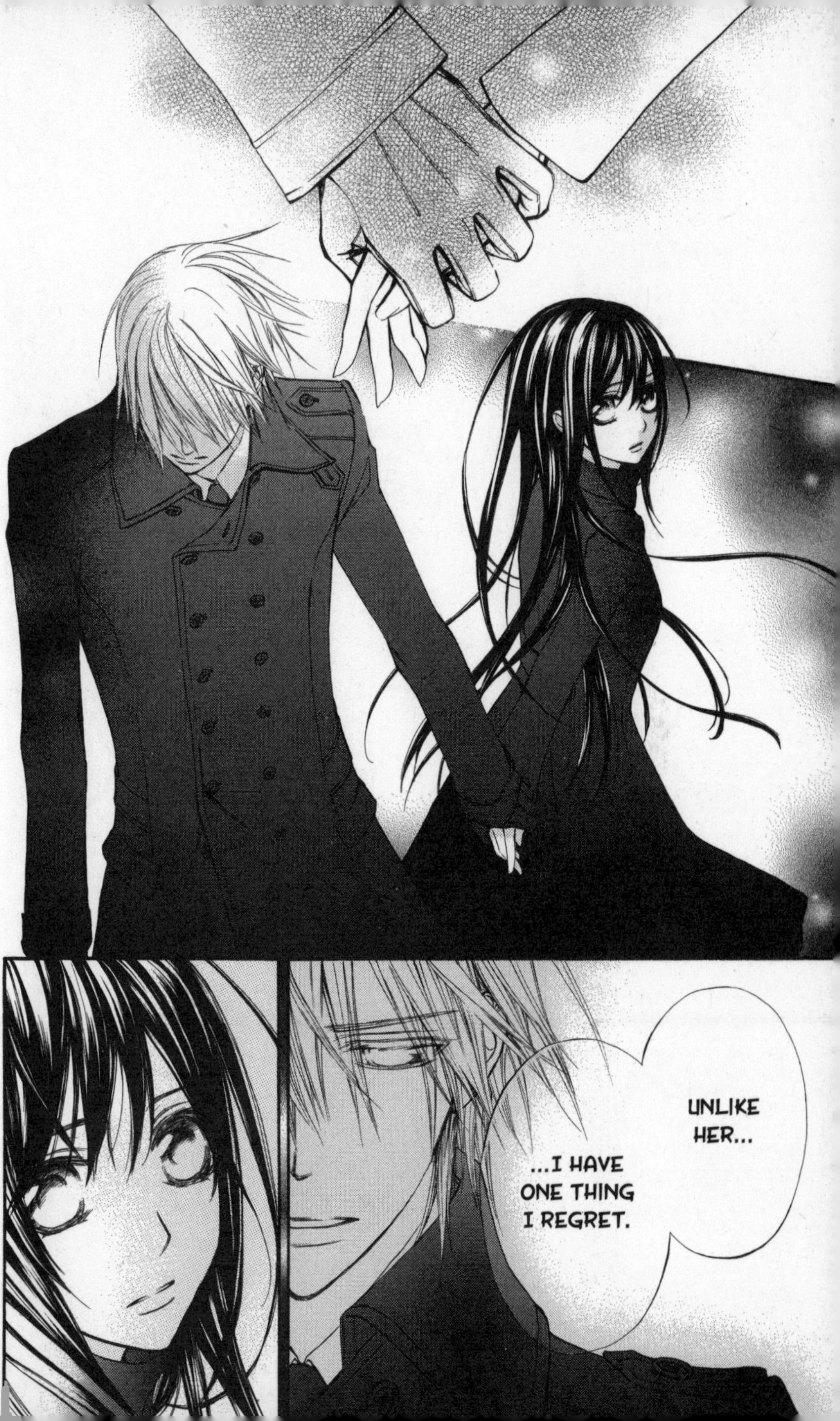
UNLIKE HER...
...I HAVE ONE THING I REGRET.

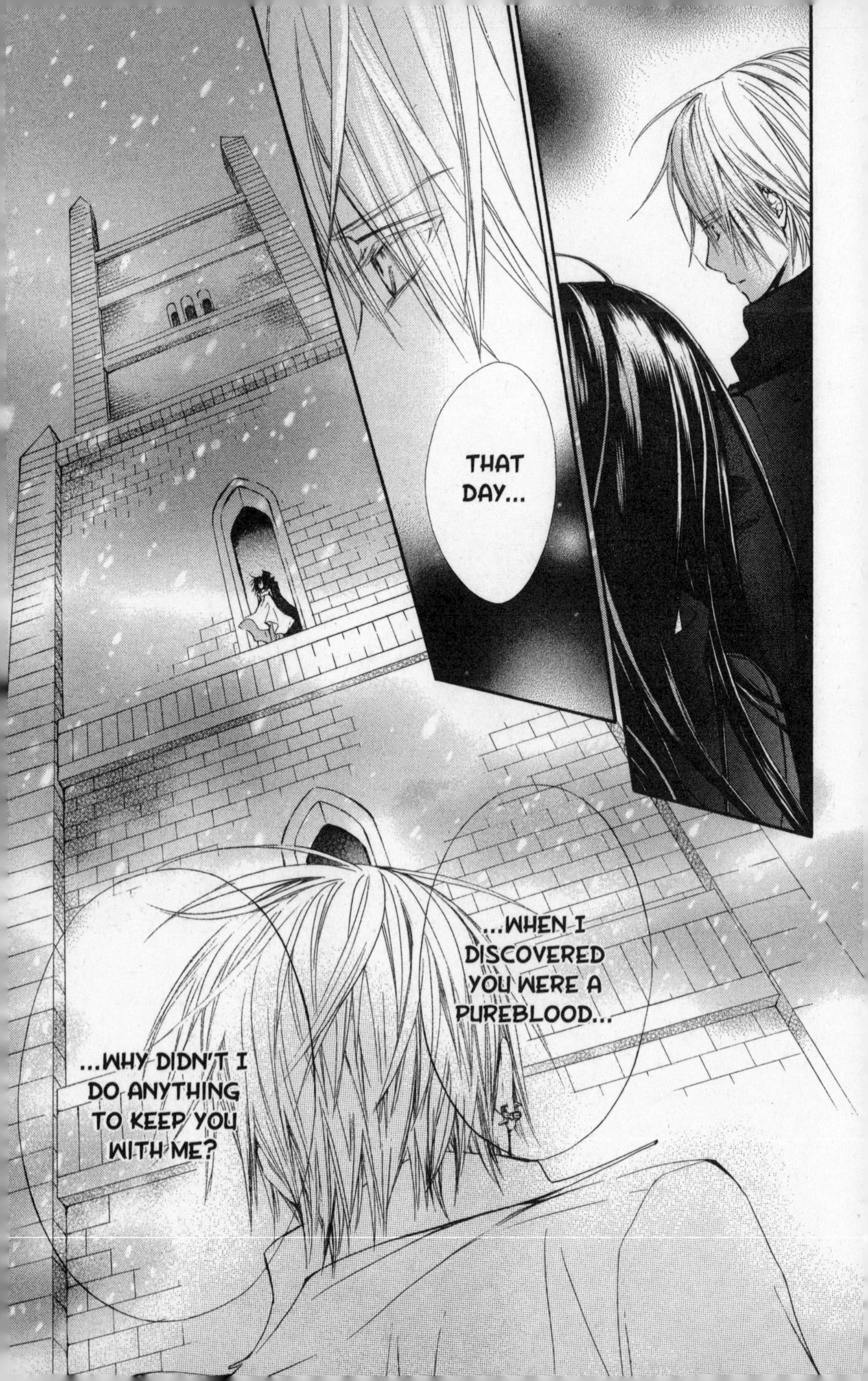
THAT DAY...
...WHEN I DISCOVERED YOU WERE A PUREBLOOD...
...WHY DIDN'T I DO ANYTHING TO KEEP YOU WITH ME?

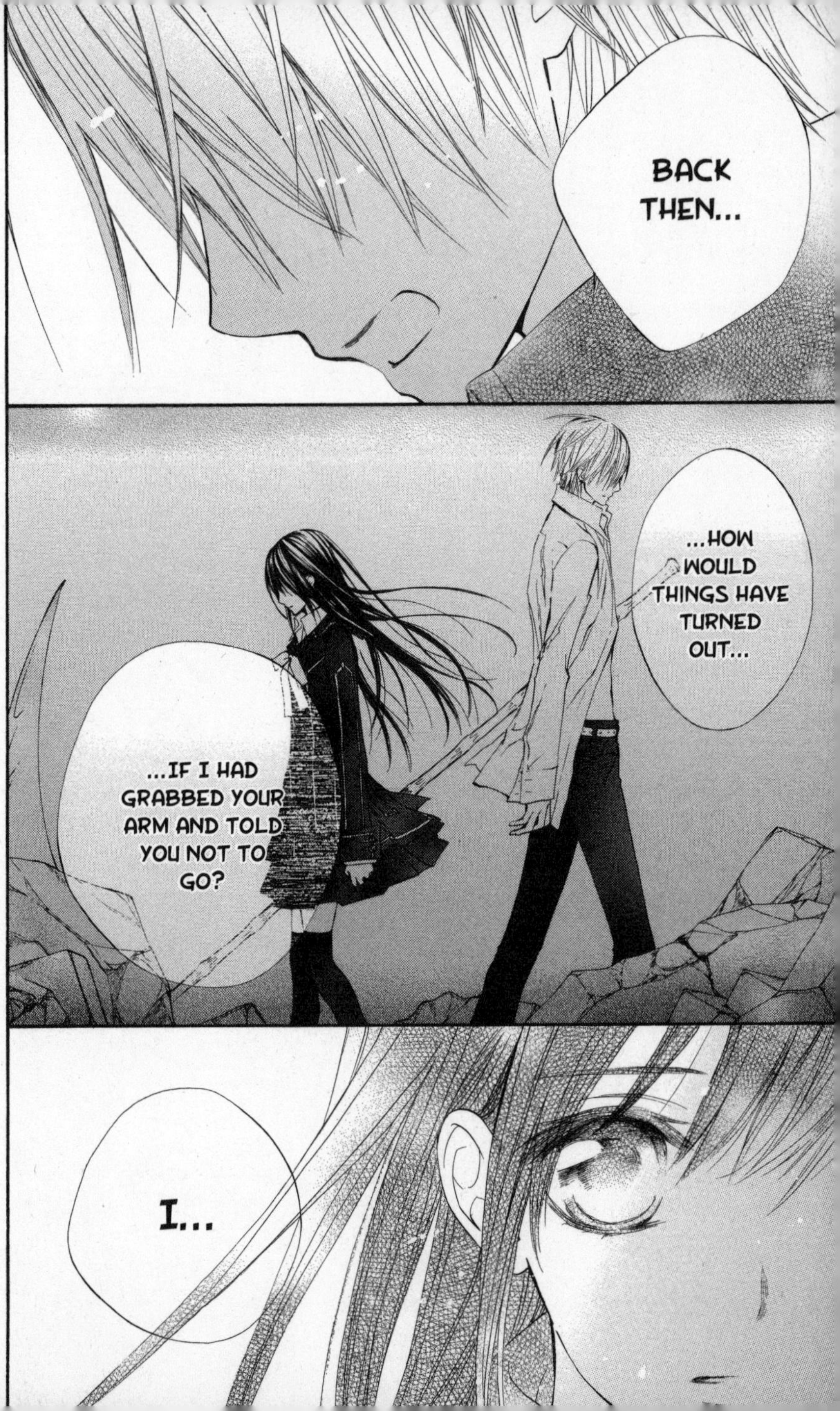
BACK THEN...
...HOW WOULD THINGS HAVE TURNED OUT...
...IF I HAD GRABBED YOUR ARM AND TOLD YOU NOT TO GO?
I...

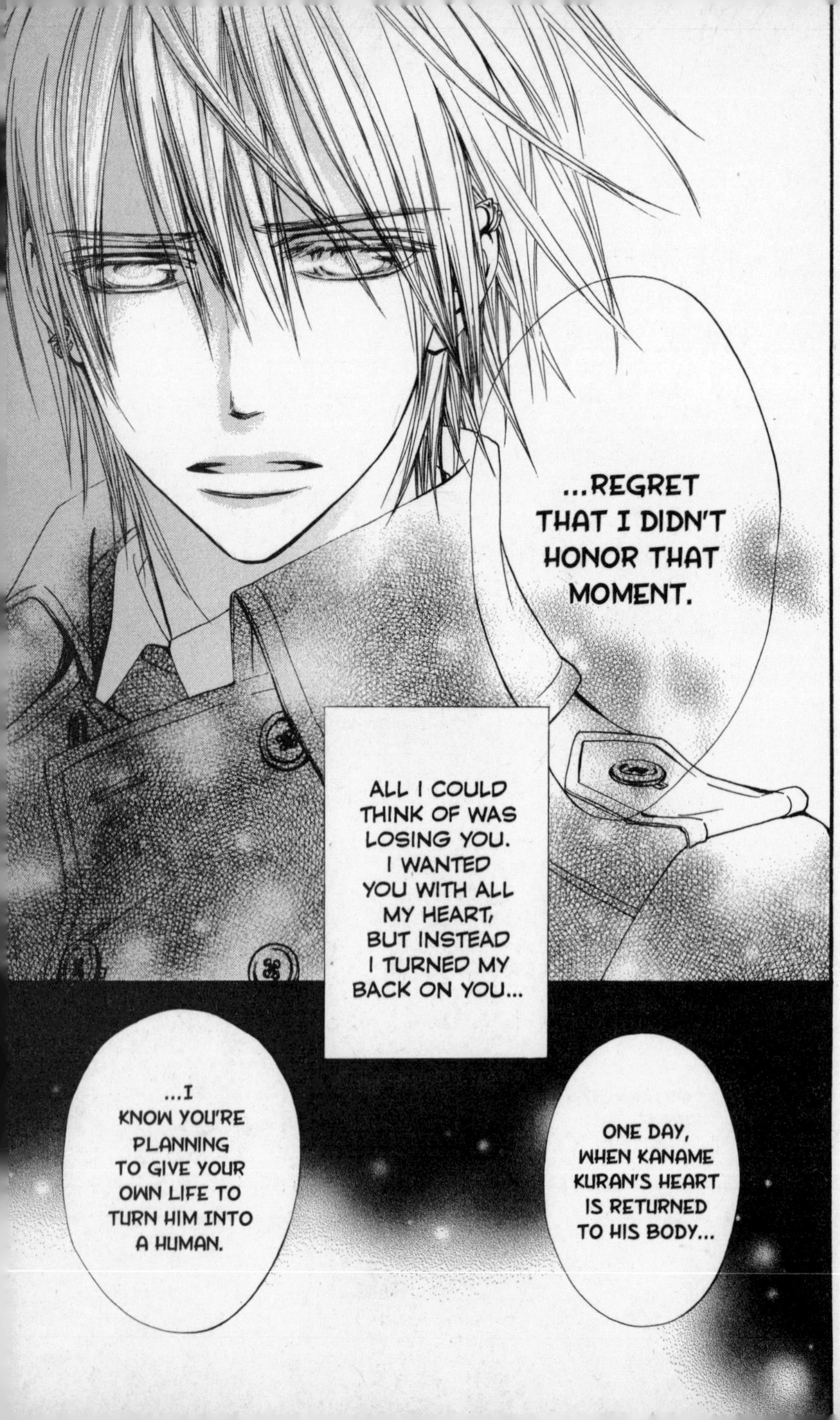
...REGRET THAT I DIDN'T HONOR THAT MOMENT.
ALL I COULD THINK OF WAS LOSING YOU. I WANTED YOU WITH ALL MY HEART, BUT INSTEAD I TURNED MY BACK ON YOU...
ONE DAY, WHEN KANAME KURAN'S HEART IS RETURNED TO HIS BODY...
...I KNOW YOU'RE PLANNING TO GIVE YOUR OWN LIFE TO TURN HIM INTO A HUMAN.

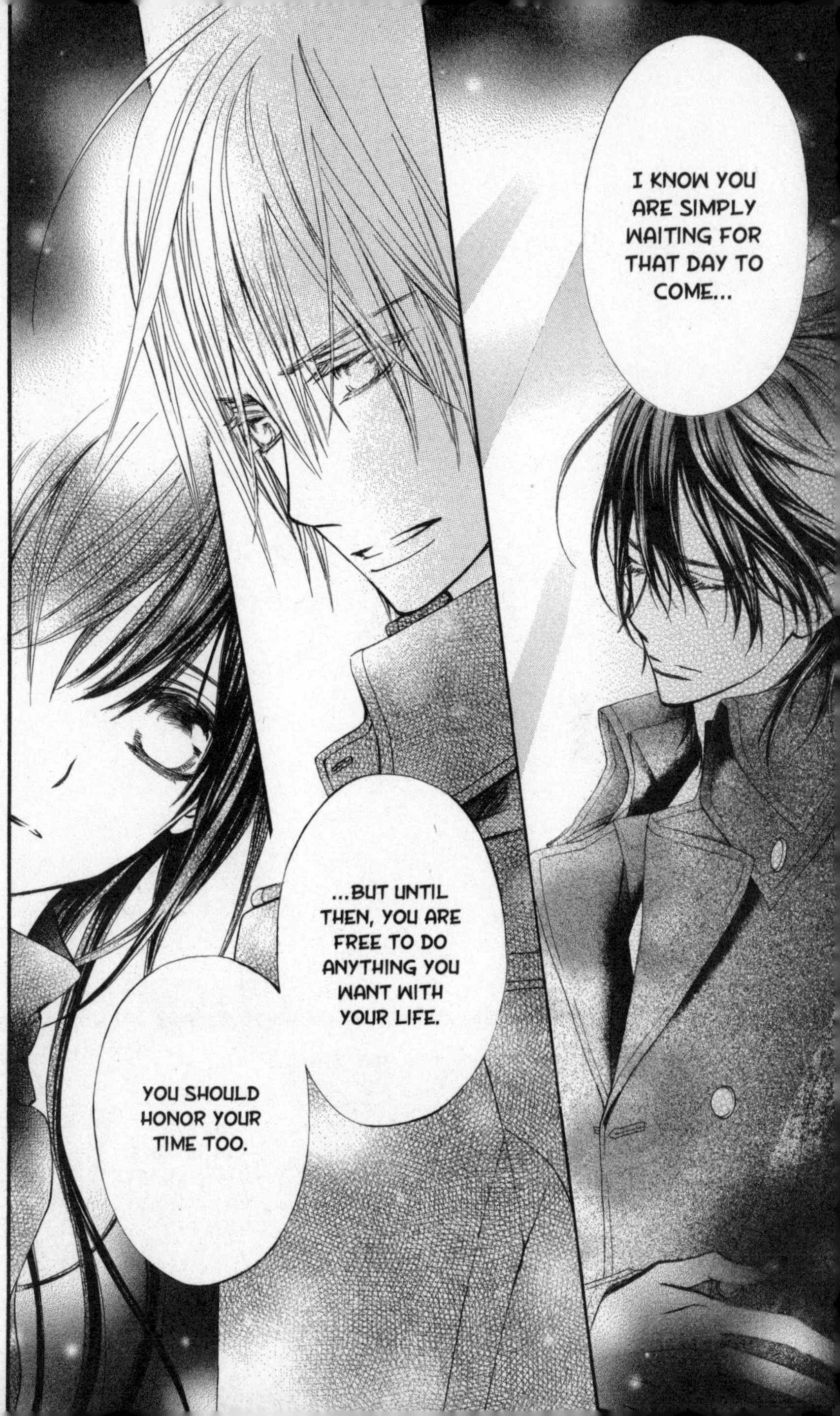
I KNOW YOU ARE SIMPLY WAITING FOR THAT DAY TO COME...
...BUT UNTIL THEN, YOU ARE FREE TO DO ANYTHING YOU WANT WITH YOUR LIFE.
YOU SHOULD HONOR YOUR TIME TOO.

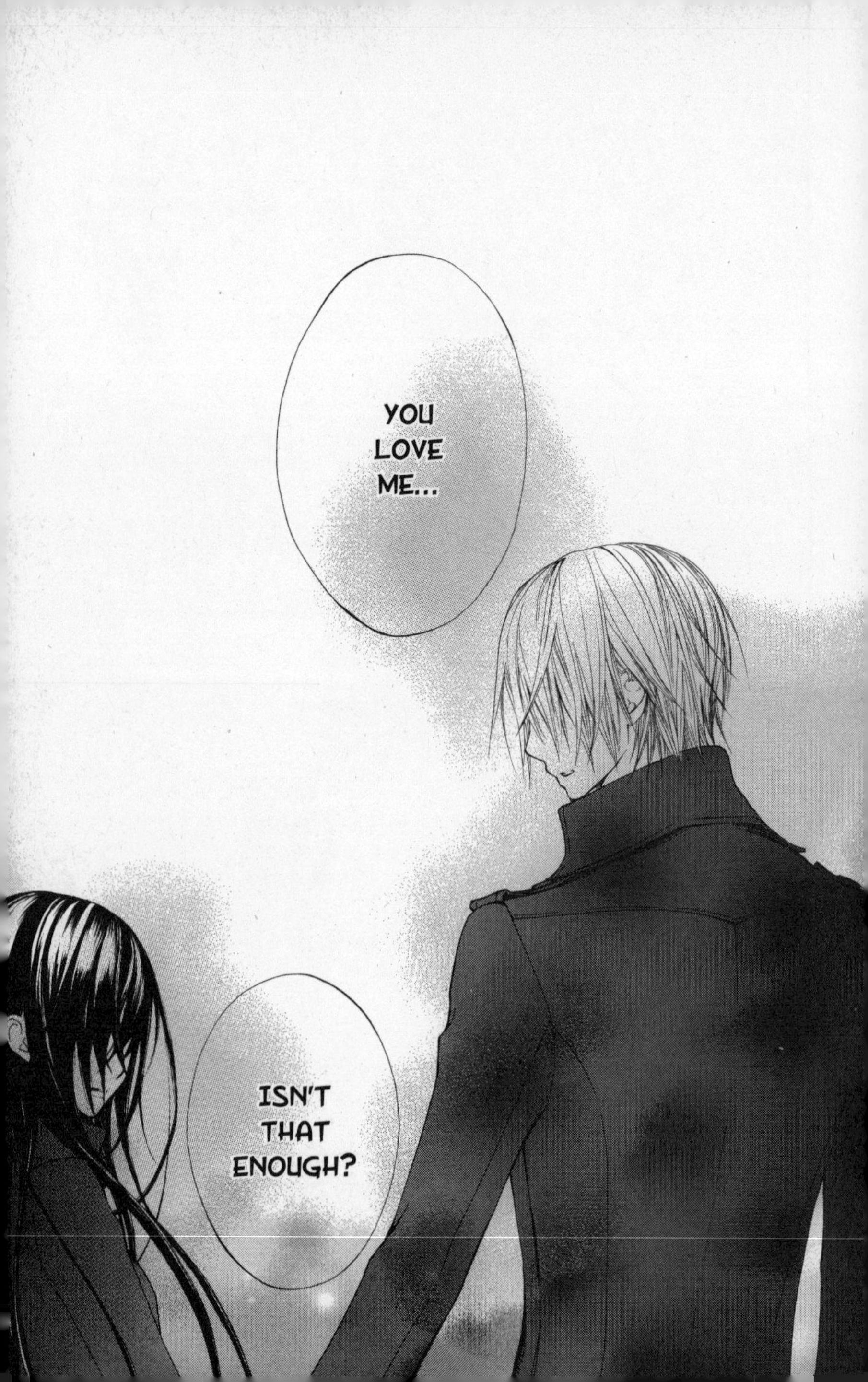
YOU LOVE ME...
ISN'T THAT ENOUGH?

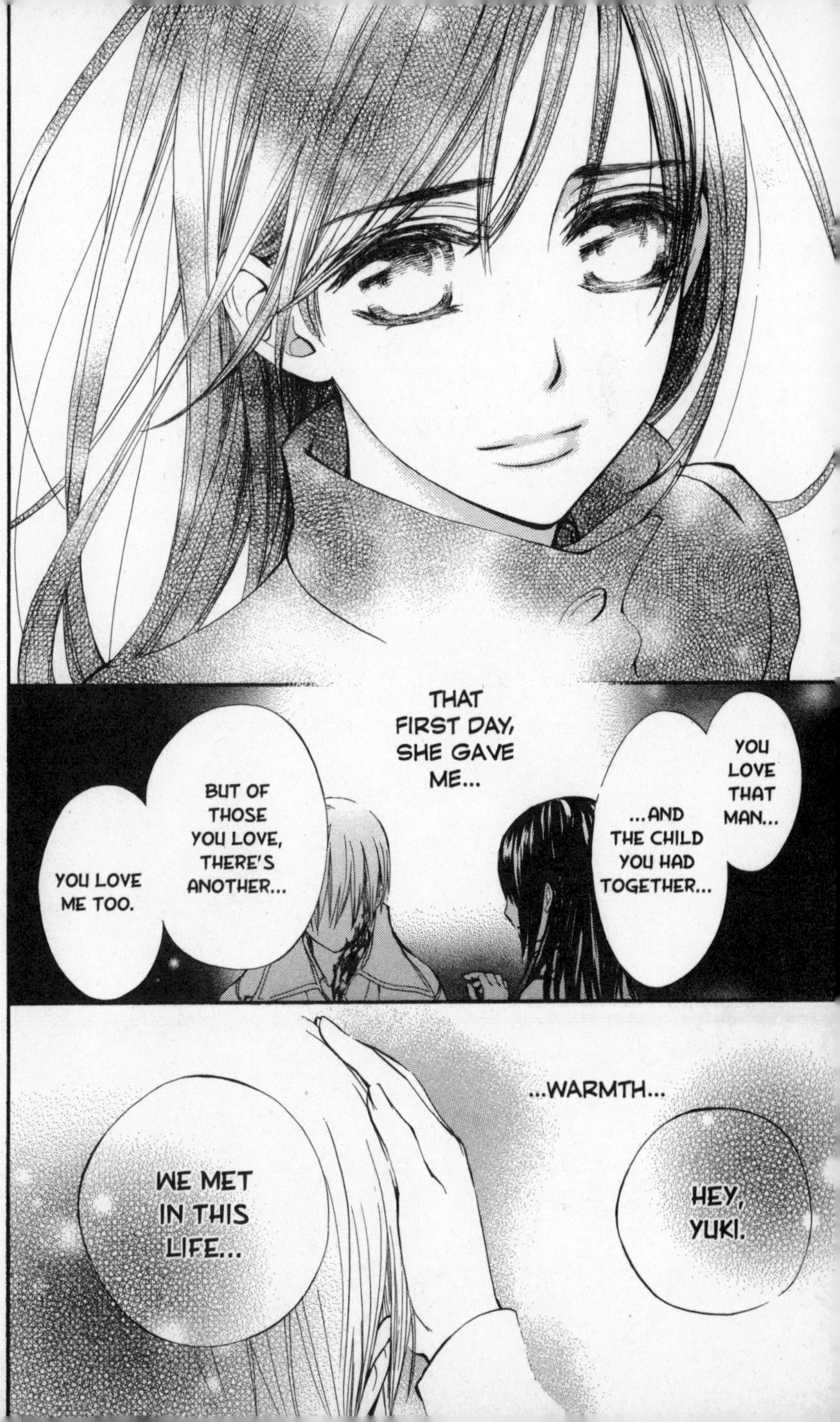
YOU LOVE THAT MAN...
THAT FIRST DAY, SHE GAVE ME...
...AND THE CHILD YOU HAD TOGETHER...
BUT OF THOSE YOU LOVE, THERE'S ANOTHER...
YOU LOVE ME TOO.
...WARMTH...
HEY, YUKI.
WE MET IN THIS LIFE...

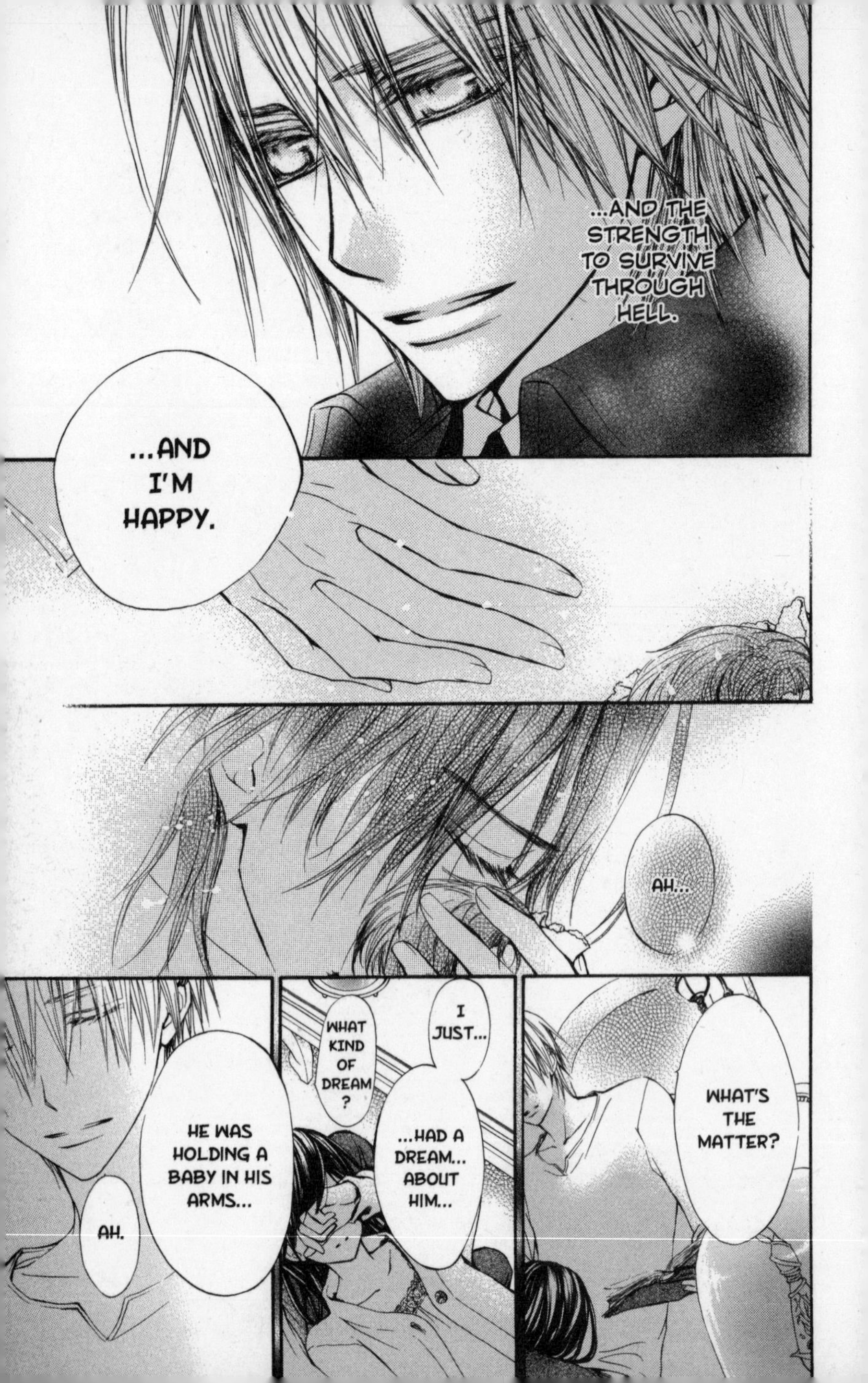
...AND THE STRENGTH TO SURVIVE THROUGH HELL.
...AND I'M HAPPY.
AH...
WHAT'S THE MATTER?
I JUST...
...HAD A DREAM... ABOUT HIM...
WHAT KIND OF DREAM?
HE WAS HOLDING A BABY IN HIS ARMS...
AH.

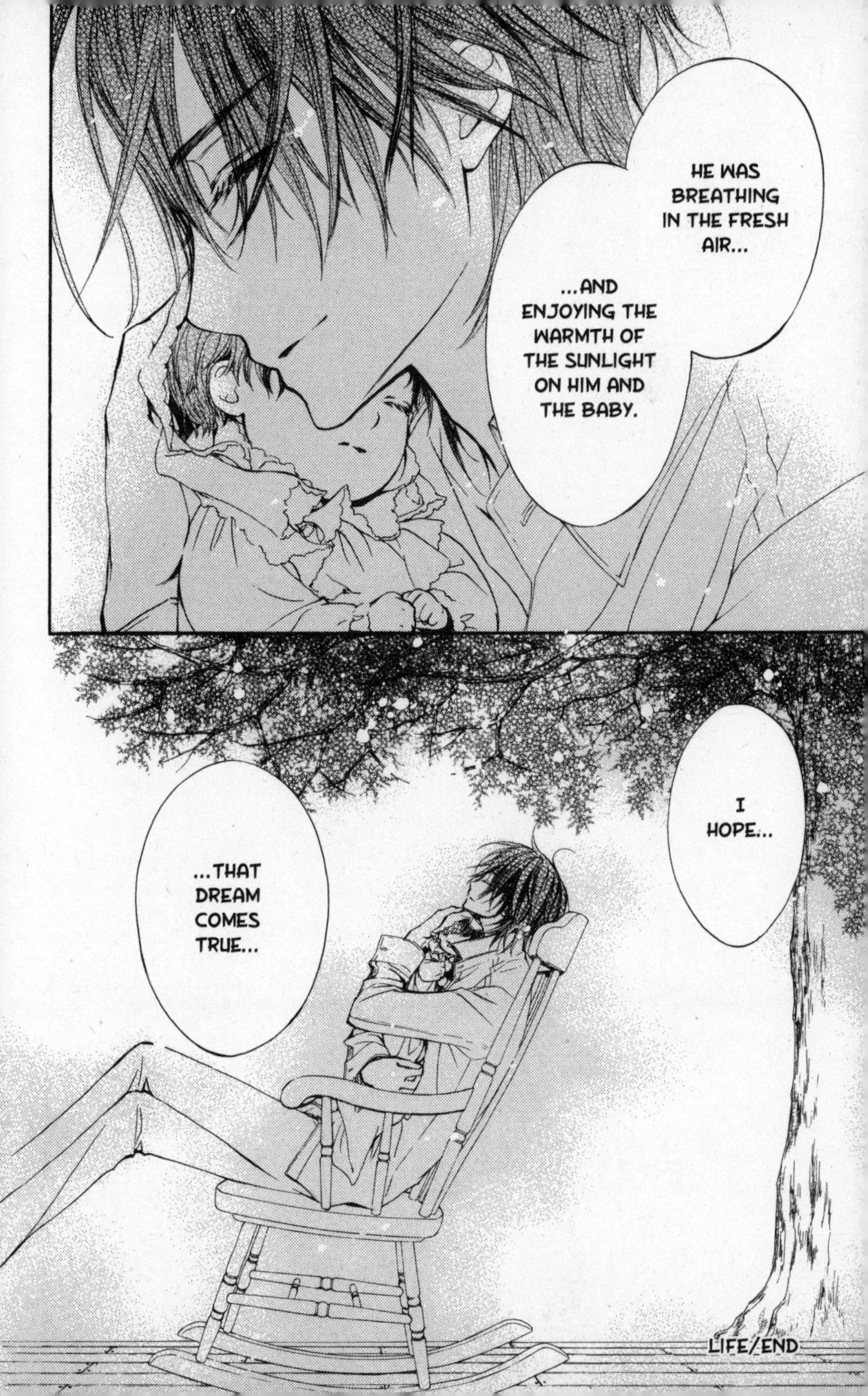
HE WAS BREATHING IN THE FRESH AIR...
...AND ENJOYING THE WARMTH OF THE SUNLIGHT ON HIM AND THE BABY.
I HOPE...
...THAT DREAM COMES TRUE...
LIFE/END

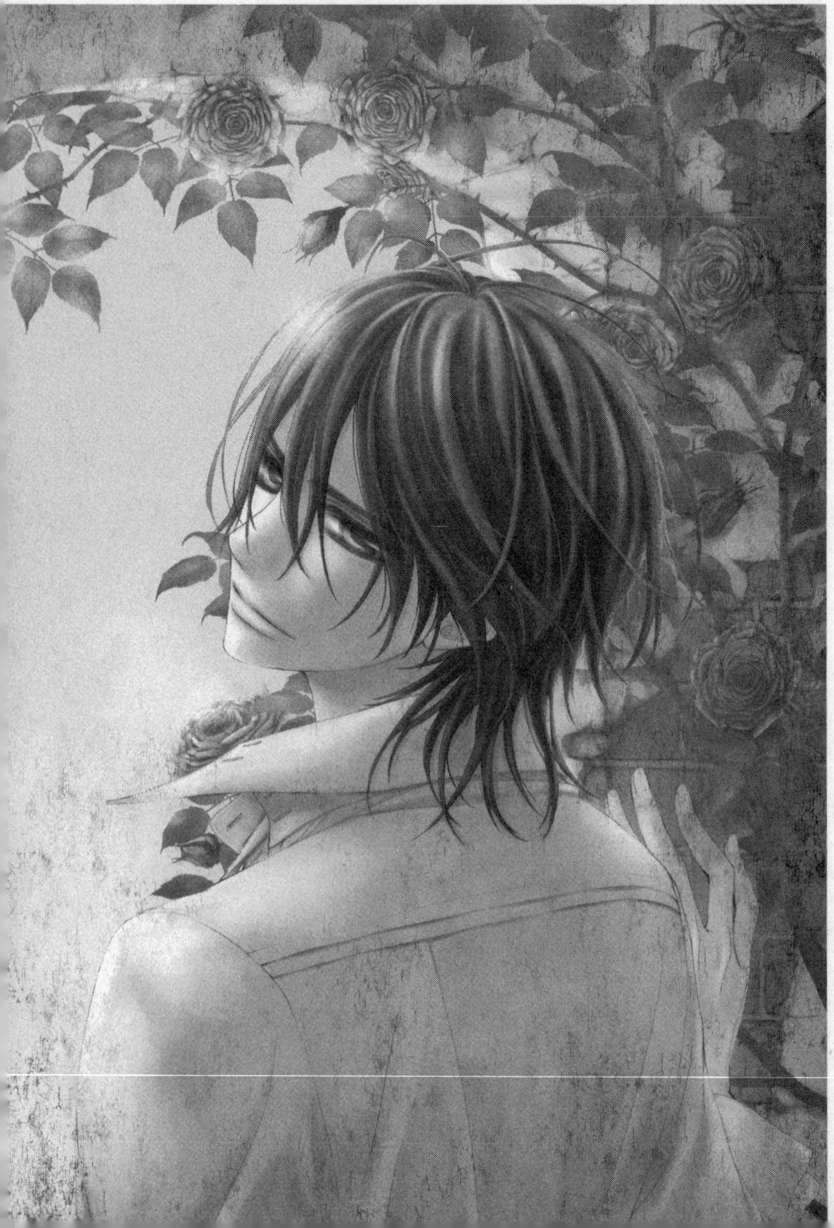

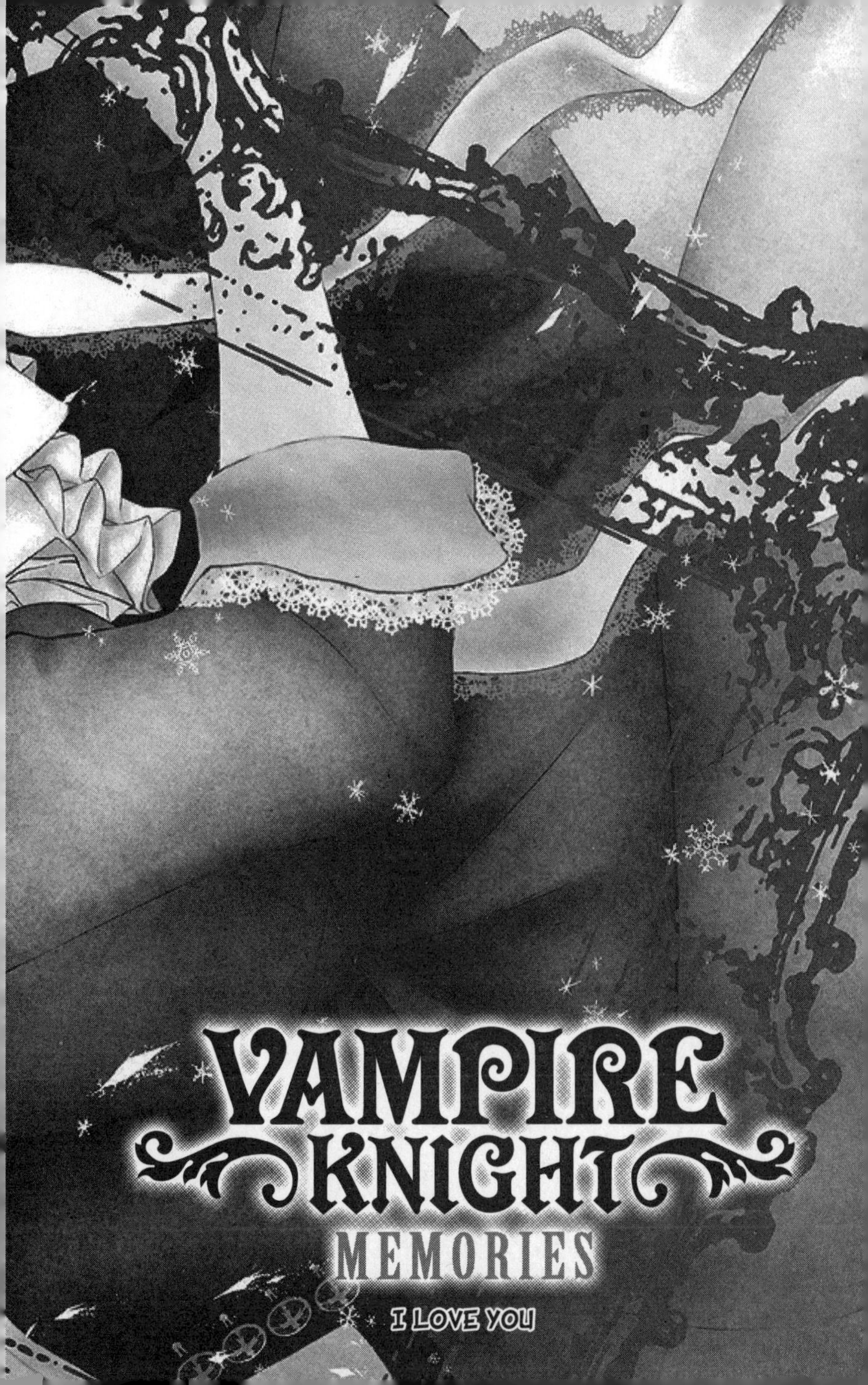
VAMPIRE KNIGHT
MEMORIES
I LOVE YOU

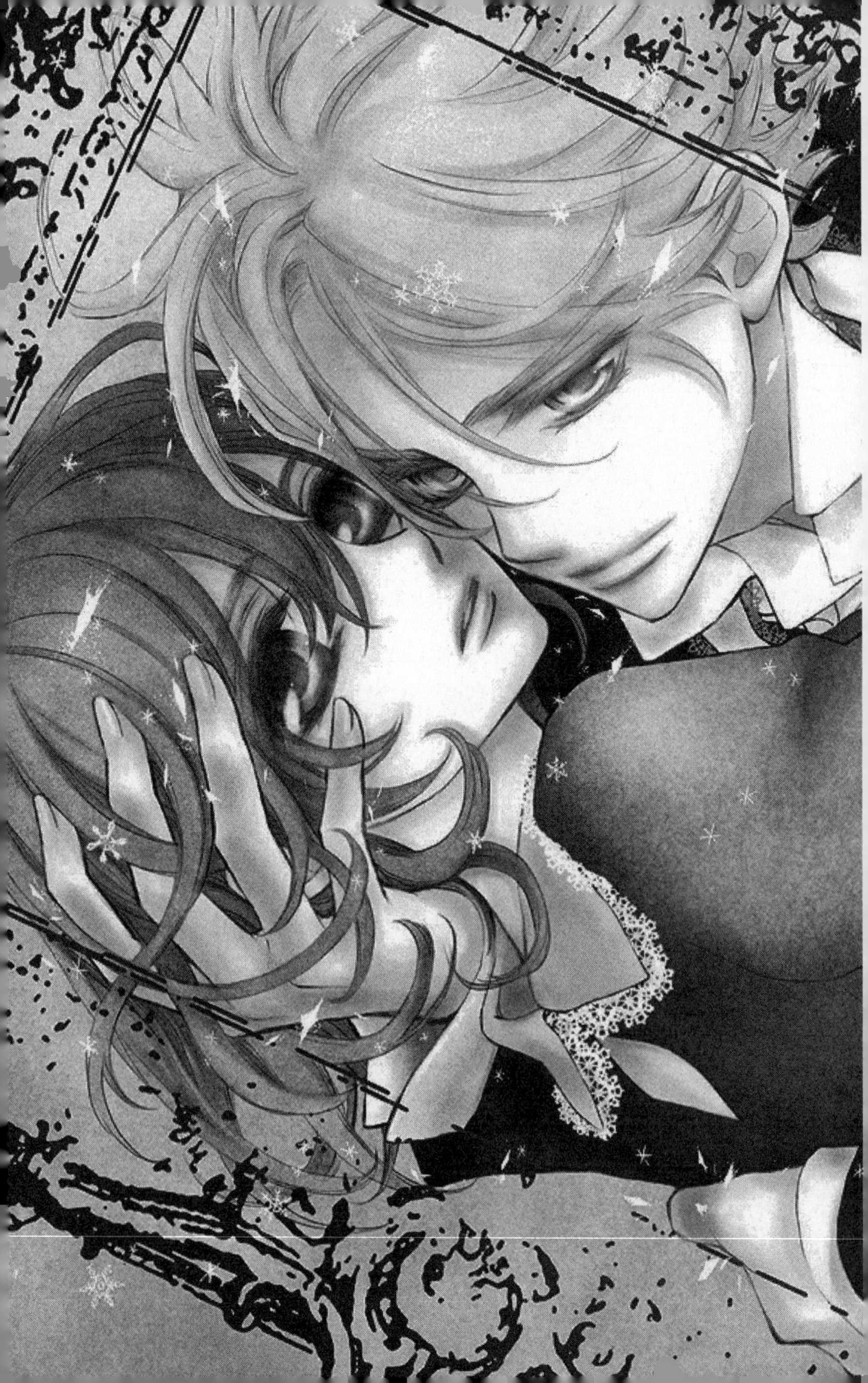

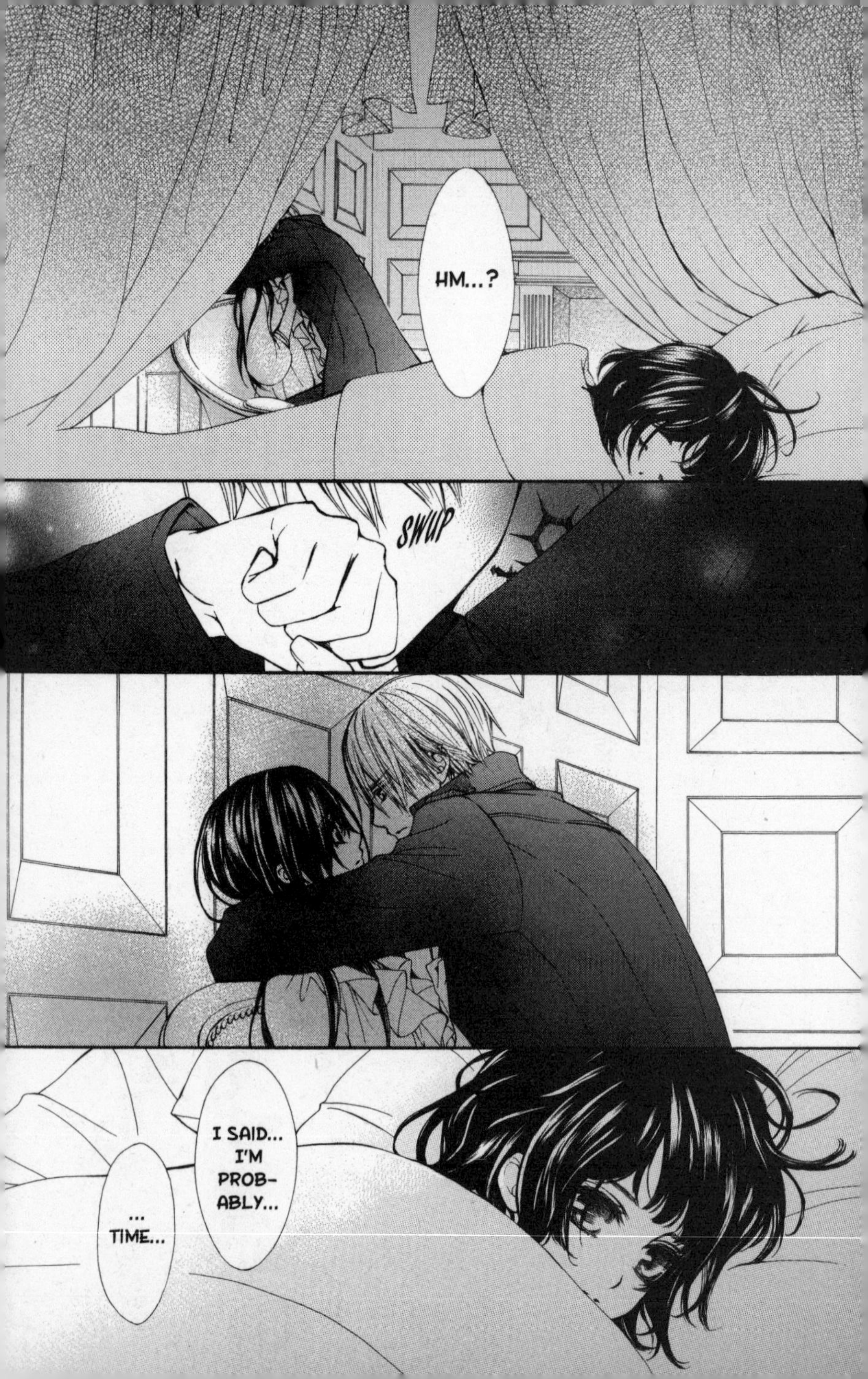
HM...?
SWUP
I SAID... I'M PROB-ABLY...
... TIME...

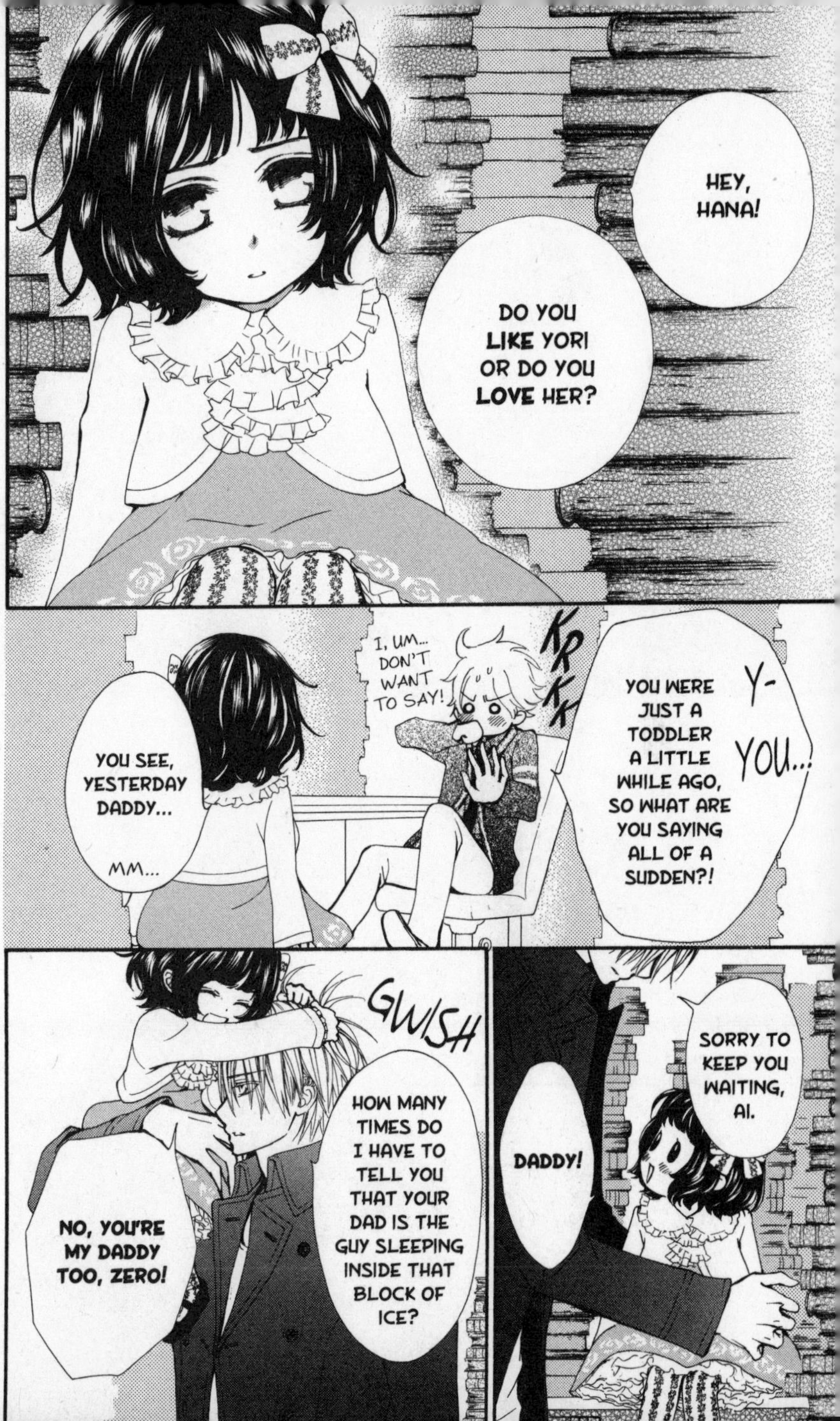

HEY, HANA!
DO YOU LIKE YORI OR DO YOU LOVE HER?
Y- YOU...
KRKK
YOU WERE JUST A TODDLER A LITTLE WHILE AGO, SO WHAT ARE YOU SAYING ALL OF A SUDDEN?!
I, UM... DON'T WANT TO SAY!
YOU SEE, YESTERDAY DADDY...
MM...
SORRY TO KEEP YOU WAITING, AI.
DADDY!
GWISH
HOW MANY TIMES DO I HAVE TO TELL YOU THAT YOUR DAD IS THE GUY SLEEPING INSIDE THAT BLOCK OF ICE?
NO, YOU'RE MY DADDY TOO, ZERO!

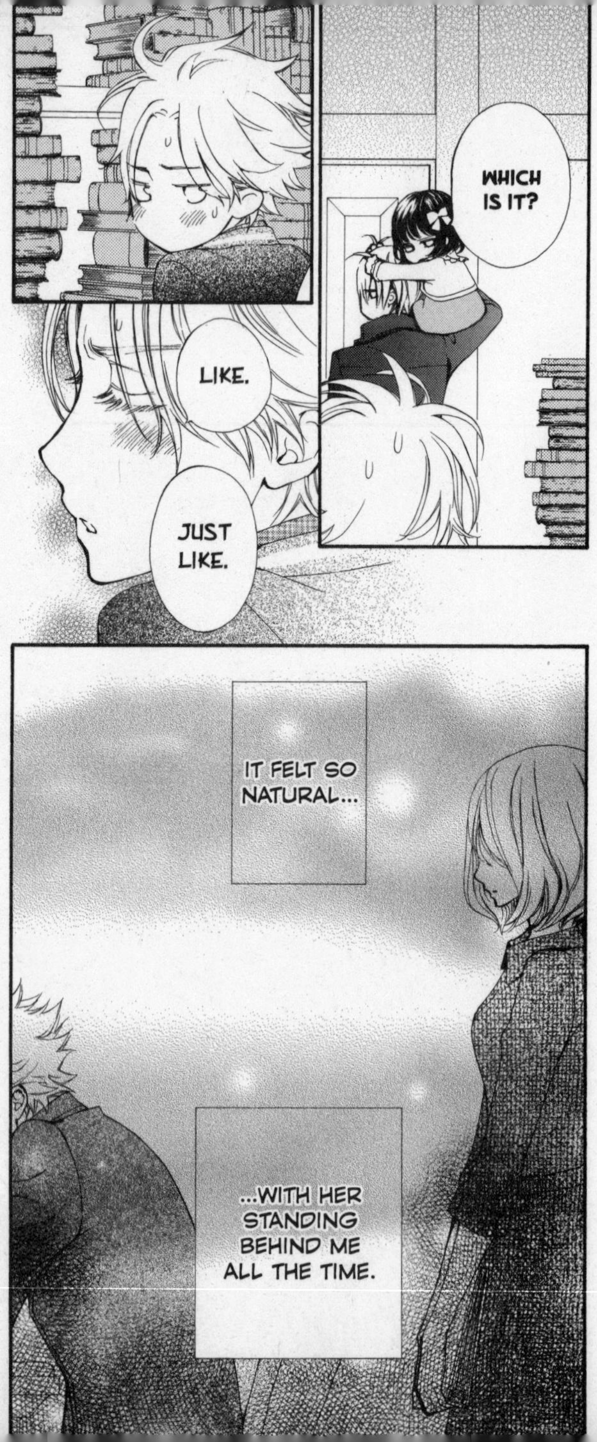
WHICH IS IT?
LIKE.
JUST LIKE.
IT FELT SO NATURAL...
...WITH HER STANDING BEHIND ME ALL THE TIME.

-2-

(I wrote about this in my BLOG, But...) I was strongly conflicted about whether to create special one-shot chapters for a series I had Brought to an end.

I'd Been fretting and pondering over that since I was asked to create the first special one-shot for *Vampire Knight*. I Began to feel strongly that I want to continue working on this series as long as I have the opportunity to do so.

I'm going to avoid saying what time period or scene I will create in future chapters, But as long as I'm working on this, I would like to cherish the 1,000 years that have passed, the future after those 1,000 years and all the characters.

So please sit Back and support *Vampire Knight* for just a little longer. It will Be serialized in *LaLa DX* (Lala Deluxe), a Bi-monthly magazine published on the tenth of even-numbered months in Japan.

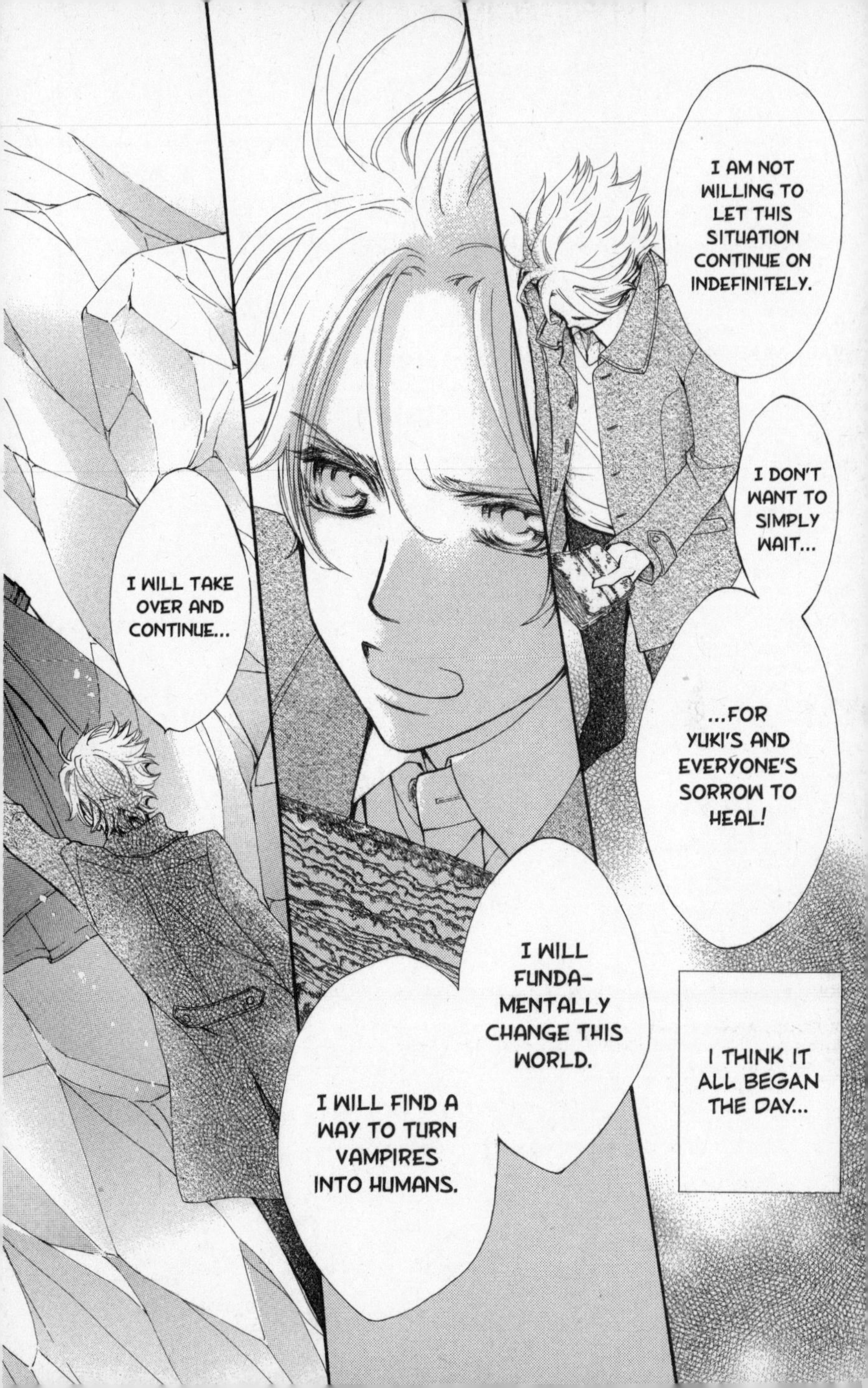
I AM NOT WILLING TO LET THIS SITUATION CONTINUE ON INDEFINITELY.
I DON'T WANT TO SIMPLY WAIT...
...FOR YUKI'S AND EVERYONE'S SORROW TO HEAL!
I WILL FUNDA-MENTALLY CHANGE THIS WORLD.
I WILL FIND A WAY TO TURN VAMPIRES INTO HUMANS.
I WILL TAKE OVER AND CONTINUE...
I THINK IT ALL BEGAN THE DAY...

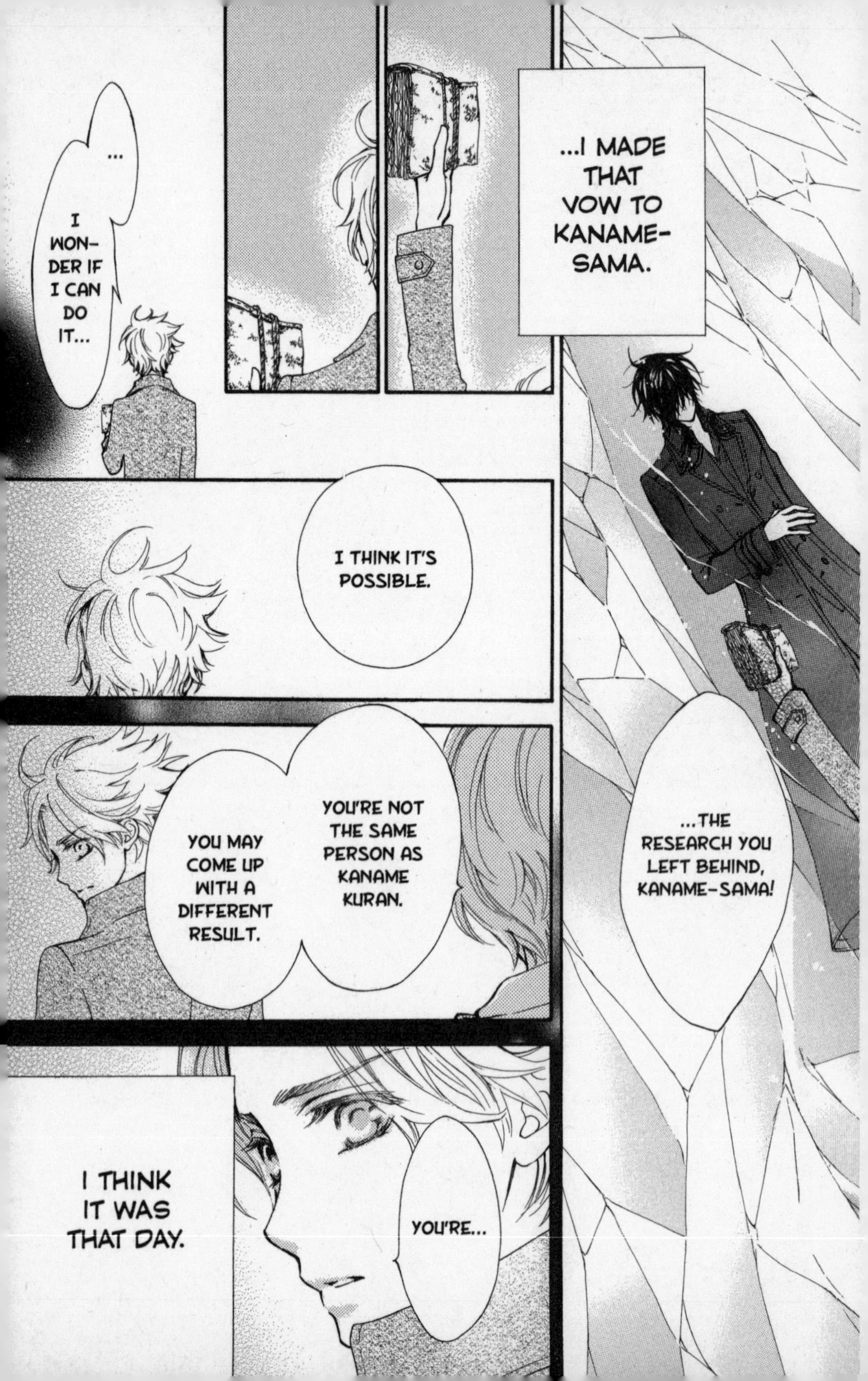
...I MADE THAT VOW TO KANAME-SAMA.
...THE RESEARCH YOU LEFT BEHIND, KANAME-SAMA!
...
I WONDER IF I CAN DO IT...
I THINK IT'S POSSIBLE.
YOU'RE NOT THE SAME PERSON AS KANAME KURAN.
YOU MAY COME UP WITH A DIFFERENT RESULT.
YOU'RE...
I THINK IT WAS THAT DAY.

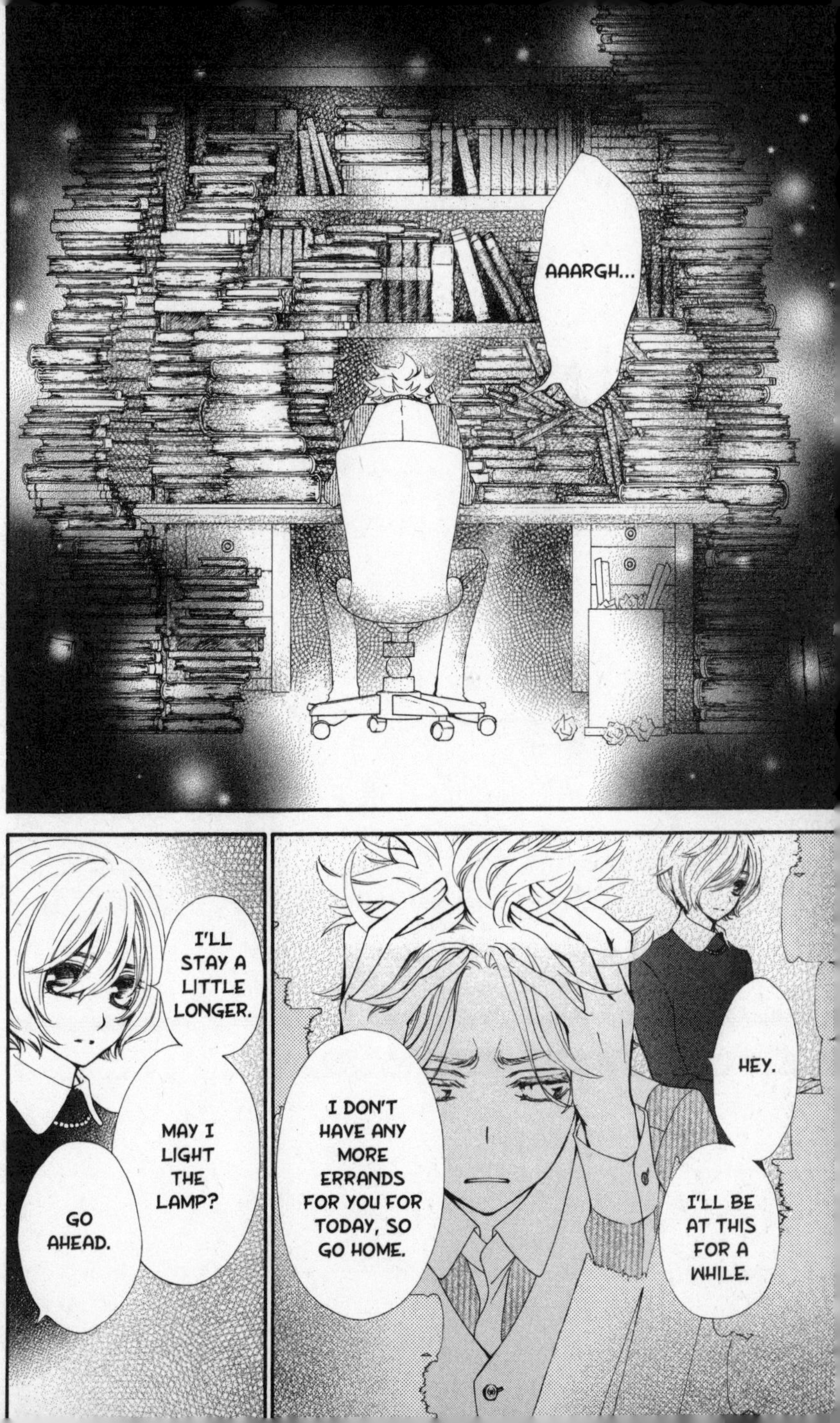
AAARGH...
HEY.
I'LL BE AT THIS FOR A WHILE.
I DON'T HAVE ANY MORE ERRANDS FOR YOU FOR TODAY, SO GO HOME.
I'LL STAY A LITTLE LONGER.
MAY I LIGHT THE LAMP?
GO AHEAD.

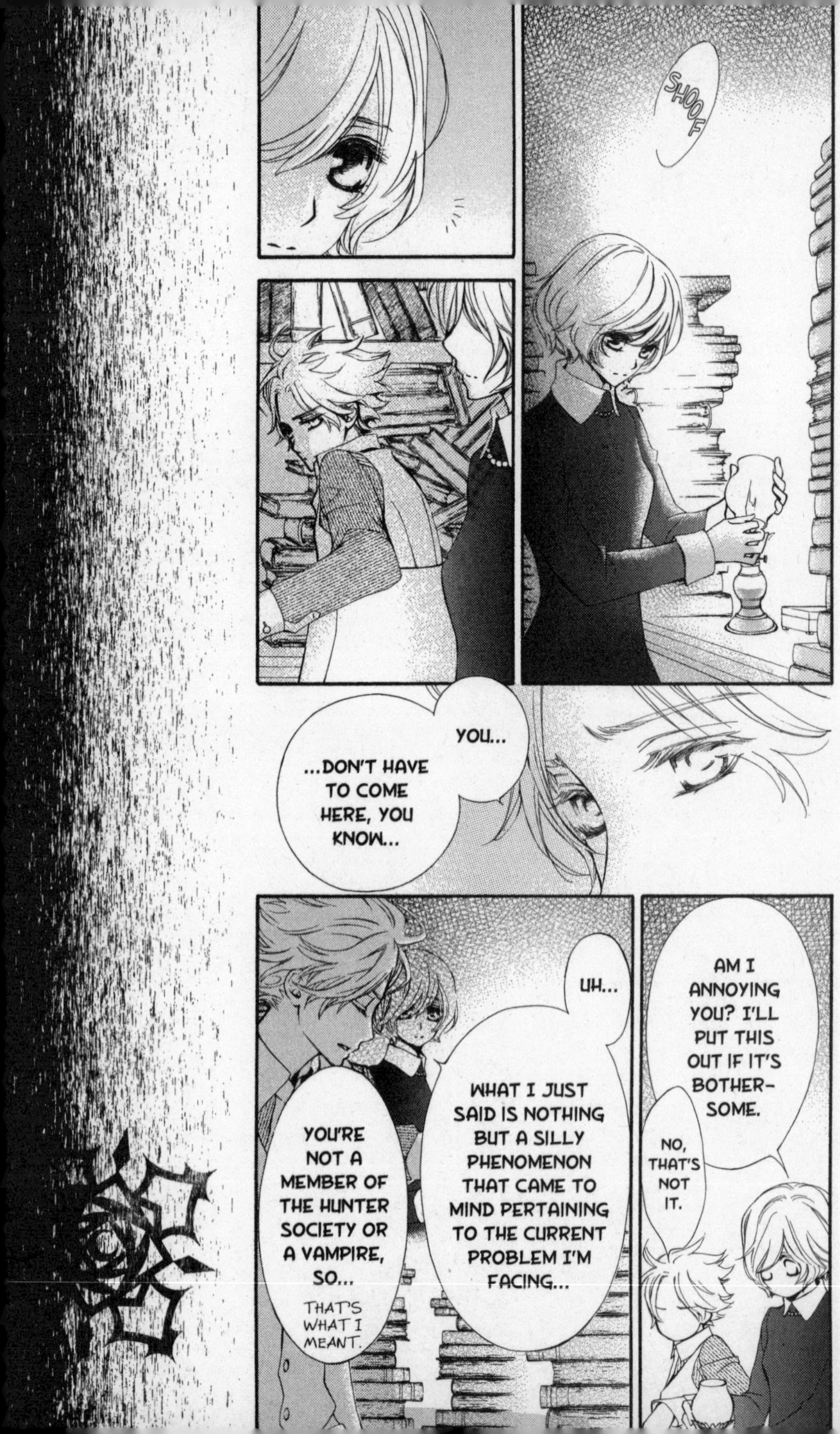
SHOOF
YOU...
...DON'T HAVE TO COME HERE, YOU KNOW...
AM I ANNOYING YOU? I'LL PUT THIS OUT IF IT'S BOTHER-SOME.
NO, THAT'S NOT IT.
UH...
WHAT I JUST SAID IS NOTHING BUT A SILLY PHENOMENON THAT CAME TO MIND PERTAINING TO THE CURRENT PROBLEM I'M FACING...
YOU'RE NOT A MEMBER OF THE HUNTER SOCIETY OR A VAMPIRE, SO...
THAT'S WHAT I MEANT.

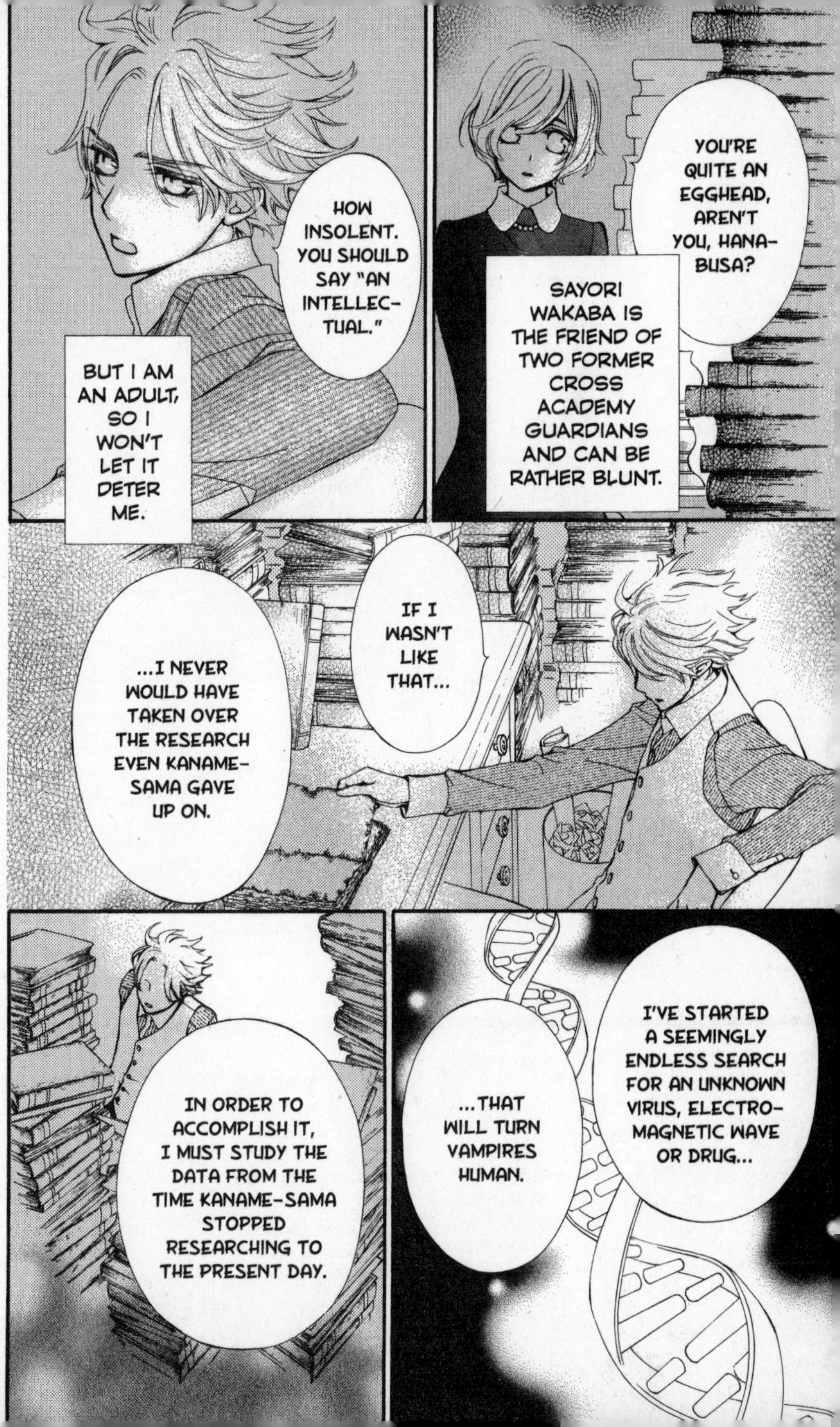
YOU'RE QUITE AN EGGHEAD, AREN'T YOU, HANA-BUSA?
SAYORI WAKABA IS THE FRIEND OF TWO FORMER CROSS ACADEMY GUARDIANS AND CAN BE RATHER BLUNT.
HOW INSOLENT. YOU SHOULD SAY "AN INTELLEC-TUAL."
BUT I AM AN ADULT, SO I WON'T LET IT DETER ME.
IF I WASN'T LIKE THAT...
...I NEVER WOULD HAVE TAKEN OVER THE RESEARCH EVEN KANAME-SAMA GAVE UP ON.
I'VE STARTED A SEEMINGLY ENDLESS SEARCH FOR AN UNKNOWN VIRUS, ELECTRO-MAGNETIC WAVE OR DRUG...
...THAT WILL TURN VAMPIRES HUMAN.
IN ORDER TO ACCOMPLISH IT, I MUST STUDY THE DATA FROM THE TIME KANAME-SAMA STOPPED RESEARCHING TO THE PRESENT DAY.

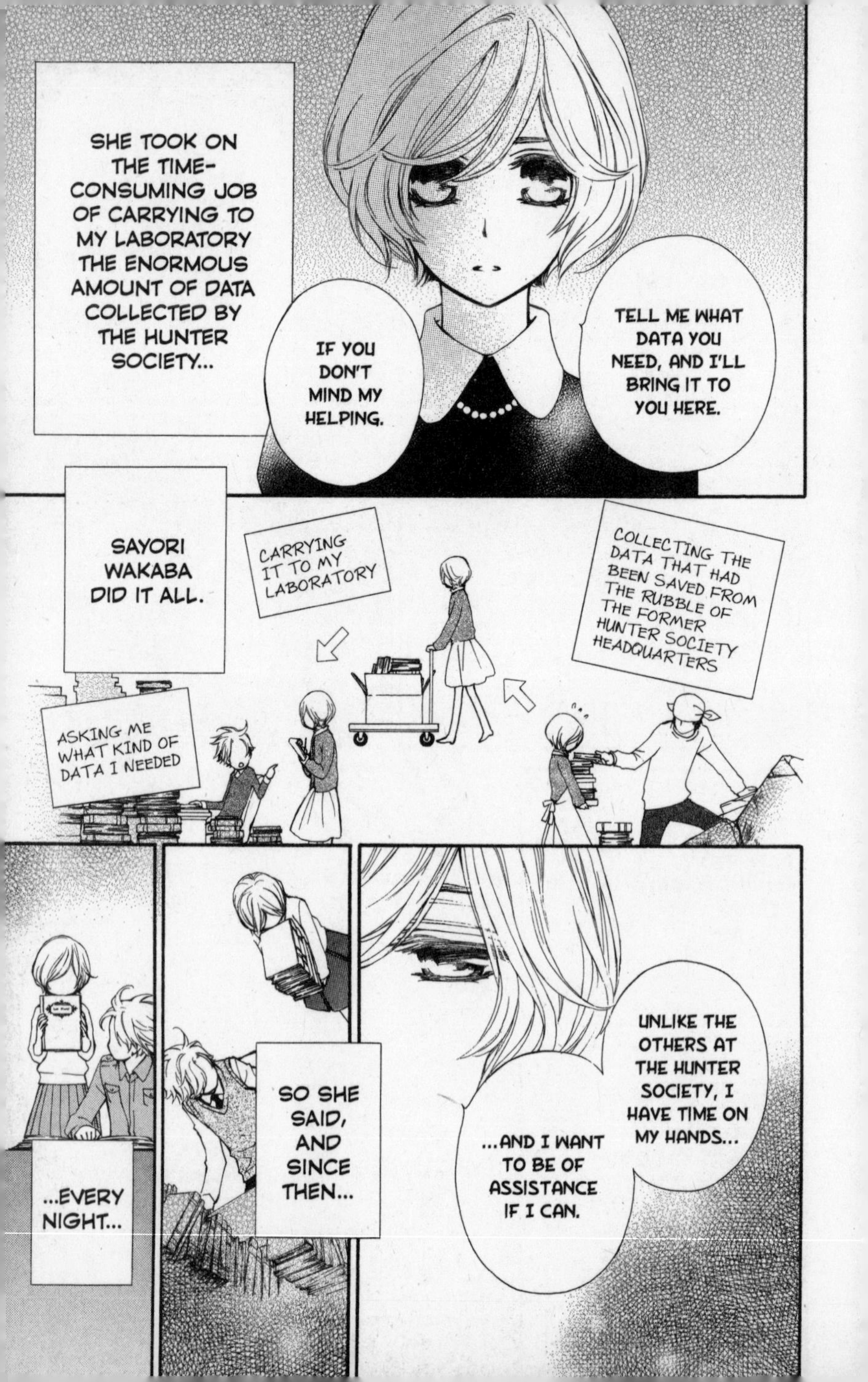
TELL ME WHAT DATA YOU NEED, AND I'LL BRING IT TO YOU HERE.
IF YOU DON'T MIND MY HELPING.
SHE TOOK ON THE TIME-CONSUMING JOB OF CARRYING TO MY LABORATORY THE ENORMOUS AMOUNT OF DATA COLLECTED BY THE HUNTER SOCIETY...
COLLECTING THE DATA THAT HAD BEEN SAVED FROM THE RUBBLE OF THE FORMER HUNTER SOCIETY HEADQUARTERS
CARRYING IT TO MY LABORATORY
SAYORI WAKABA DID IT ALL.
ASKING ME WHAT KIND OF DATA I NEEDED
UNLIKE THE OTHERS AT THE HUNTER SOCIETY, I HAVE TIME ON MY HANDS...
...AND I WANT TO BE OF ASSISTANCE IF I CAN.
SO SHE SAID, AND SINCE THEN...
...EVERY NIGHT...

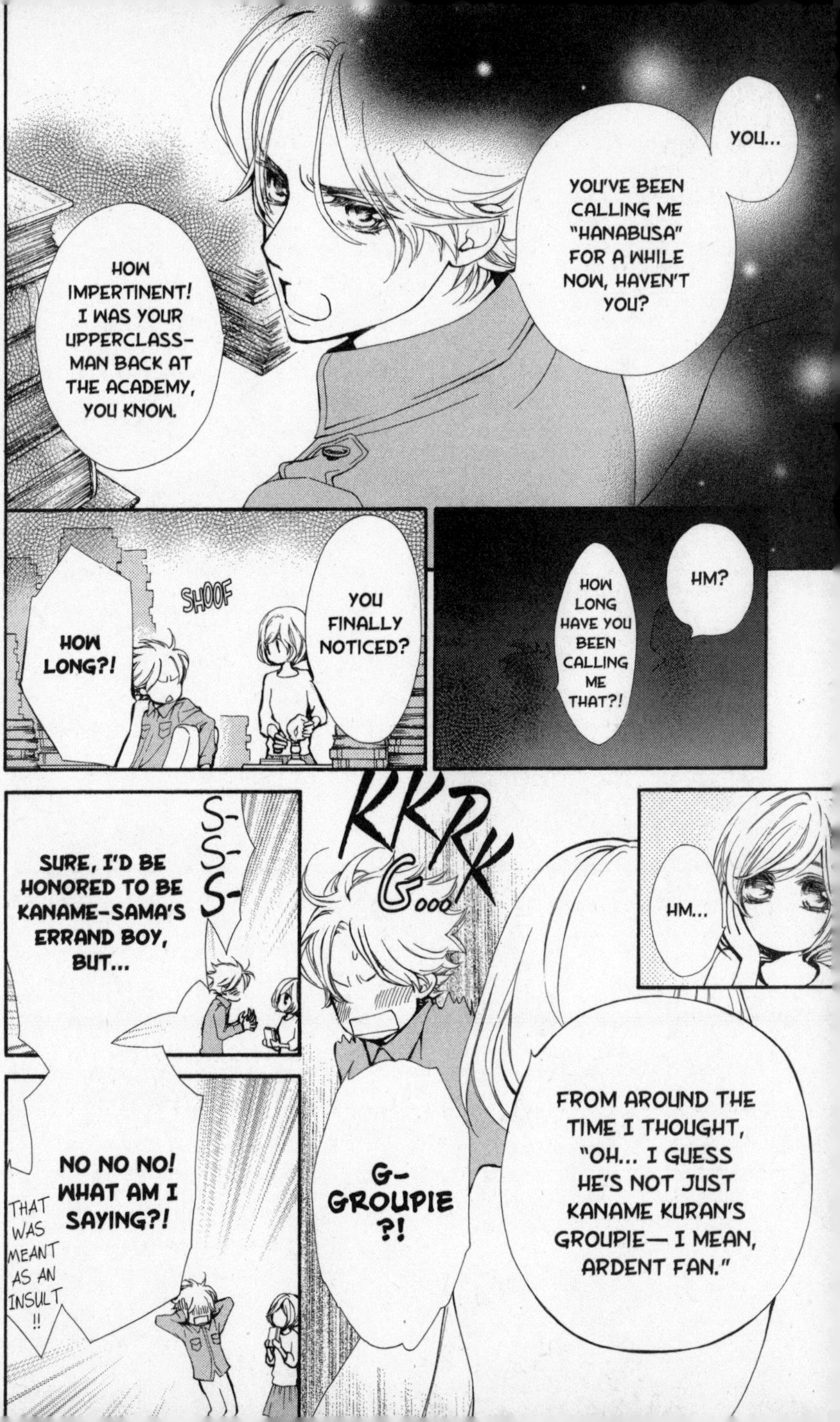
YOU...
YOU'VE BEEN CALLING ME "HANABUSA" FOR A WHILE NOW, HAVEN'T YOU?
HOW IMPERTINENT! I WAS YOUR UPPERCLASS-MAN BACK AT THE ACADEMY, YOU KNOW.
HM?
HOW LONG HAVE YOU BEEN CALLING ME THAT?!
YOU FINALLY NOTICED?
SHOOF
HOW LONG?!
HM...
FROM AROUND THE TIME I THOUGHT, "OH... I GUESS HE'S NOT JUST KANAME KURAN'S GROUPIE— I MEAN, ARDENT FAN."
KKRK
Gooo
G-GROUPIE?!
S-S-S-
SURE, I'D BE HONORED TO BE KANAME-SAMA'S ERRAND BOY, BUT...
NO NO NO! WHAT AM I SAYING?!
THAT WAS MEANT AS AN INSULT!!

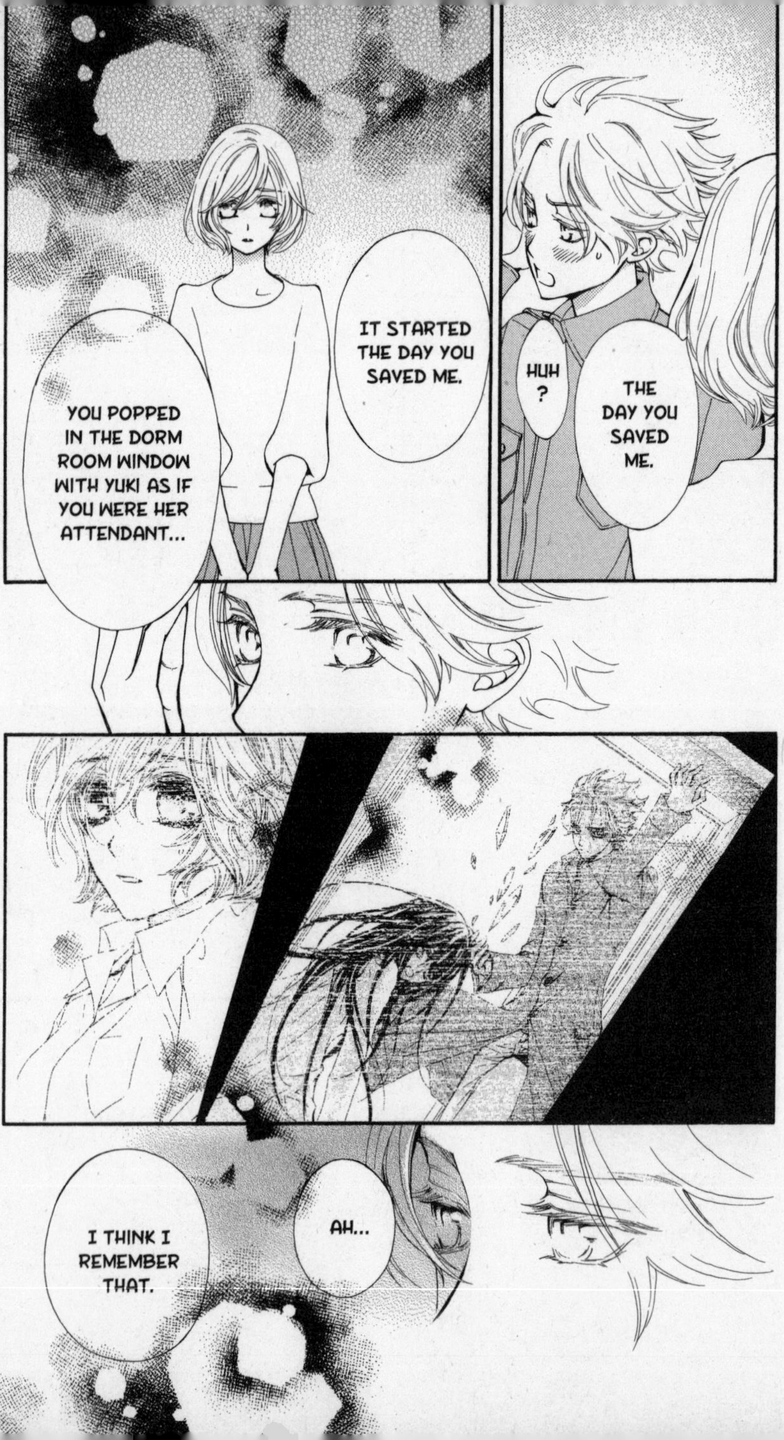
HUH ?
THE DAY YOU SAVED ME.
IT STARTED THE DAY YOU SAVED ME.
YOU POPPED IN THE DORM ROOM WINDOW WITH YUKI AS IF YOU WERE HER ATTENDANT...
AH...
I THINK I REMEMBER THAT.

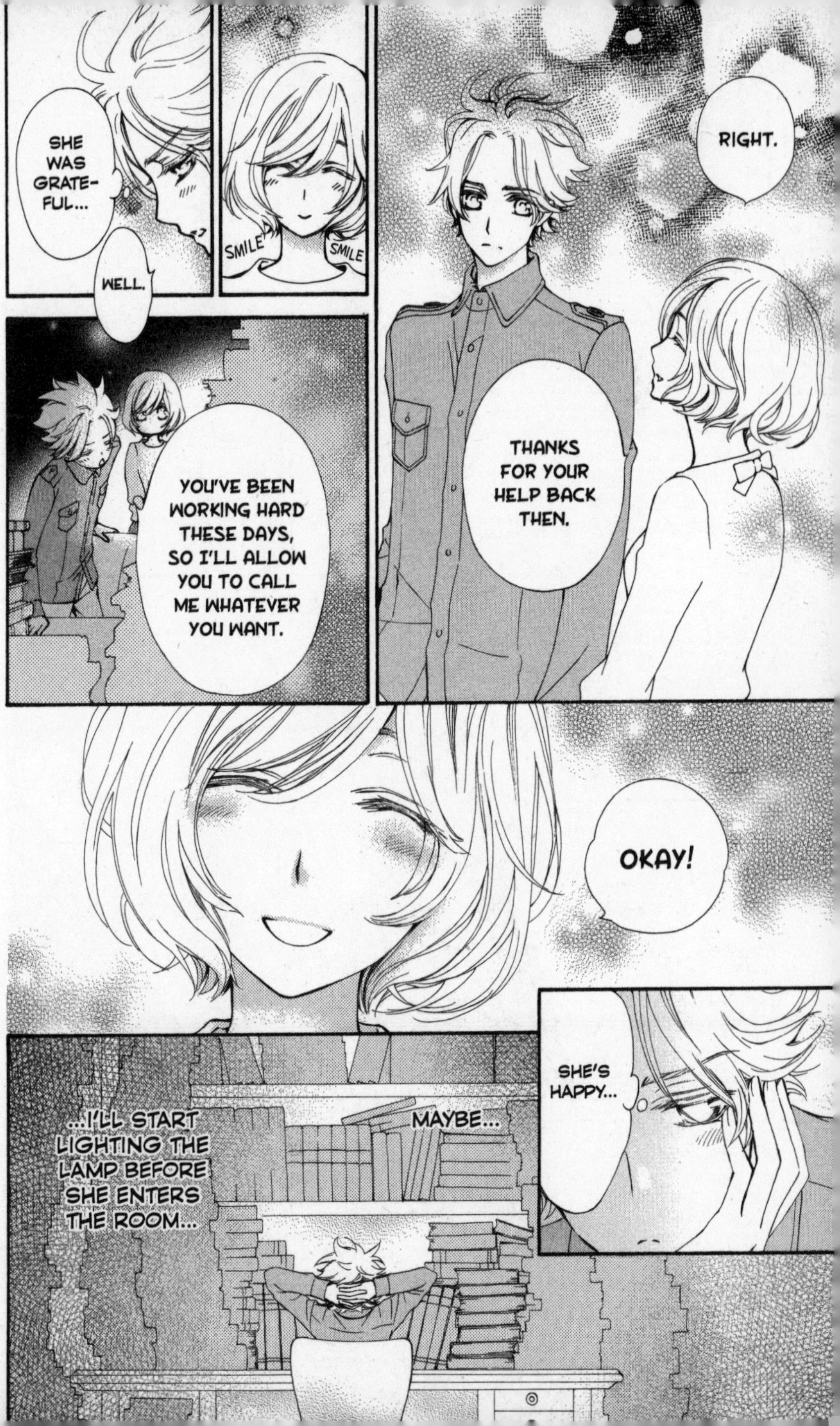
RIGHT.
THANKS FOR YOUR HELP BACK THEN.
SMILE
SMILE
SHE WAS GRATEFUL...
WELL.
YOU'VE BEEN WORKING HARD THESE DAYS, SO I'LL ALLOW YOU TO CALL ME WHATEVER YOU WANT.
OKAY!
SHE'S HAPPY...
MAYBE...
...I'LL START LIGHTING THE LAMP BEFORE SHE ENTERS THE ROOM...

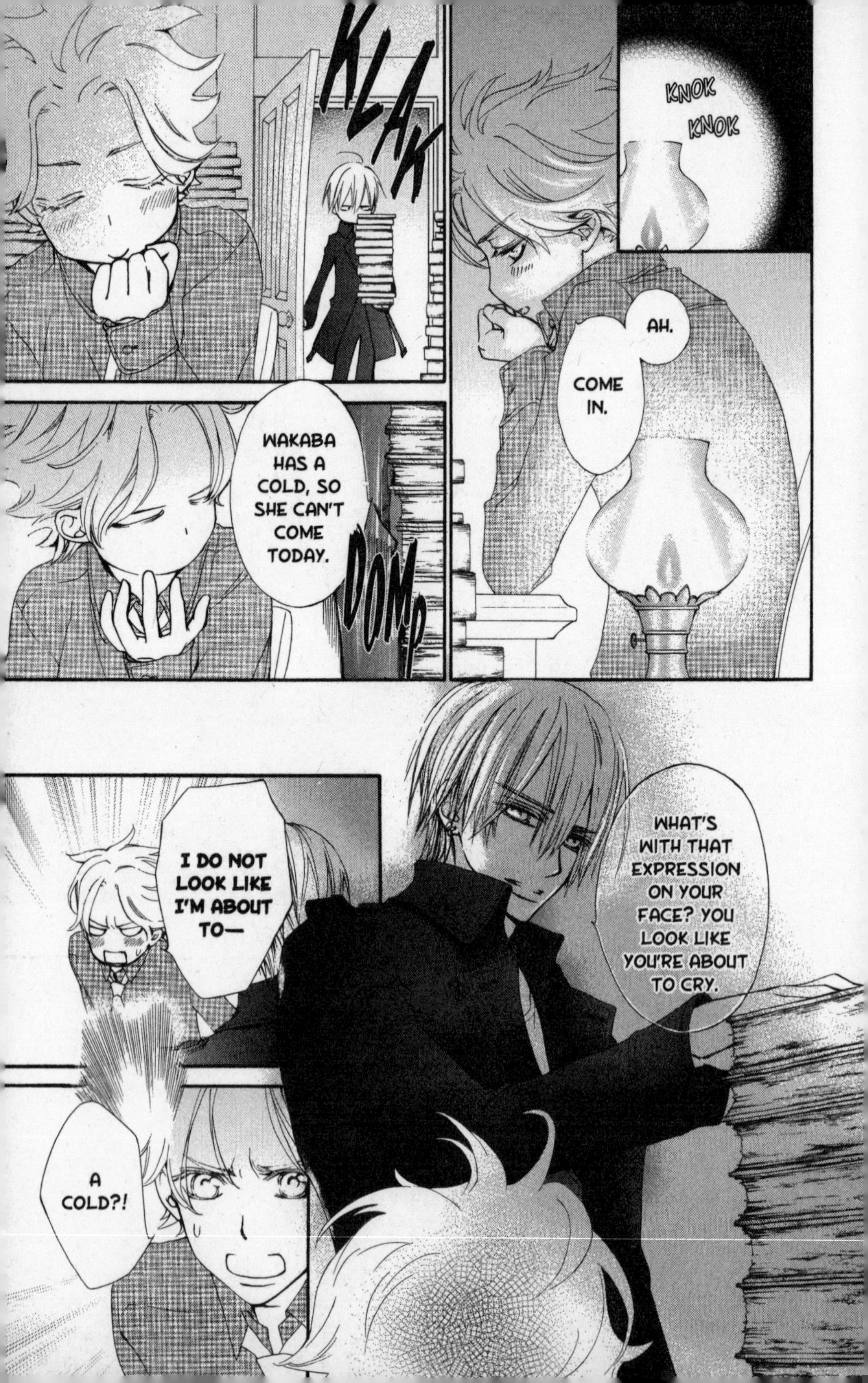
KNOK KNOK
AH.
COME IN.
KLAK
WAKABA HAS A COLD, SO SHE CAN'T COME TODAY.
DOMP
WHAT'S WITH THAT EXPRESSION ON YOUR FACE? YOU LOOK LIKE YOU'RE ABOUT TO CRY.
I DO NOT LOOK LIKE I'M ABOUT TO—
A COLD?!

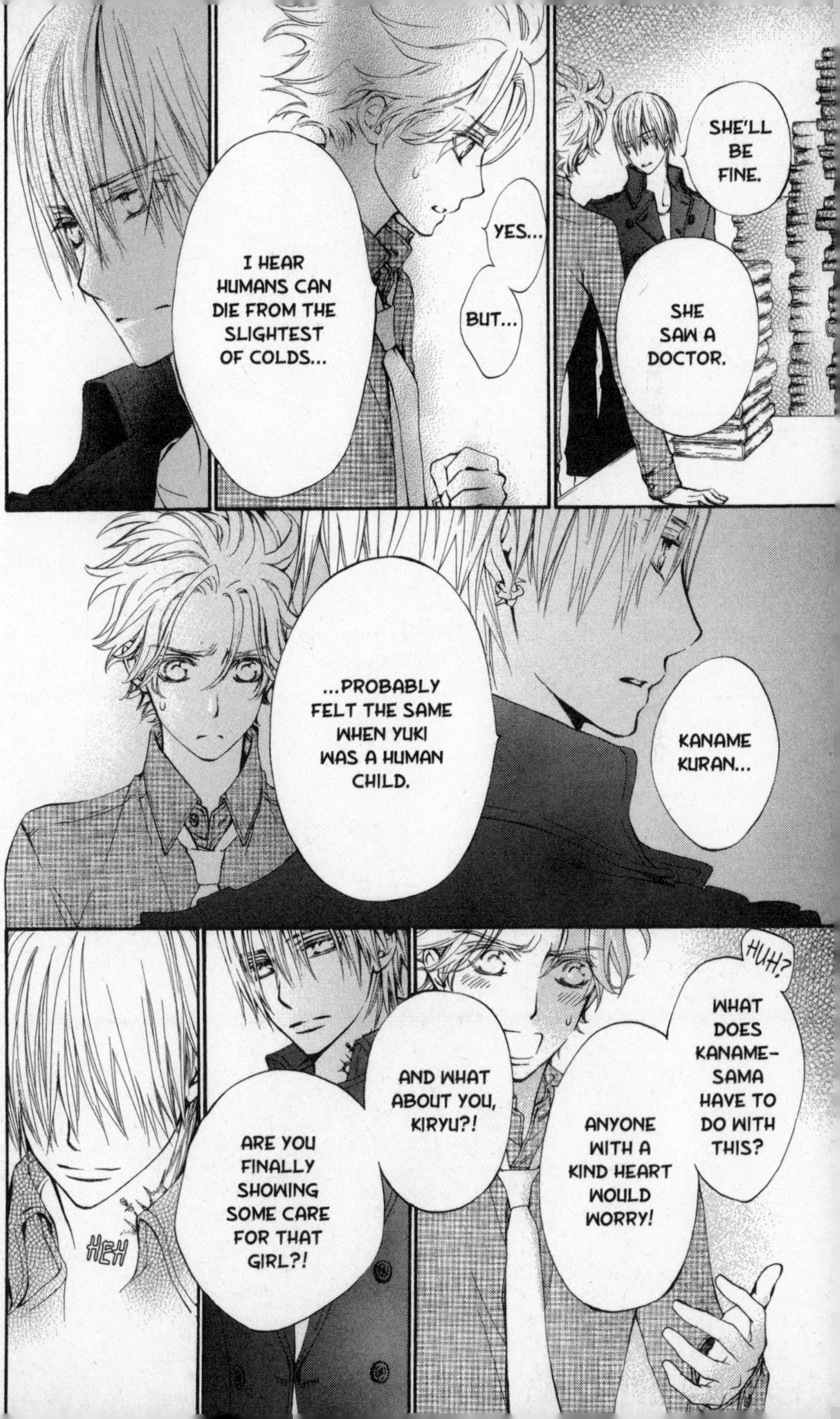
SHE'LL BE FINE.
SHE SAW A DOCTOR.
YES...
BUT...
I HEAR HUMANS CAN DIE FROM THE SLIGHTEST OF COLDS...
KANAME KURAN...
...PROBABLY FELT THE SAME WHEN YUKI WAS A HUMAN CHILD.
HUH?
WHAT DOES KANAME-SAMA HAVE TO DO WITH THIS?
ANYONE WITH A KIND HEART WOULD WORRY!
AND WHAT ABOUT YOU, KIRYU?!
ARE YOU FINALLY SHOWING SOME CARE FOR THAT GIRL?!
HEH

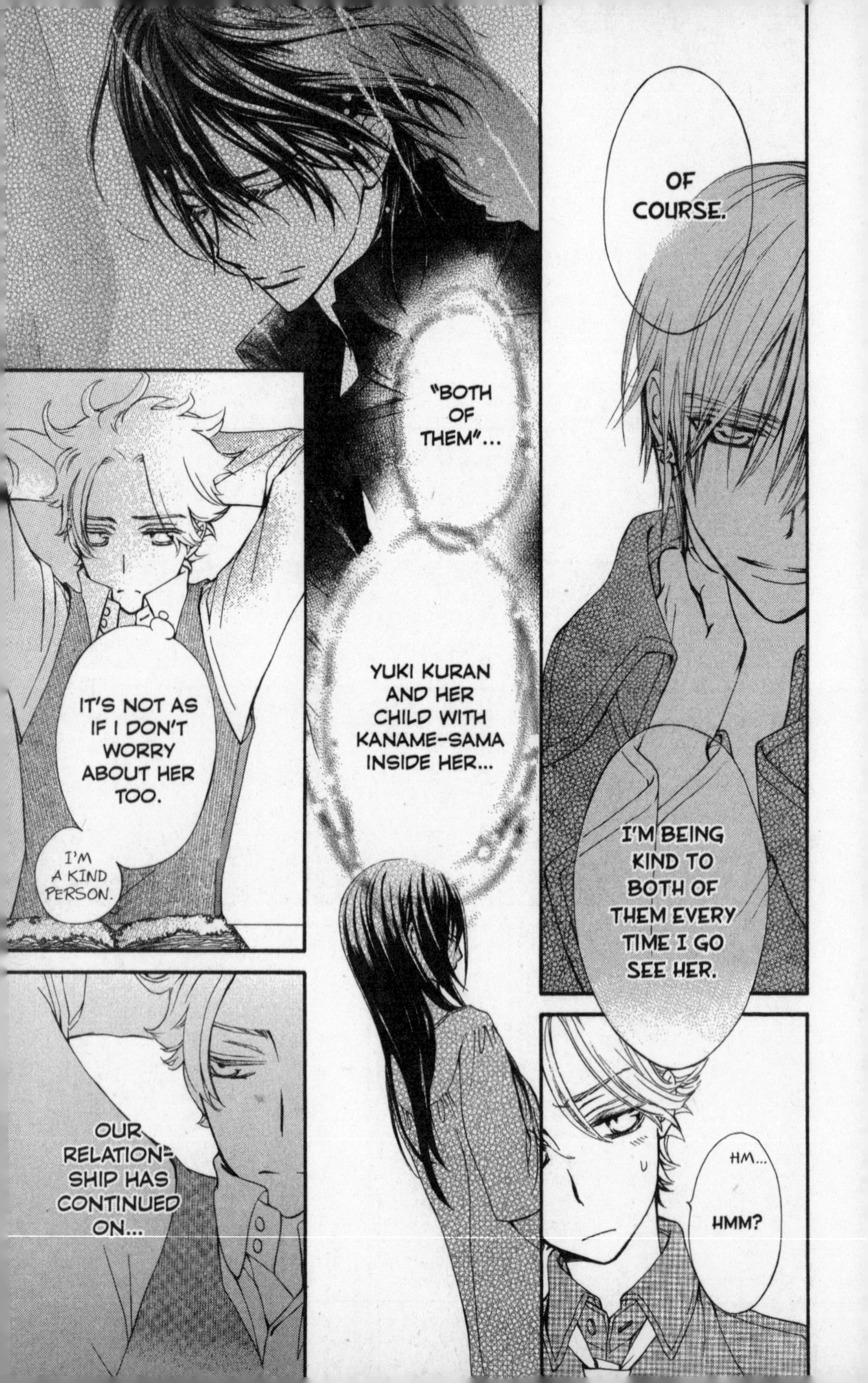

OF COURSE.
I'M BEING KIND TO BOTH OF THEM EVERY TIME I GO SEE HER.
HM...
HMM?
"BOTH OF THEM"...
YUKI KURAN AND HER CHILD WITH KANAME-SAMA INSIDE HER...
IT'S NOT AS IF I DON'T WORRY ABOUT HER TOO.
I'M A KIND PERSON.
OUR RELATION-SHIP HAS CONTINUED ON...

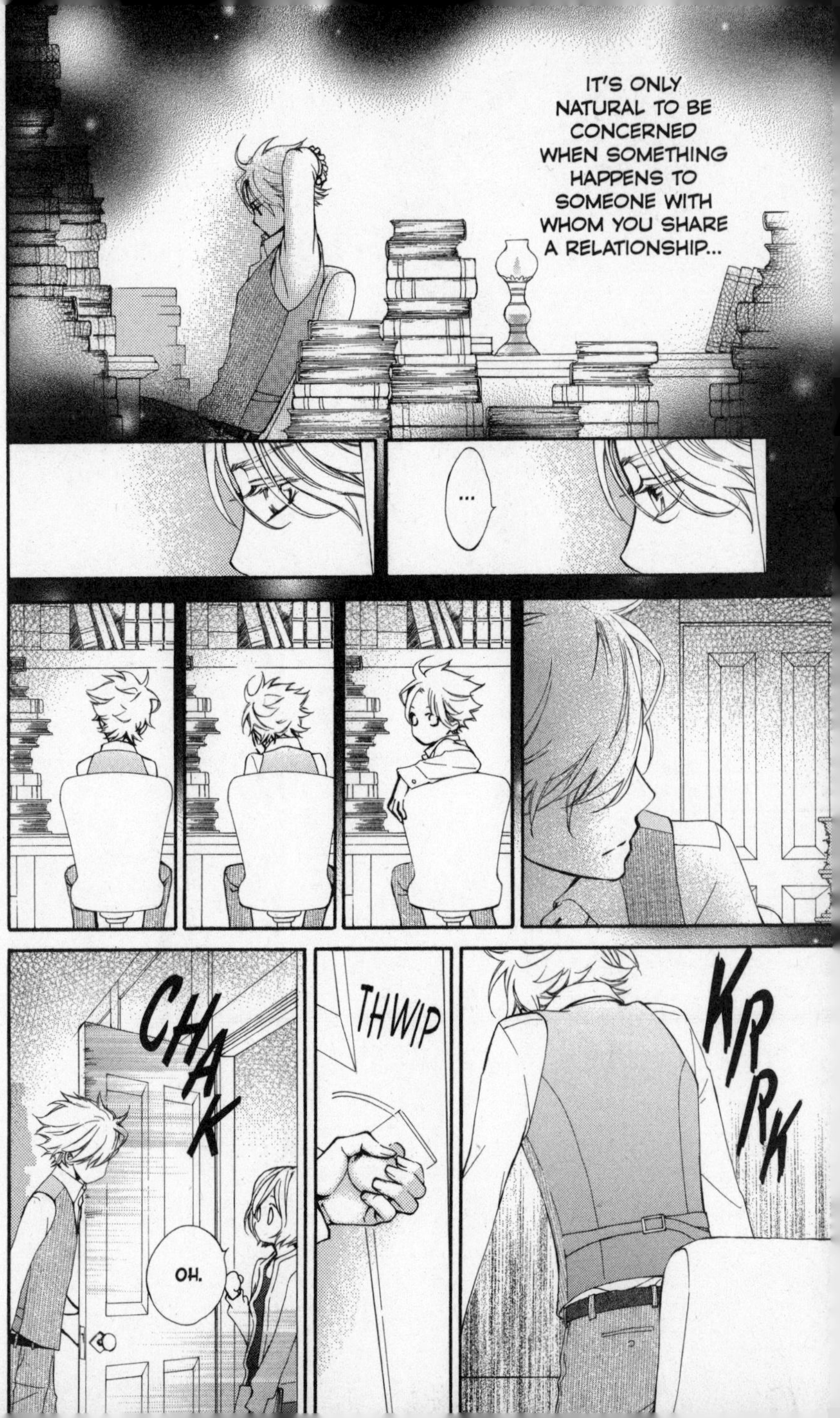
IT'S ONLY NATURAL TO BE CONCERNED WHEN SOMETHING HAPPENS TO SOMEONE WITH WHOM YOU SHARE A RELATIONSHIP...
...
KRRK
THWIP
CHAK
OH.

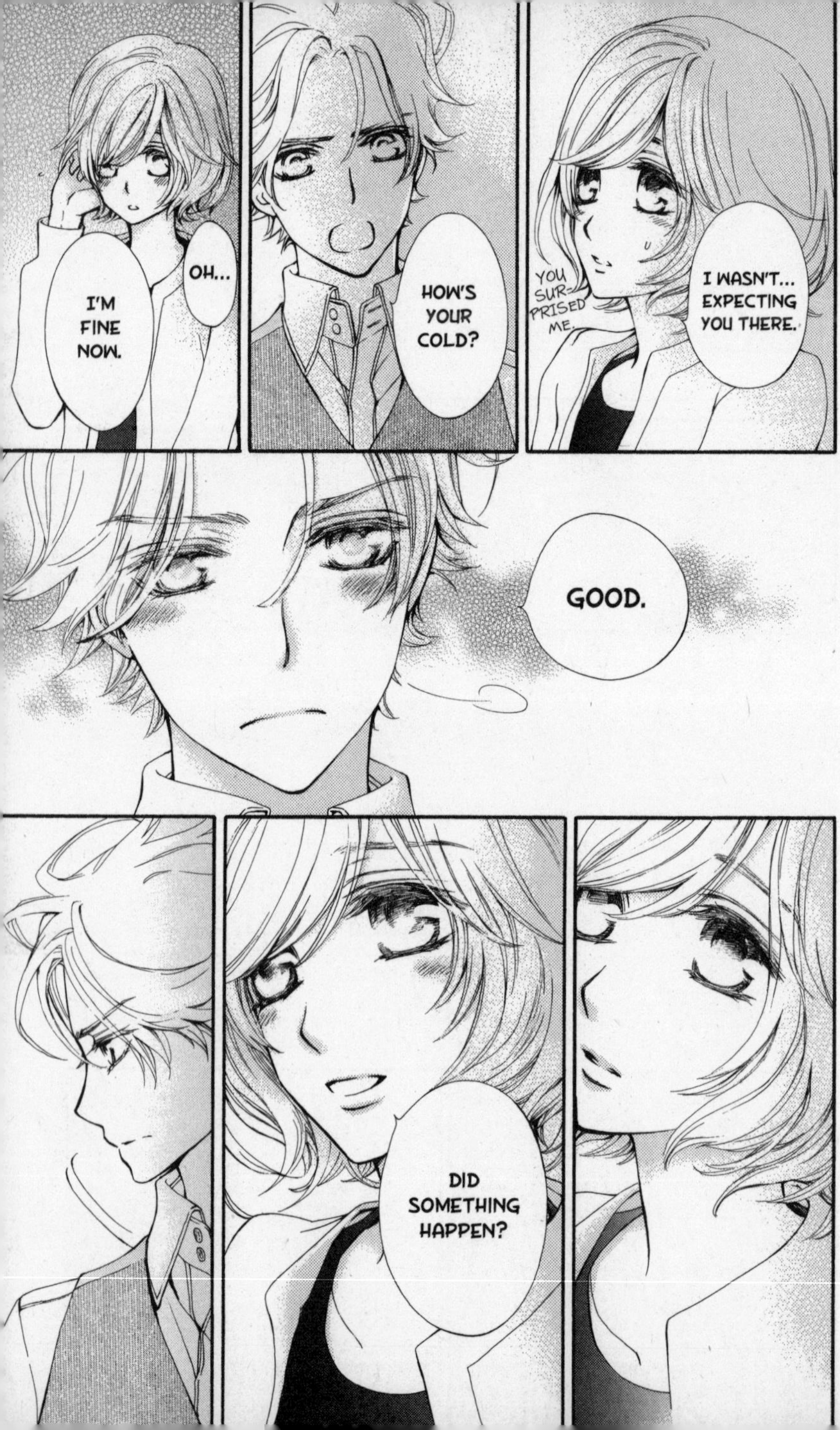
I WASN'T... EXPECTING YOU THERE.
YOU SUR-PRISED ME.
HOW'S YOUR COLD?
OH...
I'M FINE NOW.
GOOD.
DID SOMETHING HAPPEN?

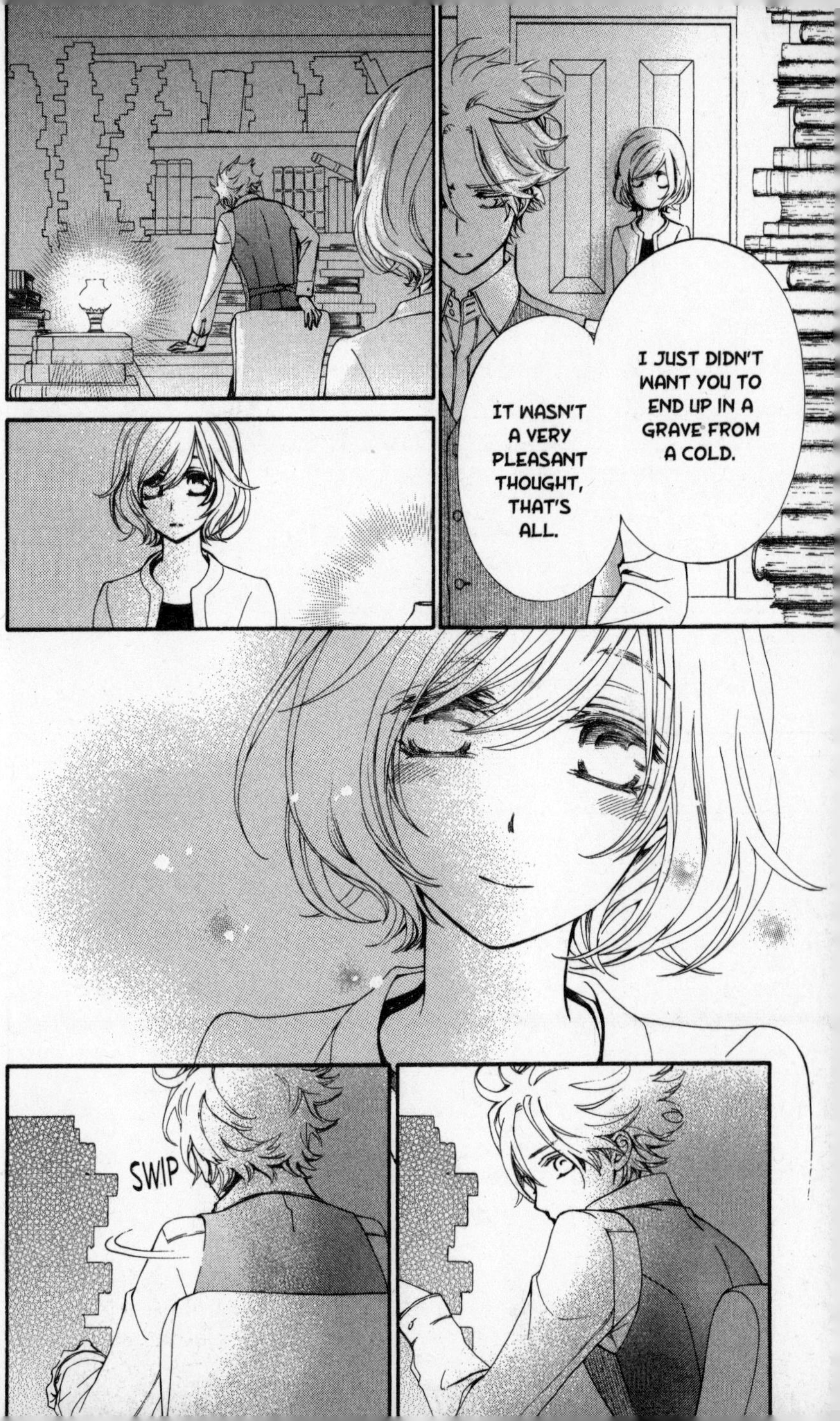
I JUST DIDN'T WANT YOU TO END UP IN A GRAVE FROM A COLD.
IT WASN'T A VERY PLEASANT THOUGHT, THAT'S ALL.
SWIP

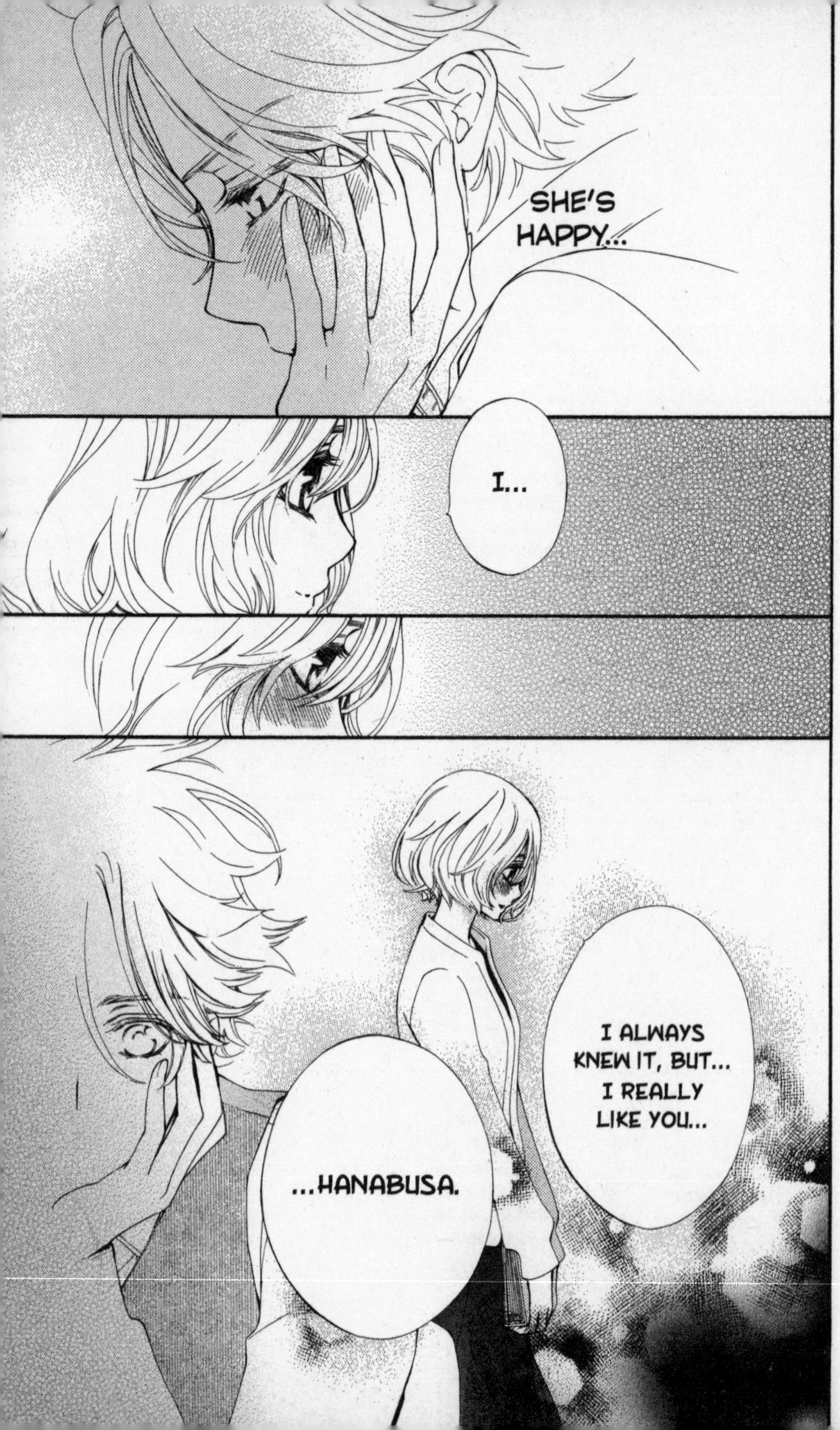
SHE'S HAPPY...
I...
I ALWAYS KNEW IT, BUT... I REALLY LIKE YOU...
...HANABUSA.

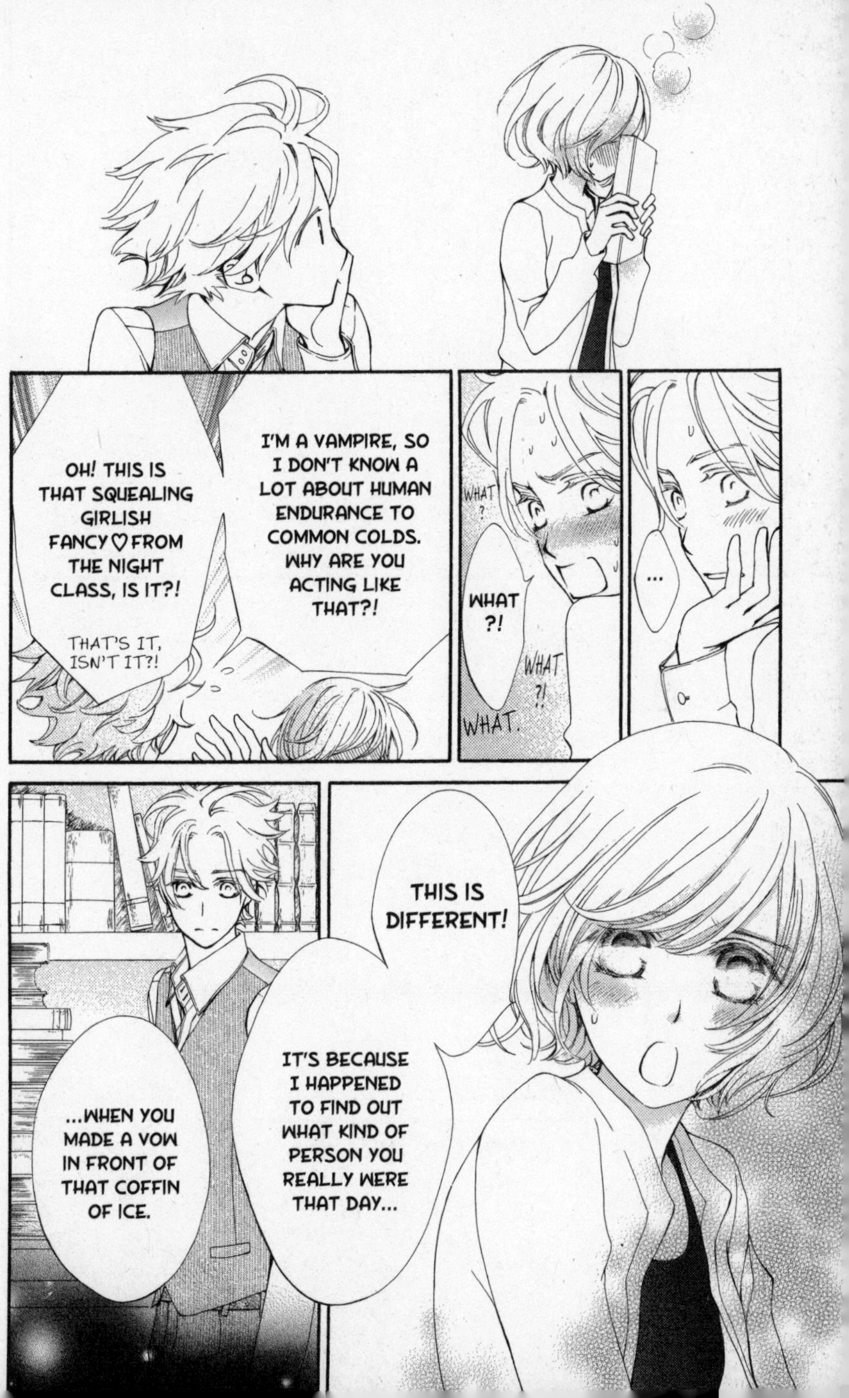
...
WHAT ?
WHAT ?!
WHAT ?!
WHAT.
I'M A VAMPIRE, SO I DON'T KNOW A LOT ABOUT HUMAN ENDURANCE TO COMMON COLDS. WHY ARE YOU ACTING LIKE THAT?!
OH! THIS IS THAT SQUEALING GIRLISH FANCY♡FROM THE NIGHT CLASS, IS IT?!
THAT'S IT, ISN'T IT?!
THIS IS DIFFERENT!
IT'S BECAUSE I HAPPENED TO FIND OUT WHAT KIND OF PERSON YOU REALLY WERE THAT DAY...
...WHEN YOU MADE A VOW IN FRONT OF THAT COFFIN OF ICE.

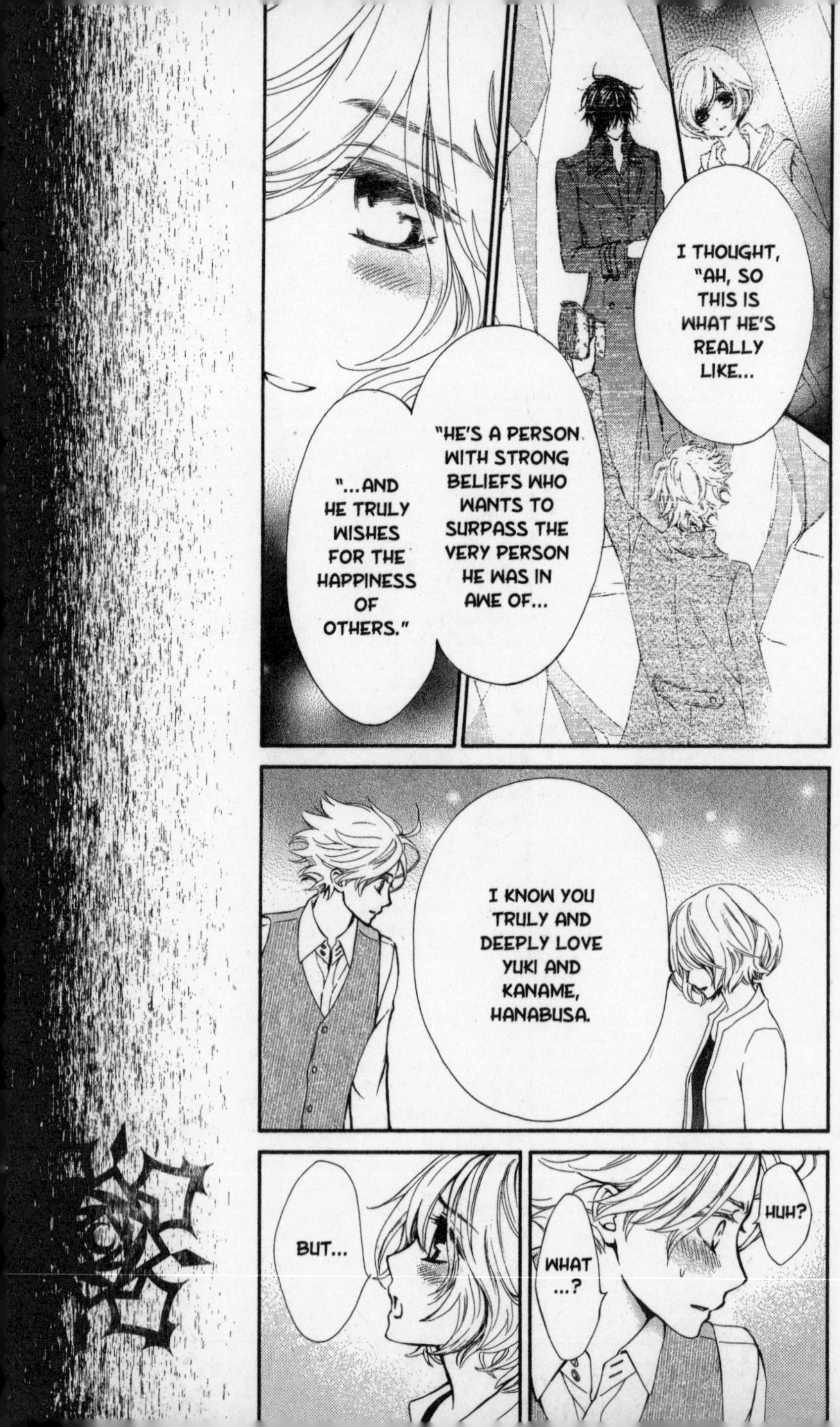
I THOUGHT, "AH, SO THIS IS WHAT HE'S REALLY LIKE...
"HE'S A PERSON WITH STRONG BELIEFS WHO WANTS TO SURPASS THE VERY PERSON HE WAS IN AWE OF...
"...AND HE TRULY WISHES FOR THE HAPPINESS OF OTHERS."
I KNOW YOU TRULY AND DEEPLY LOVE YUKI AND KANAME, HANABUSA.
HUH?
WHAT ...?
BUT...

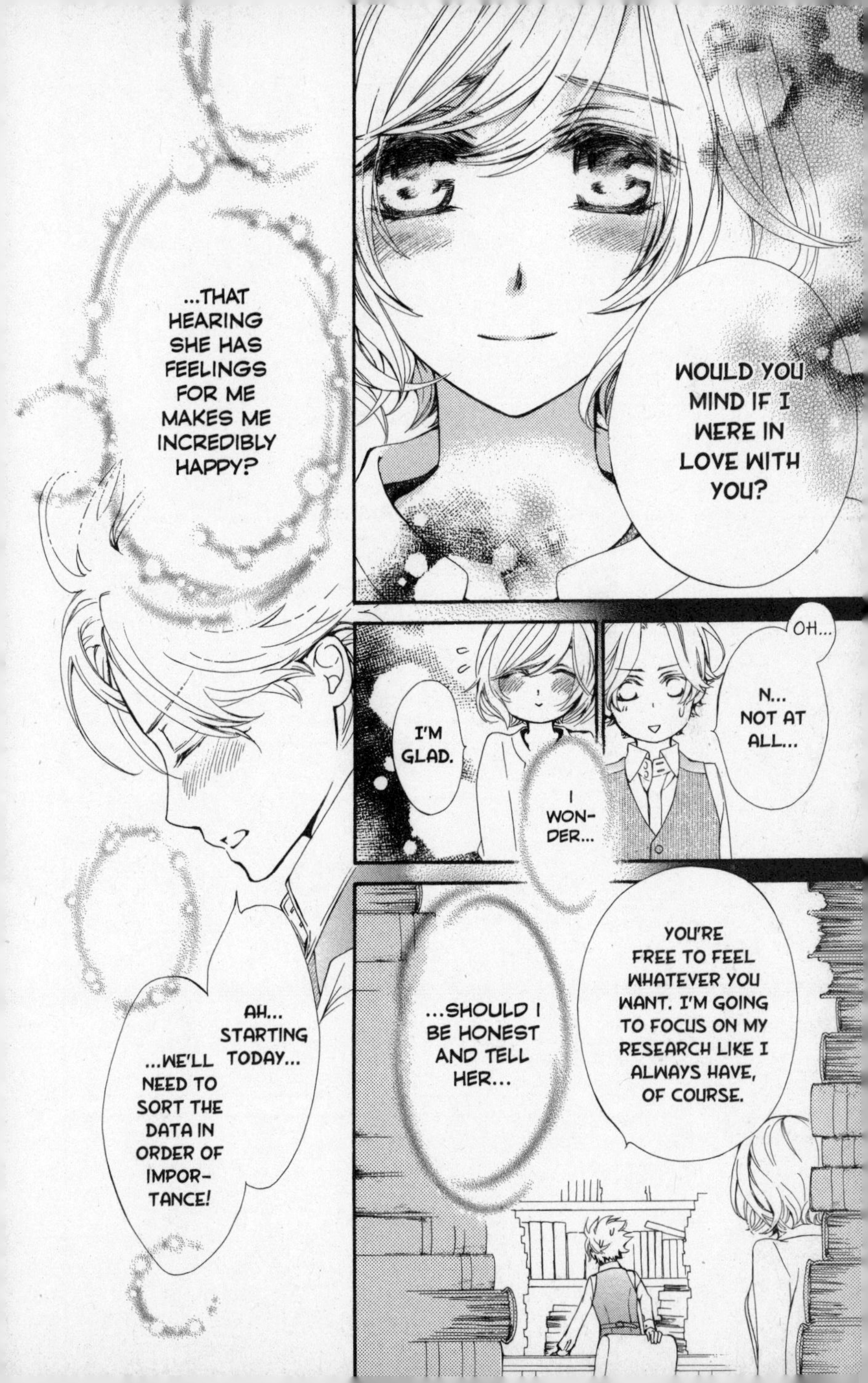
WOULD YOU MIND IF I WERE IN LOVE WITH YOU?
OH...
N... NOT AT ALL...
I'M GLAD.
I WONDER...
YOU'RE FREE TO FEEL WHATEVER YOU WANT. I'M GOING TO FOCUS ON MY RESEARCH LIKE I ALWAYS HAVE, OF COURSE.
...SHOULD I BE HONEST AND TELL HER...
...THAT HEARING SHE HAS FEELINGS FOR ME MAKES ME INCREDIBLY HAPPY?
AH... STARTING TODAY...
...WE'LL NEED TO SORT THE DATA IN ORDER OF IMPOR-TANCE!

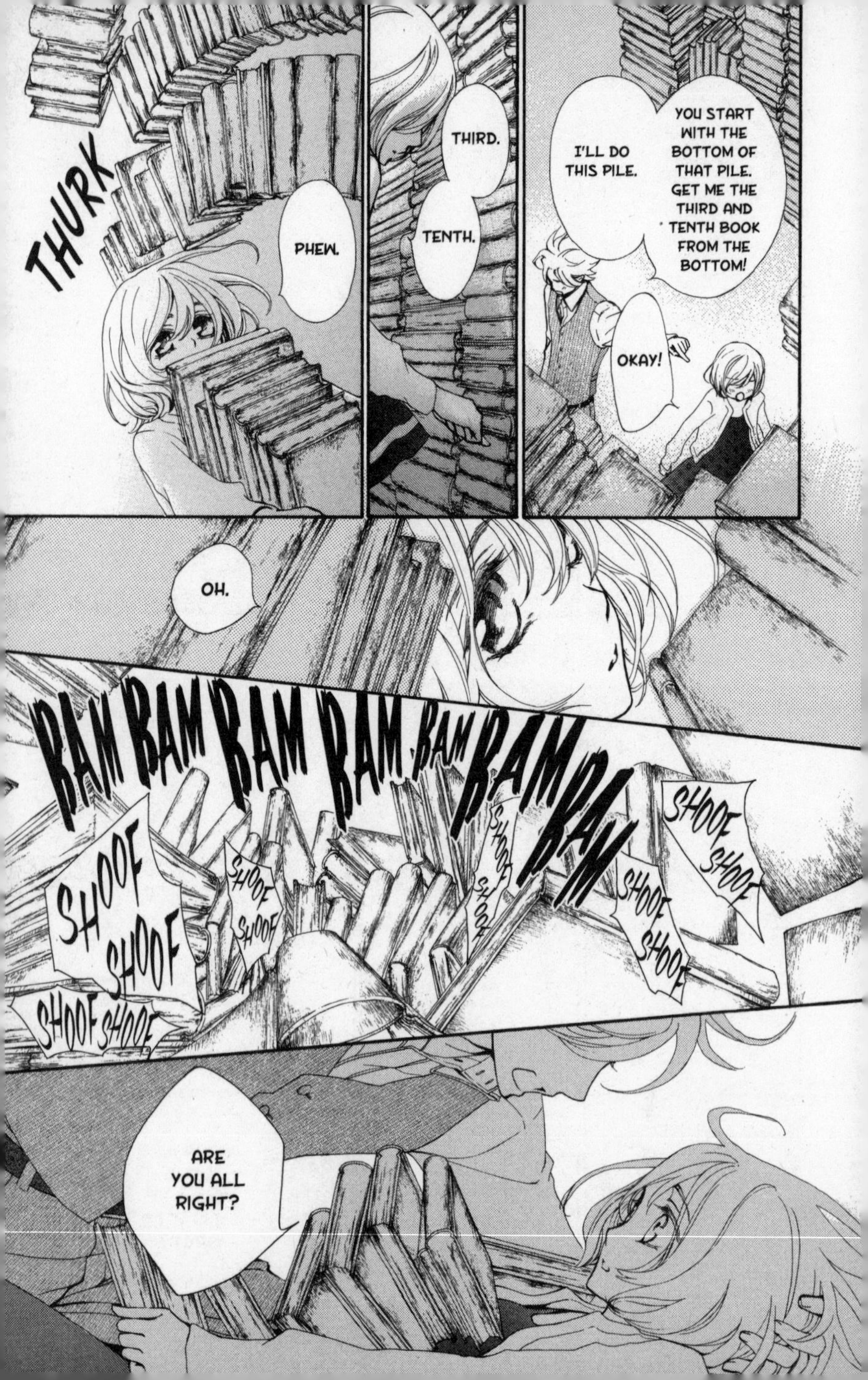

YOU START WITH THE BOTTOM OF THAT PILE. GET ME THE THIRD AND TENTH BOOK FROM THE BOTTOM!
I'LL DO THIS PILE.
OKAY!
THIRD.
TENTH.
THURK
PHEW.
OH.
BAM BAM BAM BAM BAM BAM BAM BAM
SHOOF SHOOF
SHOOF SHOOF
SHOOF SHOOF
SHOOF SHOOF
SHOOF SHOOF
SHOOF SHOOF
ARE YOU ALL RIGHT?

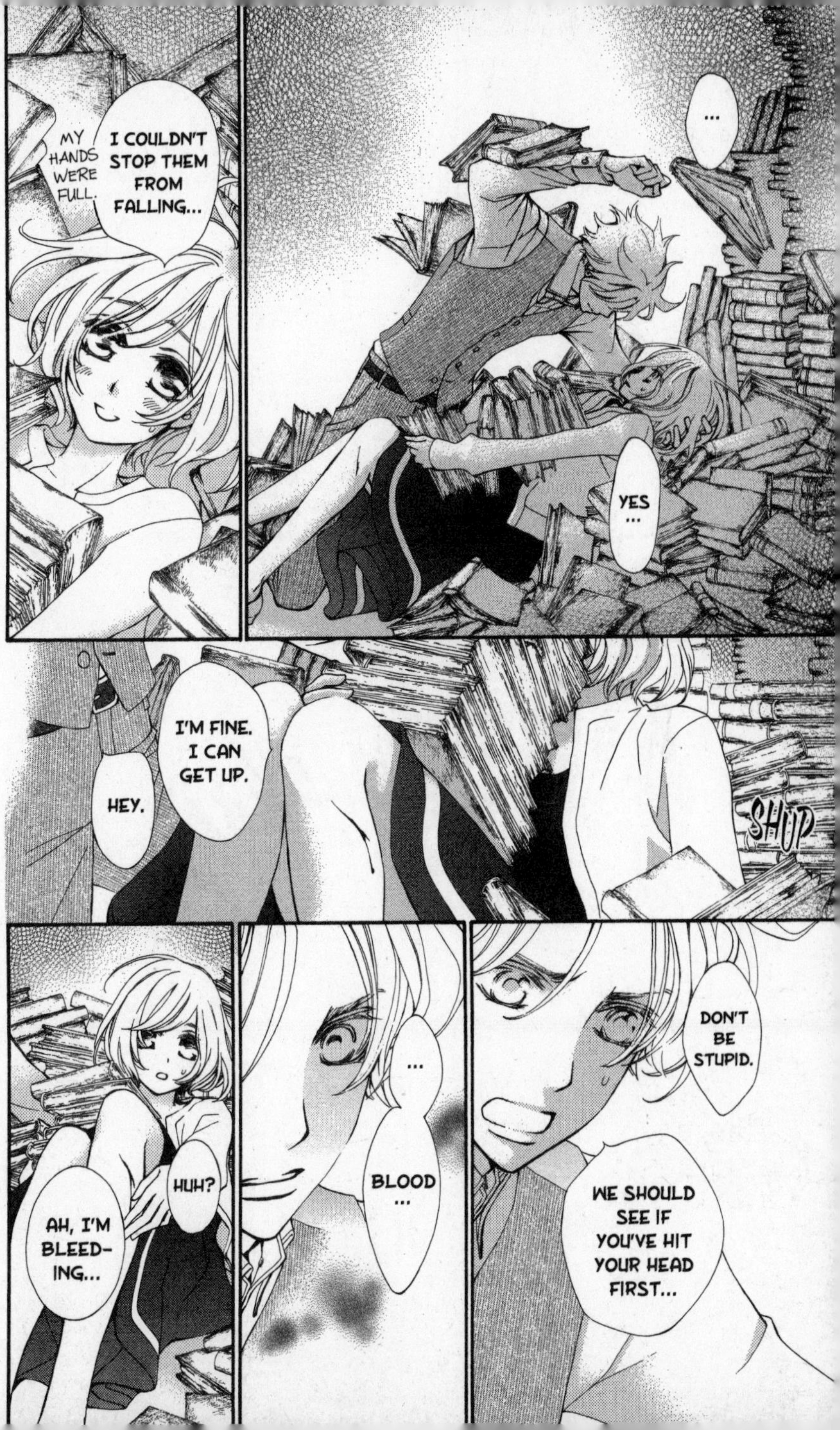
...
YES ...
I COULDN'T STOP THEM FROM FALLING...
MY HANDS WERE FULL.
SHUP
I'M FINE. I CAN GET UP.
HEY.
DON'T BE STUPID.
WE SHOULD SEE IF YOU'VE HIT YOUR HEAD FIRST...
...
BLOOD ...
HUH?
AH, I'M BLEED-ING...

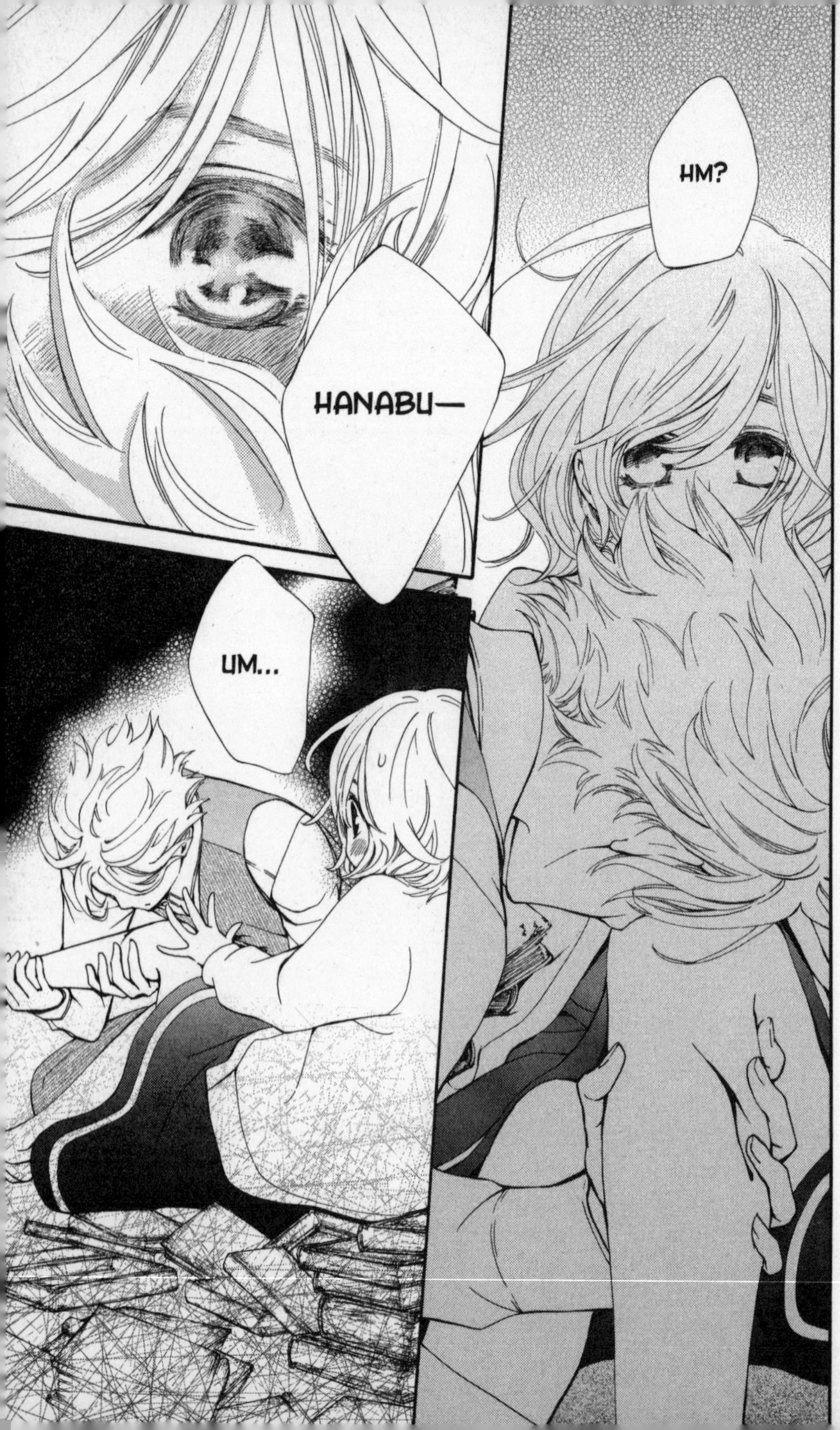
HM?
HANABU—
UM...

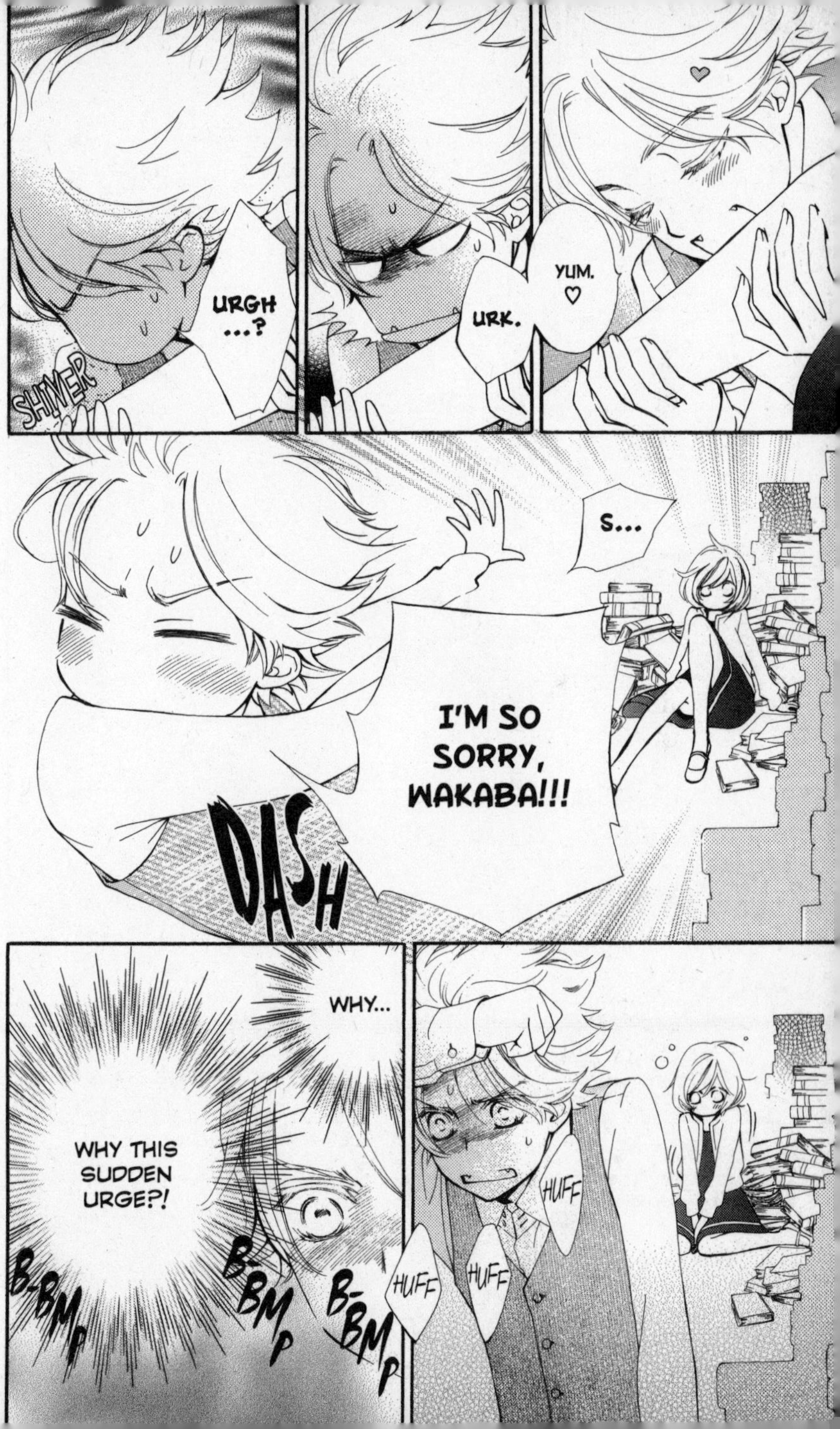
YUM. ♥
URK.
URGH ...?
SHIVER
S...
I'M SO SORRY, WAKABA!!!
DASH
HUFF
HUFF
HUFF
WHY...
WHY THIS SUDDEN URGE?!
B-BMP
B-BMP
B-BMP

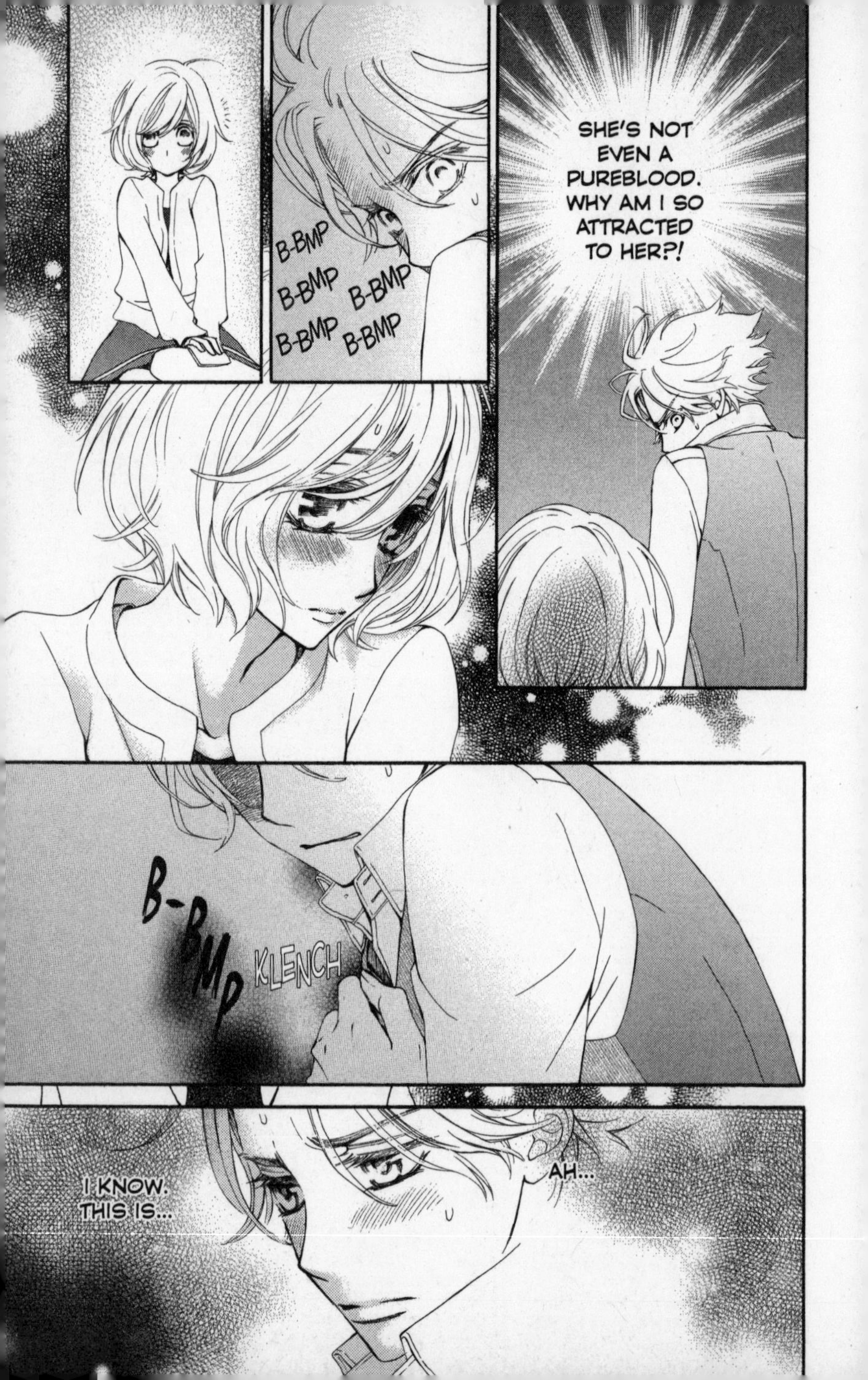
SHE'S NOT EVEN A PUREBLOOD. WHY AM I SO ATTRACTED TO HER?!
B-BMP
B-BMP
B-BMP
B-BMP
B-BMP
KLENCH
B-BMP
AH...
I KNOW. THIS IS...

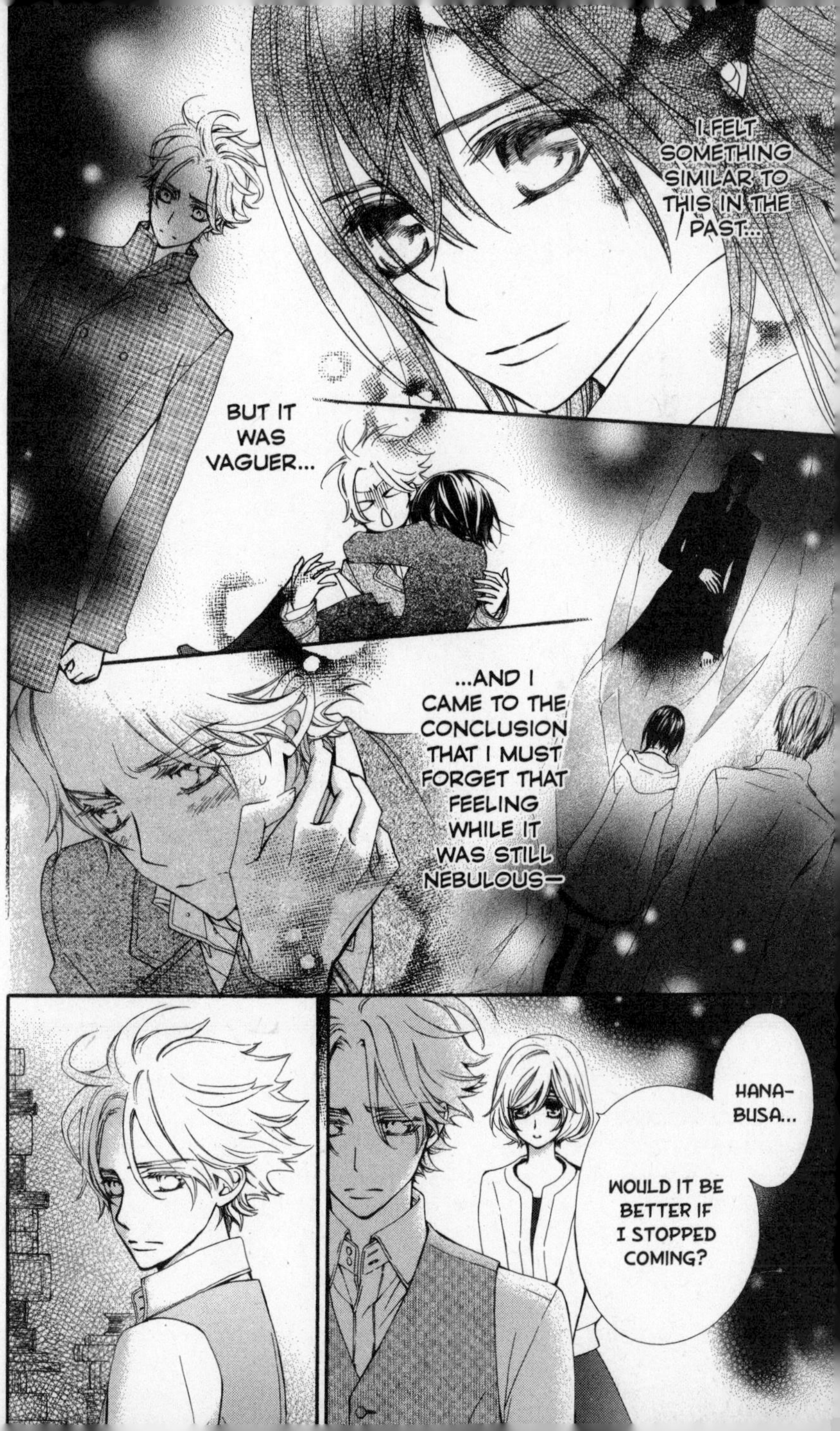
I FELT SOMETHING SIMILAR TO THIS IN THE PAST...
BUT IT WAS VAGUER...
...AND I CAME TO THE CONCLUSION THAT I MUST FORGET THAT FEELING WHILE IT WAS STILL NEBULOUS—
HANA-BUSA...
WOULD IT BE BETTER IF I STOPPED COMING?

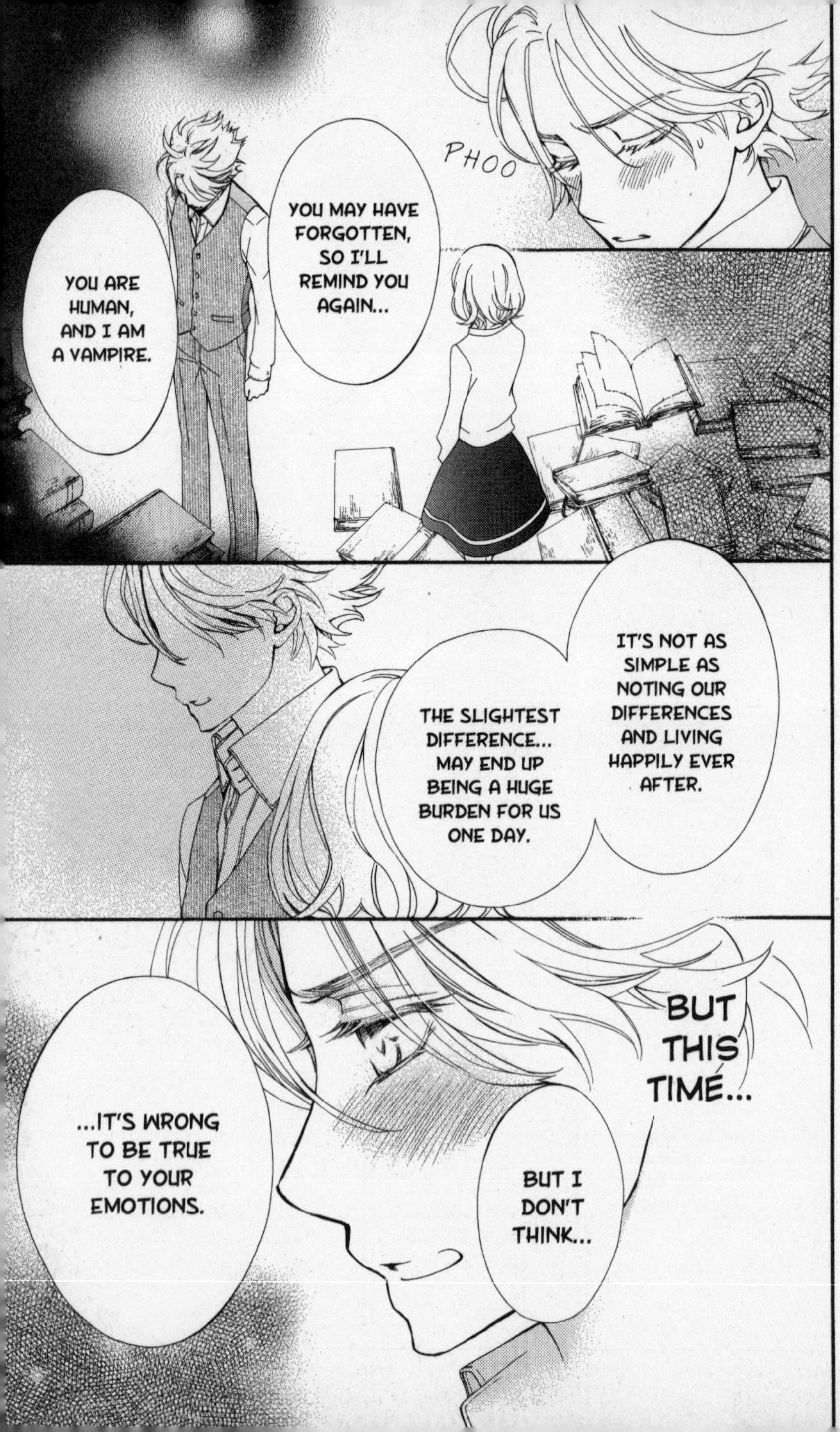
PHOO
YOU MAY HAVE FORGOTTEN, SO I'LL REMIND YOU AGAIN...
YOU ARE HUMAN, AND I AM A VAMPIRE.
IT'S NOT AS SIMPLE AS NOTING OUR DIFFERENCES AND LIVING HAPPILY EVER AFTER.
THE SLIGHTEST DIFFERENCE... MAY END UP BEING A HUGE BURDEN FOR US ONE DAY.
BUT THIS TIME...
BUT I DON'T THINK...
...IT'S WRONG TO BE TRUE TO YOUR EMOTIONS.

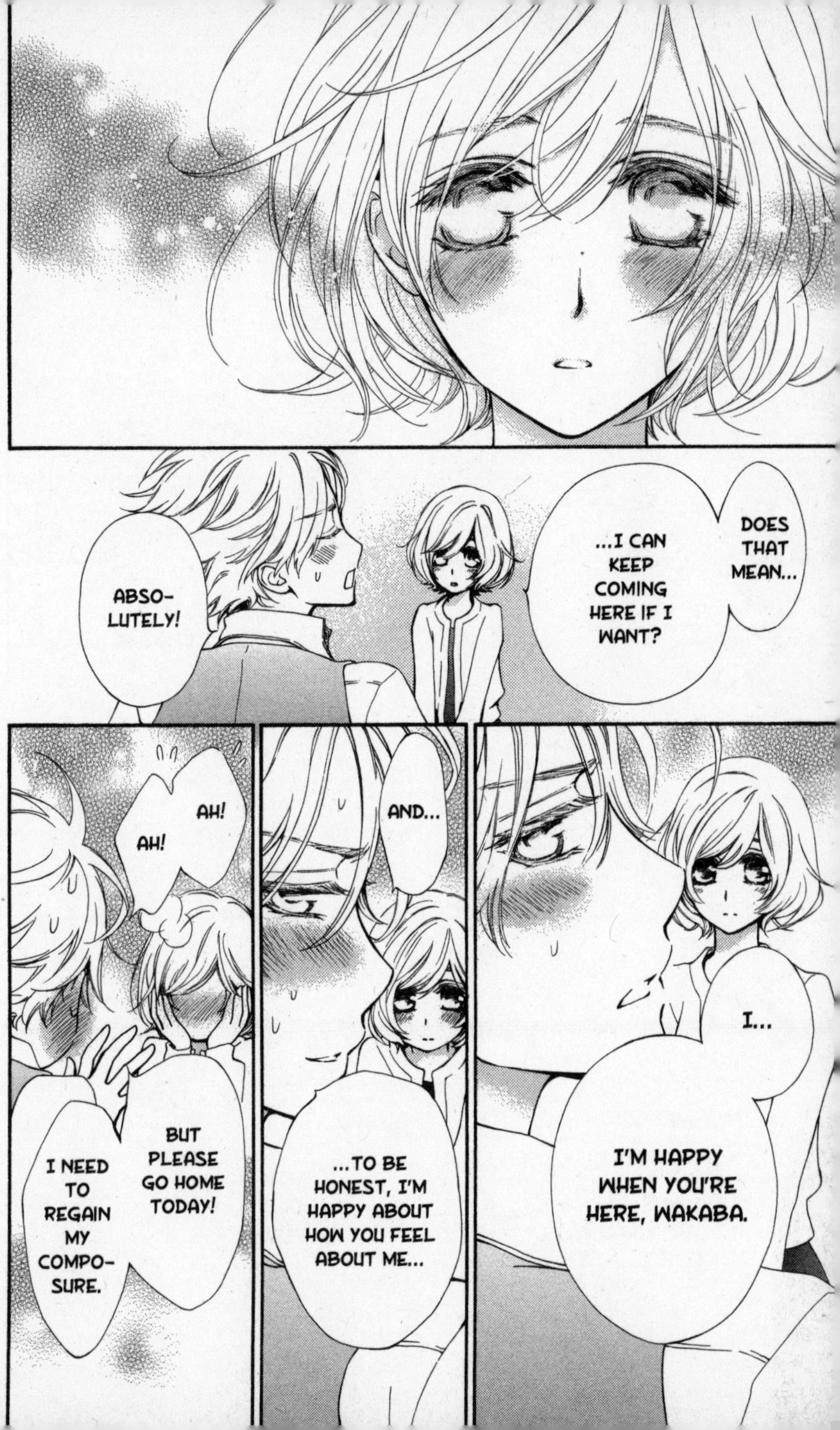
DOES THAT MEAN...
...I CAN KEEP COMING HERE IF I WANT?
ABSO-LUTELY!
I...
I'M HAPPY WHEN YOU'RE HERE, WAKABA.
AND...
...TO BE HONEST, I'M HAPPY ABOUT HOW YOU FEEL ABOUT ME...
AH!
AH!
BUT PLEASE GO HOME TODAY!
I NEED TO REGAIN MY COMPOSURE.

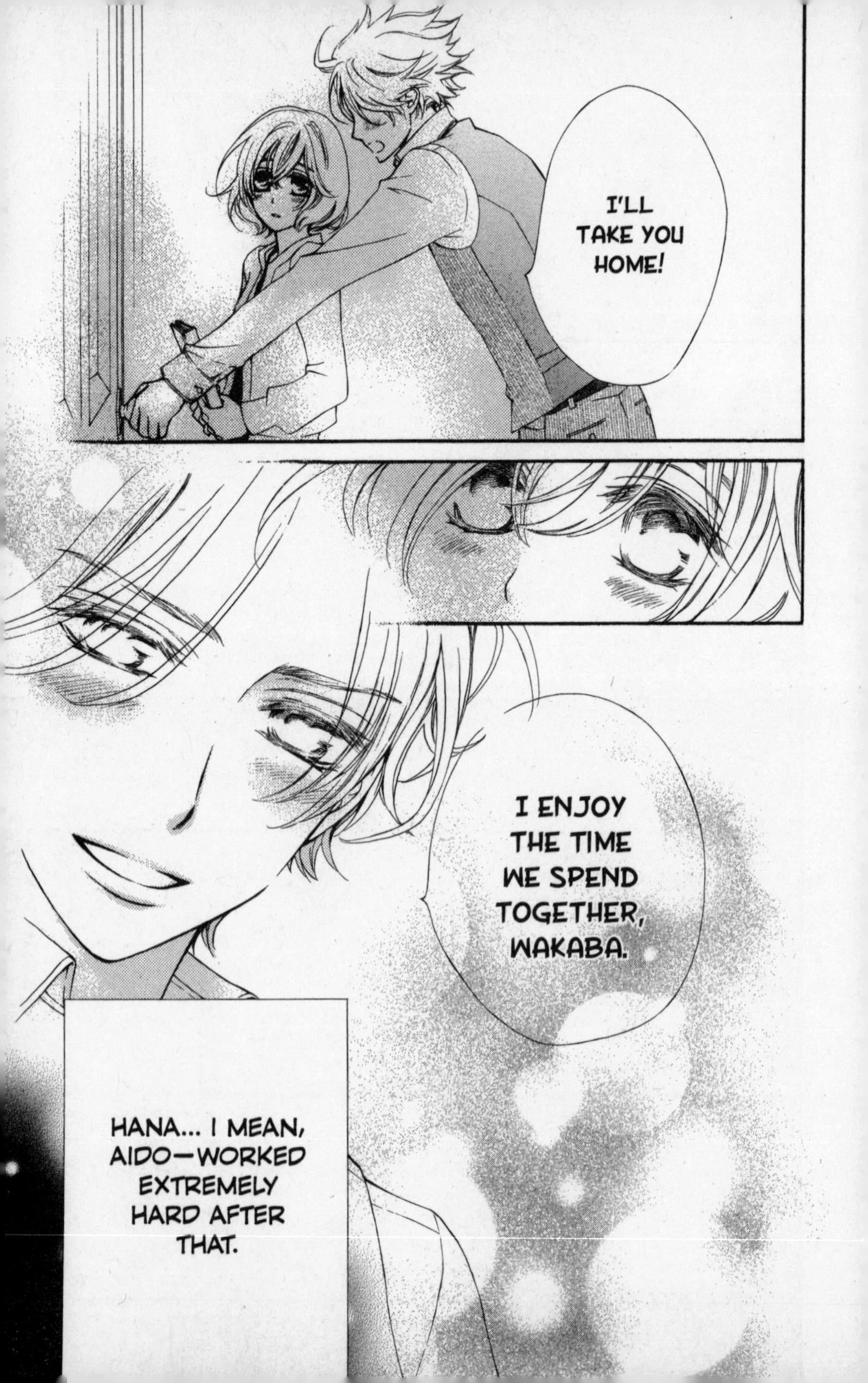
I'LL TAKE YOU HOME!
I ENJOY THE TIME WE SPEND TOGETHER, WAKABA.
HANA... I MEAN, AIDO—WORKED EXTREMELY HARD AFTER THAT.

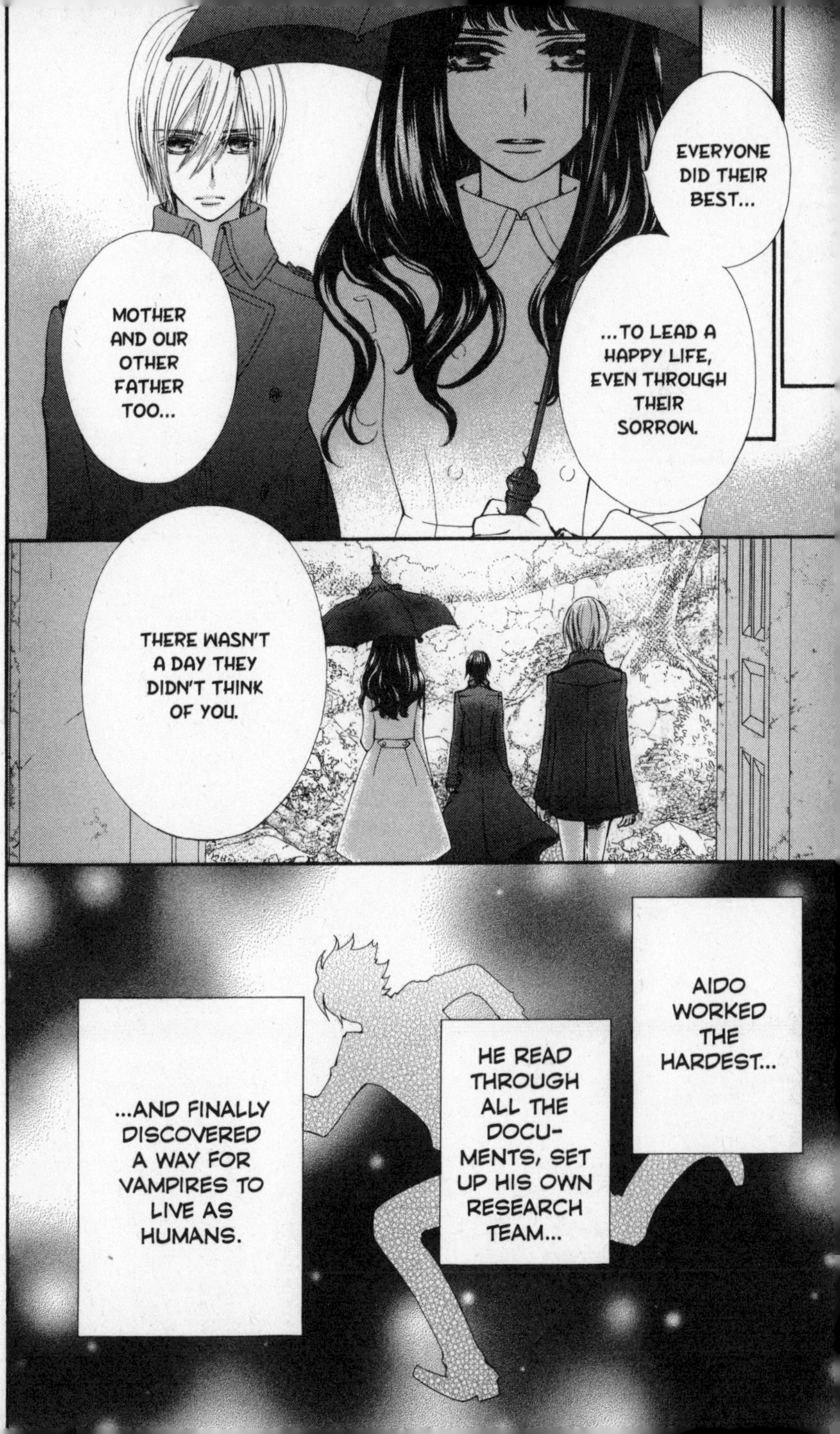
EVERYONE DID THEIR BEST...
...TO LEAD A HAPPY LIFE, EVEN THROUGH THEIR SORROW.
MOTHER AND OUR OTHER FATHER TOO...
THERE WASN'T A DAY THEY DIDN'T THINK OF YOU.
AIDO WORKED THE HARDEST...
HE READ THROUGH ALL THE DOCU-MENTS, SET UP HIS OWN RESEARCH TEAM...
...AND FINALLY DISCOVERED A WAY FOR VAMPIRES TO LIVE AS HUMANS.

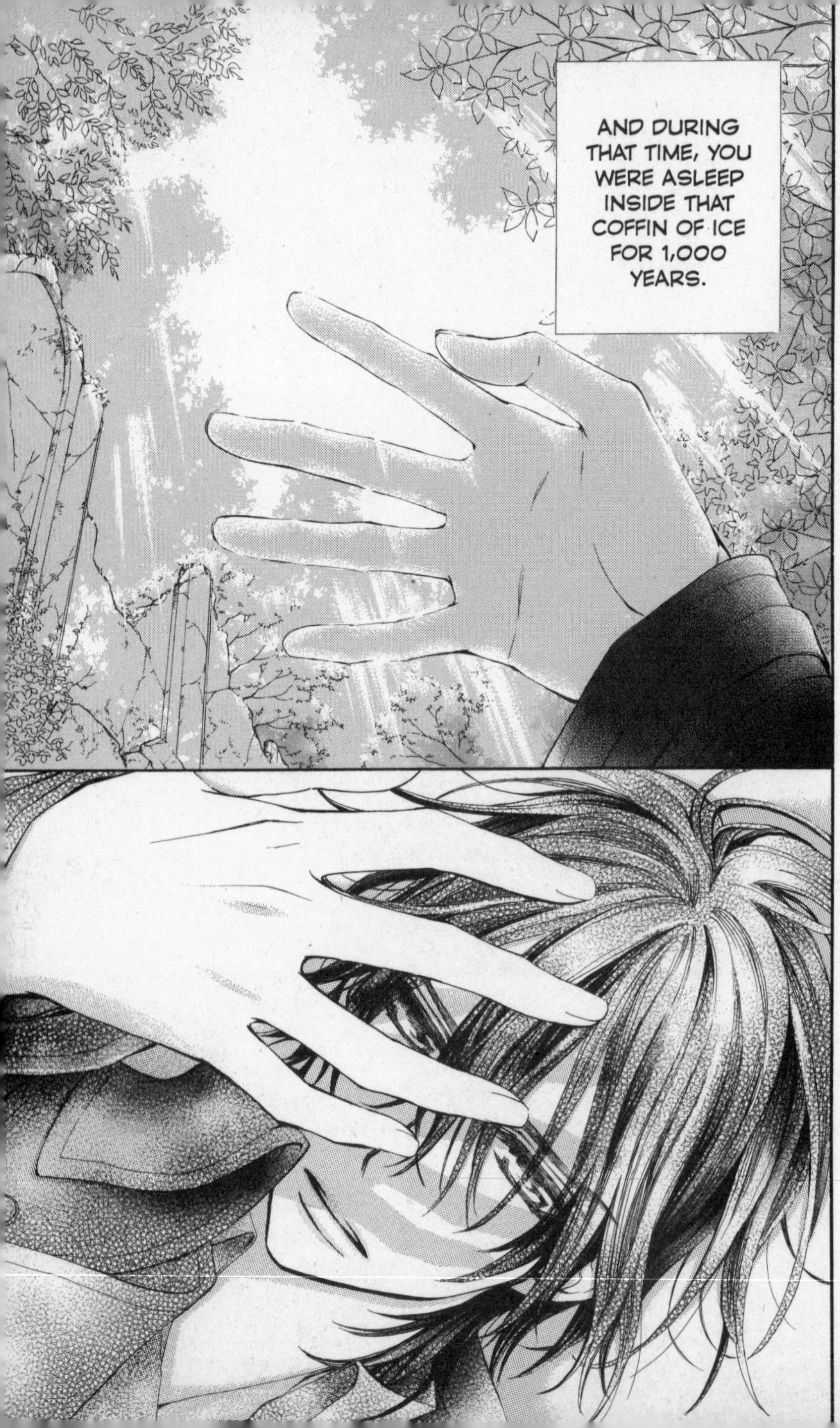
AND DURING THAT TIME, YOU WERE ASLEEP INSIDE THAT COFFIN OF ICE FOR 1,000 YEARS.

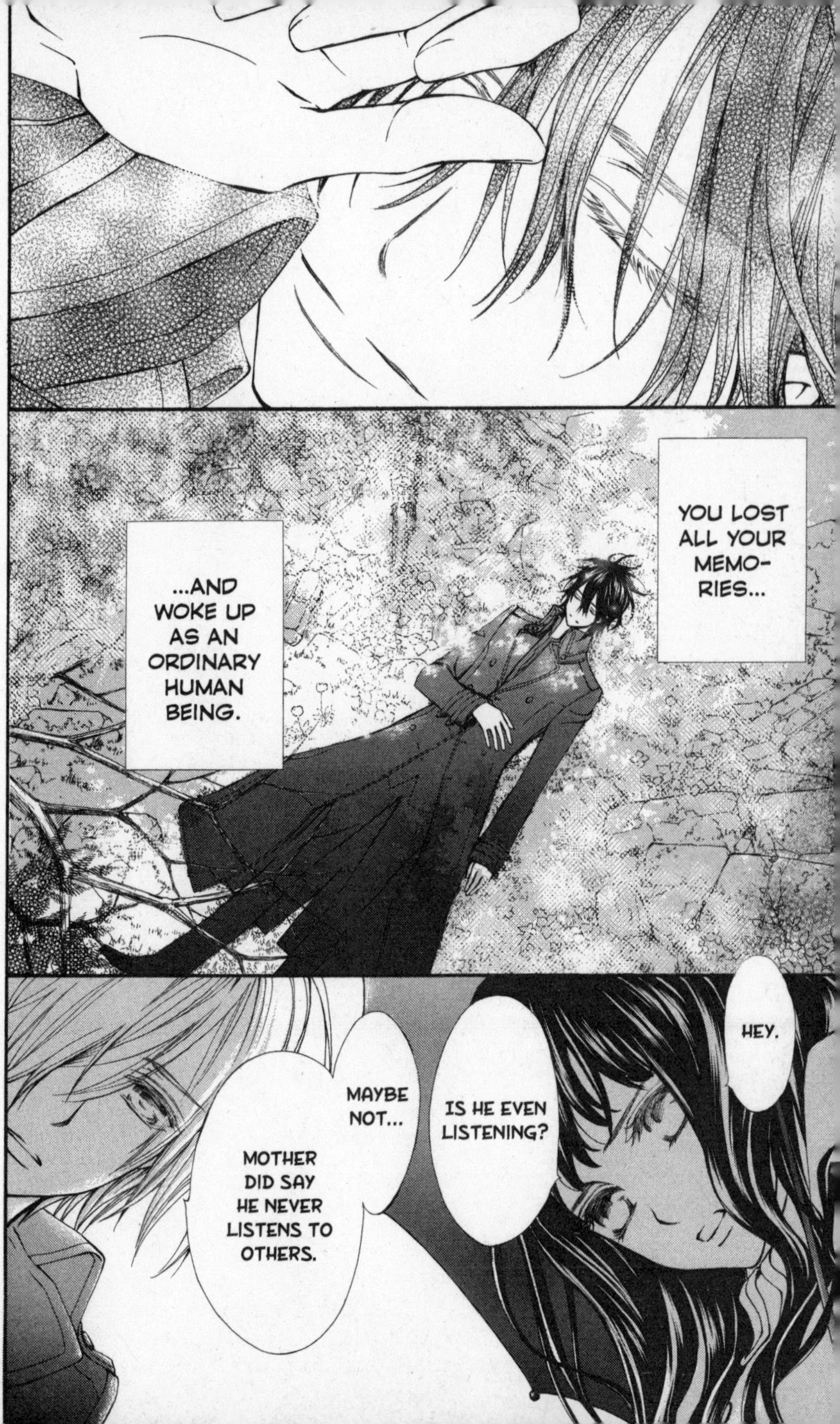
YOU LOST ALL YOUR MEMO-RIES...
...AND WOKE UP AS AN ORDINARY HUMAN BEING.
HEY.
IS HE EVEN LISTENING?
MAYBE NOT...
MOTHER DID SAY HE NEVER LISTENS TO OTHERS.

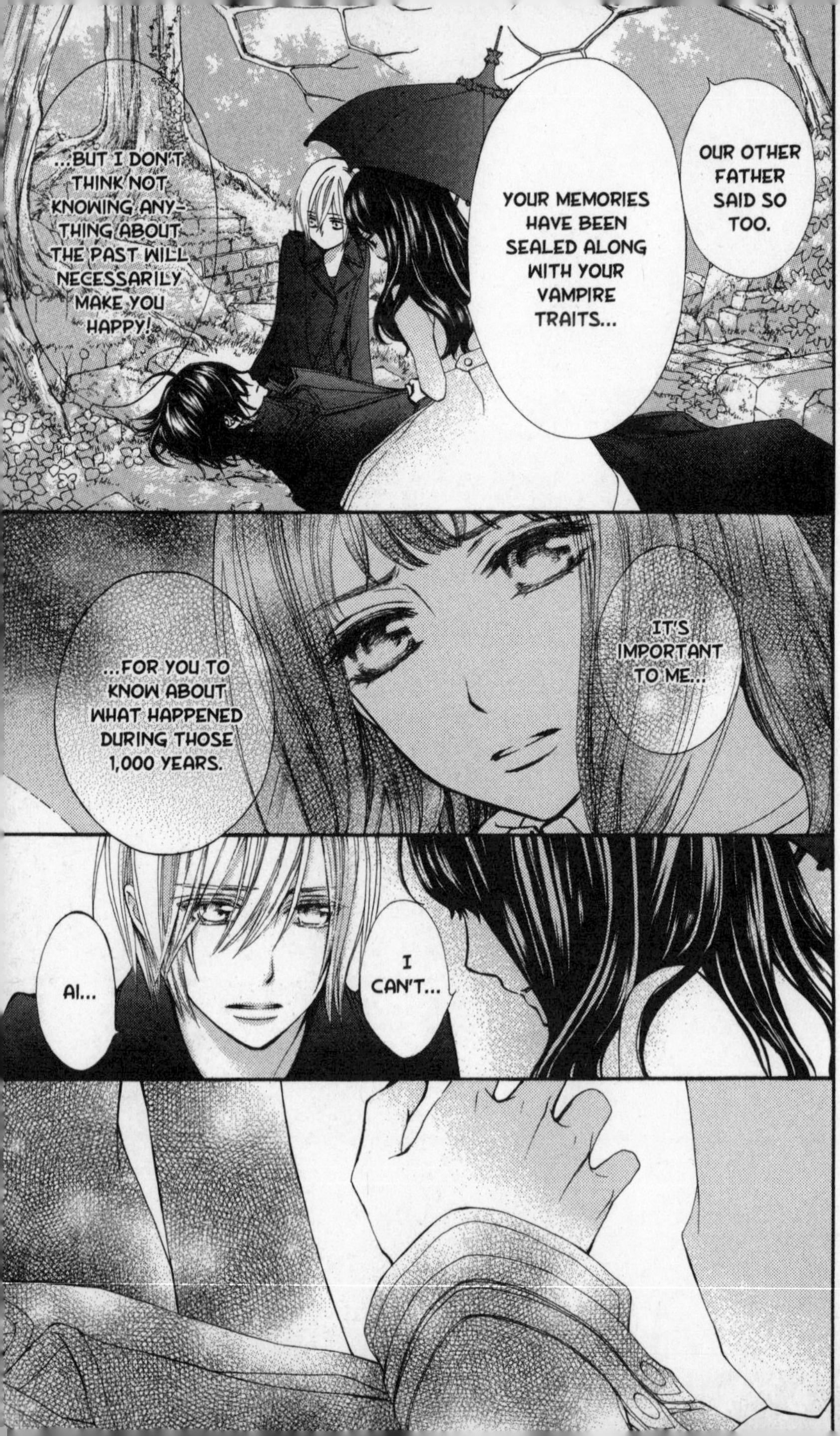
OUR OTHER FATHER SAID SO TOO.
YOUR MEMORIES HAVE BEEN SEALED ALONG WITH YOUR VAMPIRE TRAITS...
...BUT I DON'T THINK NOT KNOWING ANY-THING ABOUT THE PAST WILL NECESSARILY MAKE YOU HAPPY!
IT'S IMPORTANT TO ME...
...FOR YOU TO KNOW ABOUT WHAT HAPPENED DURING THOSE 1,000 YEARS.
I CAN'T...
AI...

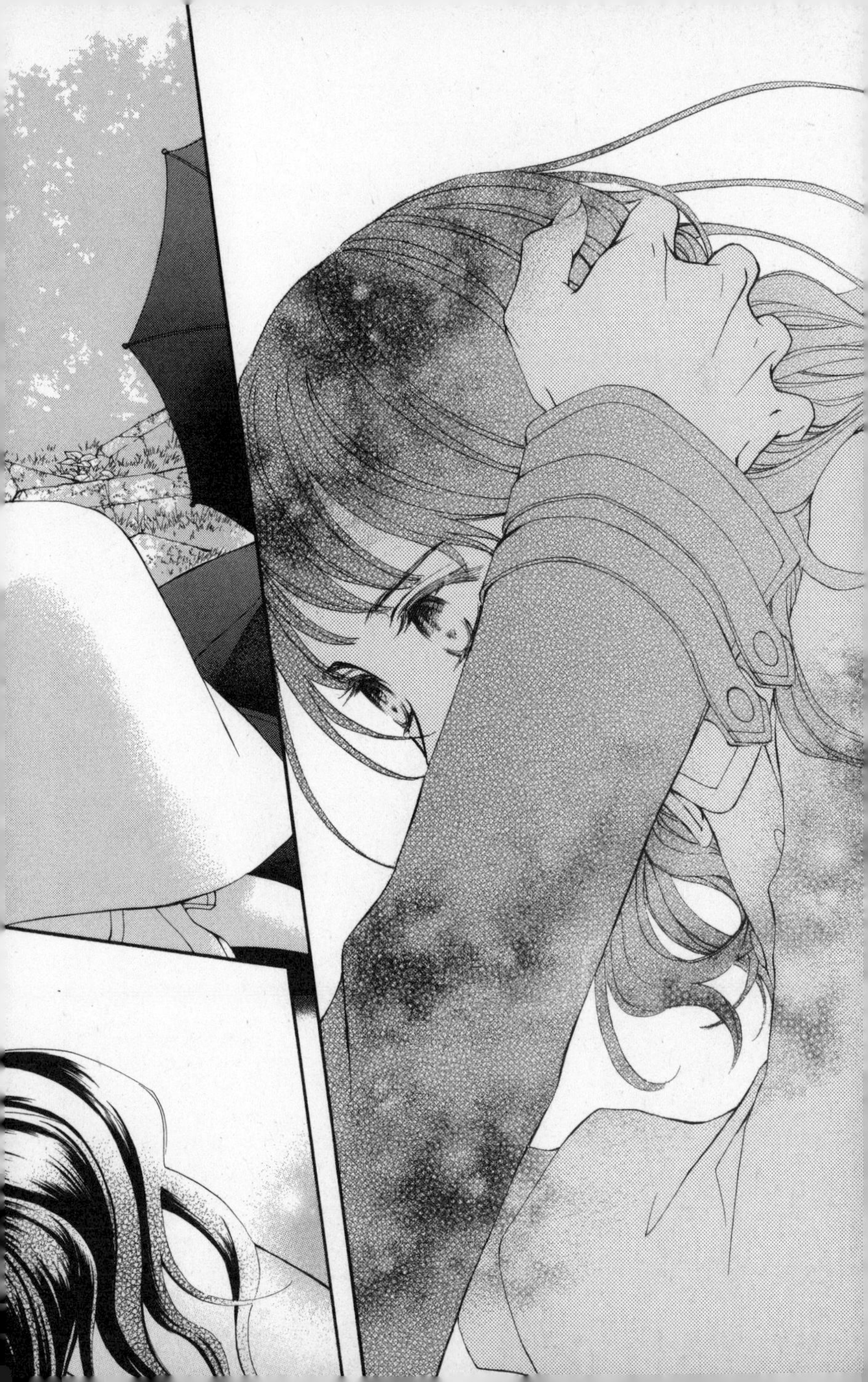

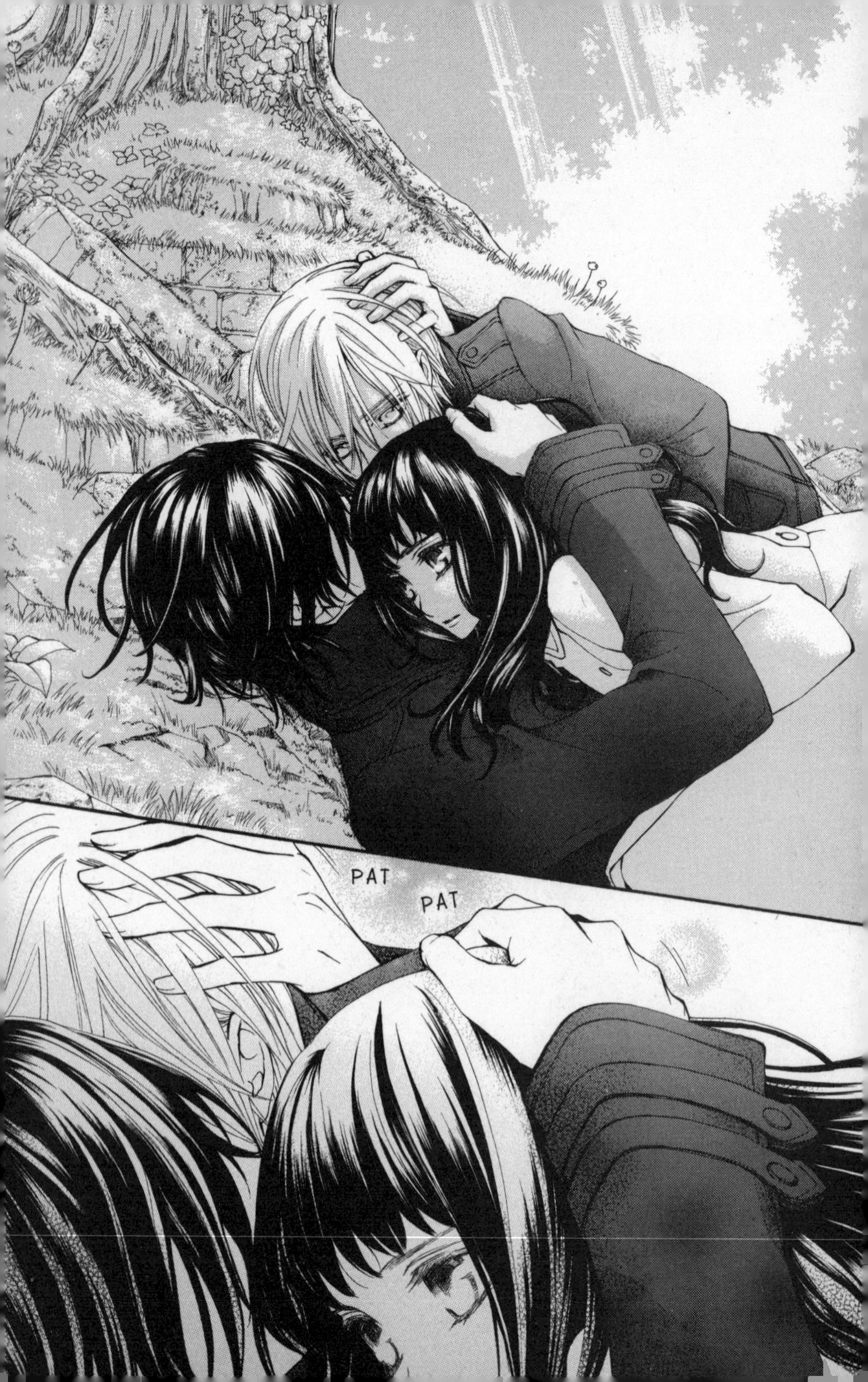
PAT
PAT

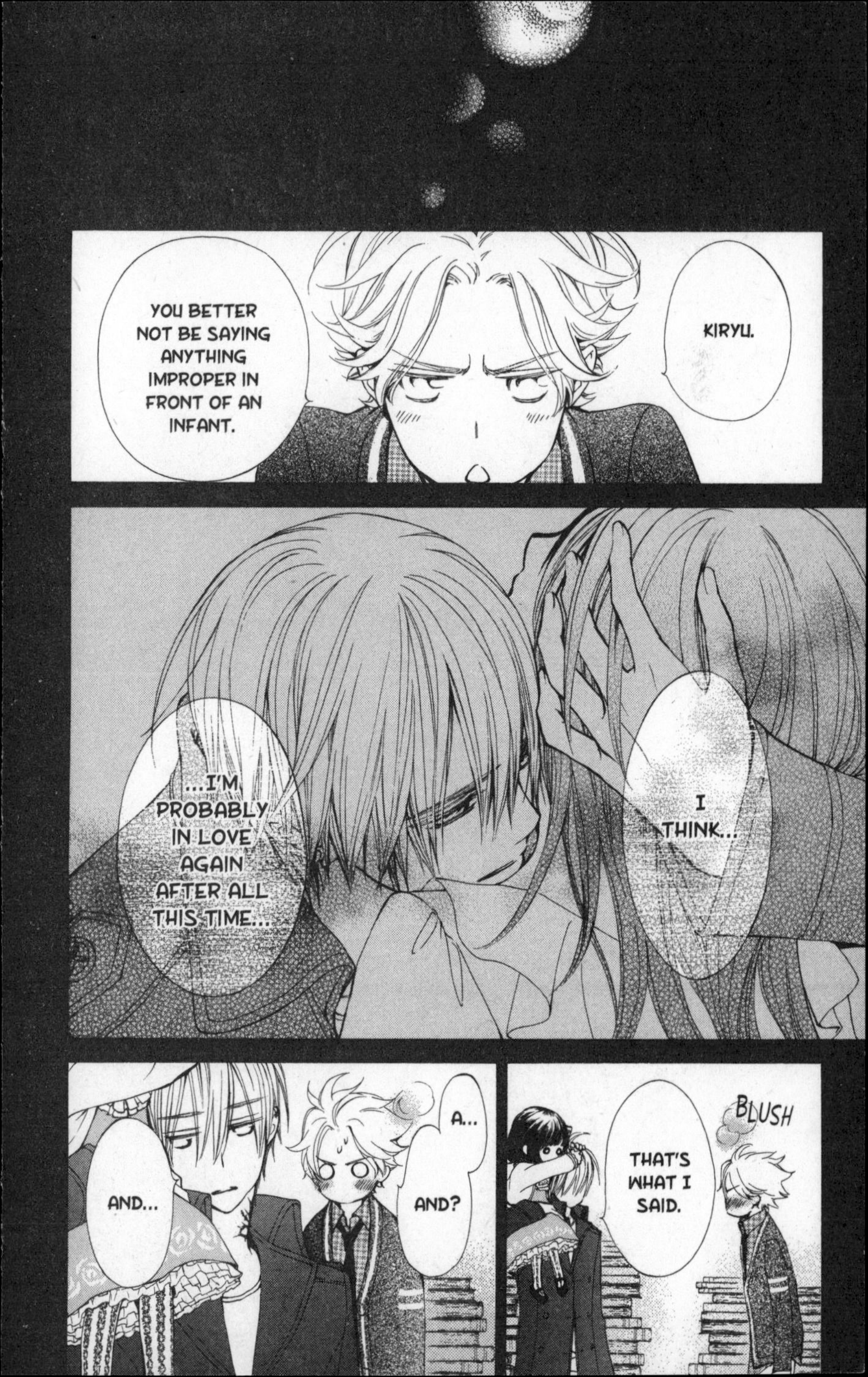
KIRYU.
YOU BETTER NOT BE SAYING ANYTHING IMPROPER IN FRONT OF AN INFANT.
I THINK...
...I'M PROBABLY IN LOVE AGAIN AFTER ALL THIS TIME...
BLUSH
THAT'S WHAT I SAID.
A... AND?
AND...

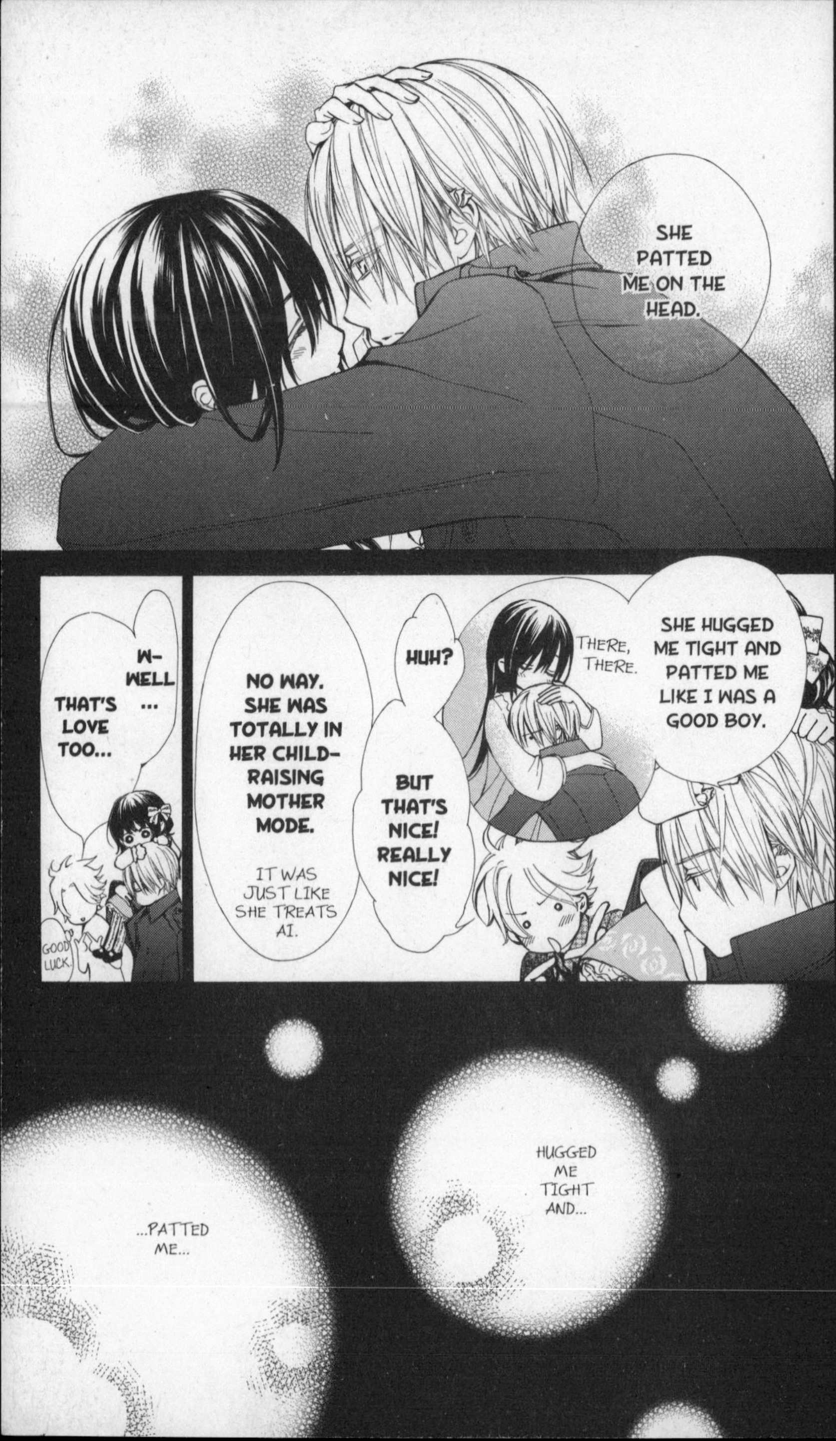
SHE PATTED ME ON THE HEAD.
SHE HUGGED ME TIGHT AND PATTED ME LIKE I WAS A GOOD BOY.
THERE, THERE.
HUH?
BUT THAT'S NICE! REALLY NICE!
NO WAY. SHE WAS TOTALLY IN HER CHILD-RAISING MOTHER MODE.
IT WAS JUST LIKE SHE TREATS AI.
W-WELL...
THAT'S LOVE TOO...
GOOD LUCK.
HUGGED ME TIGHT AND...
...PATTED ME...

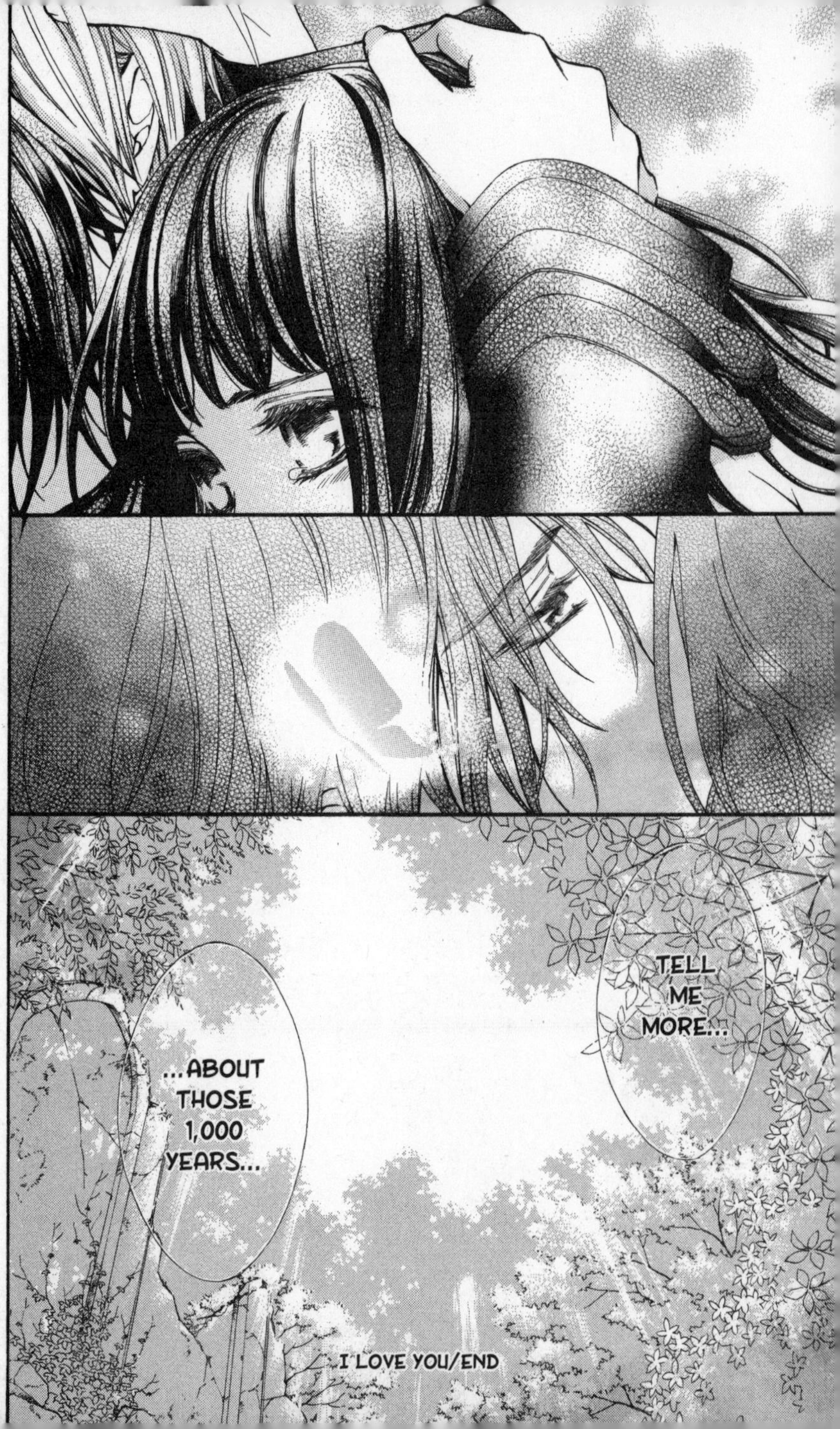
TELL ME MORE...
...ABOUT THOSE 1,000 YEARS...
I LOVE YOU/END

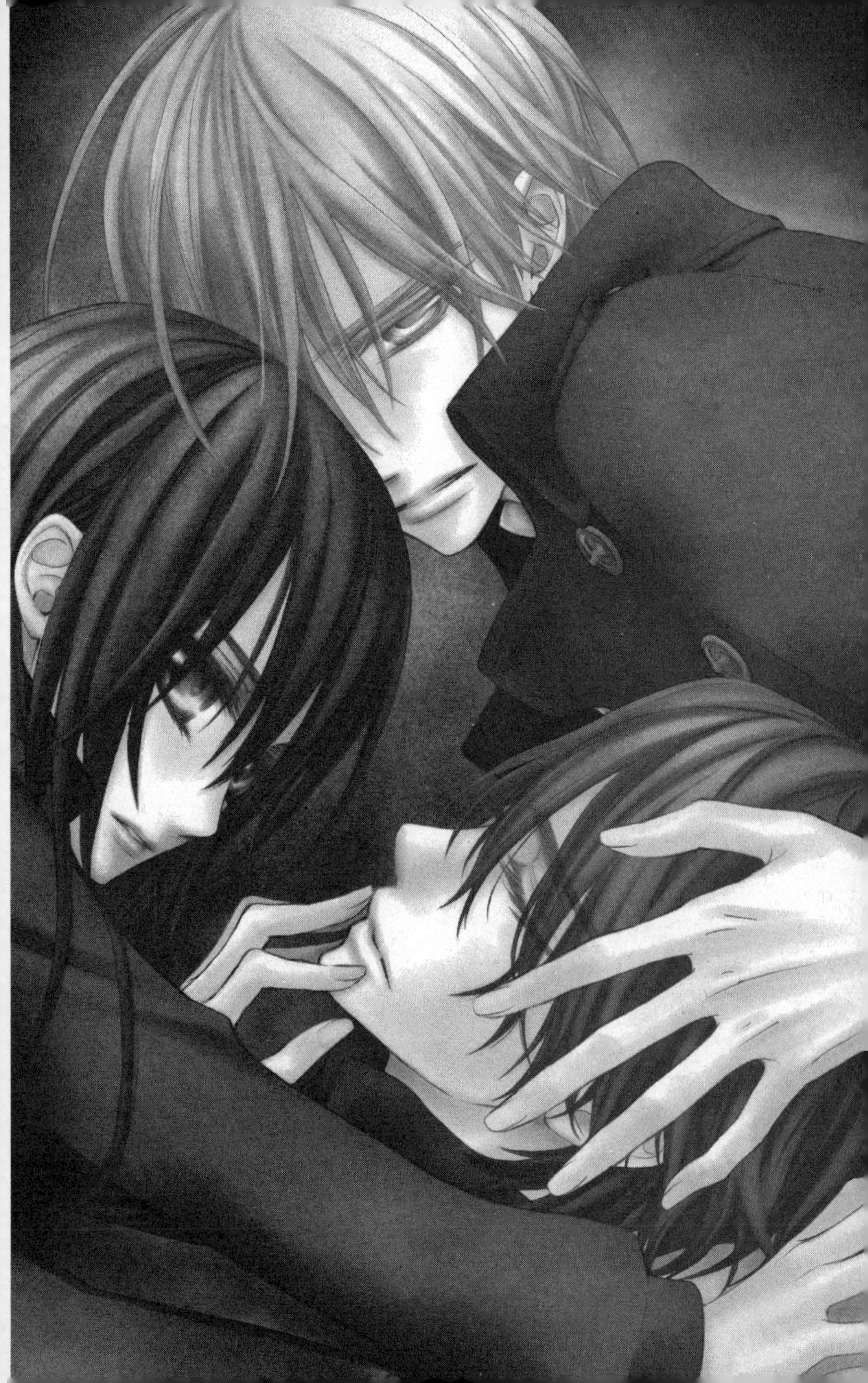

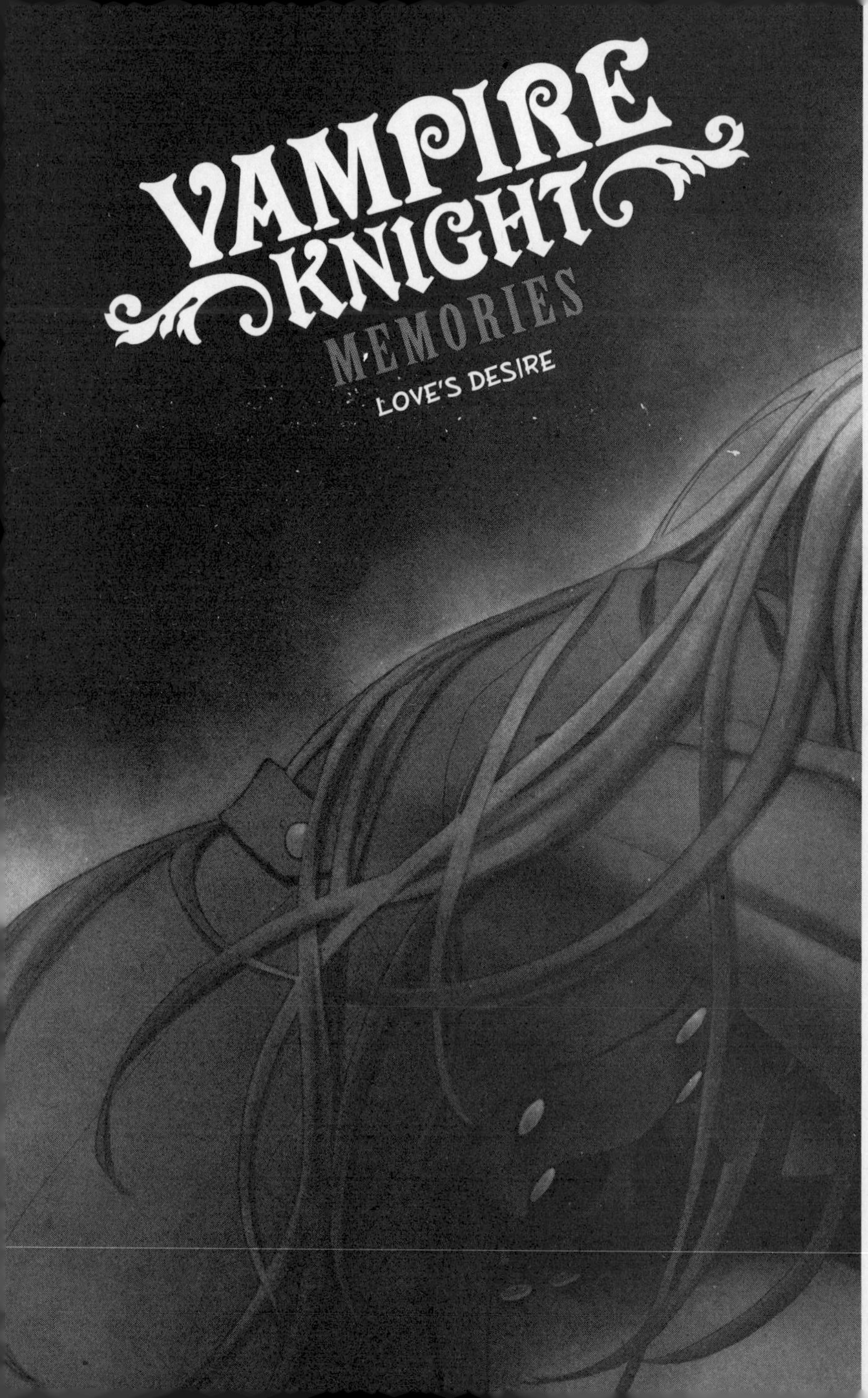
VAMPIRE KNIGHT
MEMORIES
LOVE'S DESIRE

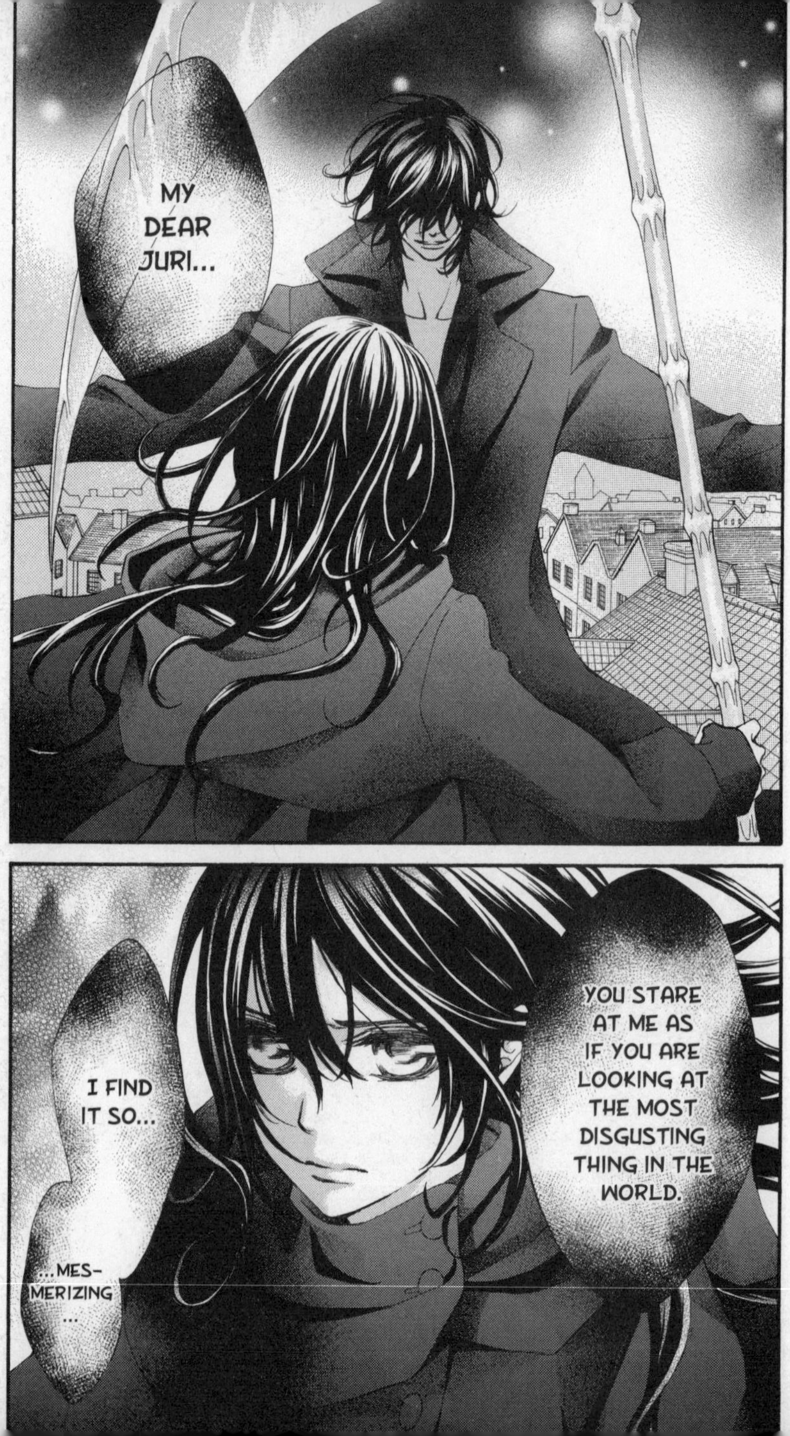
MY DEAR JURI...
YOU STARE AT ME AS IF YOU ARE LOOKING AT THE MOST DISGUSTING THING IN THE WORLD.
I FIND IT SO...
...MES-MERIZING...

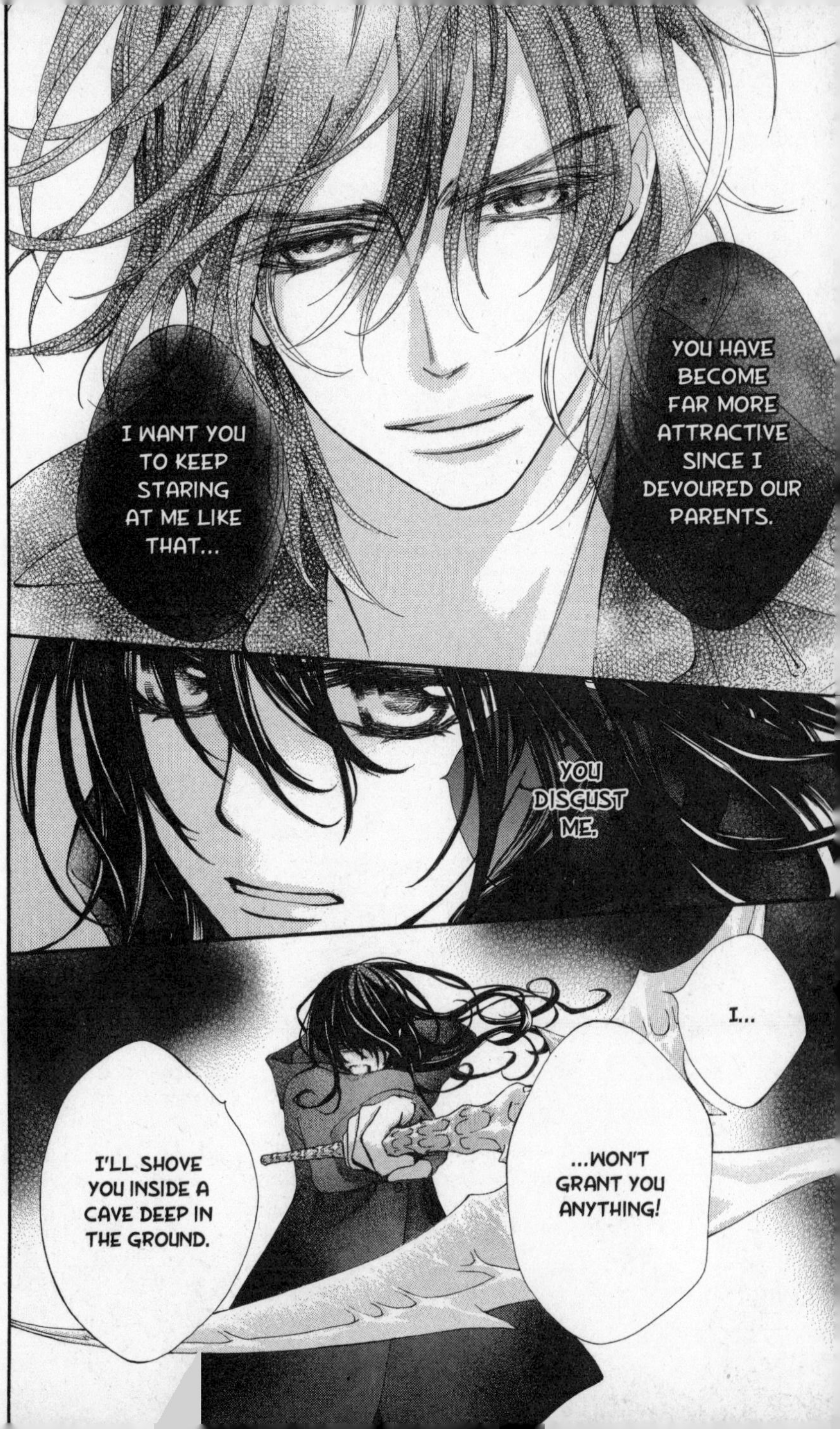
YOU HAVE BECOME FAR MORE ATTRACTIVE SINCE I DEVOURED OUR PARENTS.
I WANT YOU TO KEEP STARING AT ME LIKE THAT...
YOU DISGUST ME.
I...
...WON'T GRANT YOU ANYTHING!
I'LL SHOVE YOU INSIDE A CAVE DEEP IN THE GROUND.

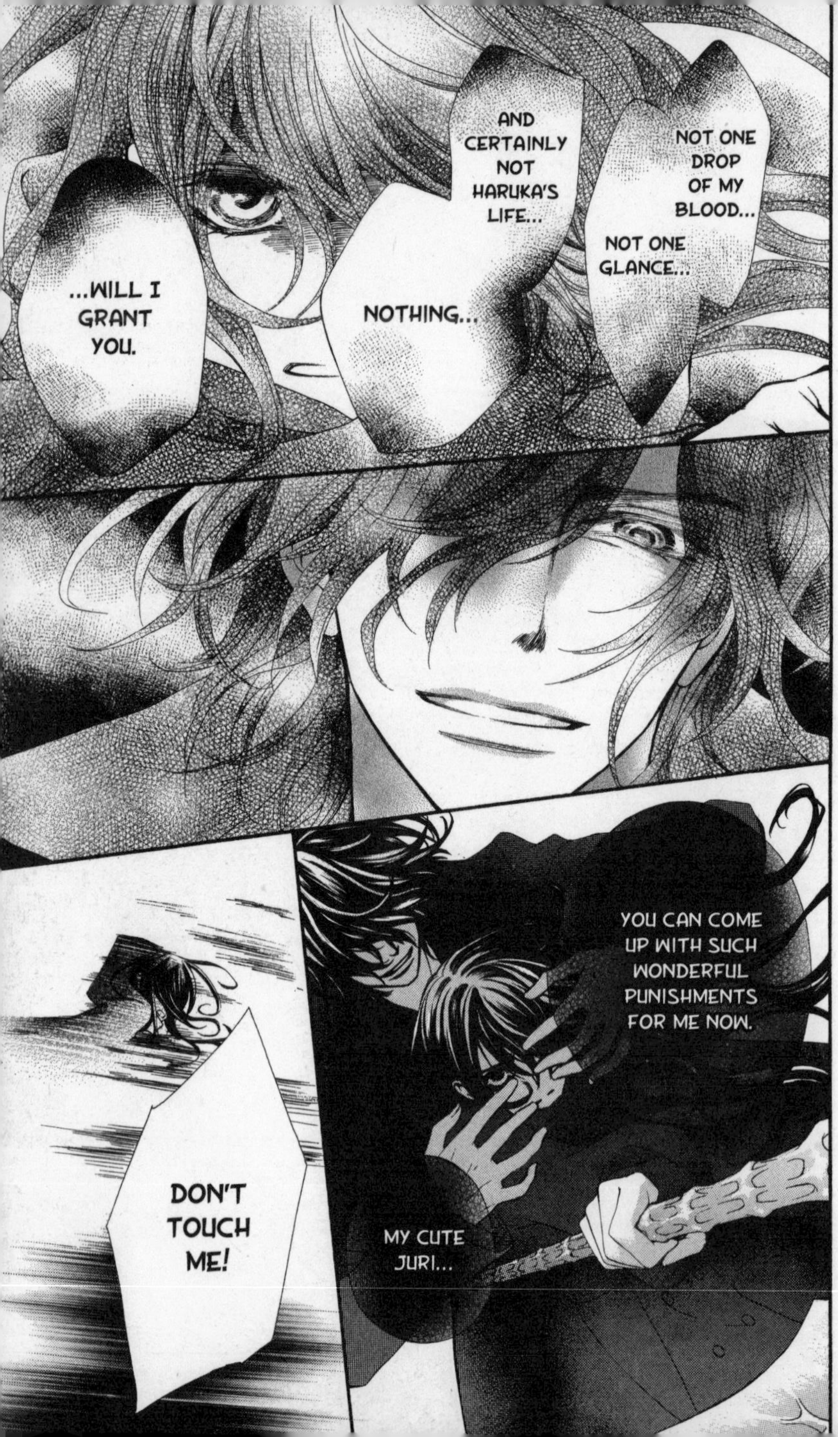
NOT ONE DROP OF MY BLOOD...
NOT ONE GLANCE...
AND CERTAINLY NOT HARUKA'S LIFE...
NOTHING...
...WILL I GRANT YOU.
YOU CAN COME UP WITH SUCH WONDERFUL PUNISHMENTS FOR ME NOW.
MY CUTE JURI...
DON'T TOUCH ME!

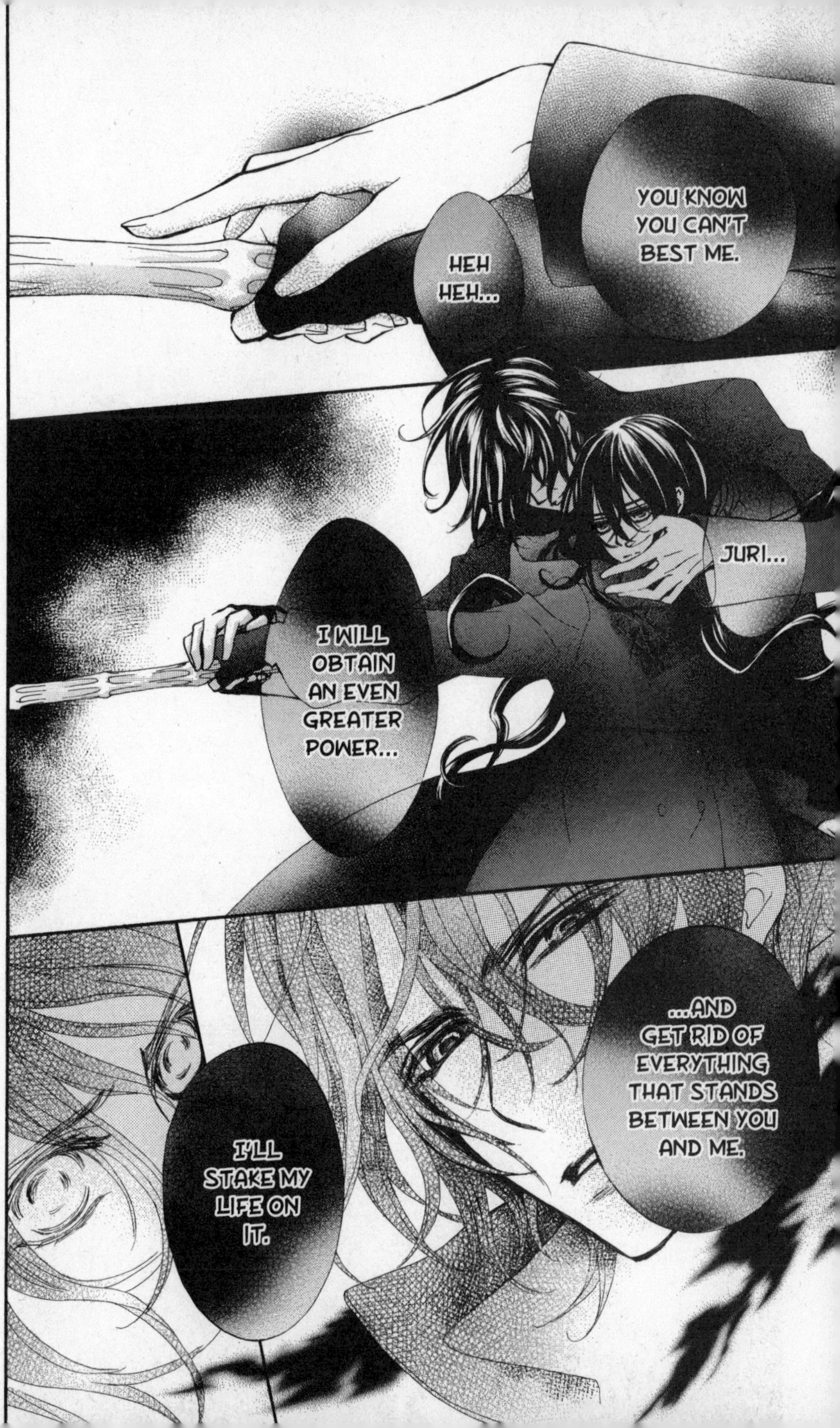
YOU KNOW YOU CAN'T BEST ME.
HEH HEH...
JURI...
I WILL OBTAIN AN EVEN GREATER POWER...
...AND GET RID OF EVERYTHING THAT STANDS BETWEEN YOU AND ME.
I'LL STAKE MY LIFE ON IT.

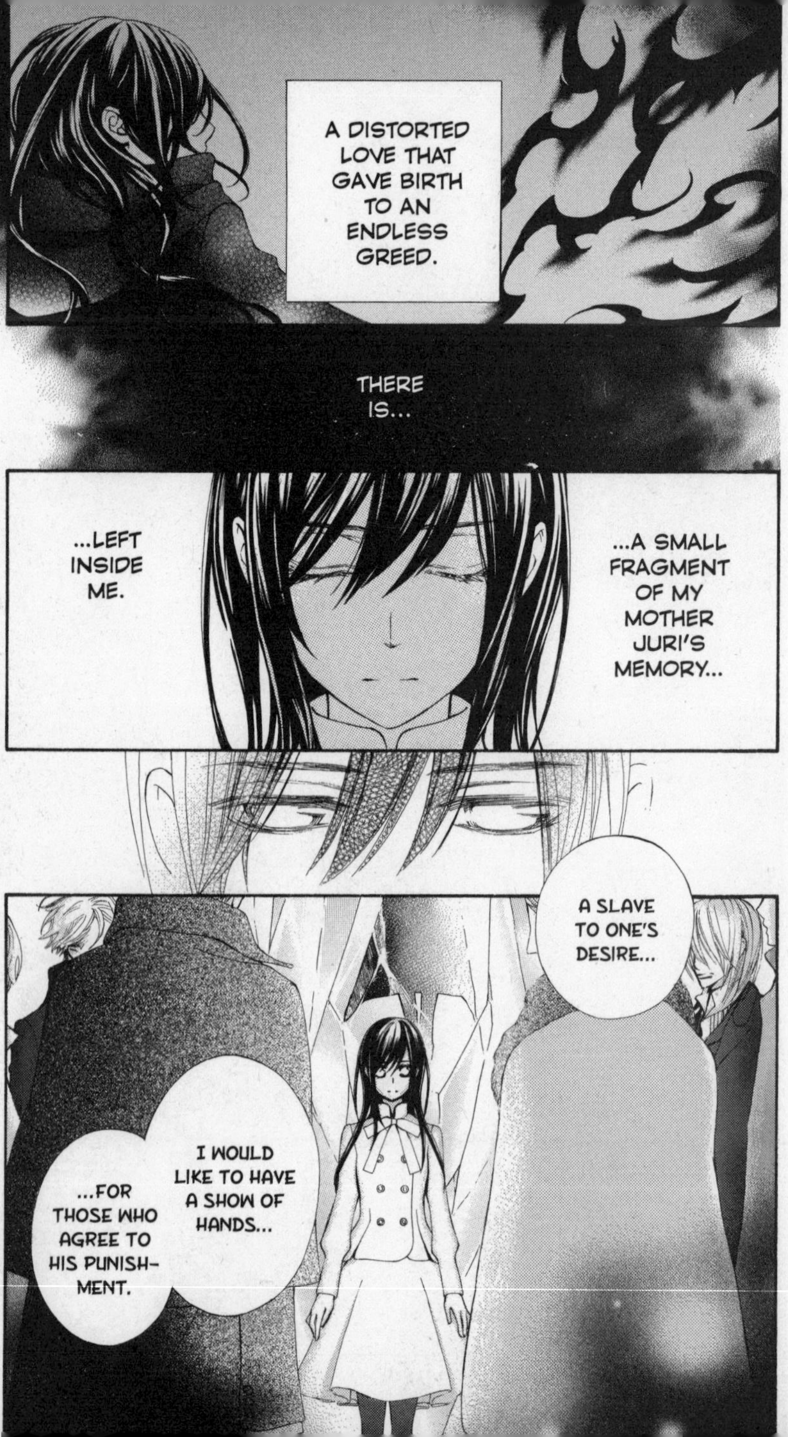
A DISTORTED LOVE THAT GAVE BIRTH TO AN ENDLESS GREED.
THERE IS...
...A SMALL FRAGMENT OF MY MOTHER JURI'S MEMORY...
...LEFT INSIDE ME.
A SLAVE TO ONE'S DESIRE...
I WOULD LIKE TO HAVE A SHOW OF HANDS...
...FOR THOSE WHO AGREE TO HIS PUNISH-MENT.

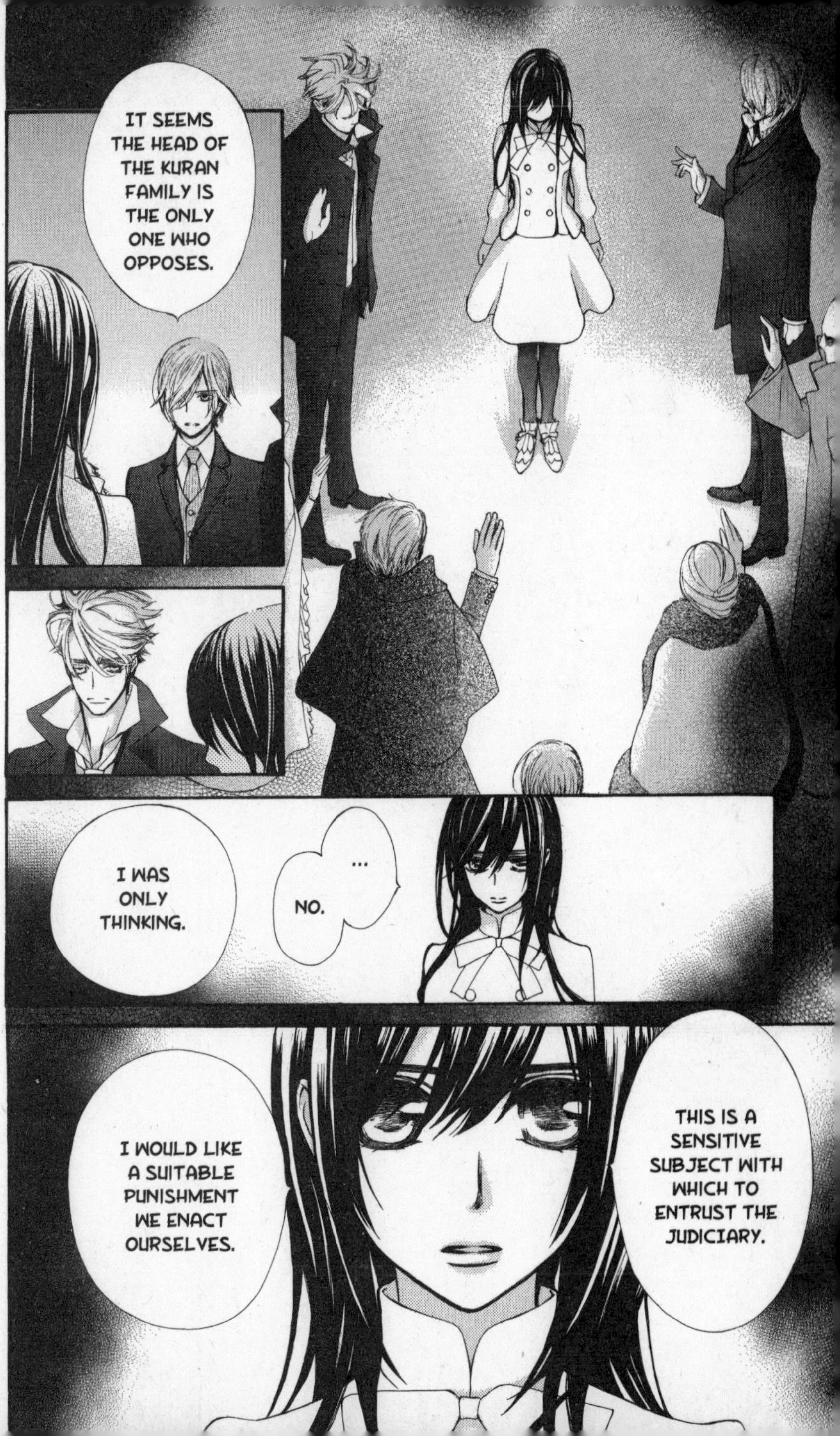
IT SEEMS THE HEAD OF THE KURAN FAMILY IS THE ONLY ONE WHO OPPOSES.
... NO.
I WAS ONLY THINKING.
THIS IS A SENSITIVE SUBJECT WITH WHICH TO ENTRUST THE JUDICIARY.
I WOULD LIKE A SUITABLE PUNISHMENT WE ENACT OURSELVES.

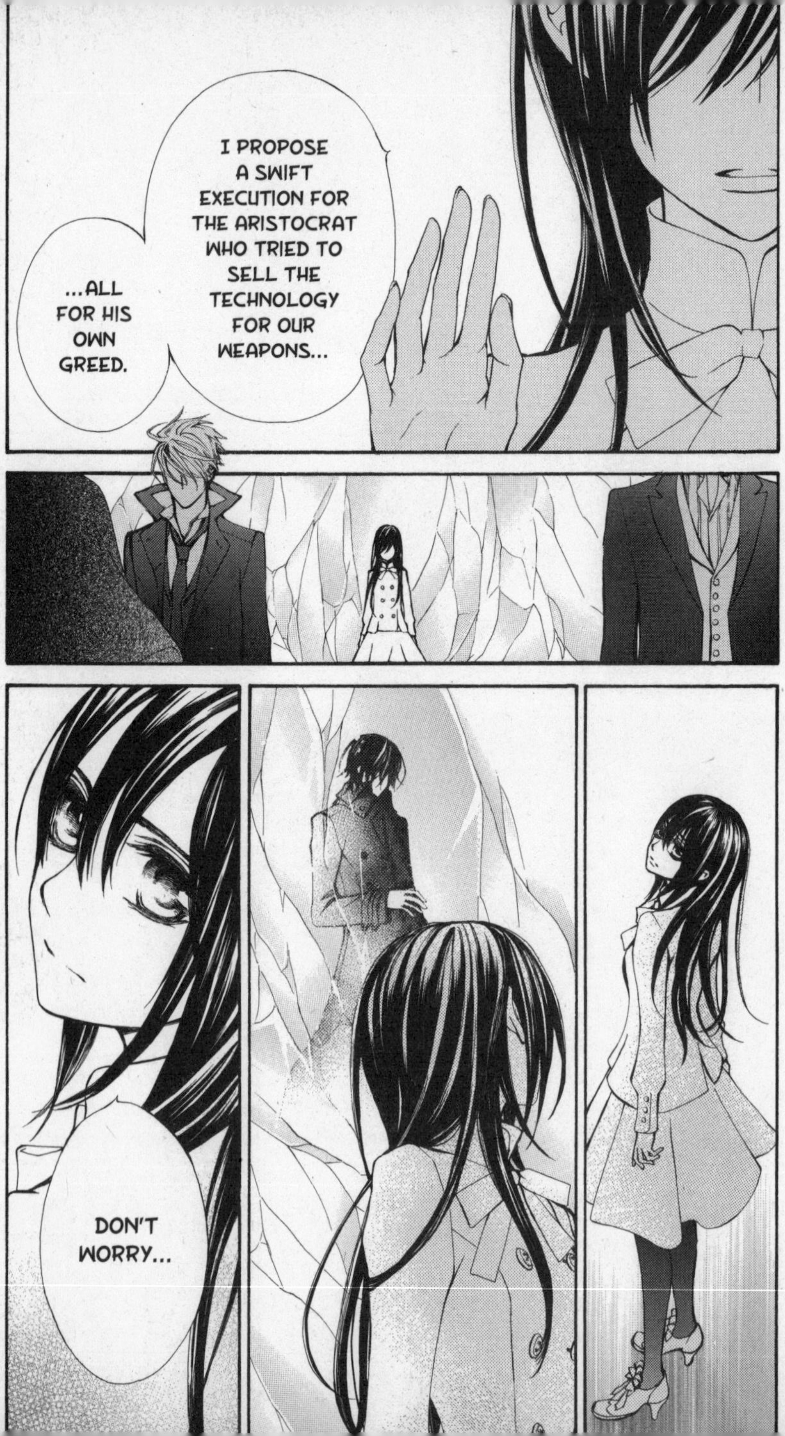
I PROPOSE A SWIFT EXECUTION FOR THE ARISTOCRAT WHO TRIED TO SELL THE TECHNOLOGY FOR OUR WEAPONS...
...ALL FOR HIS OWN GREED.
DON'T WORRY...

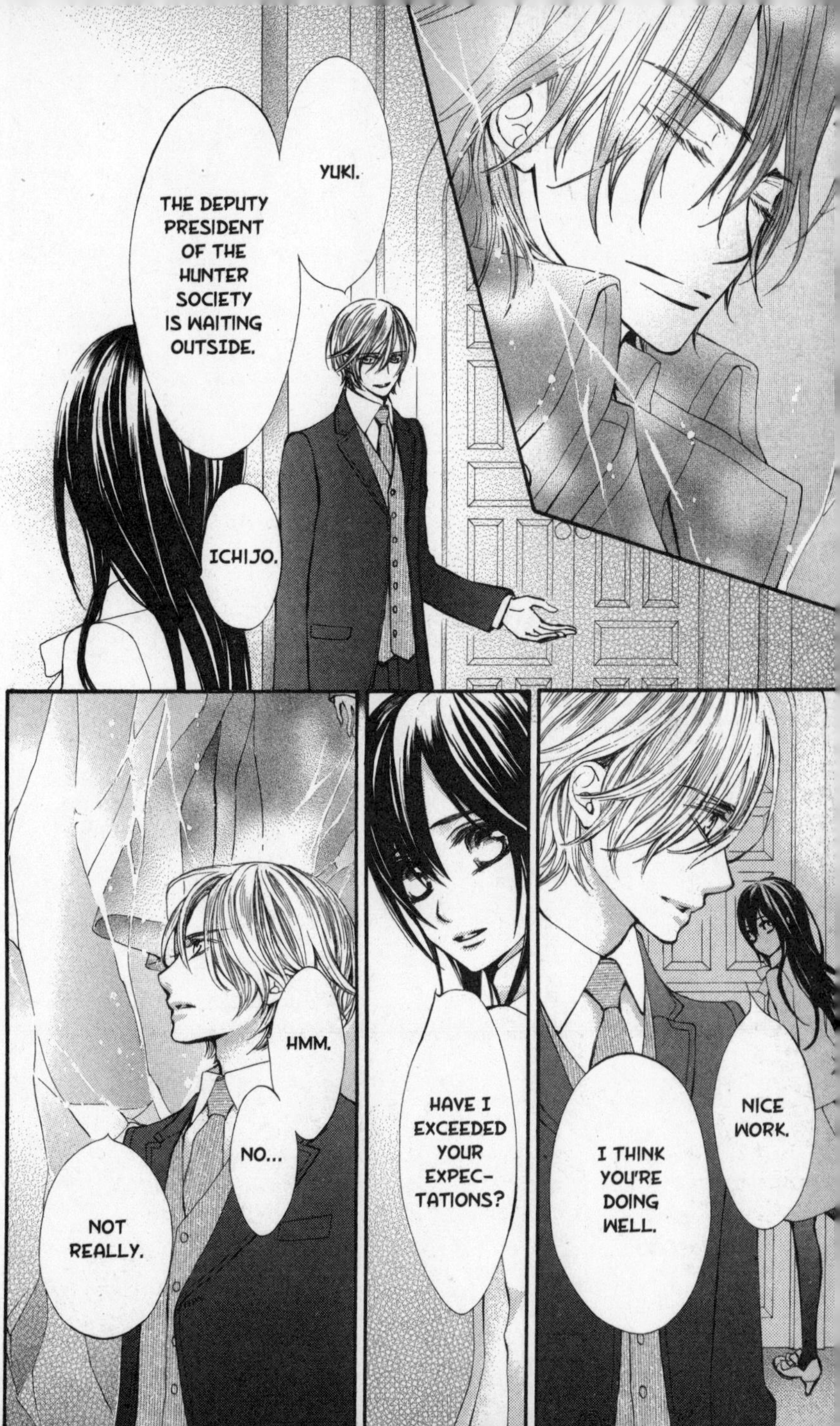
YUKI.
THE DEPUTY PRESIDENT OF THE HUNTER SOCIETY IS WAITING OUTSIDE.
ICHIJO.
NICE WORK.
I THINK YOU'RE DOING WELL.
HAVE I EXCEEDED YOUR EXPECTATIONS?
HMM.
NO...
NOT REALLY.

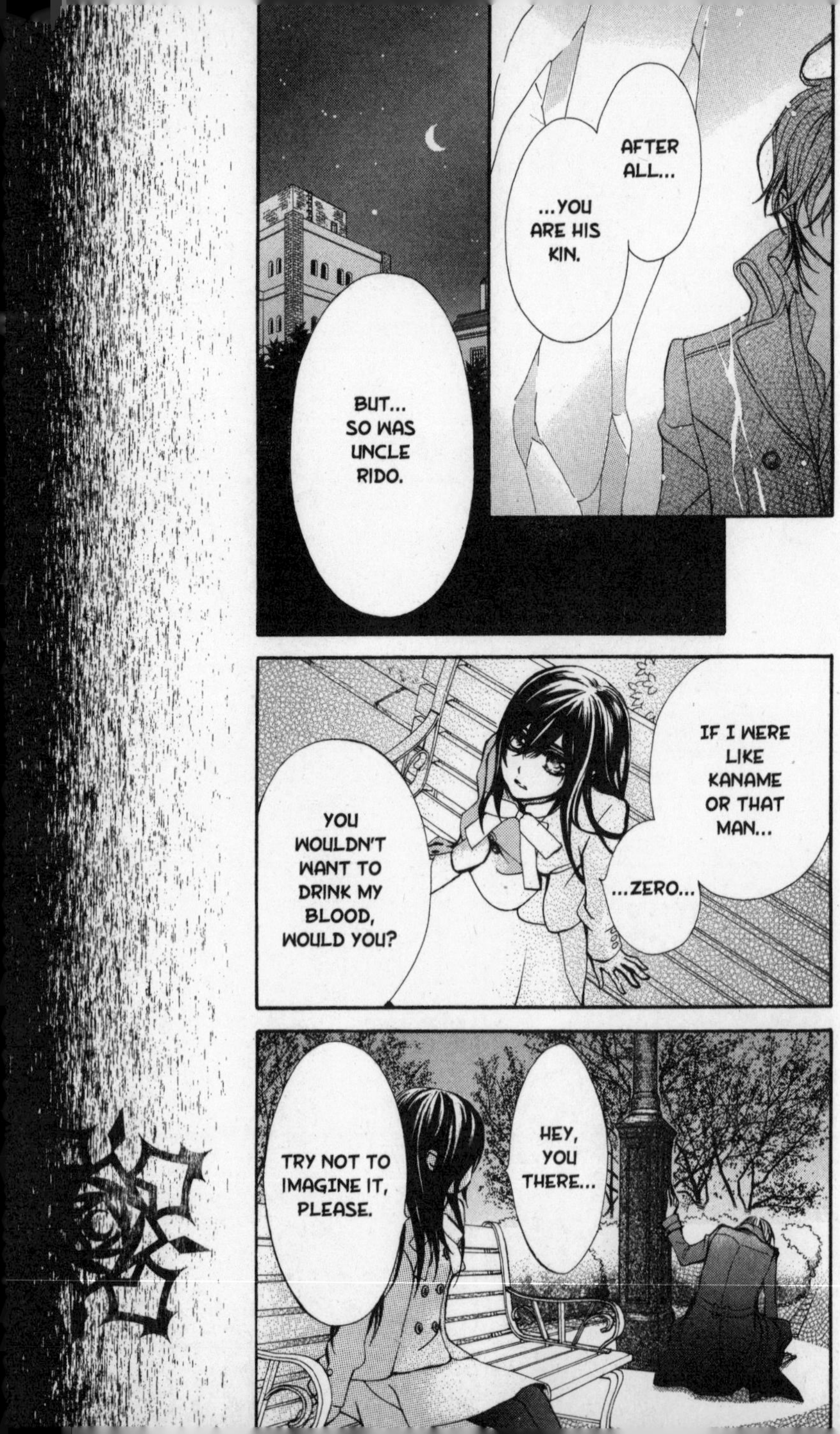
AFTER ALL...
...YOU ARE HIS KIN.
BUT... SO WAS UNCLE RIDO.
IF I WERE LIKE KANAME OR THAT MAN...
...ZERO...
YOU WOULDN'T WANT TO DRINK MY BLOOD, WOULD YOU?
HEY, YOU THERE...
TRY NOT TO IMAGINE IT, PLEASE.

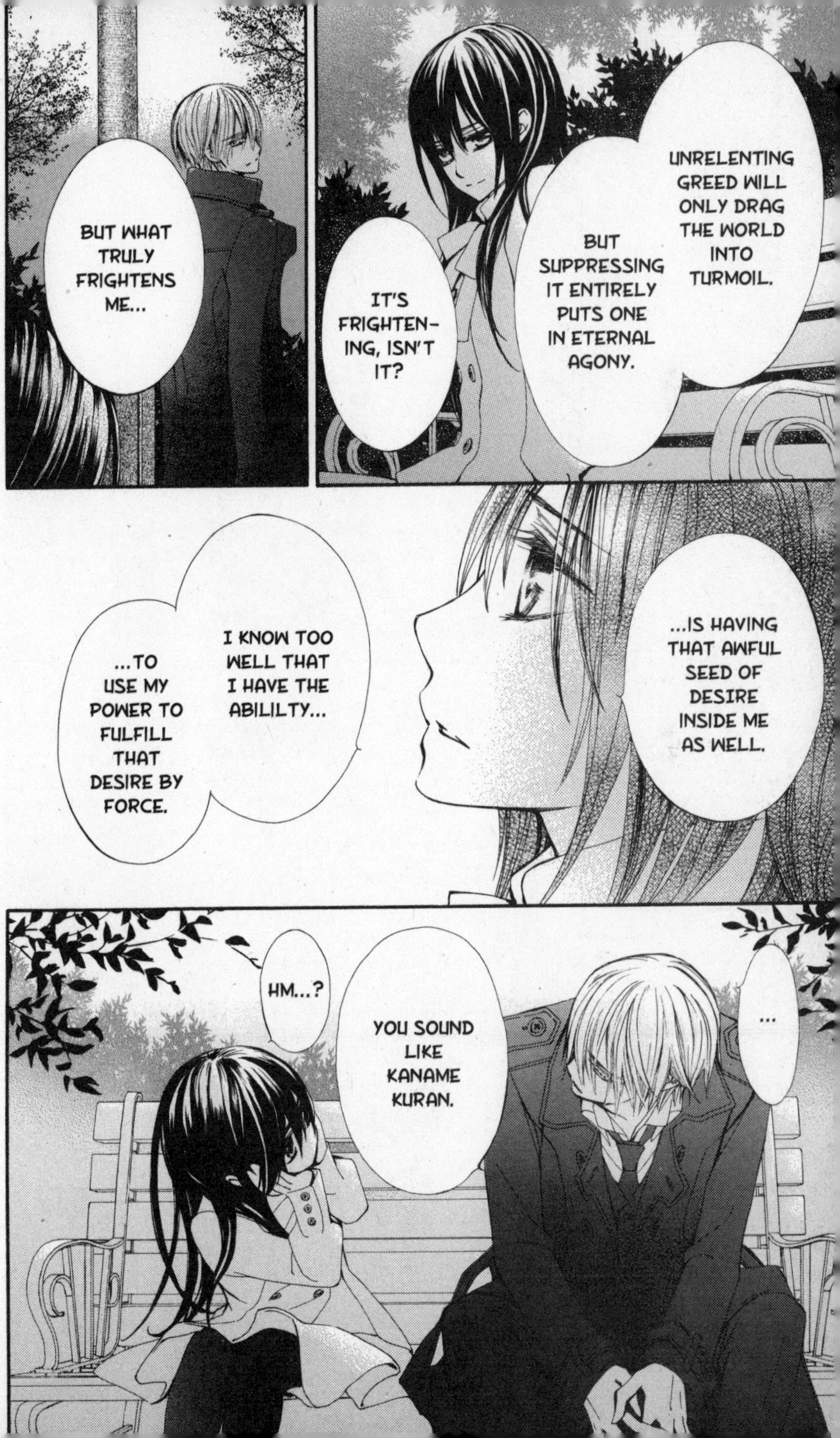
UNRELENTING GREED WILL ONLY DRAG THE WORLD INTO TURMOIL.
BUT SUPPRESSING IT ENTIRELY PUTS ONE IN ETERNAL AGONY.
IT'S FRIGHTEN-ING, ISN'T IT?
BUT WHAT TRULY FRIGHTENS ME...
...IS HAVING THAT AWFUL SEED OF DESIRE INSIDE ME AS WELL.
I KNOW TOO WELL THAT I HAVE THE ABILILTY...
...TO USE MY POWER TO FULFILL THAT DESIRE BY FORCE.
...
YOU SOUND LIKE KANAME KURAN.
HM...?

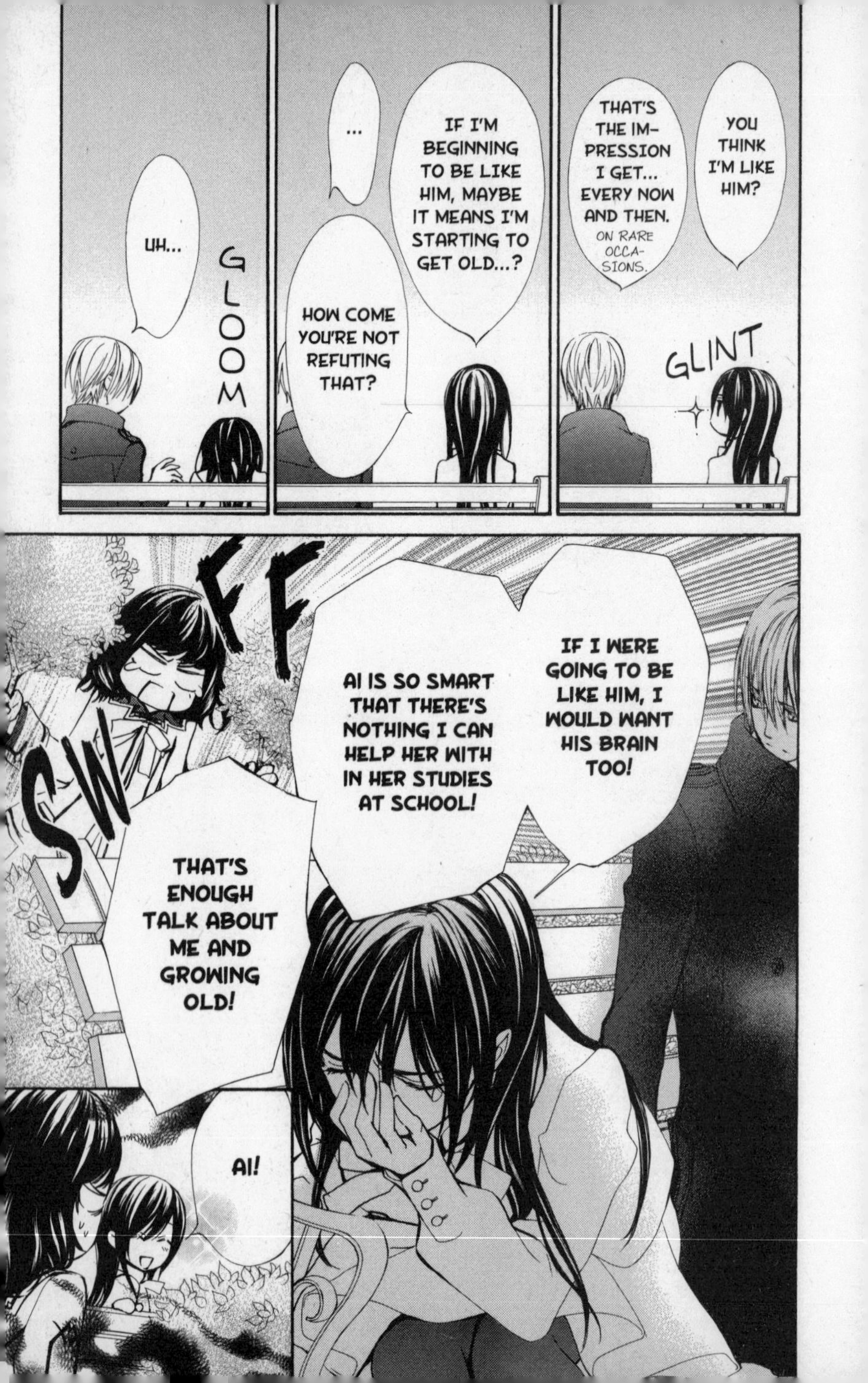
YOU THINK I'M LIKE HIM?
THAT'S THE IM-PRESSION I GET... EVERY NOW AND THEN.
ON RARE OCCA-SIONS.
GLINT
IF I'M BEGINNING TO BE LIKE HIM, MAYBE IT MEANS I'M STARTING TO GET OLD...?
...
HOW COME YOU'RE NOT REFUTING THAT?
GLOOM
UH...
IF I WERE GOING TO BE LIKE HIM, I WOULD WANT HIS BRAIN TOO!
AI IS SO SMART THAT THERE'S NOTHING I CAN HELP HER WITH IN HER STUDIES AT SCHOOL!
SWFF
THAT'S ENOUGH TALK ABOUT ME AND GROWING OLD!
AI!

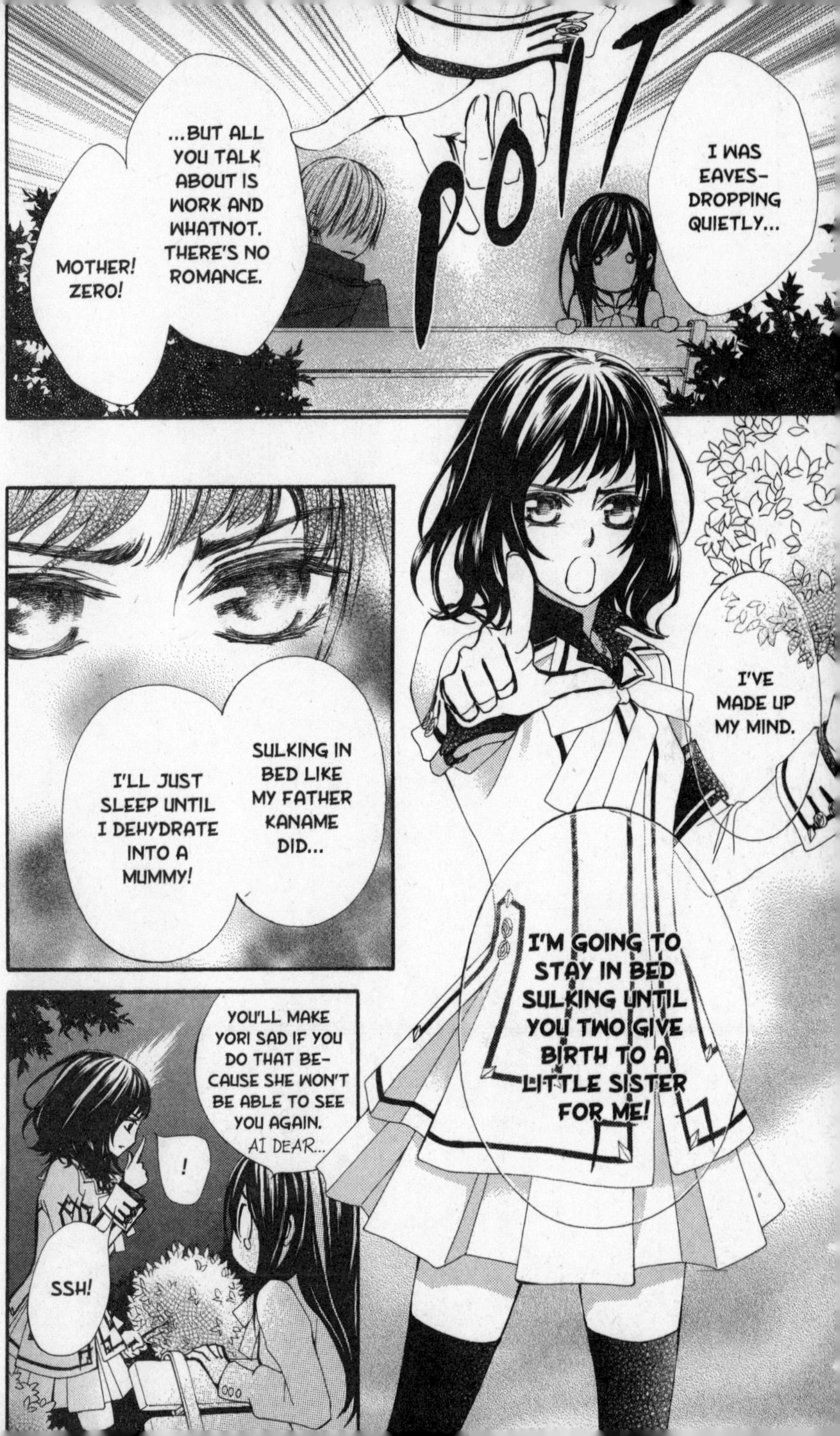
I WAS EAVES-DROPPING QUIETLY...
...BUT ALL YOU TALK ABOUT IS WORK AND WHATNOT. THERE'S NO ROMANCE.
MOTHER! ZERO!
I'VE MADE UP MY MIND.
I'M GOING TO STAY IN BED SULKING UNTIL YOU TWO GIVE BIRTH TO A LITTLE SISTER FOR ME!
SULKING IN BED LIKE MY FATHER KANAME DID...
I'LL JUST SLEEP UNTIL I DEHYDRATE INTO A MUMMY!
YOU'LL MAKE YORI SAD IF YOU DO THAT BE-CAUSE SHE WON'T BE ABLE TO SEE YOU AGAIN.
AI DEAR...
!
SSH!

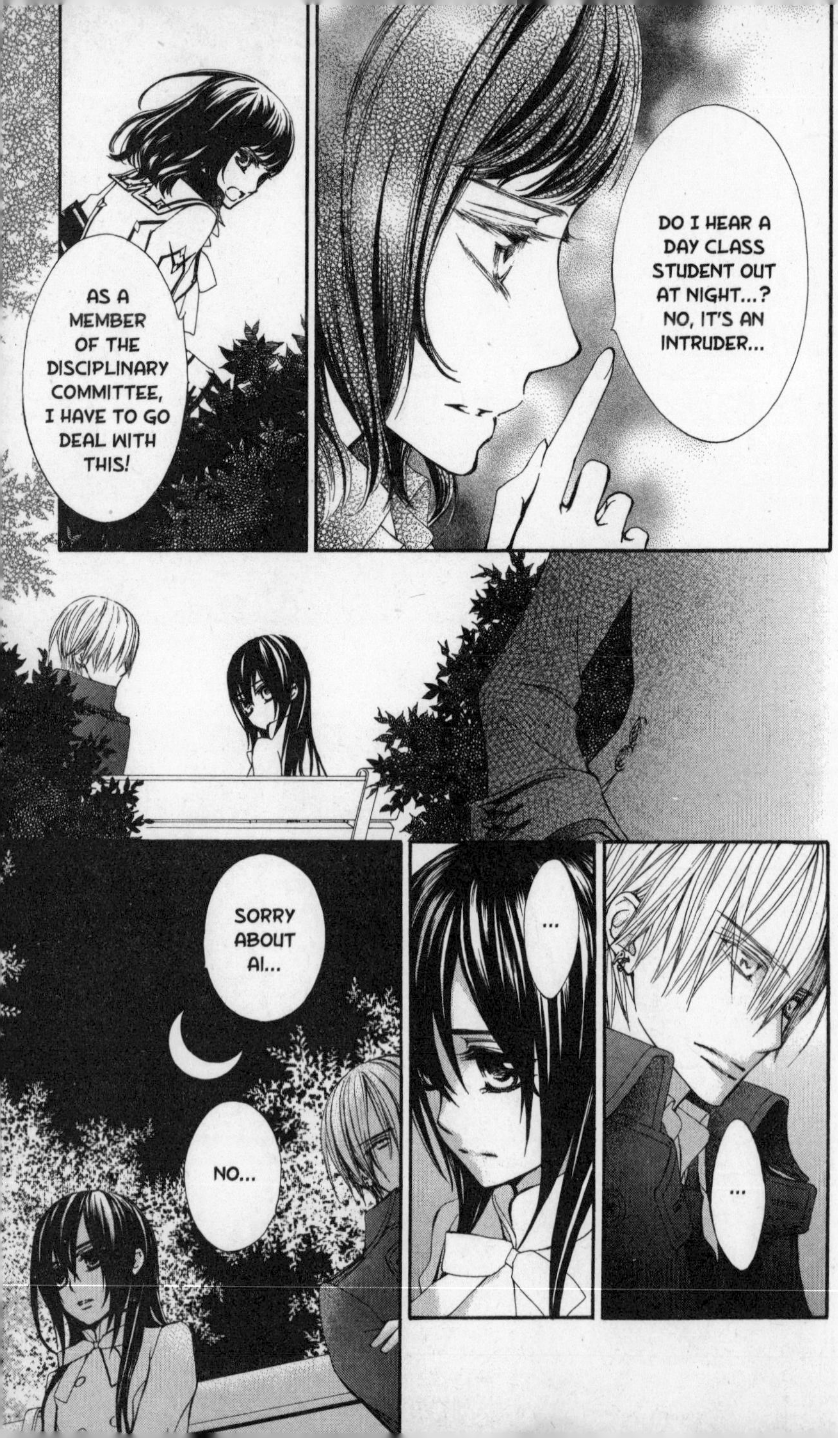
DO I HEAR A DAY CLASS STUDENT OUT AT NIGHT...? NO, IT'S AN INTRUDER...
AS A MEMBER OF THE DISCIPLINARY COMMITTEE, I HAVE TO GO DEAL WITH THIS!
...
...
SORRY ABOUT AI...
NO...

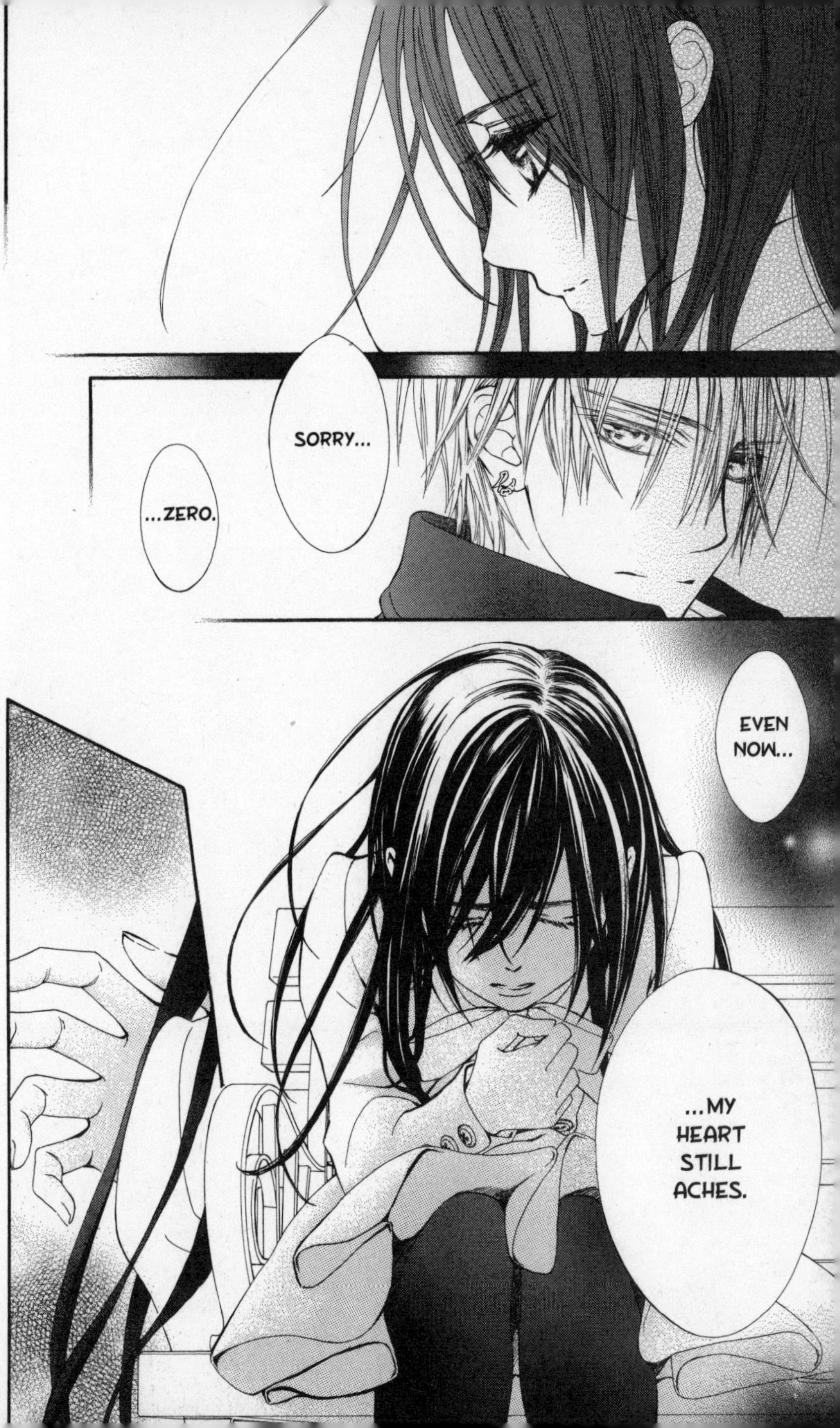
SORRY...
...ZERO.
EVEN NOW...
...MY HEART STILL ACHES.

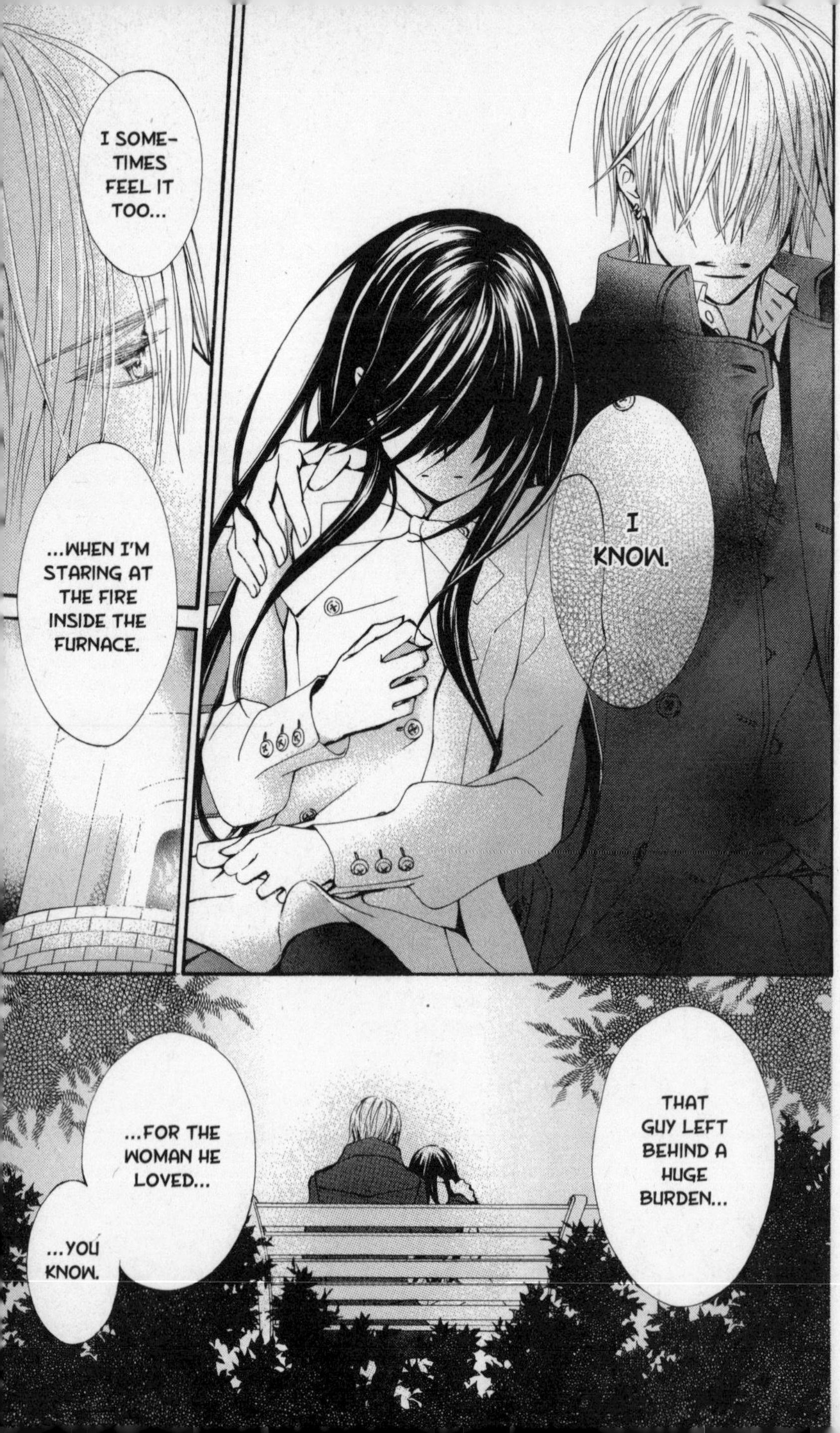
I KNOW.
I SOMETIMES FEEL IT TOO...
...WHEN I'M STARING AT THE FIRE INSIDE THE FURNACE.
THAT GUY LEFT BEHIND A HUGE BURDEN...
...FOR THE WOMAN HE LOVED...
...YOU KNOW.

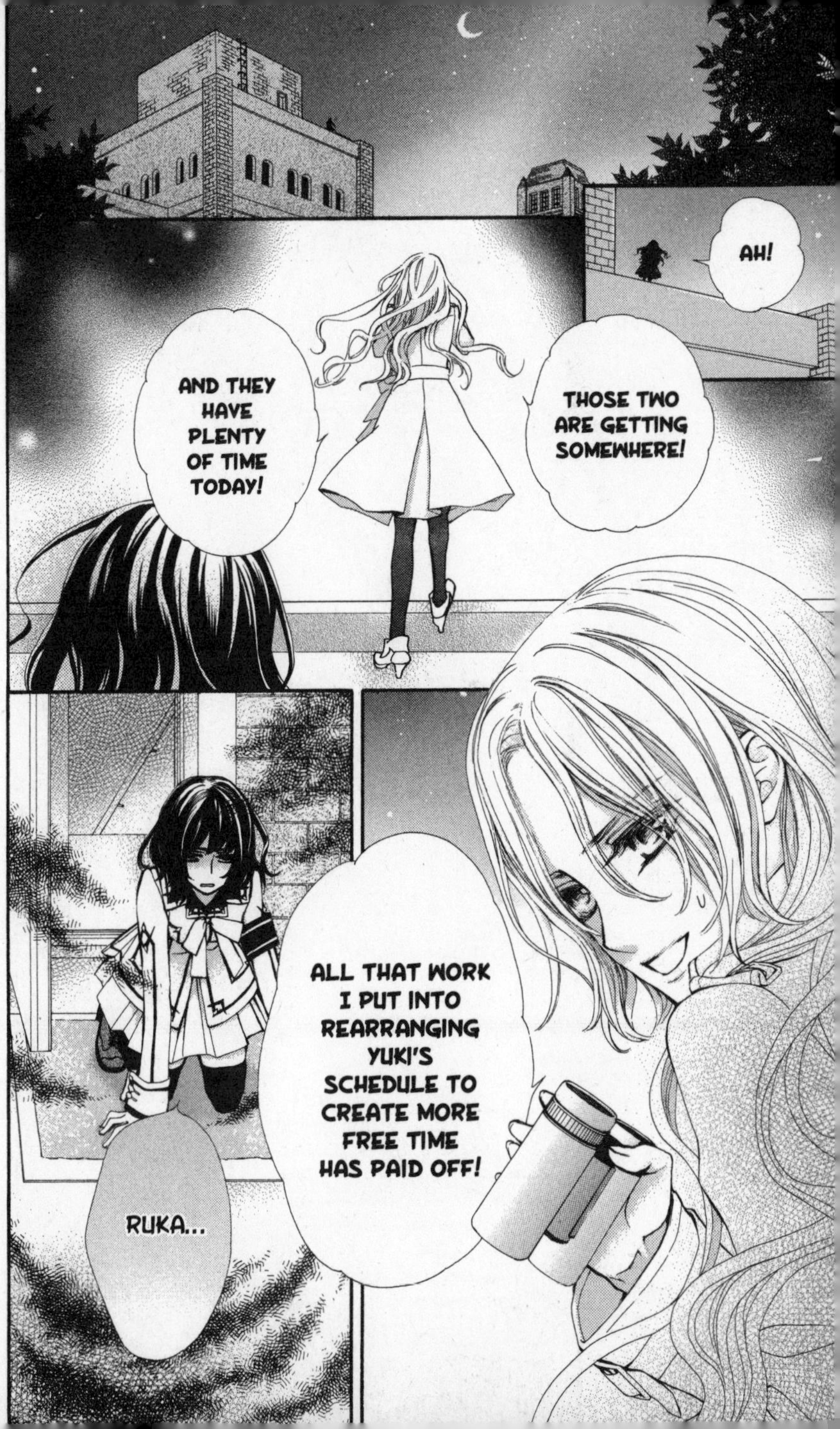
AH!
THOSE TWO ARE GETTING SOMEWHERE!
AND THEY HAVE PLENTY OF TIME TODAY!
ALL THAT WORK I PUT INTO REARRANGING YUKI'S SCHEDULE TO CREATE MORE FREE TIME HAS PAID OFF!
RUKA...

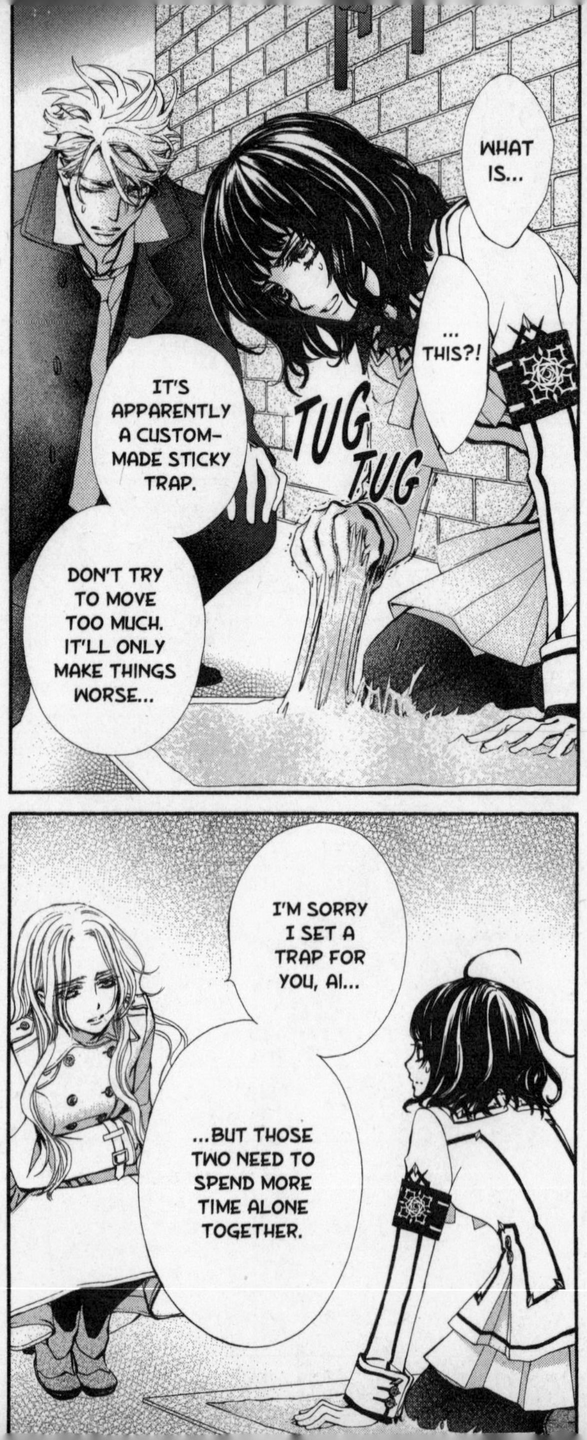
WHAT IS...
...THIS?!
TUG TUG
IT'S APPARENTLY A CUSTOM-MADE STICKY TRAP.
DON'T TRY TO MOVE TOO MUCH. IT'LL ONLY MAKE THINGS WORSE...
I'M SORRY I SET A TRAP FOR YOU, AI...
...BUT THOSE TWO NEED TO SPEND MORE TIME ALONE TOGETHER.

-3-

A gentle *kabedon* that can only be done by a strong man, as well as a scene with a certain character snapping in anger with the actual "KRIK" sound... I packed this volume with scenes I'd always wanted to draw while I was working on the series. I'll work equally hard on volume 2!

[A *kabedon* (hand-wall) is when someone hits their hand on the wall above a love interest and traps them close. See pages 120–121. —Ed.]

I would like to thank the people who were involved in getting this volume published: My four editors, the editor of the graphic novel, the designer and everyone else who helped.

Thanks also to the people who always assist me with my final drafts:
O. Mio-sama
K. Midori-sama
A. Ichiya-sama

And my family and friends.

And most of all, to my gentle readers—thank you very much!

樋野まつり 2016
Matsuri Hino

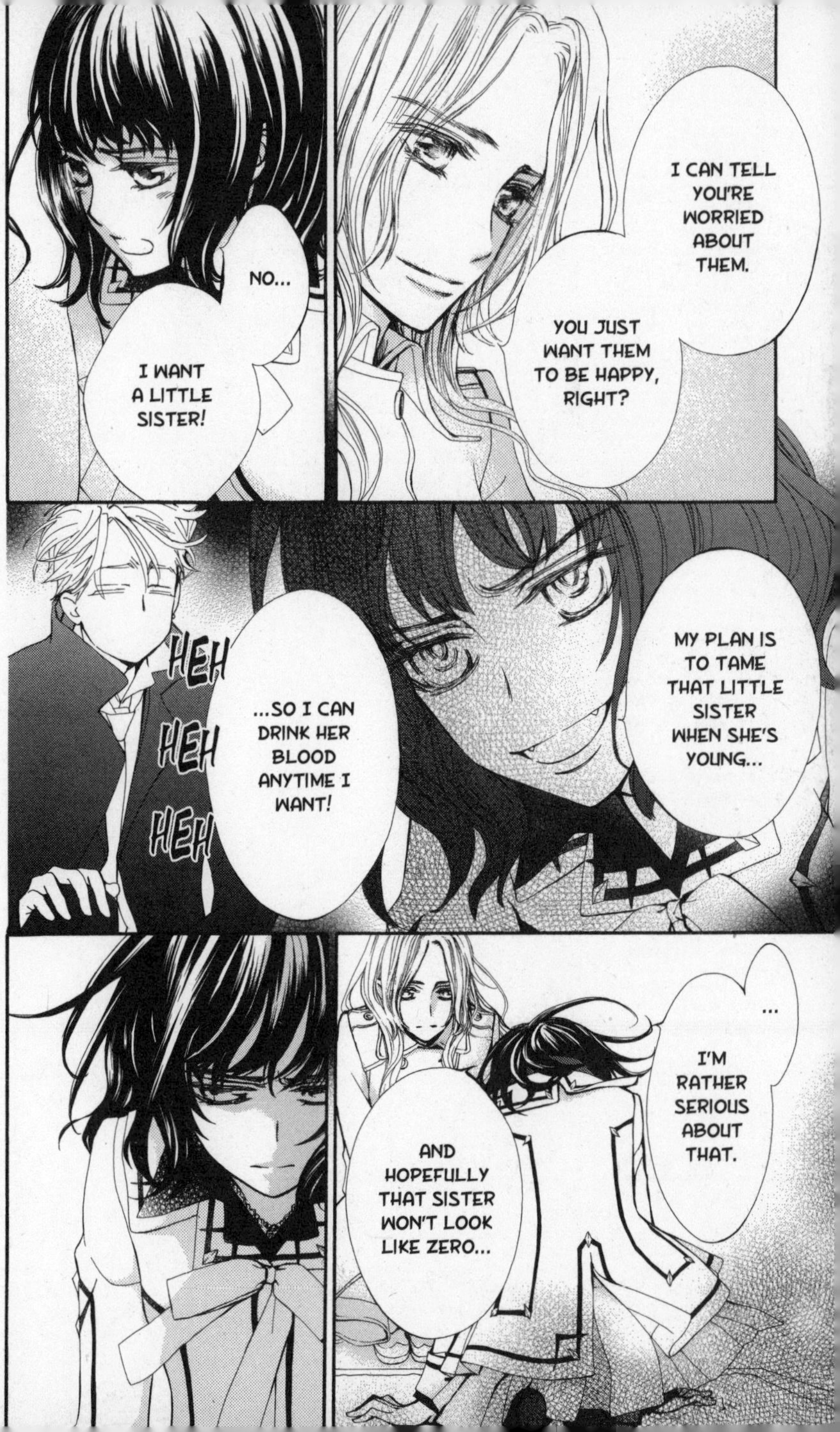
I CAN TELL YOU'RE WORRIED ABOUT THEM.
YOU JUST WANT THEM TO BE HAPPY, RIGHT?
NO...
I WANT A LITTLE SISTER!
MY PLAN IS TO TAME THAT LITTLE SISTER WHEN SHE'S YOUNG...
...SO I CAN DRINK HER BLOOD ANYTIME I WANT!
HEH
HEH
HEH
...
I'M RATHER SERIOUS ABOUT THAT.
AND HOPEFULLY THAT SISTER WON'T LOOK LIKE ZERO...

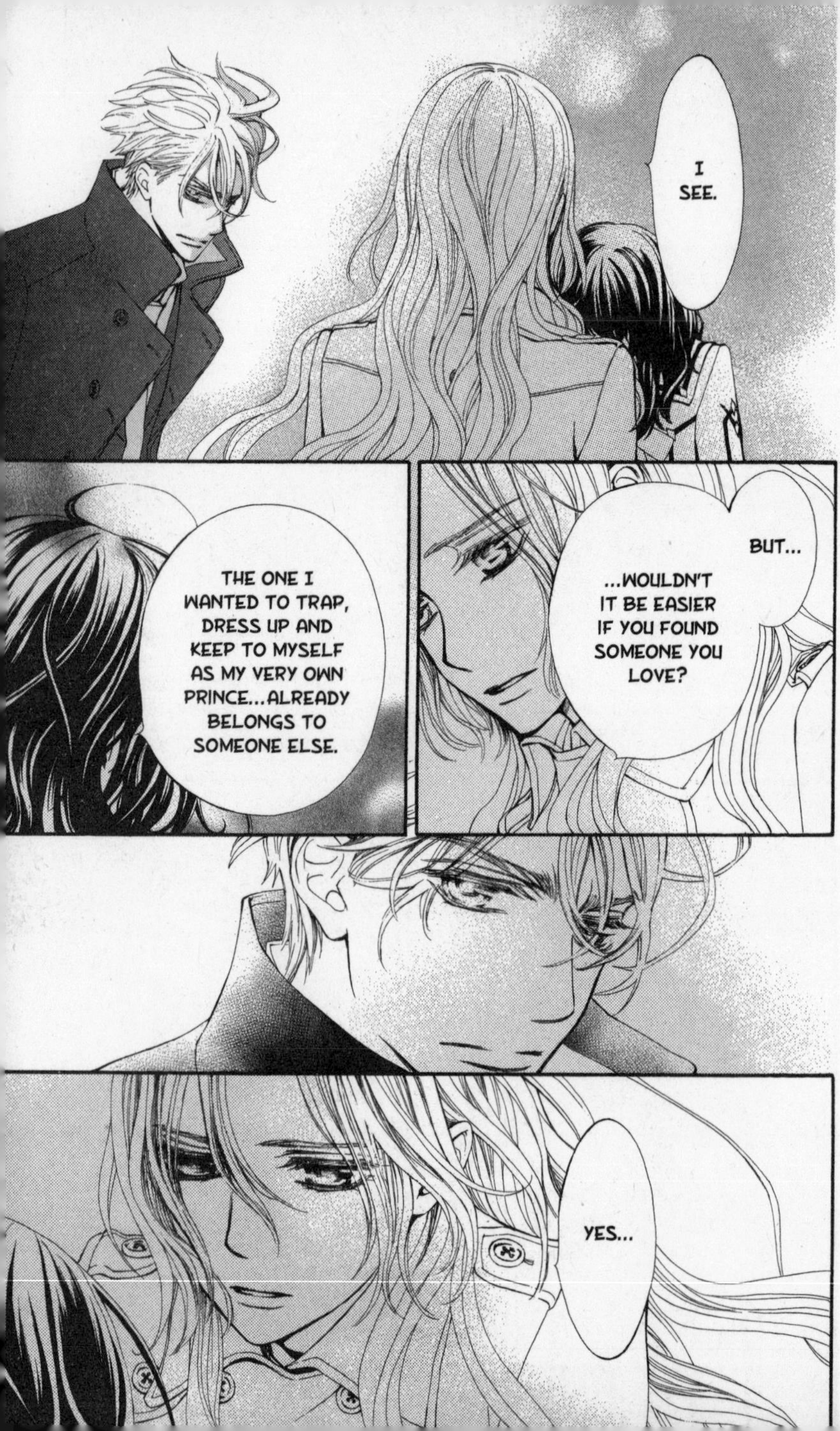
I SEE.
BUT...
...WOULDN'T IT BE EASIER IF YOU FOUND SOMEONE YOU LOVE?
THE ONE I WANTED TO TRAP, DRESS UP AND KEEP TO MYSELF AS MY VERY OWN PRINCE...ALREADY BELONGS TO SOMEONE ELSE.
YES...

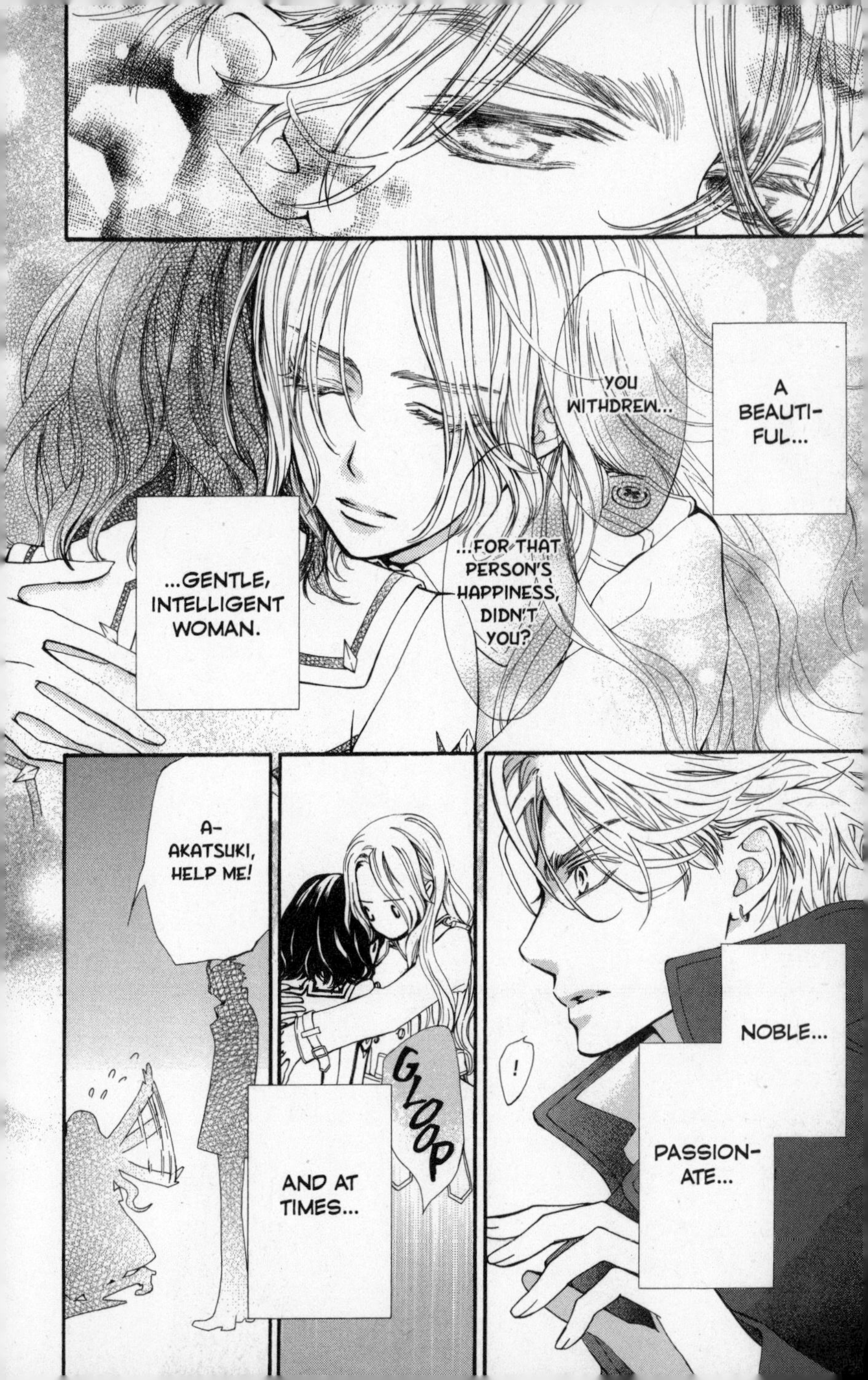
A BEAUTI-FUL...
YOU WITHDREW...
...FOR THAT PERSON'S HAPPINESS, DIDN'T YOU?
...GENTLE, INTELLIGENT WOMAN.
NOBLE...
!
PASSION-ATE...
GLOOP
AND AT TIMES...
A- AKATSUKI, HELP ME!

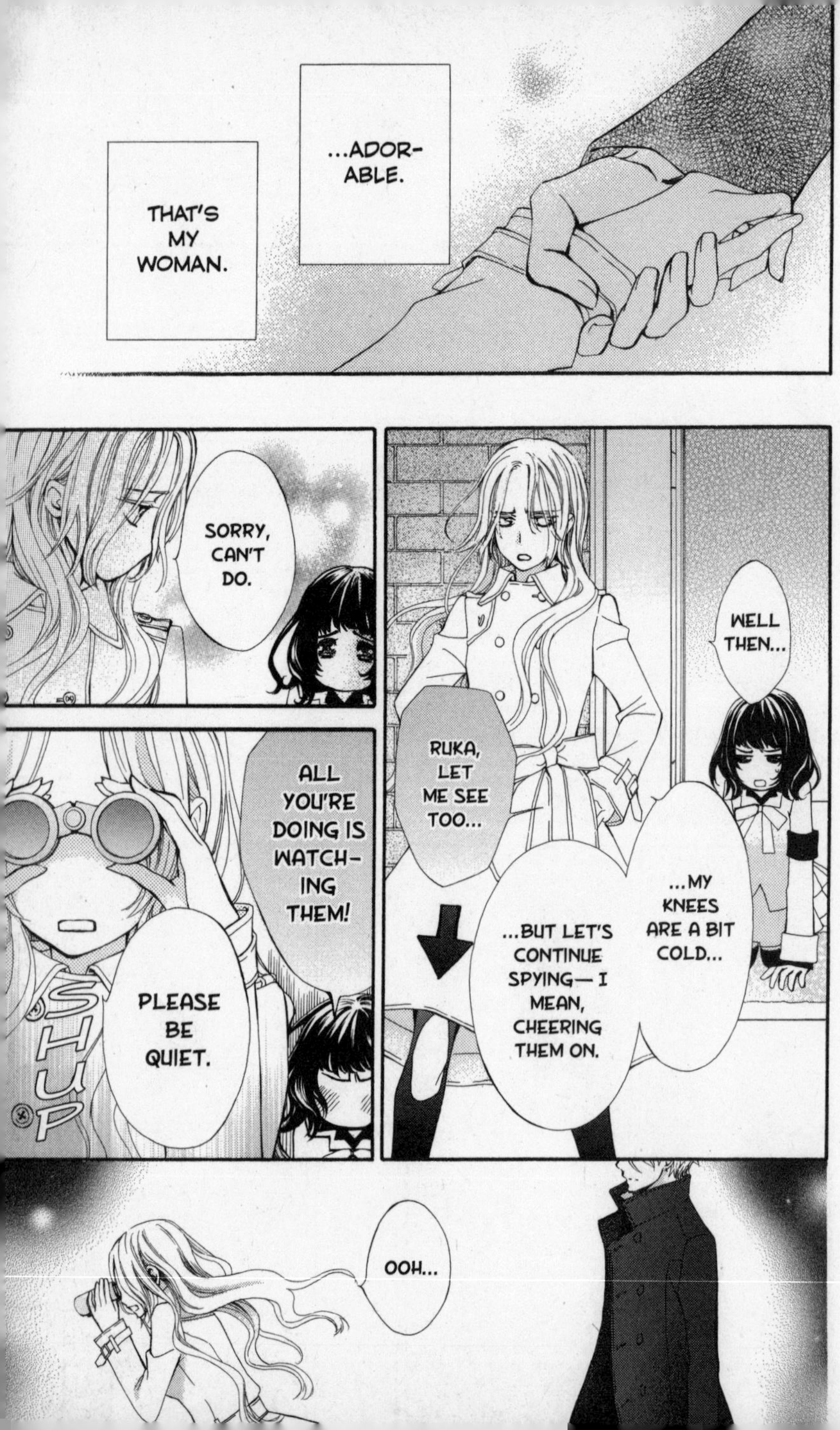
...ADOR-
ABLE.
THAT'S MY WOMAN.
WELL THEN...
...MY KNEES ARE A BIT COLD...
...BUT LET'S CONTINUE SPYING— I MEAN, CHEERING THEM ON.
RUKA, LET ME SEE TOO...
SORRY, CAN'T DO.
ALL YOU'RE DOING IS WATCH-ING THEM!
PLEASE BE QUIET.
SHUP
OOH...

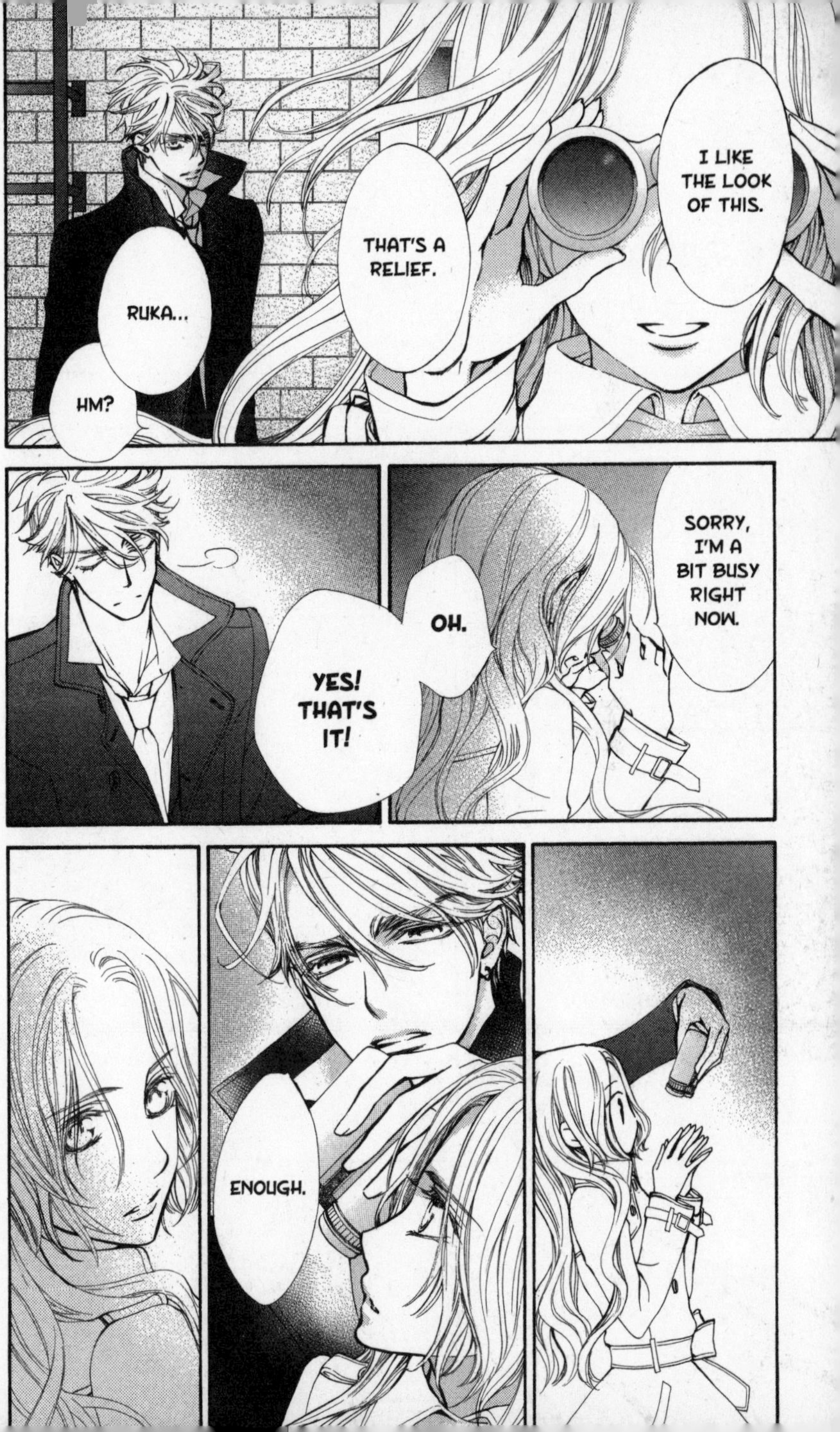
I LIKE THE LOOK OF THIS.
THAT'S A RELIEF.
RUKA...
HM?
SORRY, I'M A BIT BUSY RIGHT NOW.
OH.
YES! THAT'S IT!
ENOUGH.

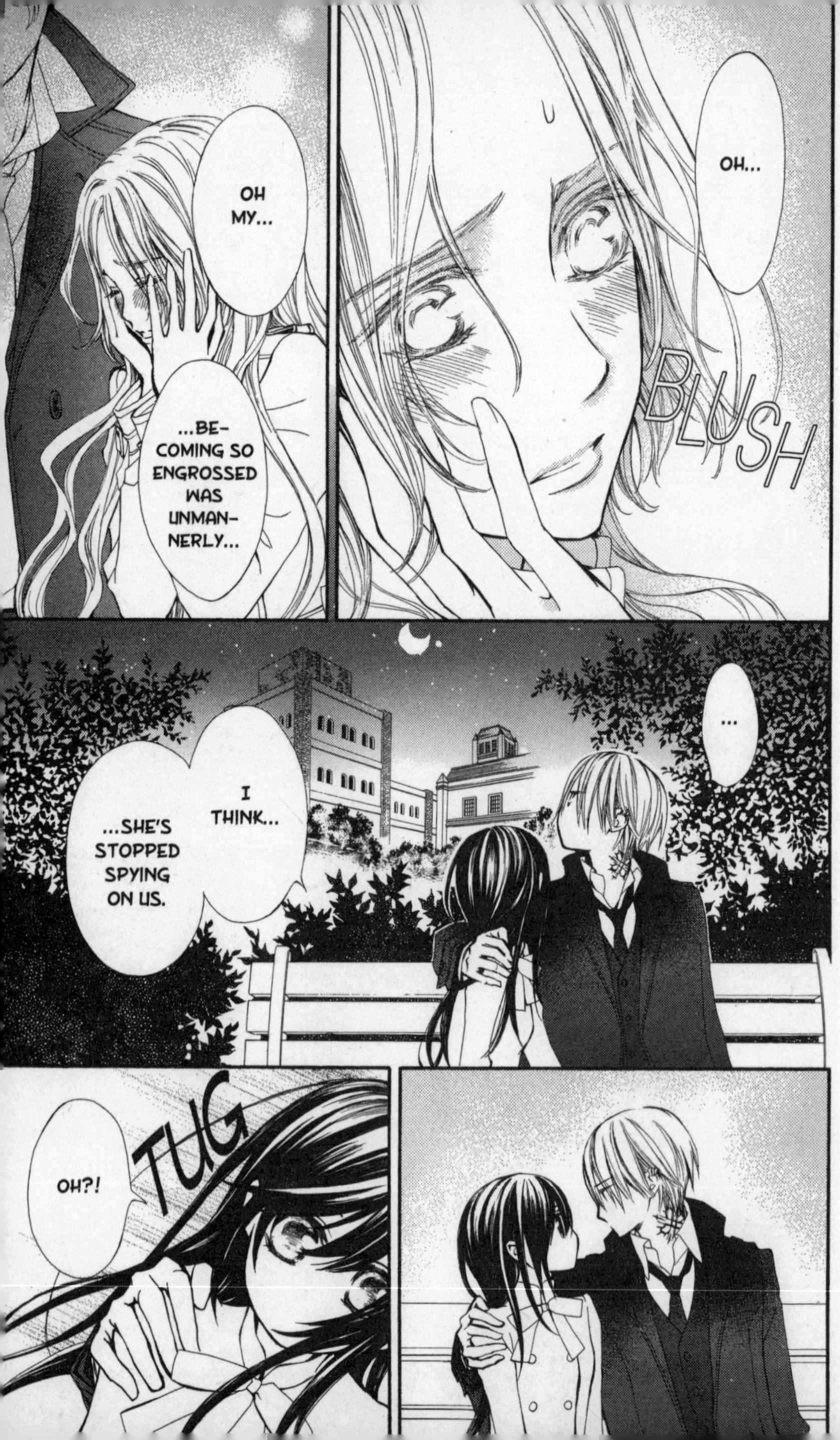
OH...
BLUSH
OH MY...
...BE-COMING SO ENGROSSED WAS UNMAN-NERLY...
...
I THINK...
...SHE'S STOPPED SPYING ON US.
TUG
OH?!

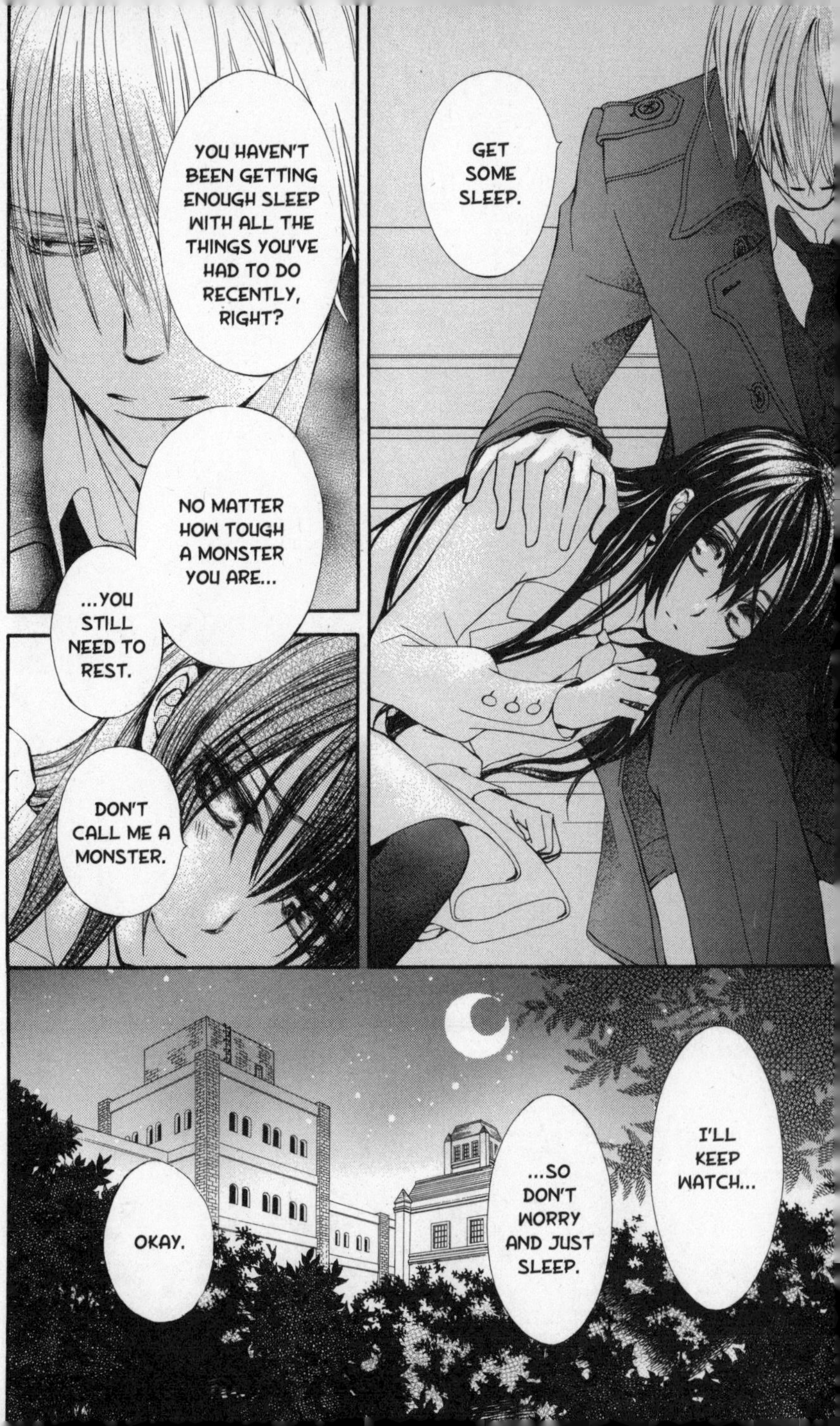
GET SOME SLEEP.
YOU HAVEN'T BEEN GETTING ENOUGH SLEEP WITH ALL THE THINGS YOU'VE HAD TO DO RECENTLY, RIGHT?
NO MATTER HOW TOUGH A MONSTER YOU ARE...
...YOU STILL NEED TO REST.
DON'T CALL ME A MONSTER.
I'LL KEEP WATCH...
...SO DON'T WORRY AND JUST SLEEP.
OKAY.

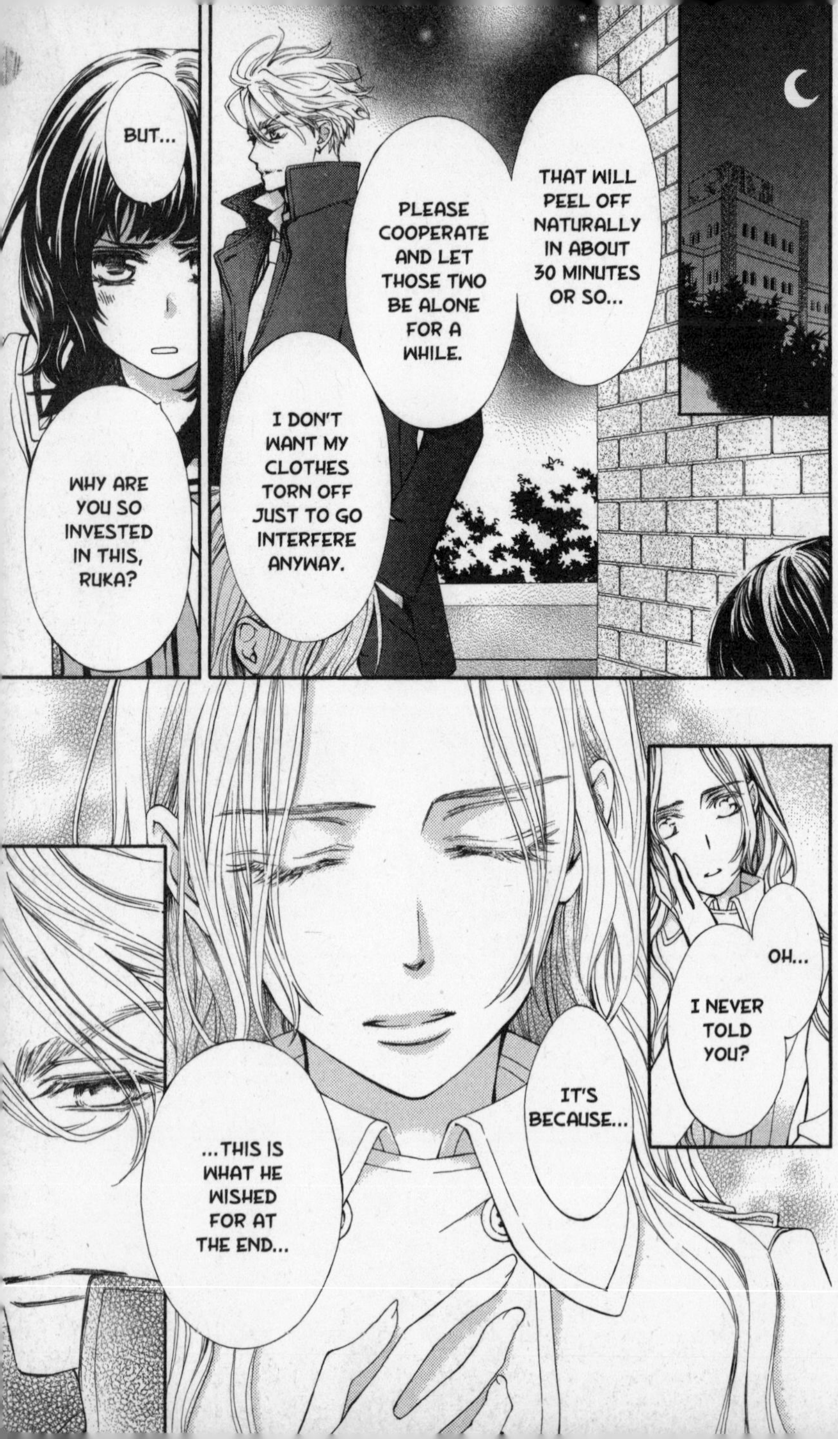
THAT WILL PEEL OFF NATURALLY IN ABOUT 30 MINUTES OR SO...
PLEASE COOPERATE AND LET THOSE TWO BE ALONE FOR A WHILE.
I DON'T WANT MY CLOTHES TORN OFF JUST TO GO INTERFERE ANYWAY.
BUT...
WHY ARE YOU SO INVESTED IN THIS, RUKA?
OH...
I NEVER TOLD YOU?
IT'S BECAUSE...
...THIS IS WHAT HE WISHED FOR AT THE END...

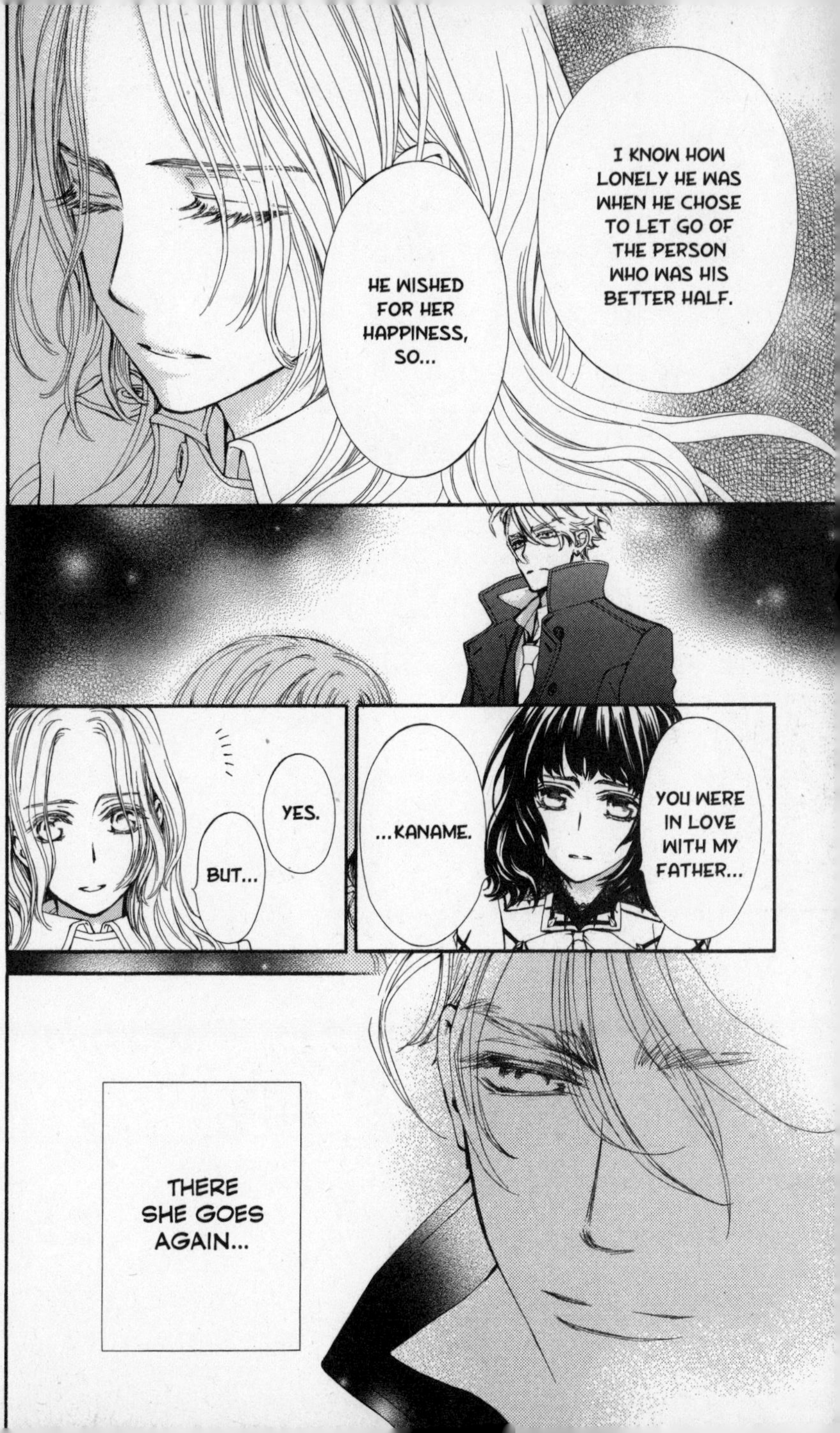
I KNOW HOW LONELY HE WAS WHEN HE CHOSE TO LET GO OF THE PERSON WHO WAS HIS BETTER HALF.
HE WISHED FOR HER HAPPINESS, SO...
YOU WERE IN LOVE WITH MY FATHER...
...KANAME.
YES.
BUT...
THERE SHE GOES AGAIN...

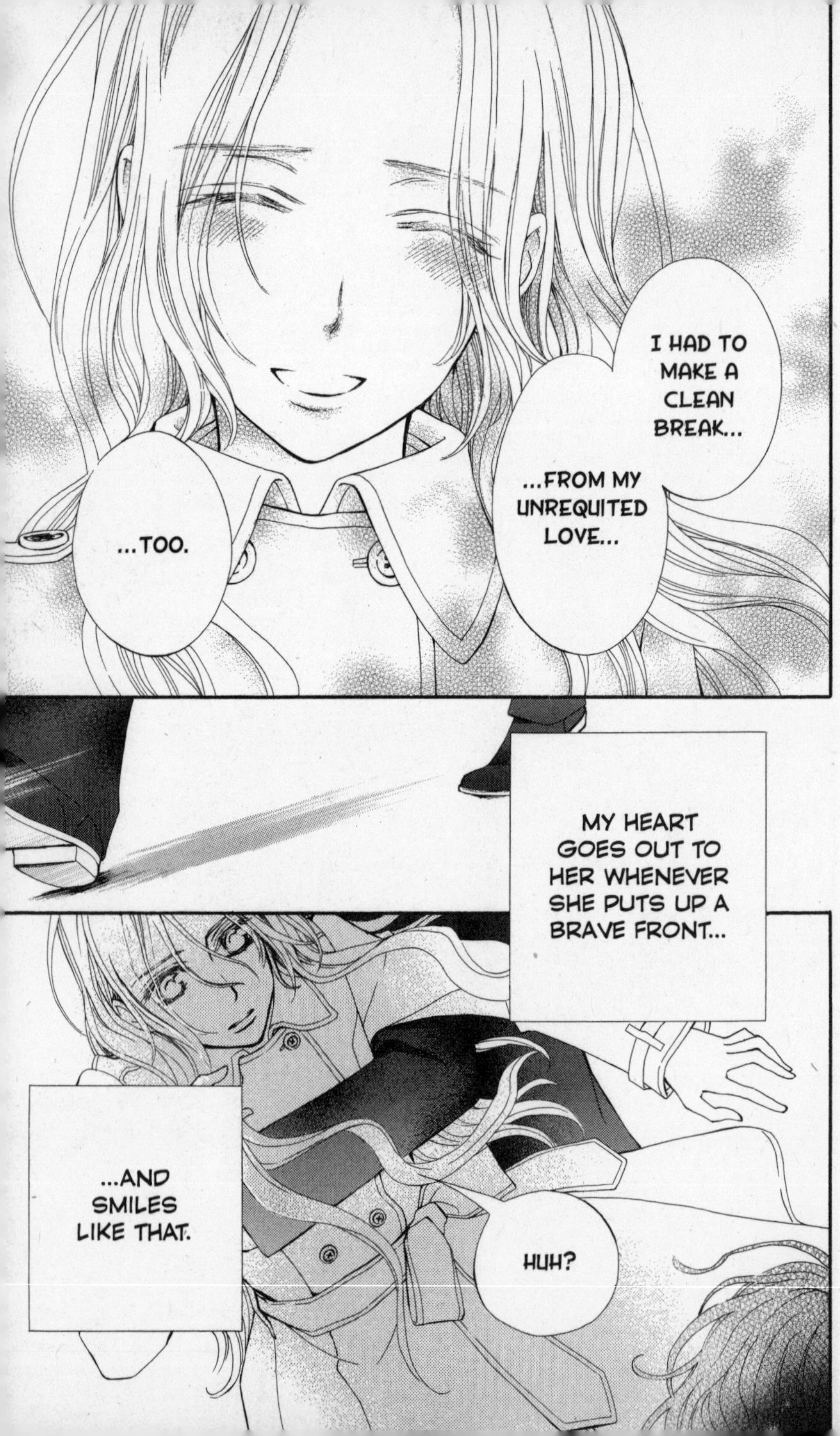
I HAD TO MAKE A CLEAN BREAK...
...FROM MY UNREQUITED LOVE...
...TOO.
MY HEART GOES OUT TO HER WHENEVER SHE PUTS UP A BRAVE FRONT...
...AND SMILES LIKE THAT.
HUH?

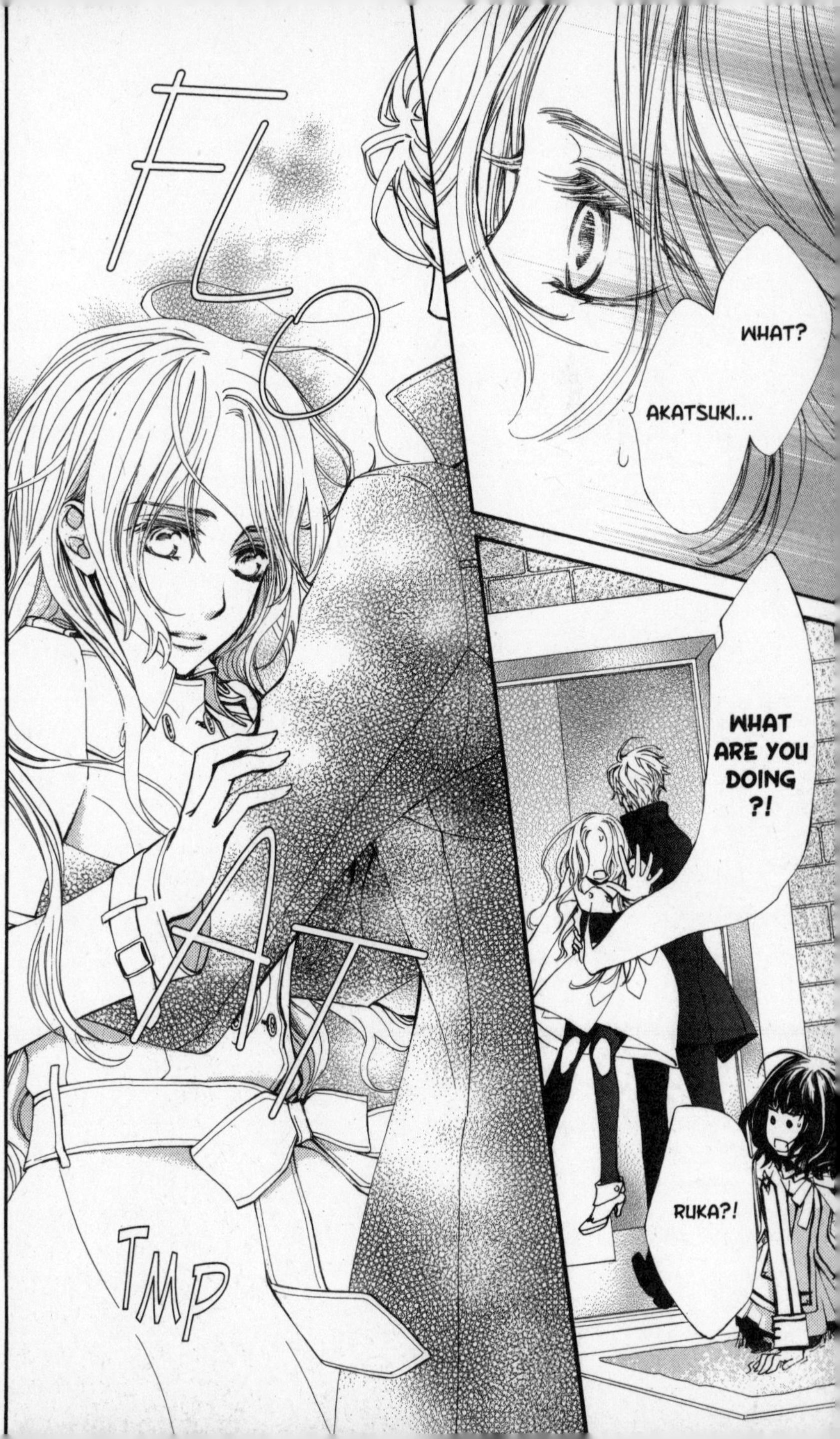
WHAT?
AKATSUKI...
WHAT ARE YOU DOING?!
RUKA?!
FLOAT
TMP

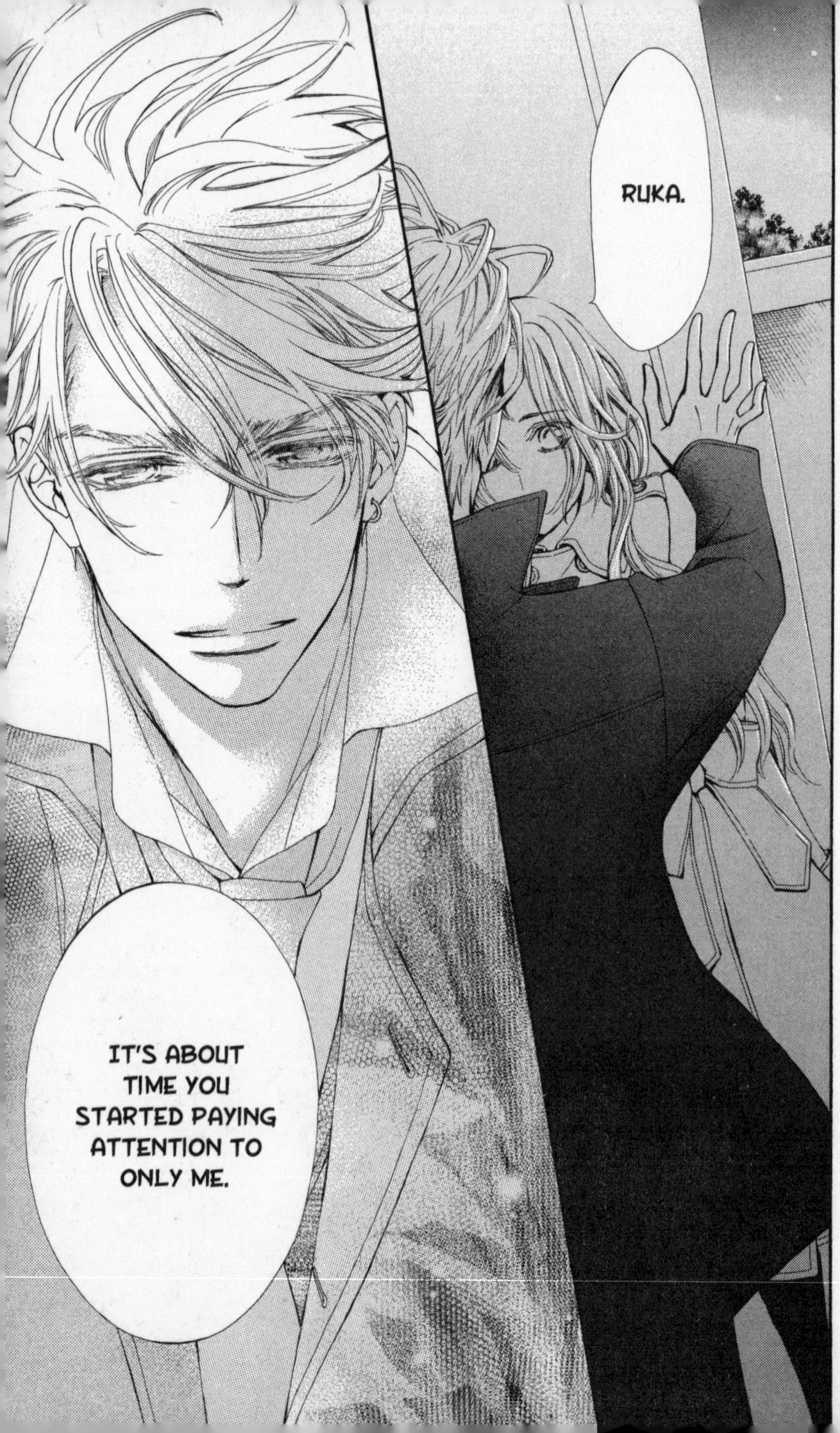
RUKA.
IT'S ABOUT TIME YOU STARTED PAYING ATTENTION TO ONLY ME.

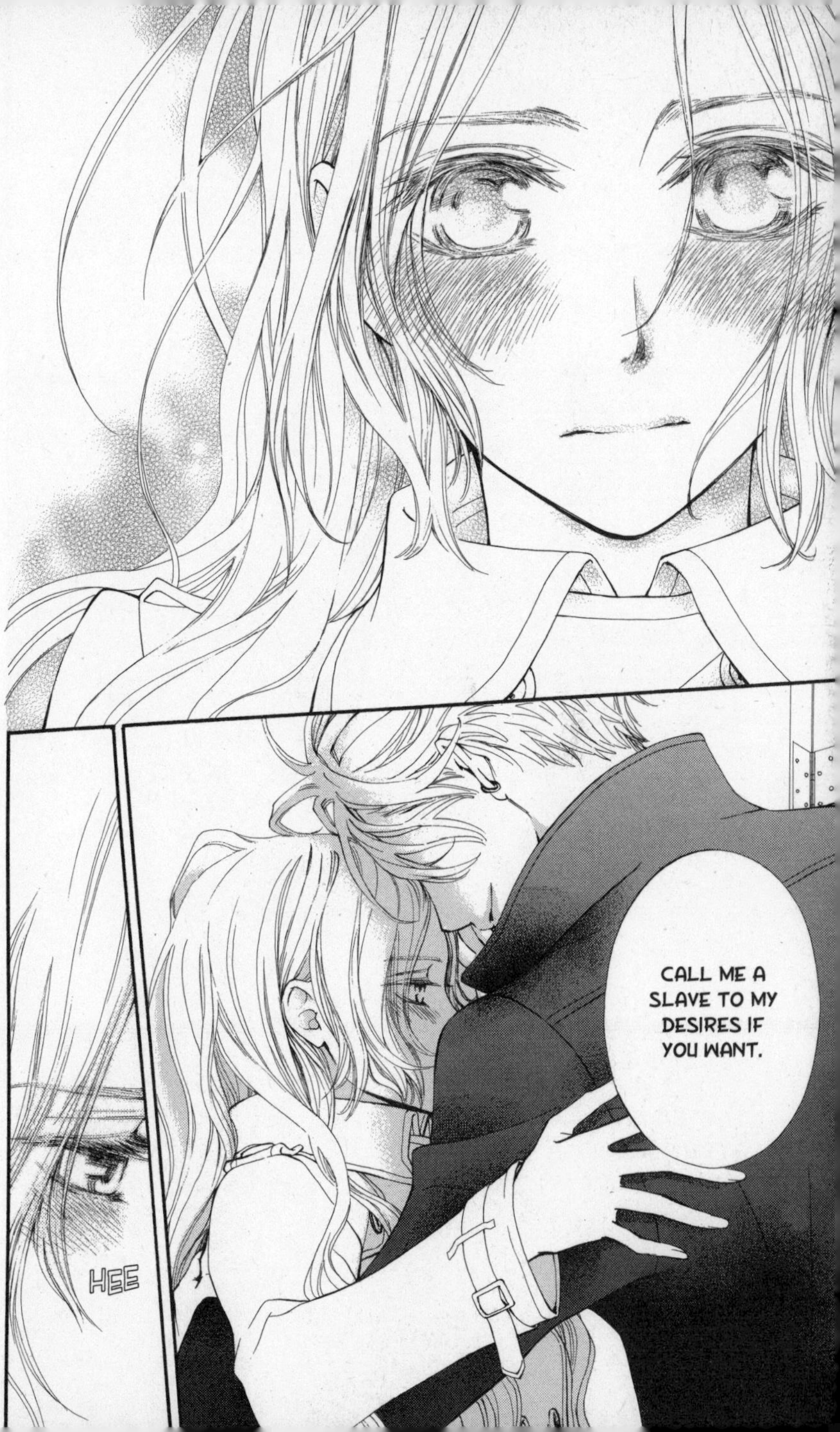
CALL ME A SLAVE TO MY DESIRES IF YOU WANT.
HEE

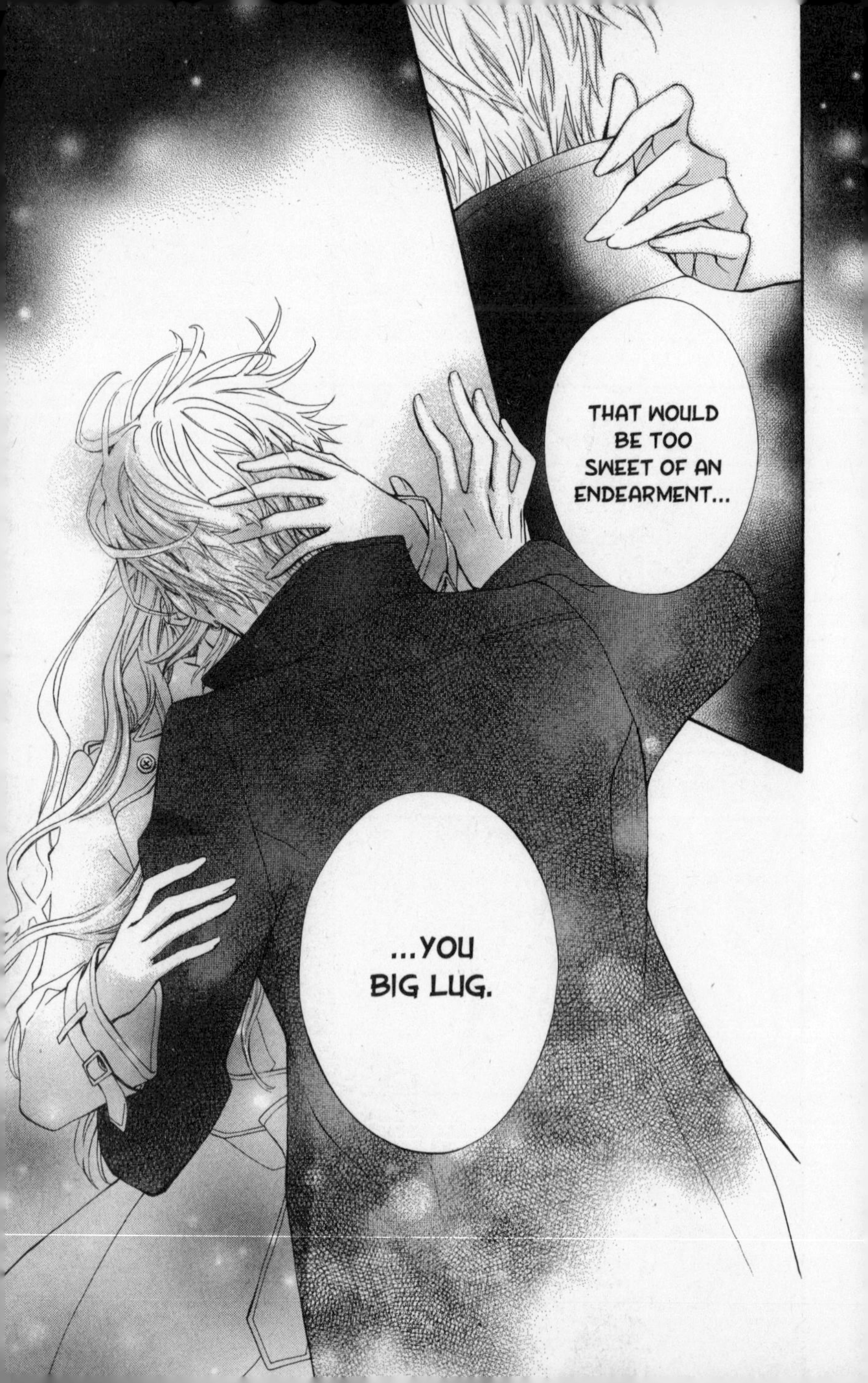
THAT WOULD BE TOO SWEET OF AN ENDEARMENT...
...YOU BIG LUG.

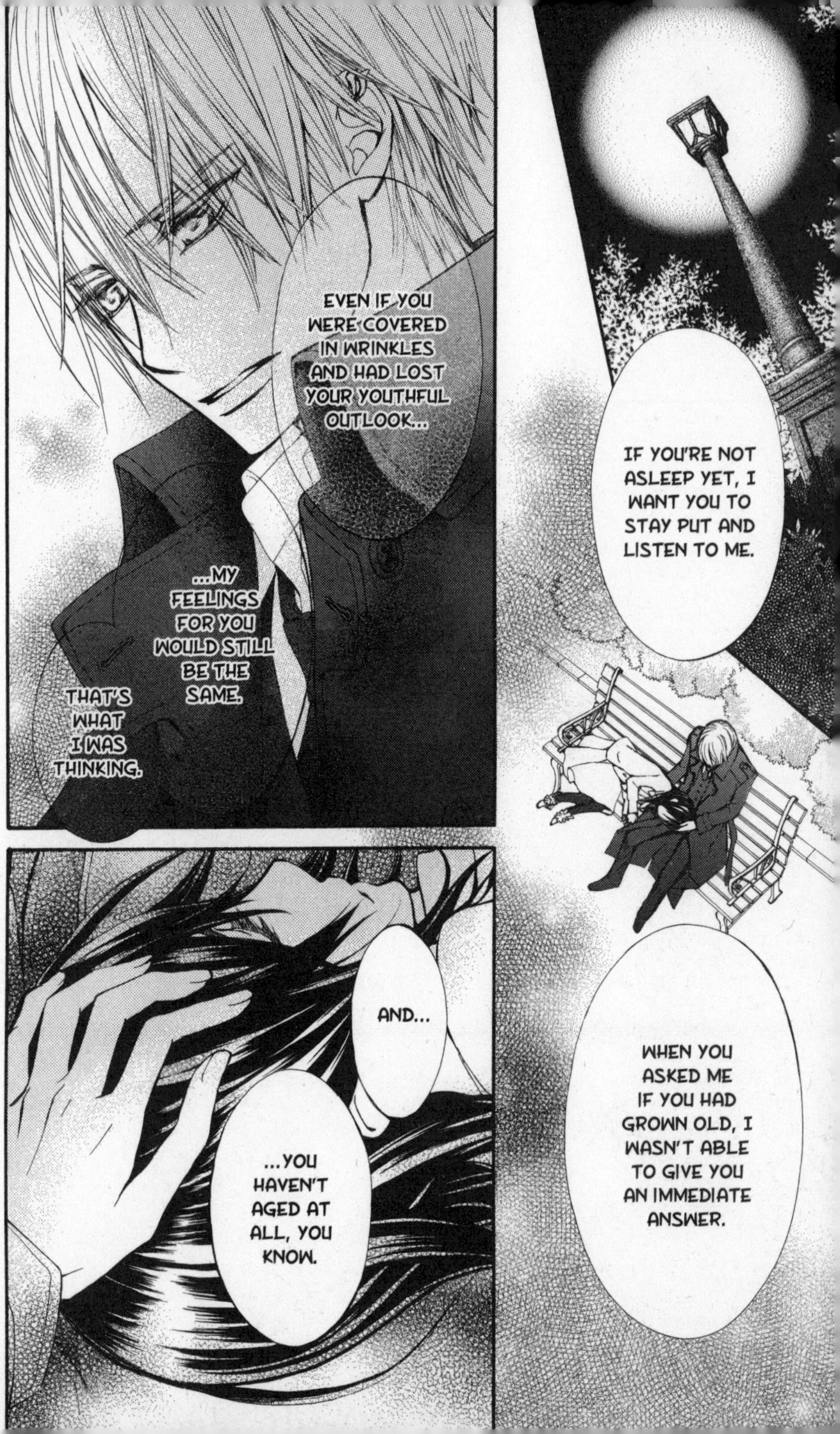
IF YOU'RE NOT ASLEEP YET, I WANT YOU TO STAY PUT AND LISTEN TO ME.
WHEN YOU ASKED ME IF YOU HAD GROWN OLD, I WASN'T ABLE TO GIVE YOU AN IMMEDIATE ANSWER.
EVEN IF YOU WERE COVERED IN WRINKLES AND HAD LOST YOUR YOUTHFUL OUTLOOK...
...MY FEELINGS FOR YOU WOULD STILL BE THE SAME.
THAT'S WHAT I WAS THINKING.
AND...
...YOU HAVEN'T AGED AT ALL, YOU KNOW.

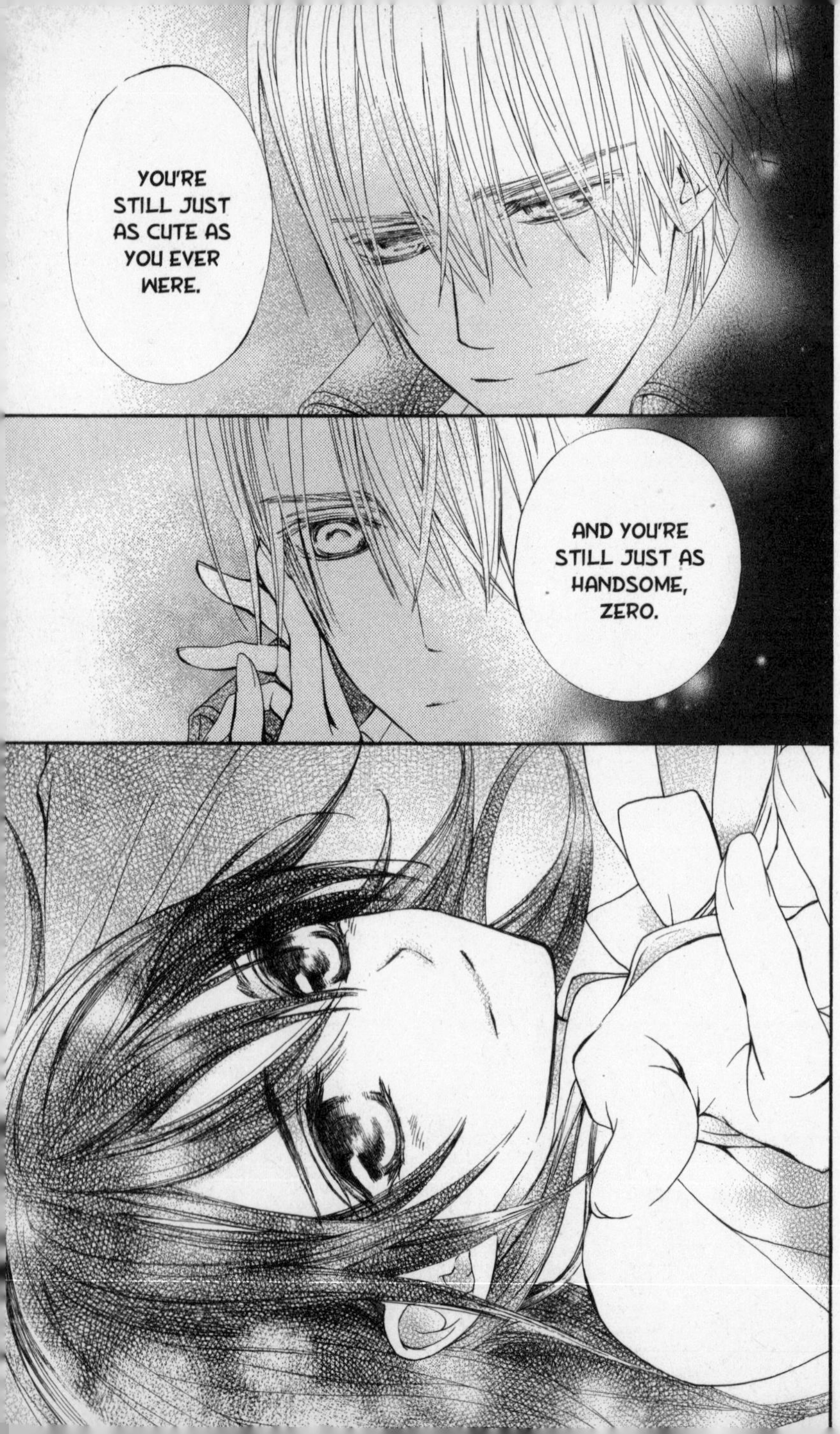
YOU'RE STILL JUST AS CUTE AS YOU EVER WERE.
AND YOU'RE STILL JUST AS HANDSOME, ZERO.

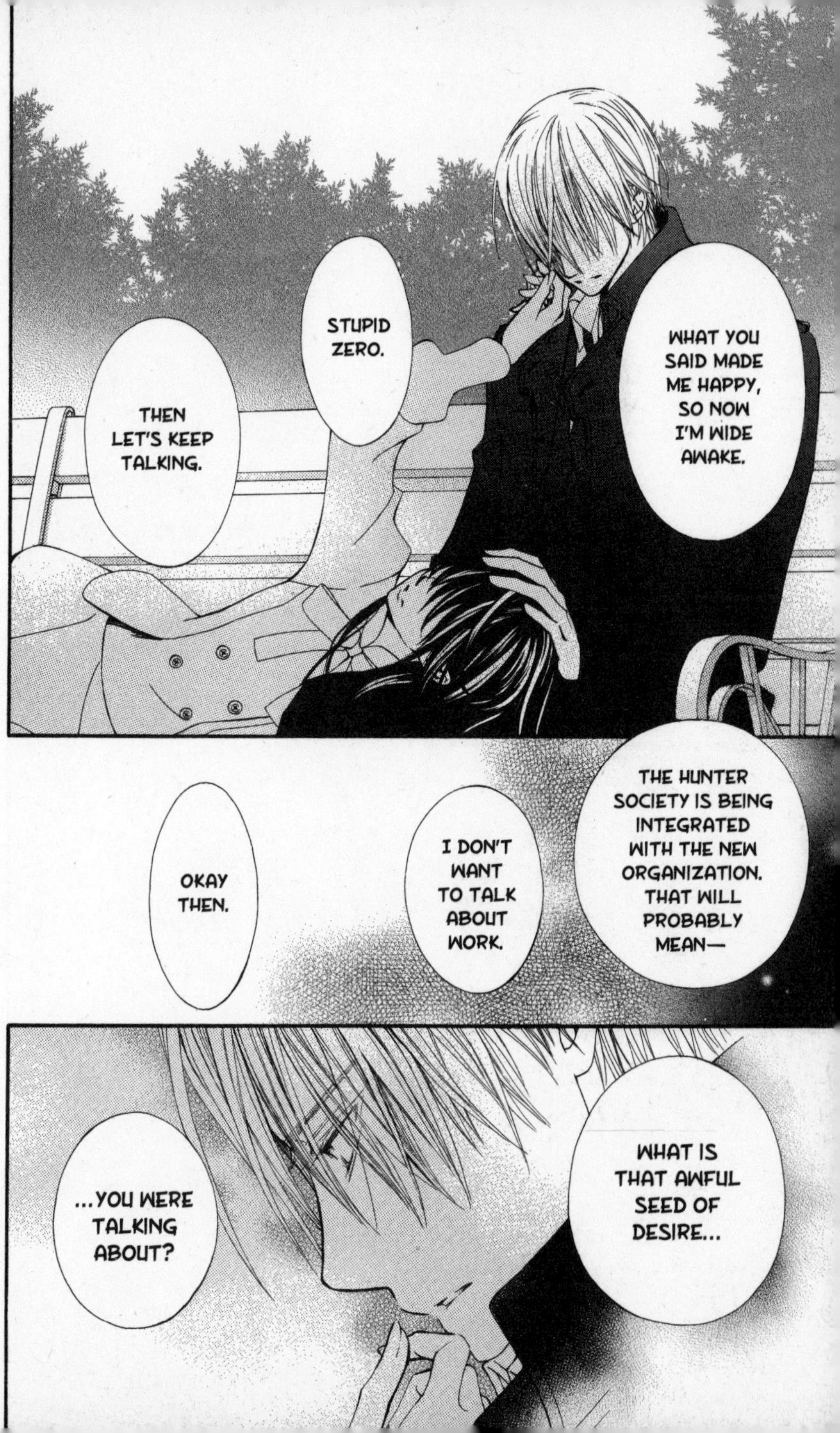
WHAT YOU SAID MADE ME HAPPY, SO NOW I'M WIDE AWAKE.
STUPID ZERO.
THEN LET'S KEEP TALKING.
THE HUNTER SOCIETY IS BEING INTEGRATED WITH THE NEW ORGANIZATION. THAT WILL PROBABLY MEAN—
I DON'T WANT TO TALK ABOUT WORK.
OKAY THEN.
WHAT IS THAT AWFUL SEED OF DESIRE...
...YOU WERE TALKING ABOUT?

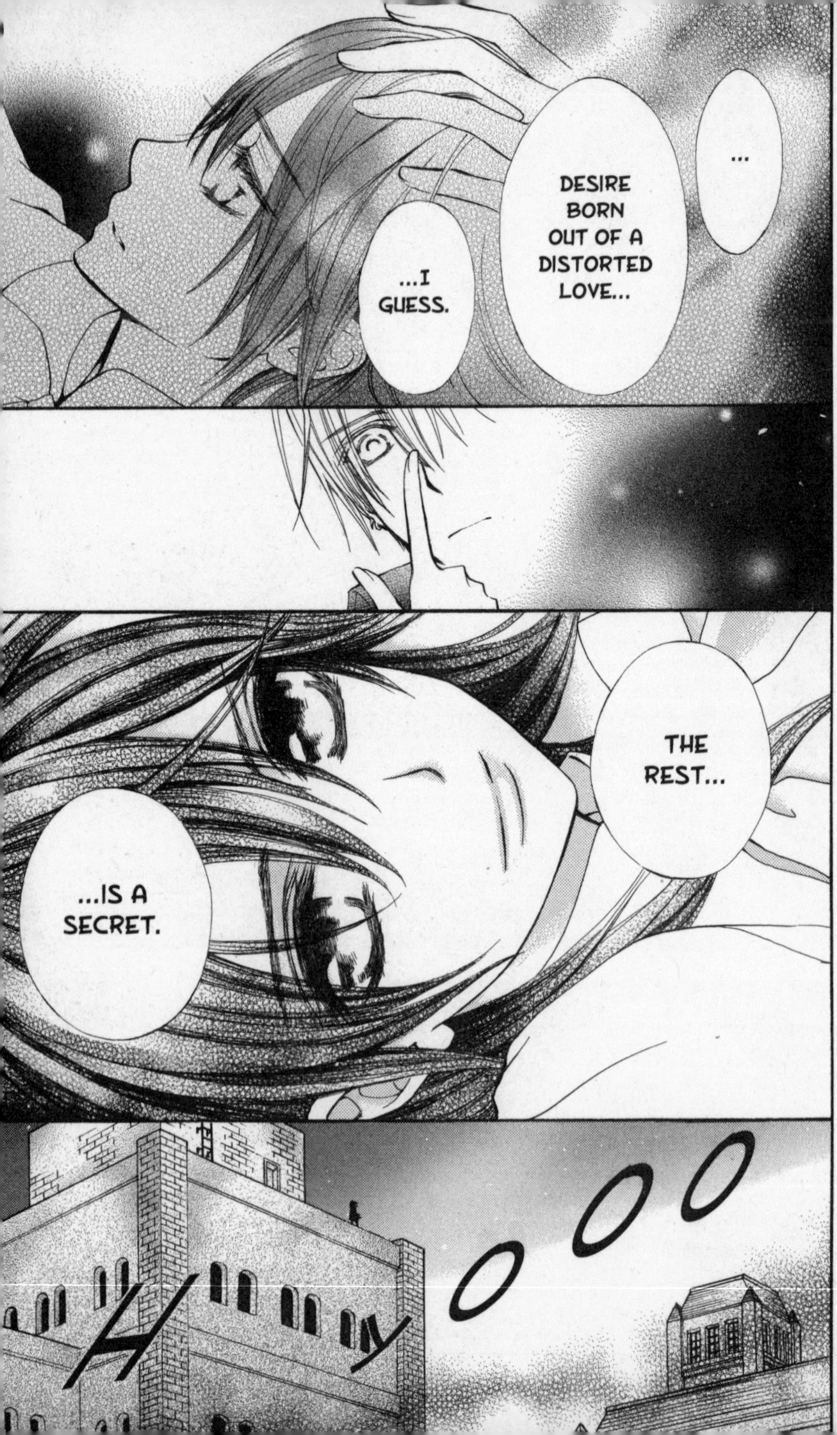
...
DESIRE BORN OUT OF A DISTORTED LOVE...
...I GUESS.
THE REST...
...IS A SECRET.
HyOOOOO

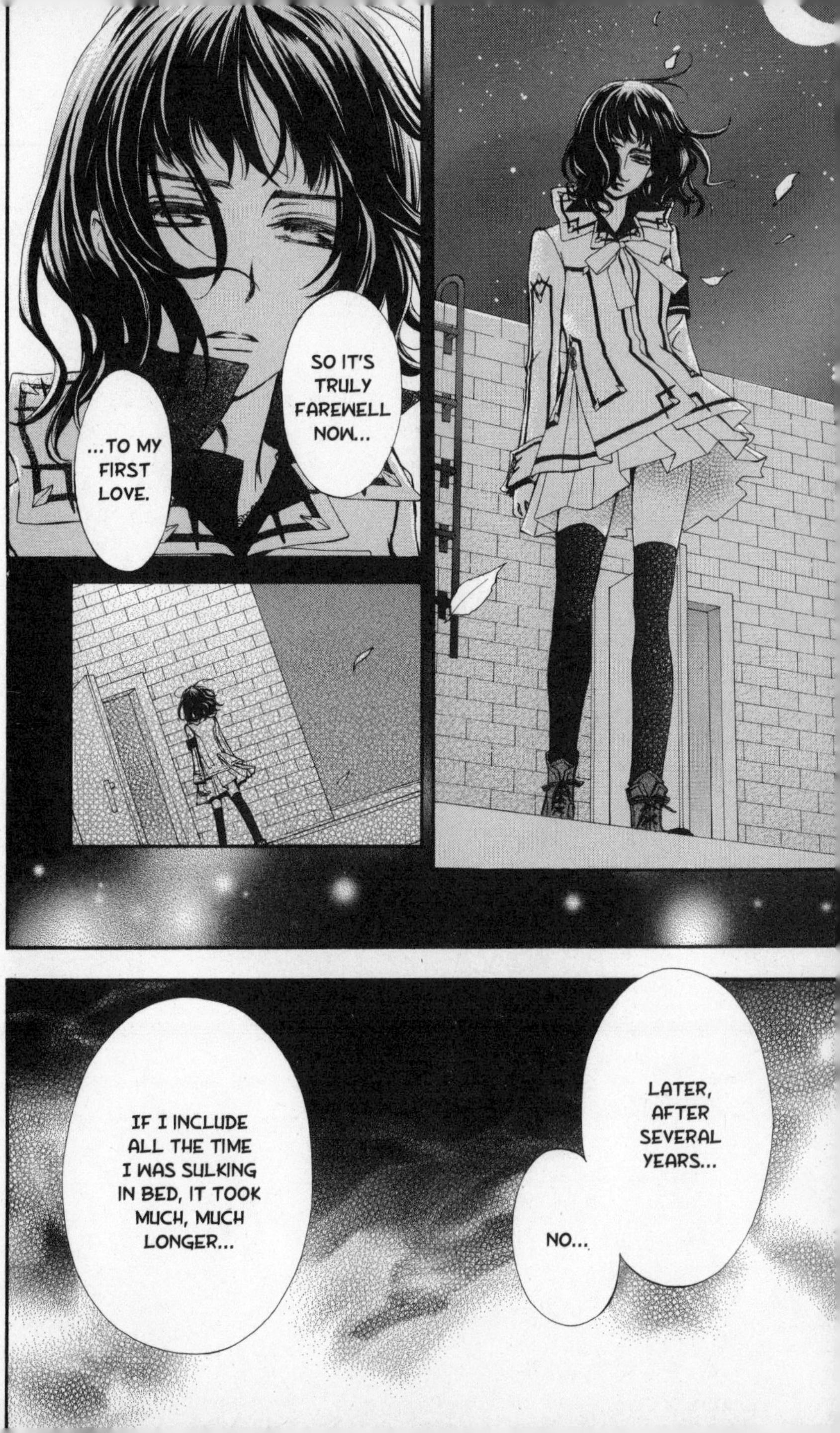
SO IT'S TRULY FAREWELL NOW...
...TO MY FIRST LOVE.
LATER, AFTER SEVERAL YEARS...
NO...
IF I INCLUDE ALL THE TIME I WAS SULKING IN BED, IT TOOK MUCH, MUCH LONGER...

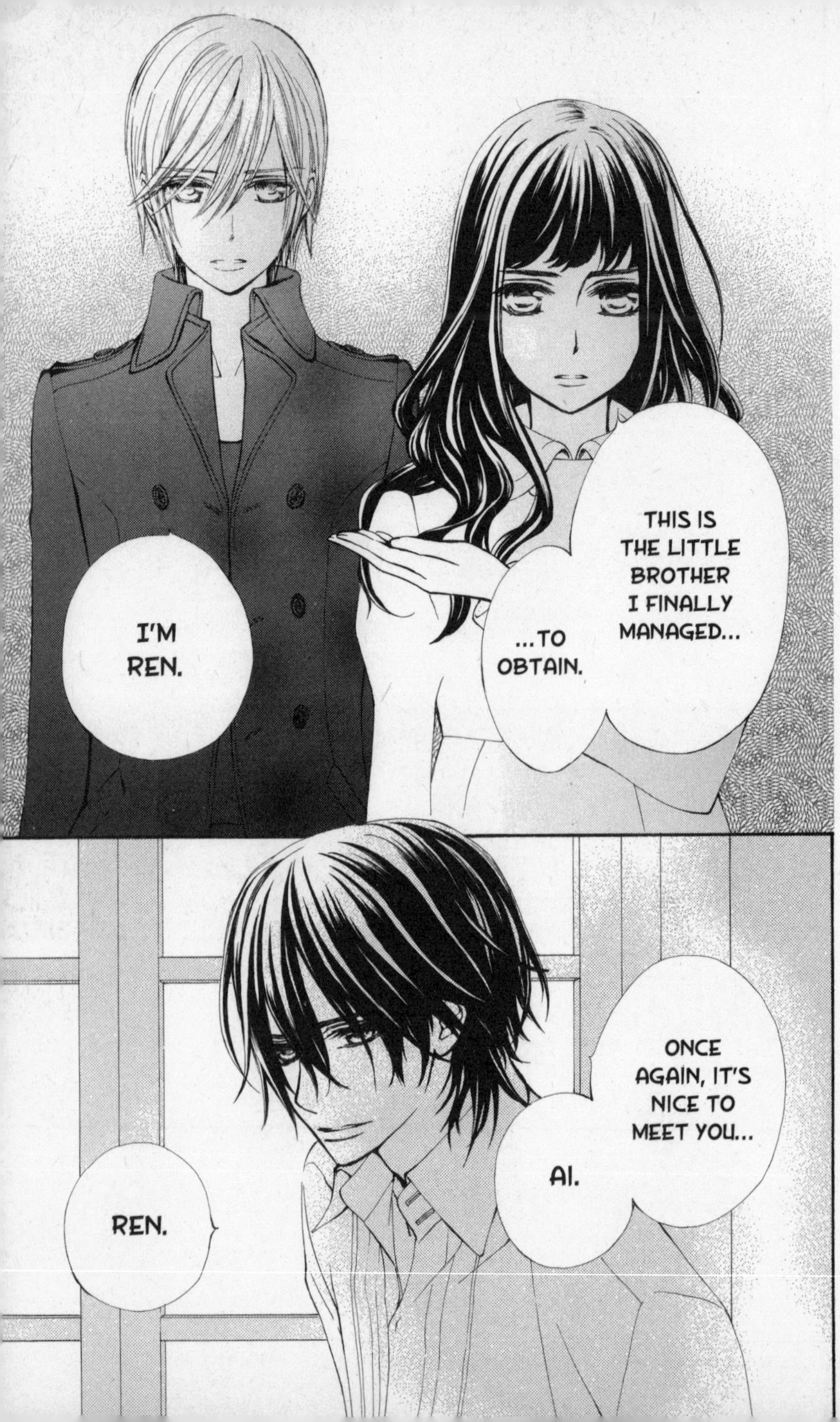
THIS IS THE LITTLE BROTHER I FINALLY MANAGED...
...TO OBTAIN.
I'M REN.
ONCE AGAIN, IT'S NICE TO MEET YOU...
AI.
REN.

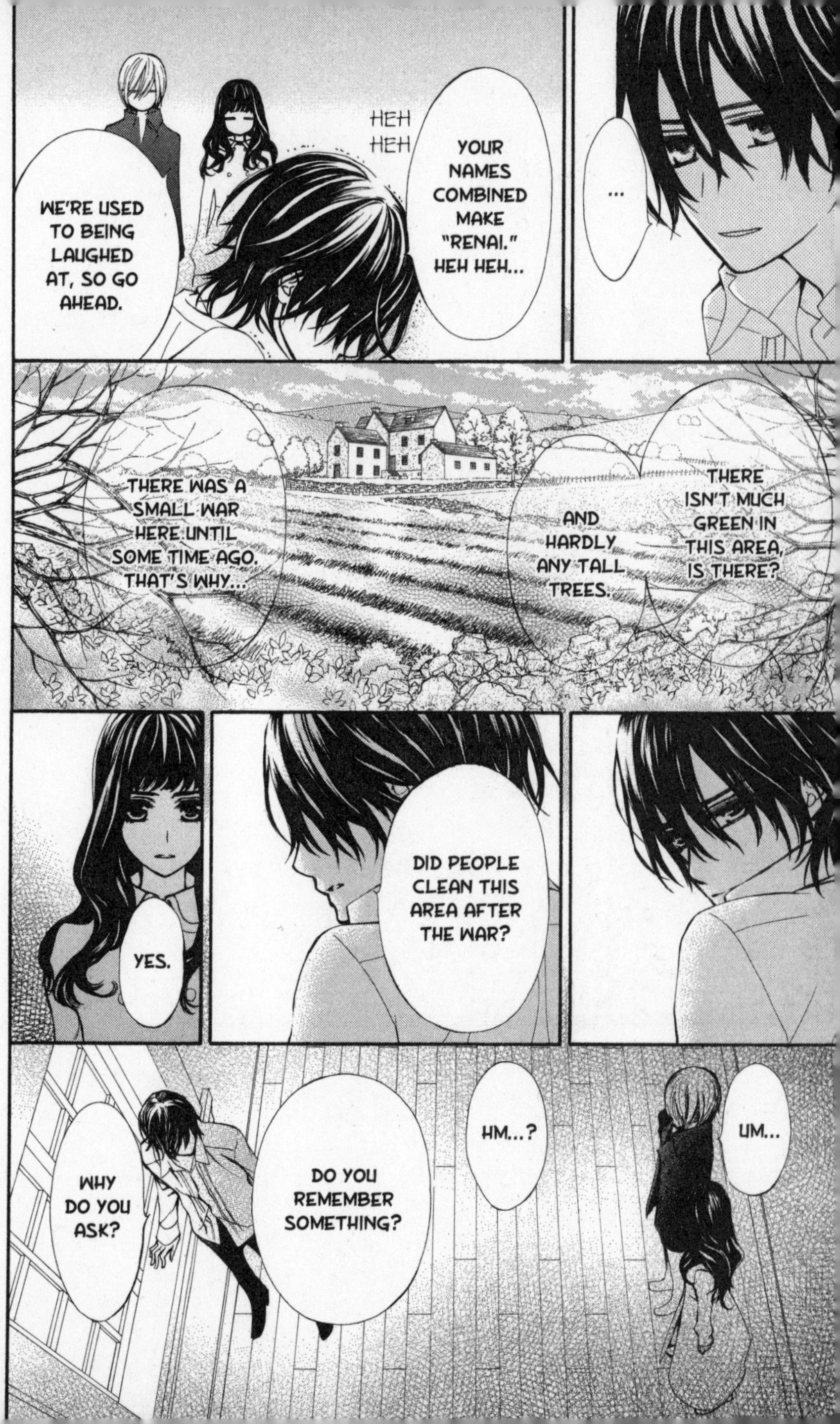
...
YOUR NAMES COMBINED MAKE "RENAI." HEH HEH...
HEH HEH
WE'RE USED TO BEING LAUGHED AT, SO GO AHEAD.
THERE ISN'T MUCH GREEN IN THIS AREA, IS THERE?
AND HARDLY ANY TALL TREES.
THERE WAS A SMALL WAR HERE UNTIL SOME TIME AGO. THAT'S WHY...
DID PEOPLE CLEAN THIS AREA AFTER THE WAR?
YES.
UM...
HM...?
DO YOU REMEMBER SOMETHING?
WHY DO YOU ASK?

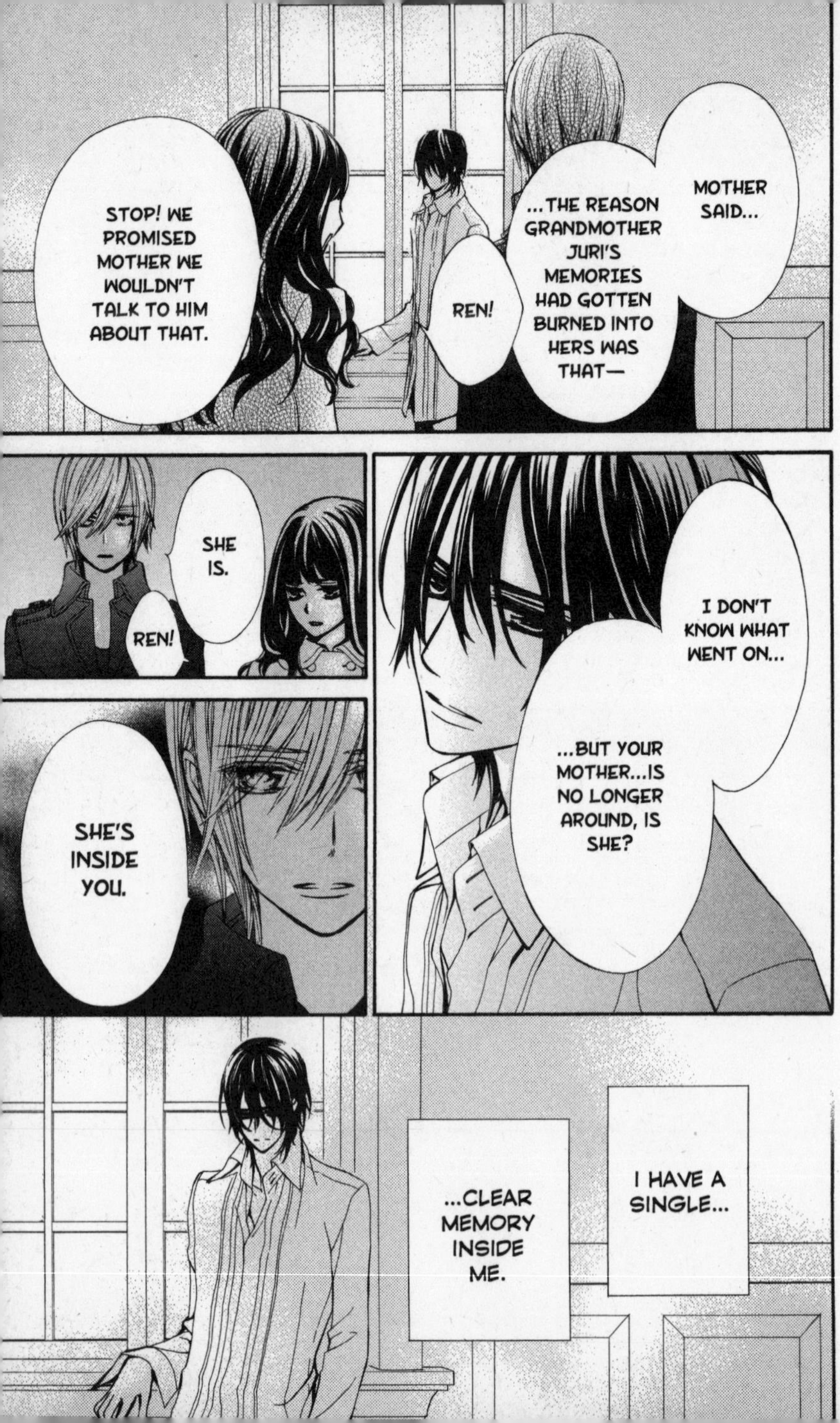
MOTHER SAID...
...THE REASON GRANDMOTHER JURI'S MEMORIES HAD GOTTEN BURNED INTO HERS WAS THAT—
REN!
STOP! WE PROMISED MOTHER WE WOULDN'T TALK TO HIM ABOUT THAT.
I DON'T KNOW WHAT WENT ON...
...BUT YOUR MOTHER...IS NO LONGER AROUND, IS SHE?
SHE IS.
REN!
SHE'S INSIDE YOU.
I HAVE A SINGLE...
...CLEAR MEMORY INSIDE ME.

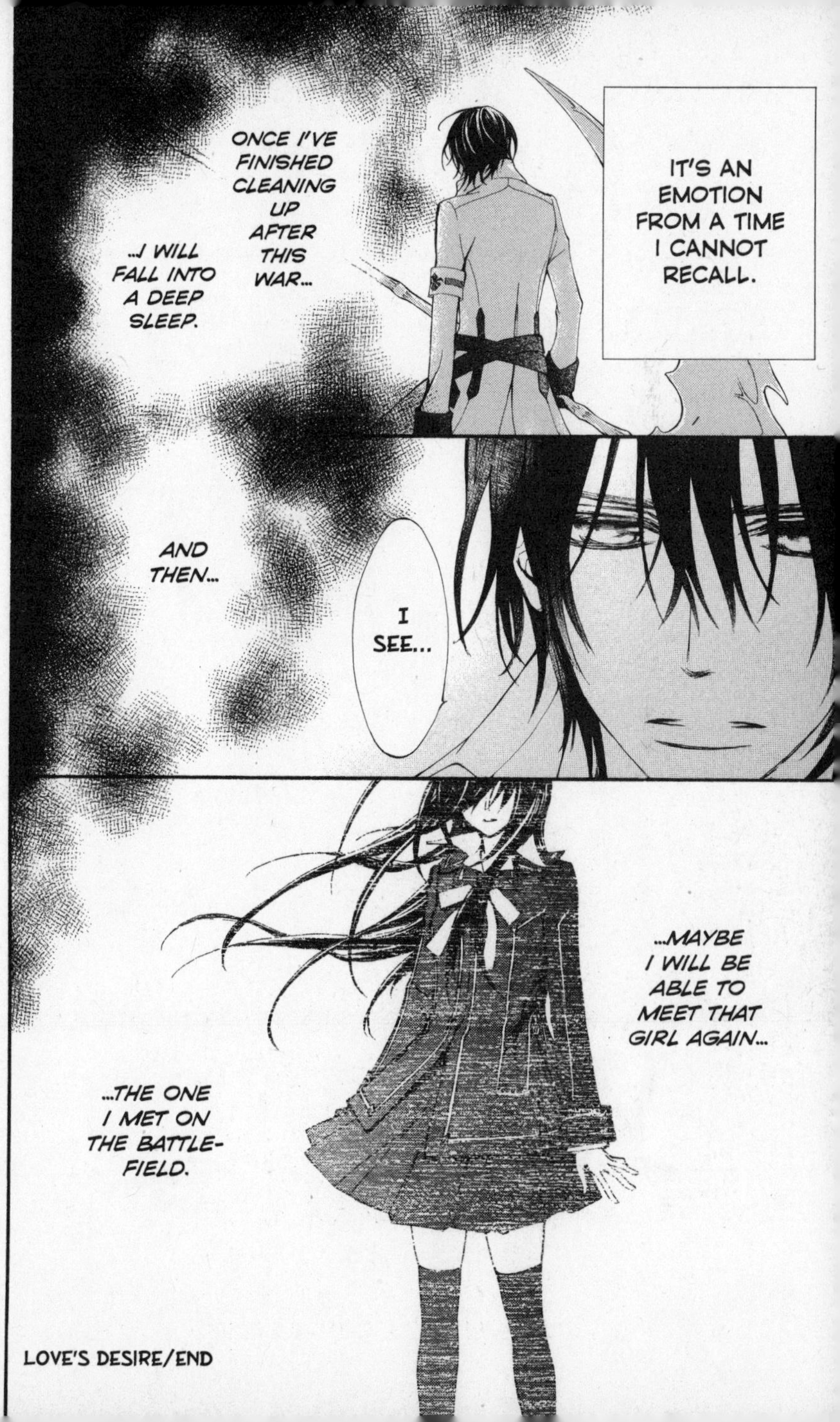
IT'S AN EMOTION FROM A TIME I CANNOT RECALL.
ONCE I'VE FINISHED CLEANING UP AFTER THIS WAR...
...I WILL FALL INTO A DEEP SLEEP.
I SEE...
AND THEN...
...MAYBE I WILL BE ABLE TO MEET THAT GIRL AGAIN...
...THE ONE I MET ON THE BATTLE-FIELD.
LOVE'S DESIRE/END

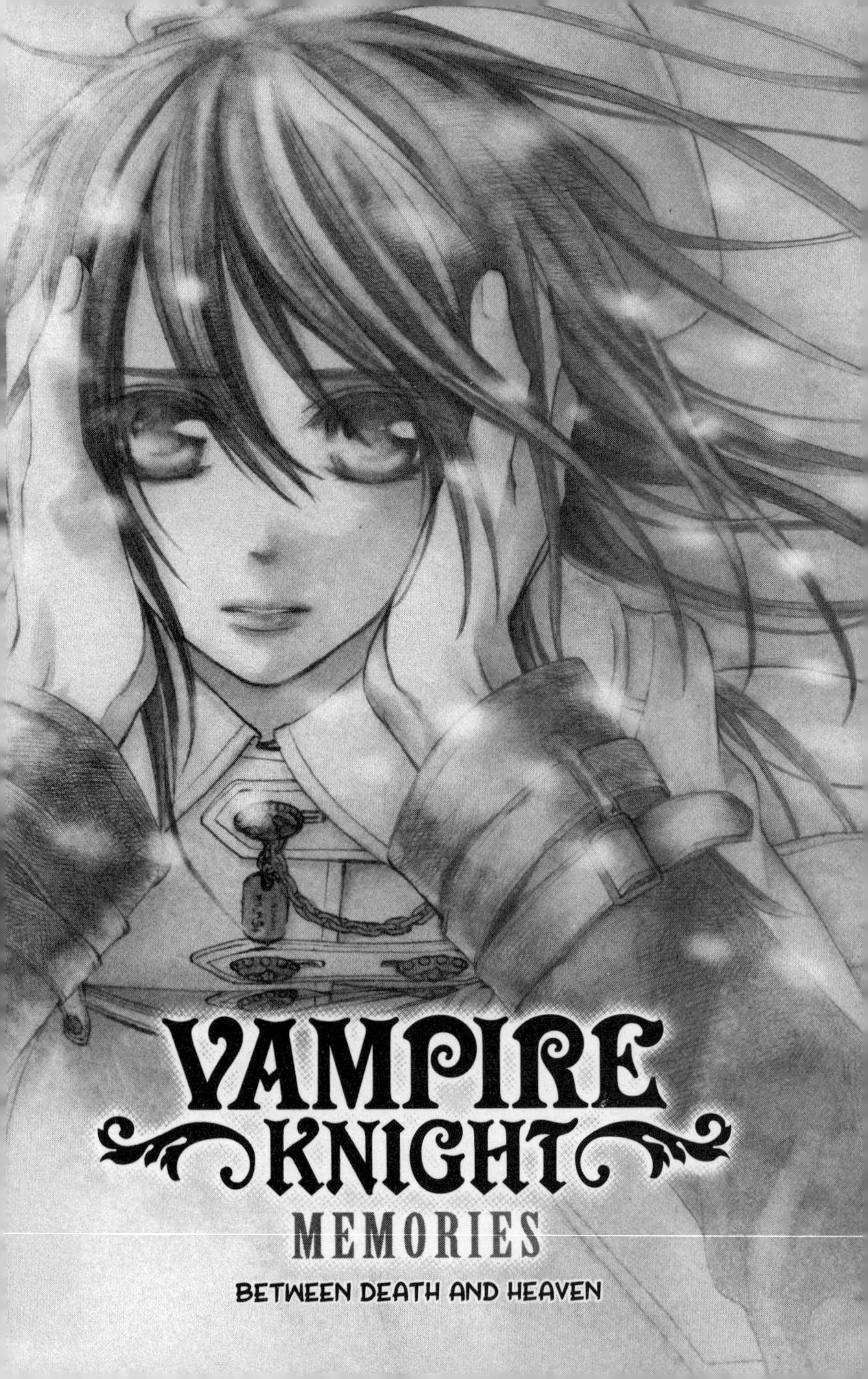
VAMPIRE KNIGHT
MEMORIES
BETWEEN DEATH AND HEAVEN

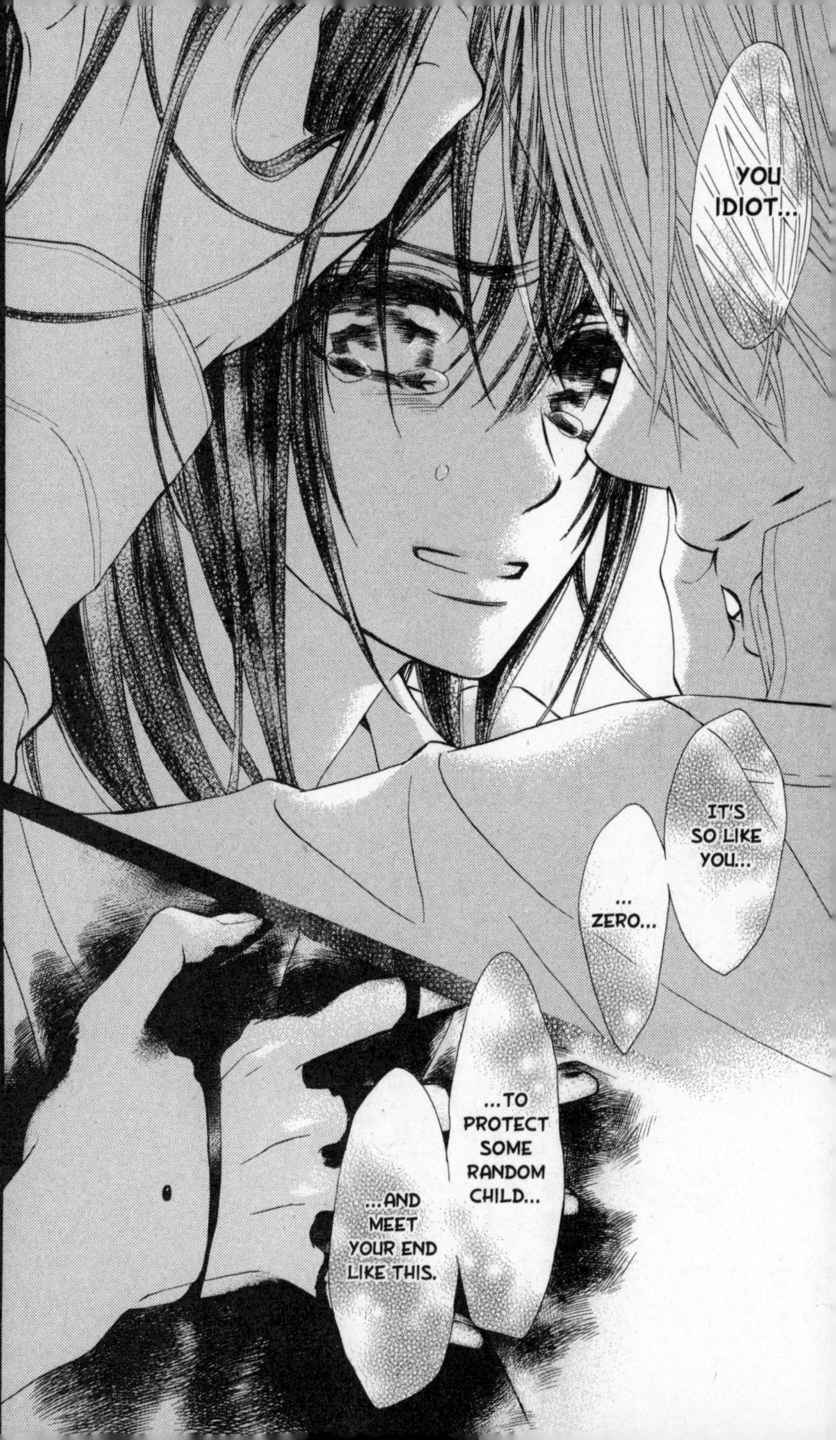
YOU IDIOT...
IT'S SO LIKE YOU...
...ZERO...
...TO PROTECT SOME RANDOM CHILD...
...AND MEET YOUR END LIKE THIS.

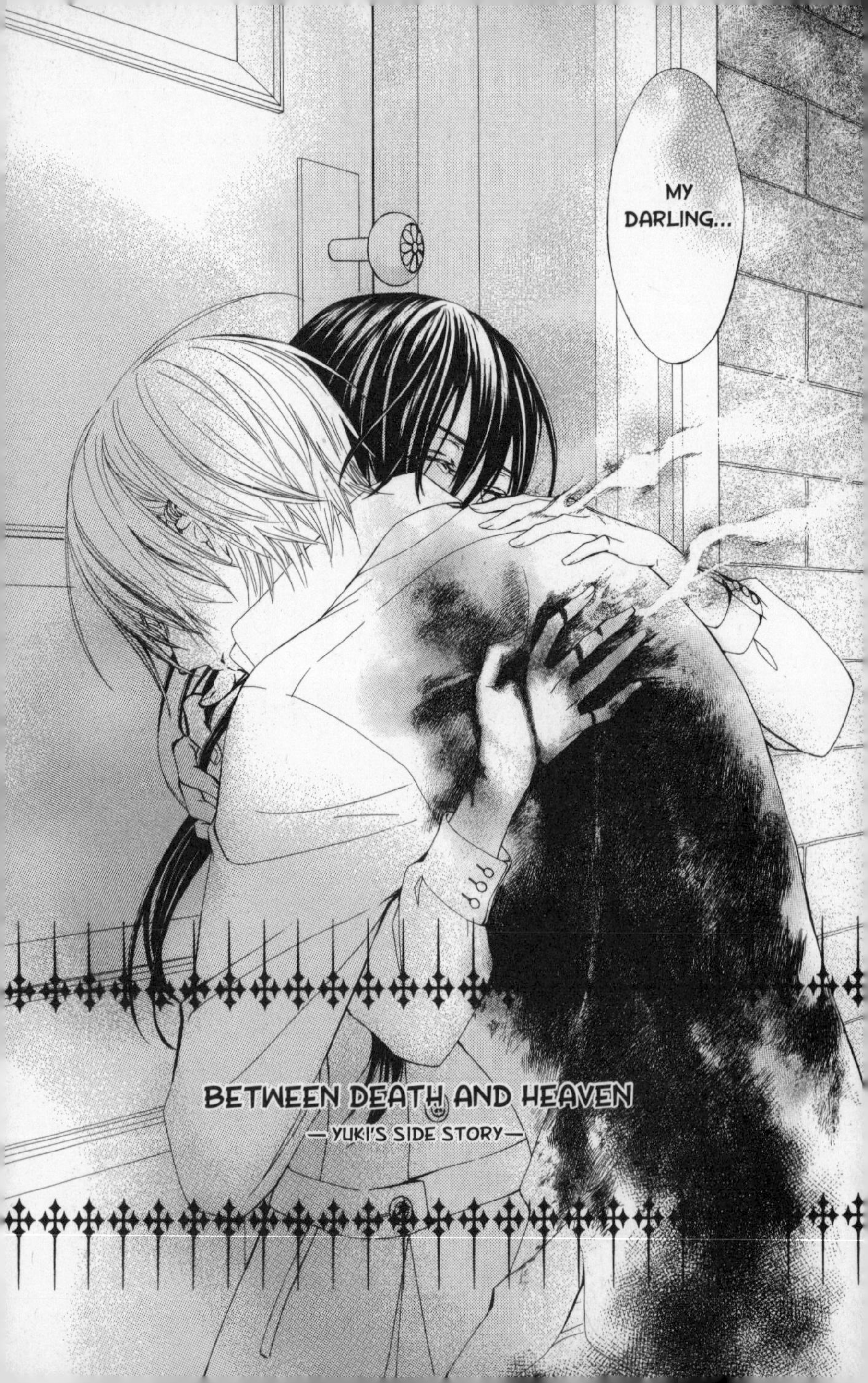
MY DARLING...
BETWEEN DEATH AND HEAVEN
—YUKI'S SIDE STORY—

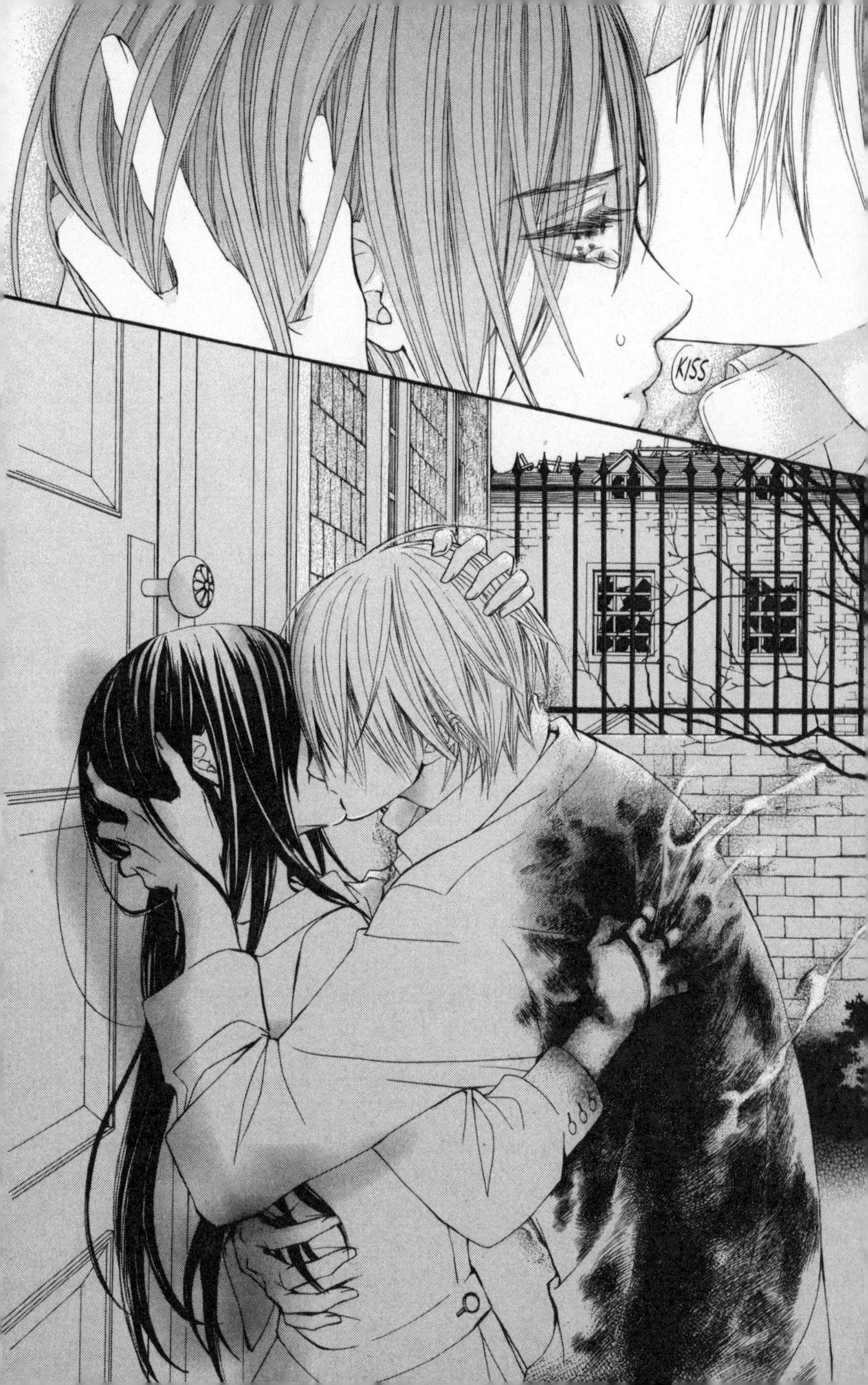
KISS

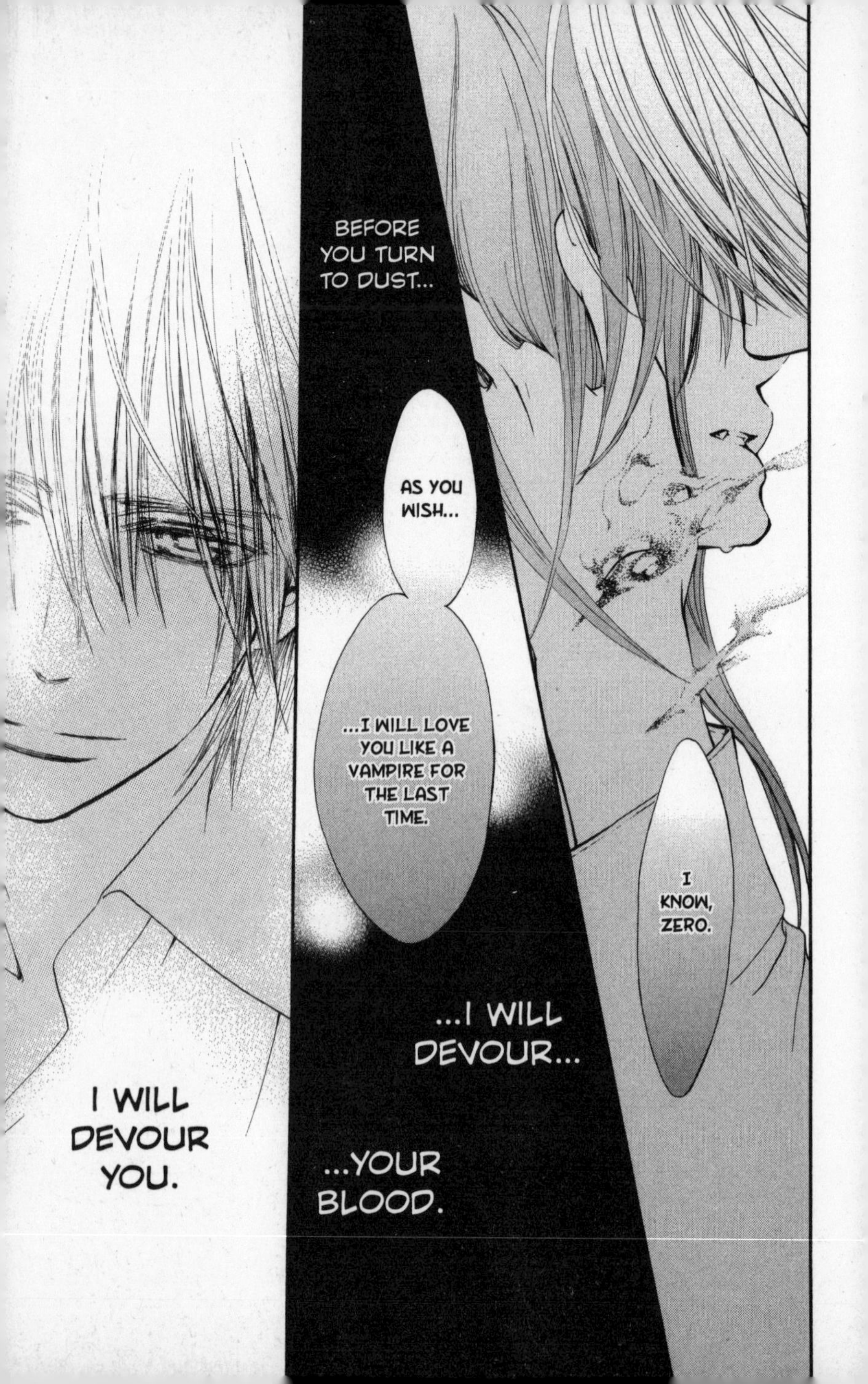
BEFORE YOU TURN TO DUST...
AS YOU WISH...
...I WILL LOVE YOU LIKE A VAMPIRE FOR THE LAST TIME.
I KNOW, ZERO.
...I WILL DEVOUR...
...YOUR BLOOD.
I WILL DEVOUR YOU.

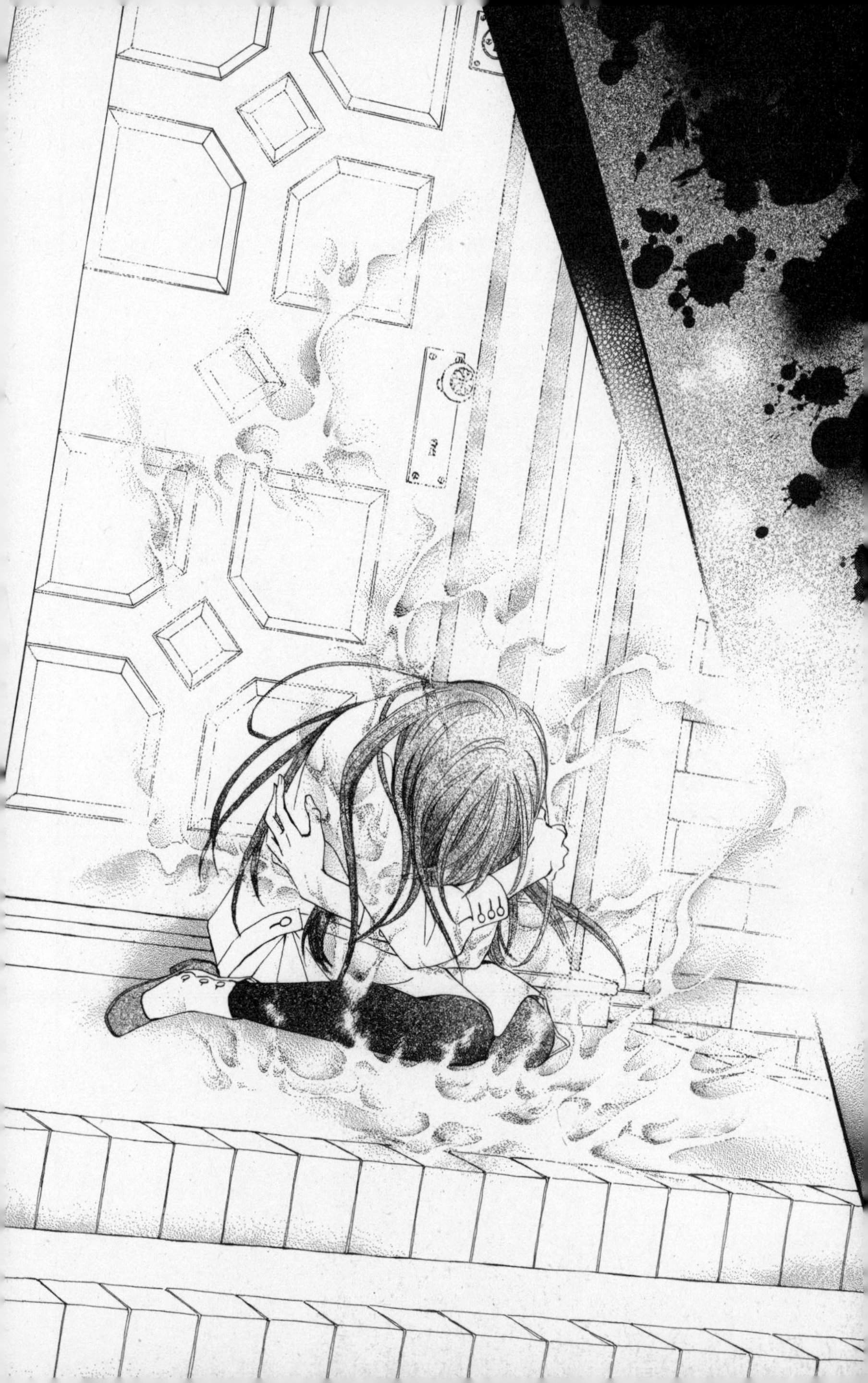

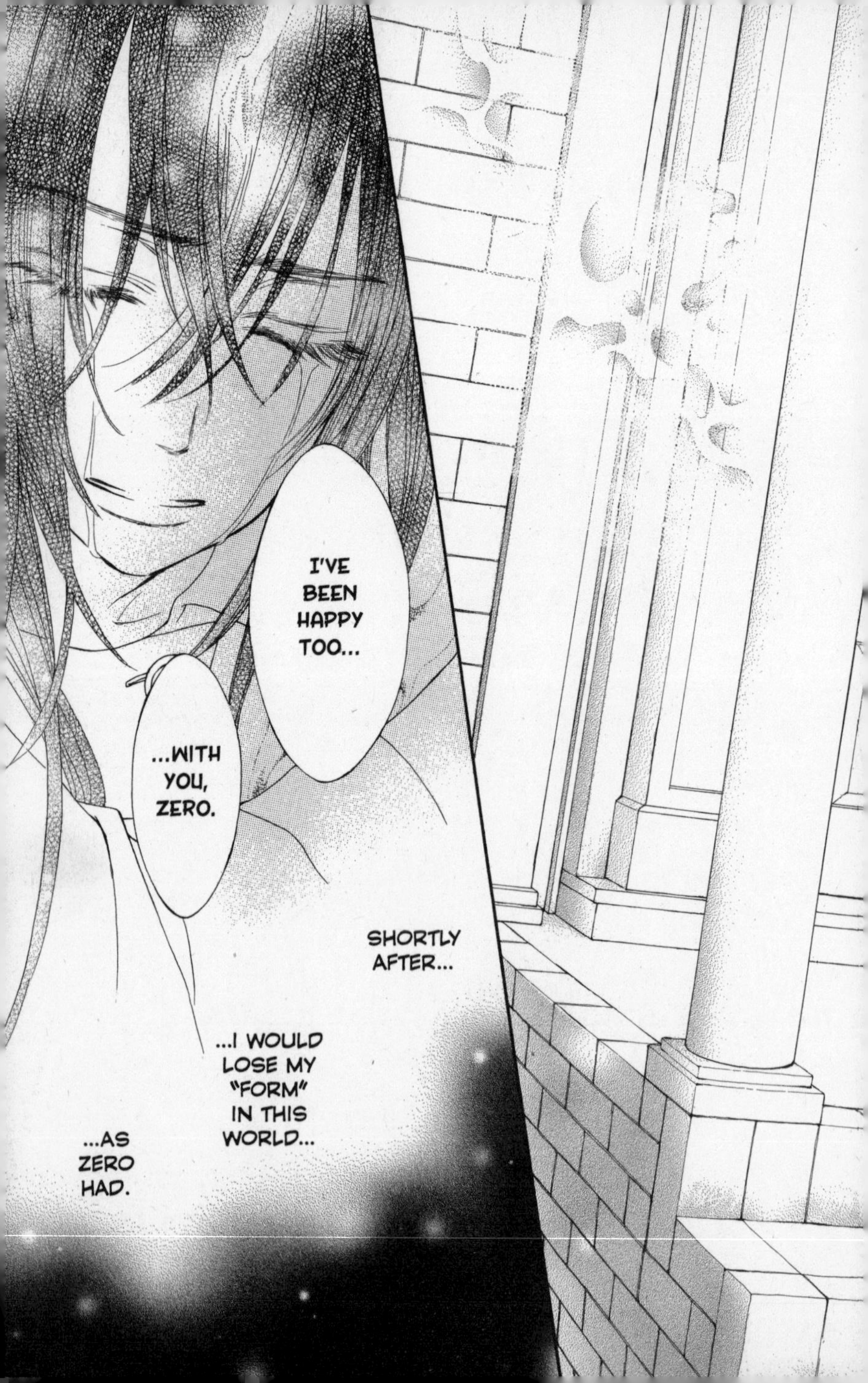
I'VE BEEN HAPPY TOO...
...WITH YOU, ZERO.
SHORTLY AFTER...
...I WOULD LOSE MY "FORM" IN THIS WORLD...
...AS ZERO HAD.

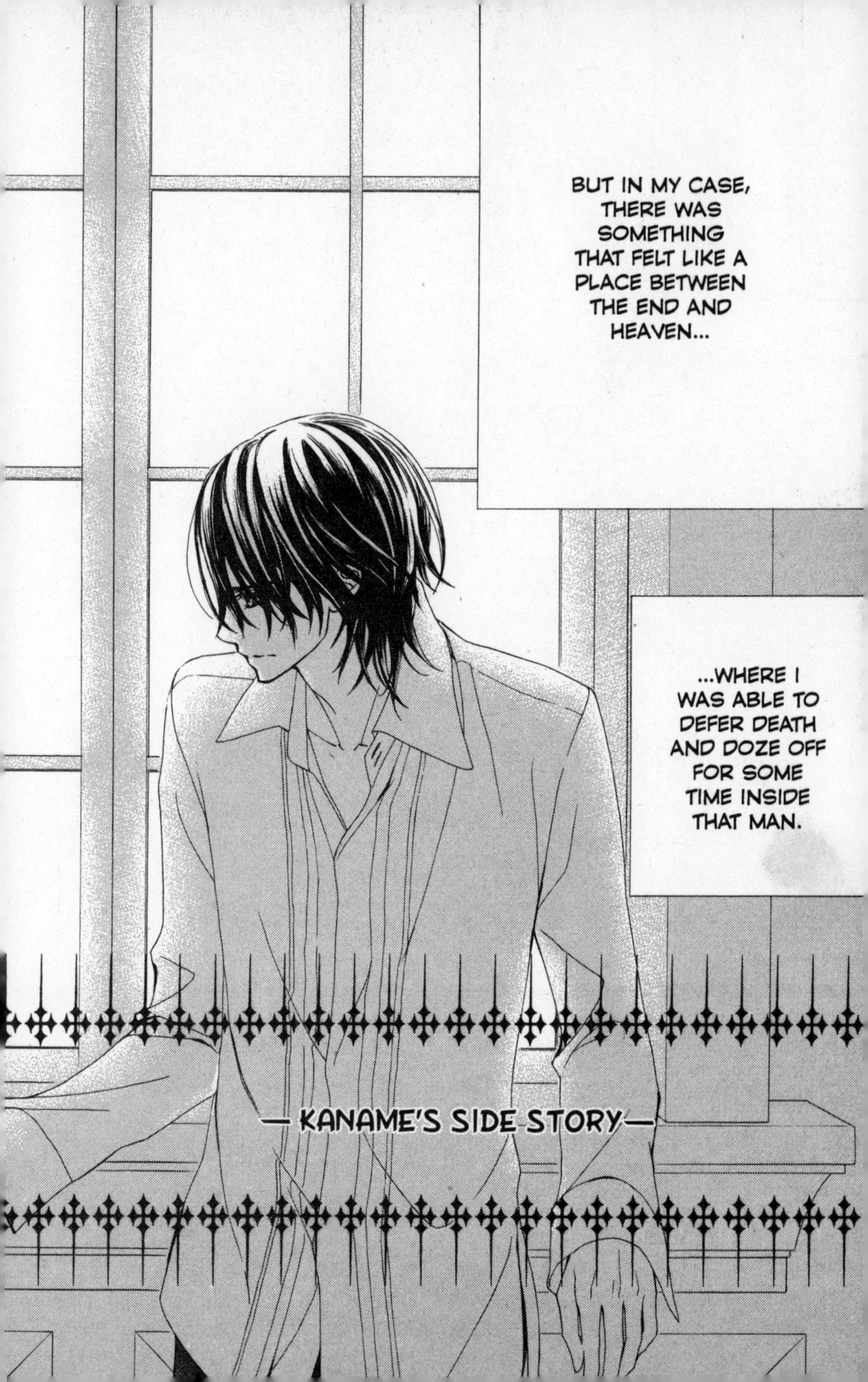
BUT IN MY CASE, THERE WAS SOMETHING THAT FELT LIKE A PLACE BETWEEN THE END AND HEAVEN...
...WHERE I WAS ABLE TO DEFER DEATH AND DOZE OFF FOR SOME TIME INSIDE THAT MAN.
— KANAME'S SIDE STORY —

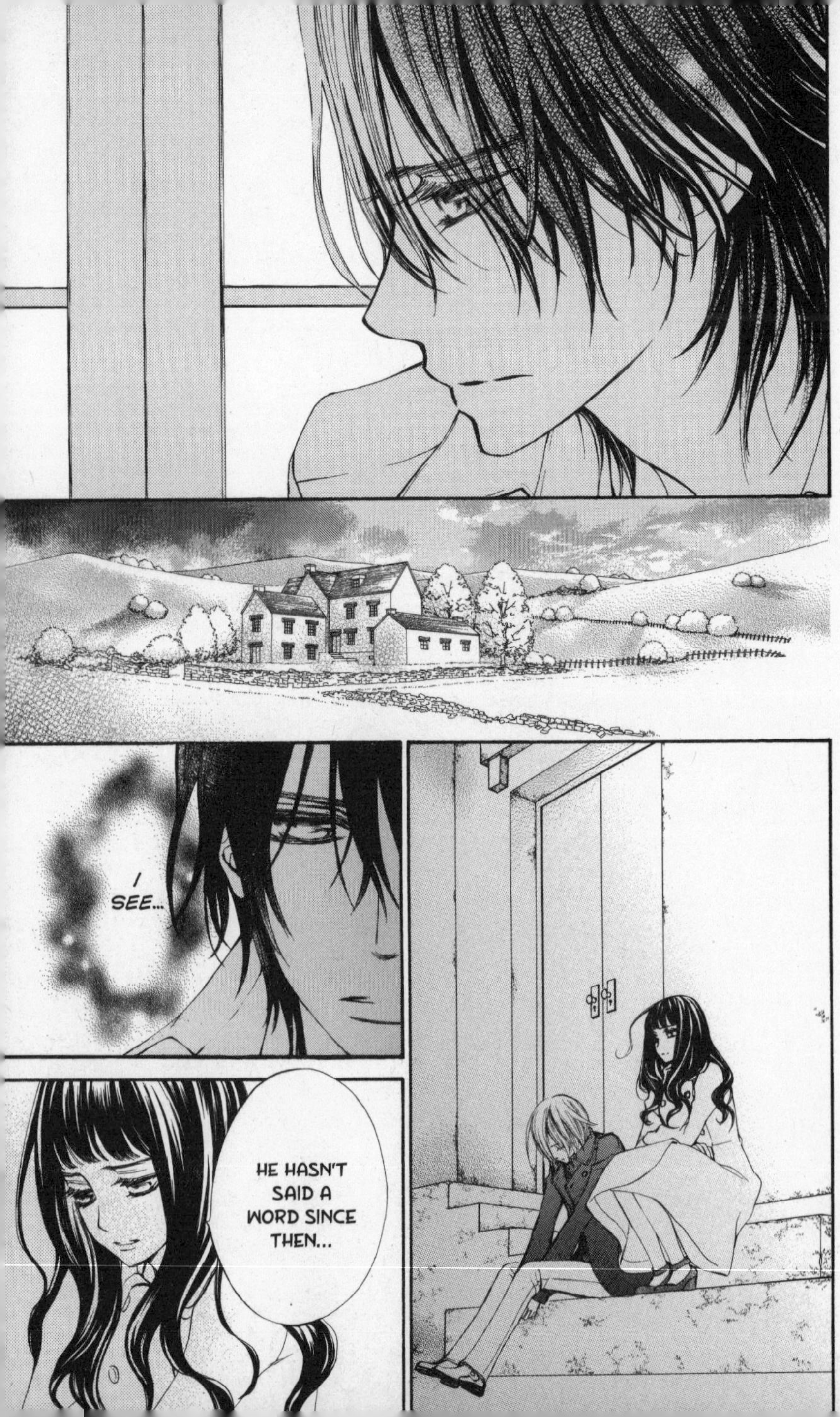
I SEE...
HE HASN'T SAID A WORD SINCE THEN...

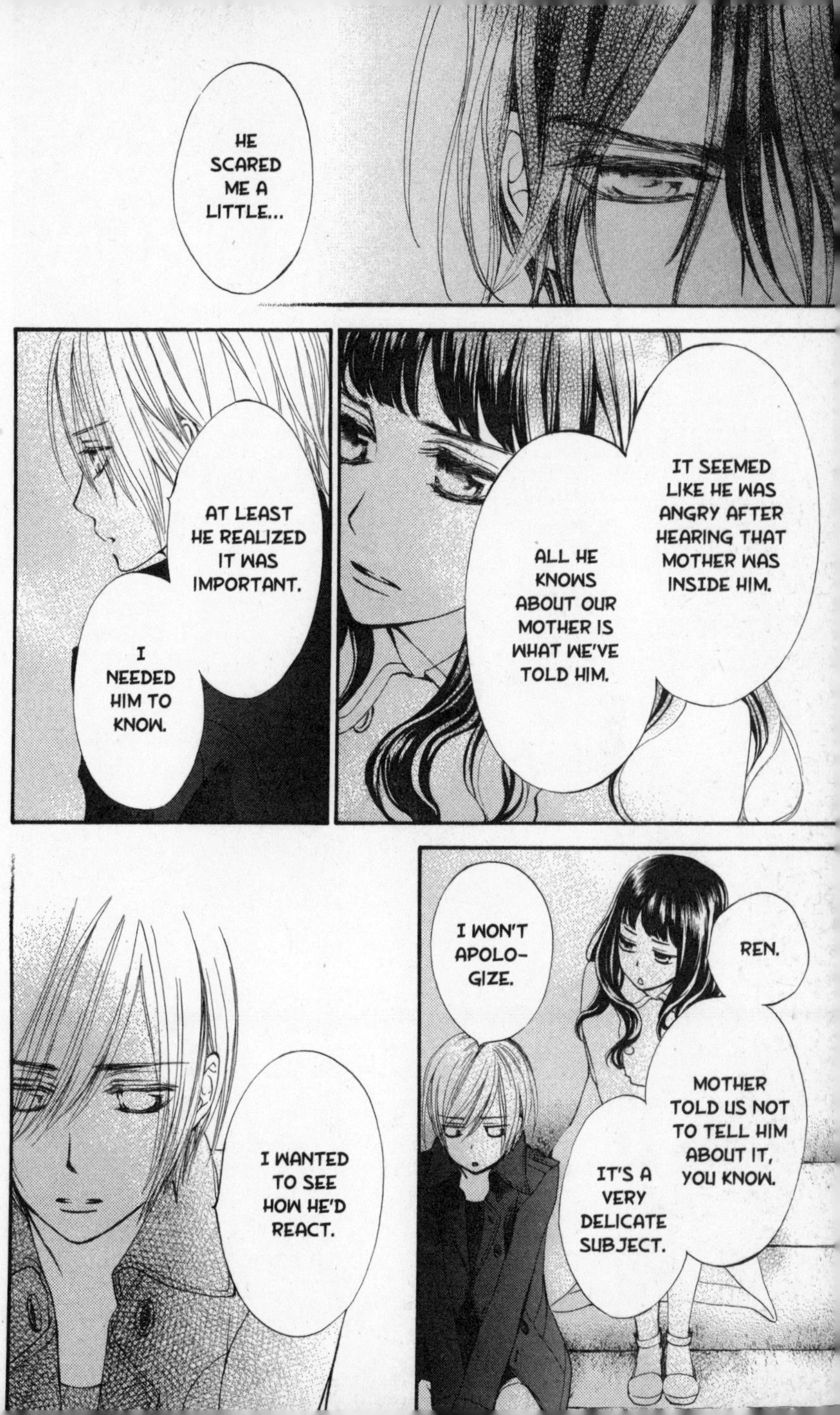
HE SCARED ME A LITTLE...
IT SEEMED LIKE HE WAS ANGRY AFTER HEARING THAT MOTHER WAS INSIDE HIM.
ALL HE KNOWS ABOUT OUR MOTHER IS WHAT WE'VE TOLD HIM.
AT LEAST HE REALIZED IT WAS IMPORTANT.
I NEEDED HIM TO KNOW.
REN.
MOTHER TOLD US NOT TO TELL HIM ABOUT IT, YOU KNOW.
IT'S A VERY DELICATE SUBJECT.
I WON'T APOLO-GIZE.
I WANTED TO SEE HOW HE'D REACT.

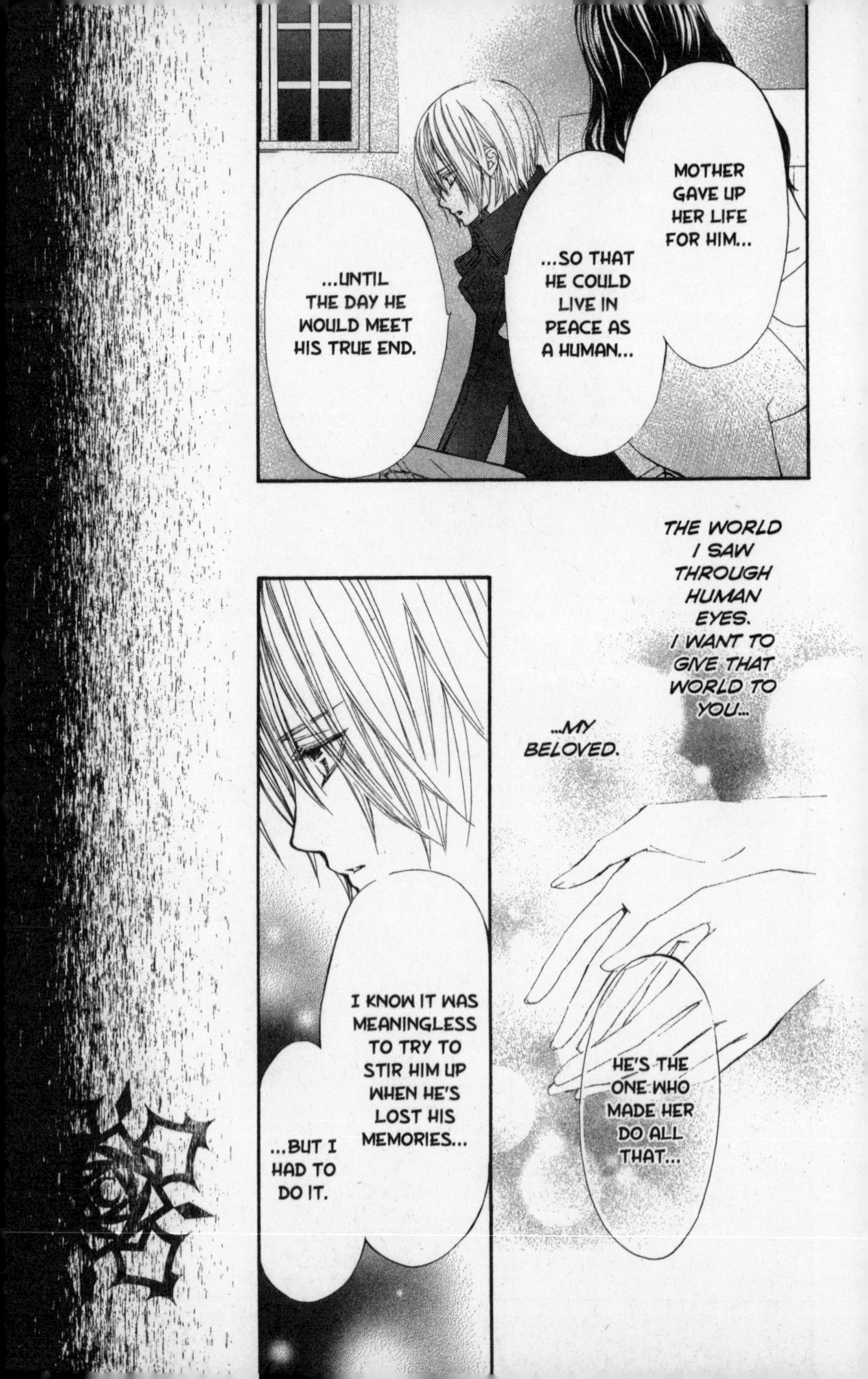
MOTHER GAVE UP HER LIFE FOR HIM...
...SO THAT HE COULD LIVE IN PEACE AS A HUMAN...
...UNTIL THE DAY HE WOULD MEET HIS TRUE END.
THE WORLD I SAW THROUGH HUMAN EYES. I WANT TO GIVE THAT WORLD TO YOU...
...MY BELOVED.
HE'S THE ONE WHO MADE HER DO ALL THAT...
I KNOW IT WAS MEANINGLESS TO TRY TO STIR HIM UP WHEN HE'S LOST HIS MEMORIES...
...BUT I HAD TO DO IT.

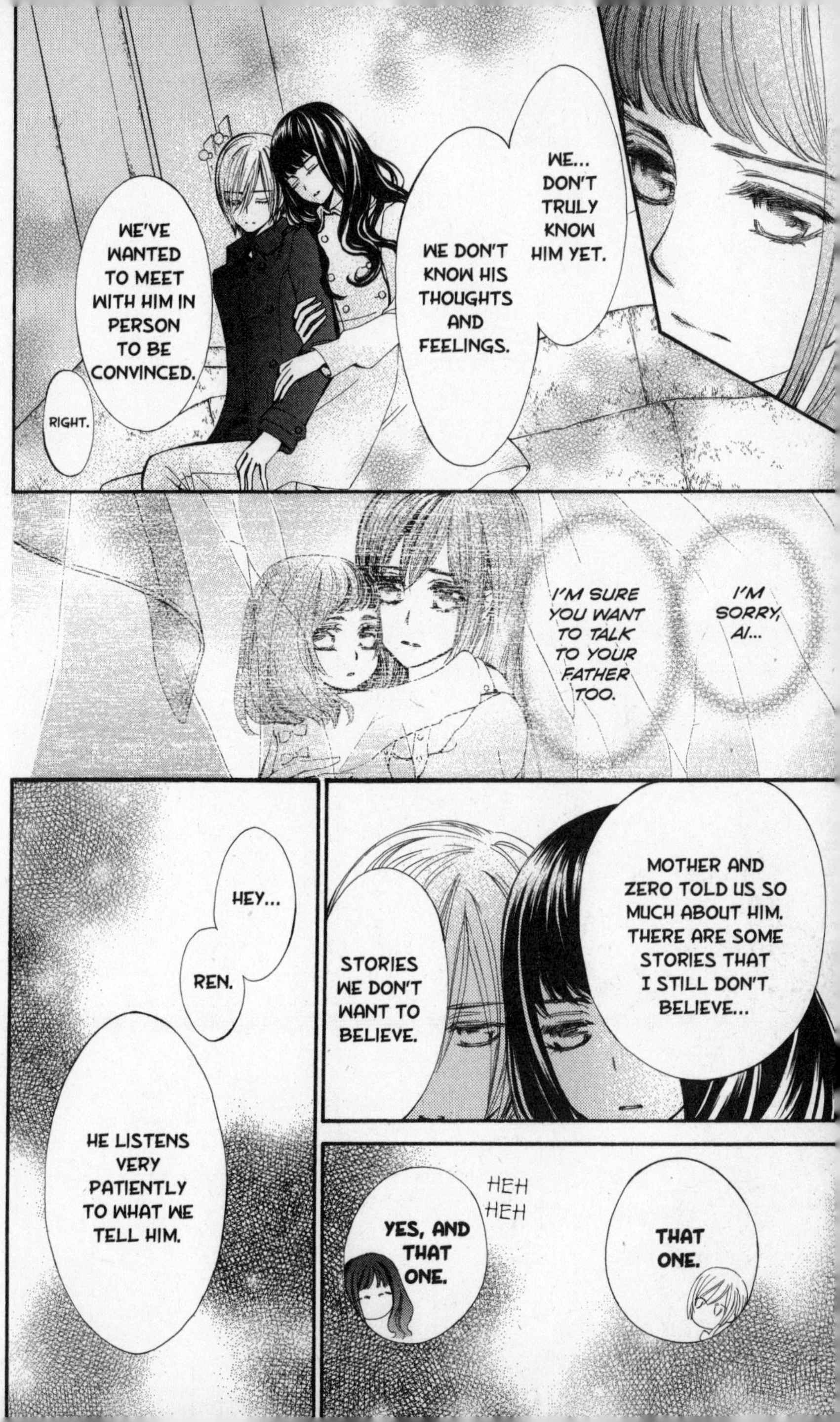
WE... DON'T TRULY KNOW HIM YET.
WE DON'T KNOW HIS THOUGHTS AND FEELINGS.
WE'VE WANTED TO MEET WITH HIM IN PERSON TO BE CONVINCED.
RIGHT.
I'M SORRY, AI...
I'M SURE YOU WANT TO TALK TO YOUR FATHER TOO.
MOTHER AND ZERO TOLD US SO MUCH ABOUT HIM. THERE ARE SOME STORIES THAT I STILL DON'T BELIEVE...
STORIES WE DON'T WANT TO BELIEVE.
THAT ONE.
HEH HEH
YES, AND THAT ONE.
HEY...
REN.
HE LISTENS VERY PATIENTLY TO WHAT WE TELL HIM.

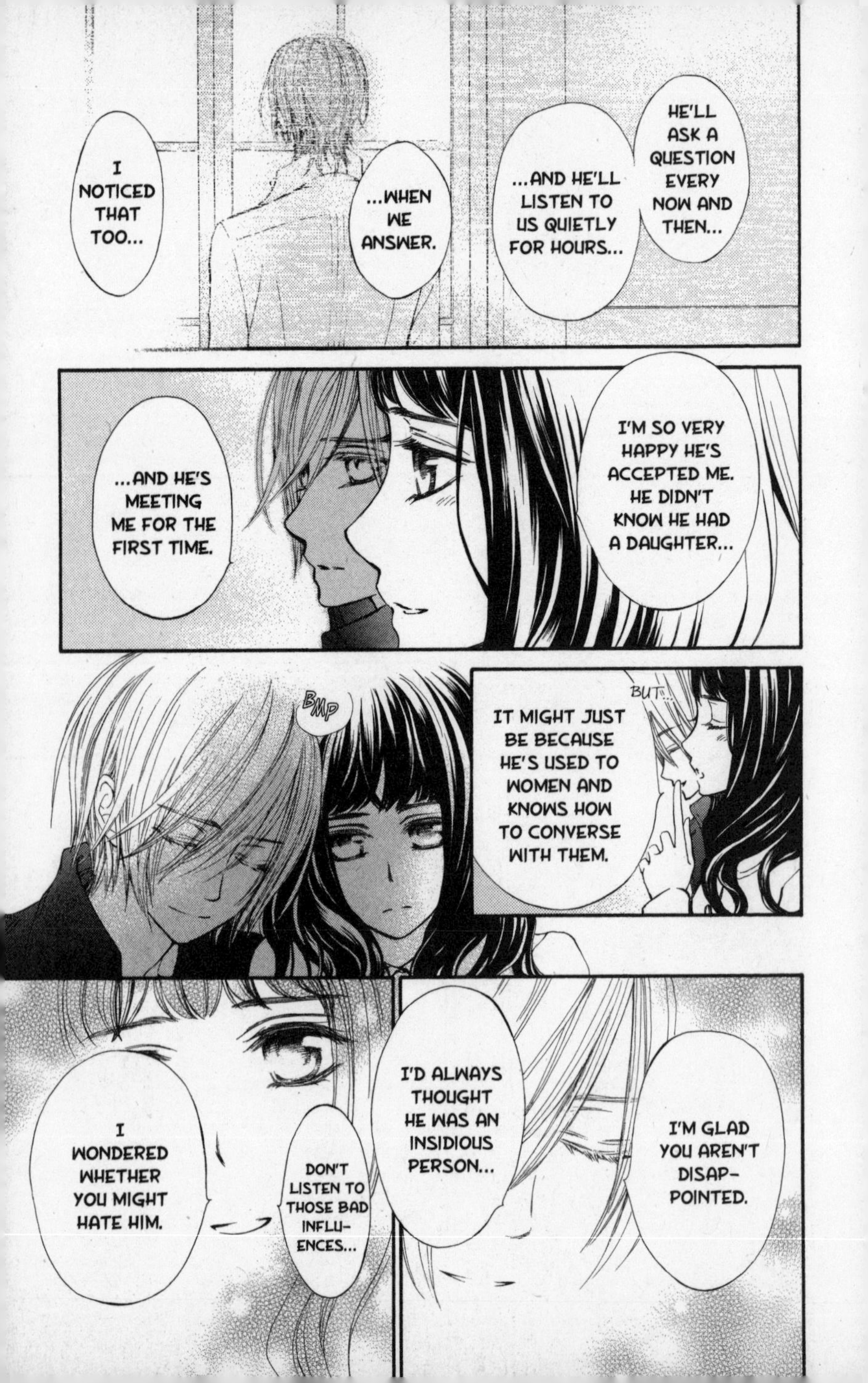
HE'LL ASK A QUESTION EVERY NOW AND THEN...
...AND HE'LL LISTEN TO US QUIETLY FOR HOURS...
...WHEN WE ANSWER.
I NOTICED THAT TOO...
I'M SO VERY HAPPY HE'S ACCEPTED ME. HE DIDN'T KNOW HE HAD A DAUGHTER...
...AND HE'S MEETING ME FOR THE FIRST TIME.
BUT!!...
IT MIGHT JUST BE BECAUSE HE'S USED TO WOMEN AND KNOWS HOW TO CONVERSE WITH THEM.
BMP
I'M GLAD YOU AREN'T DISAP-POINTED.
I'D ALWAYS THOUGHT HE WAS AN INSIDIOUS PERSON...
DON'T LISTEN TO THOSE BAD INFLU-ENCES...
I WONDERED WHETHER YOU MIGHT HATE HIM.

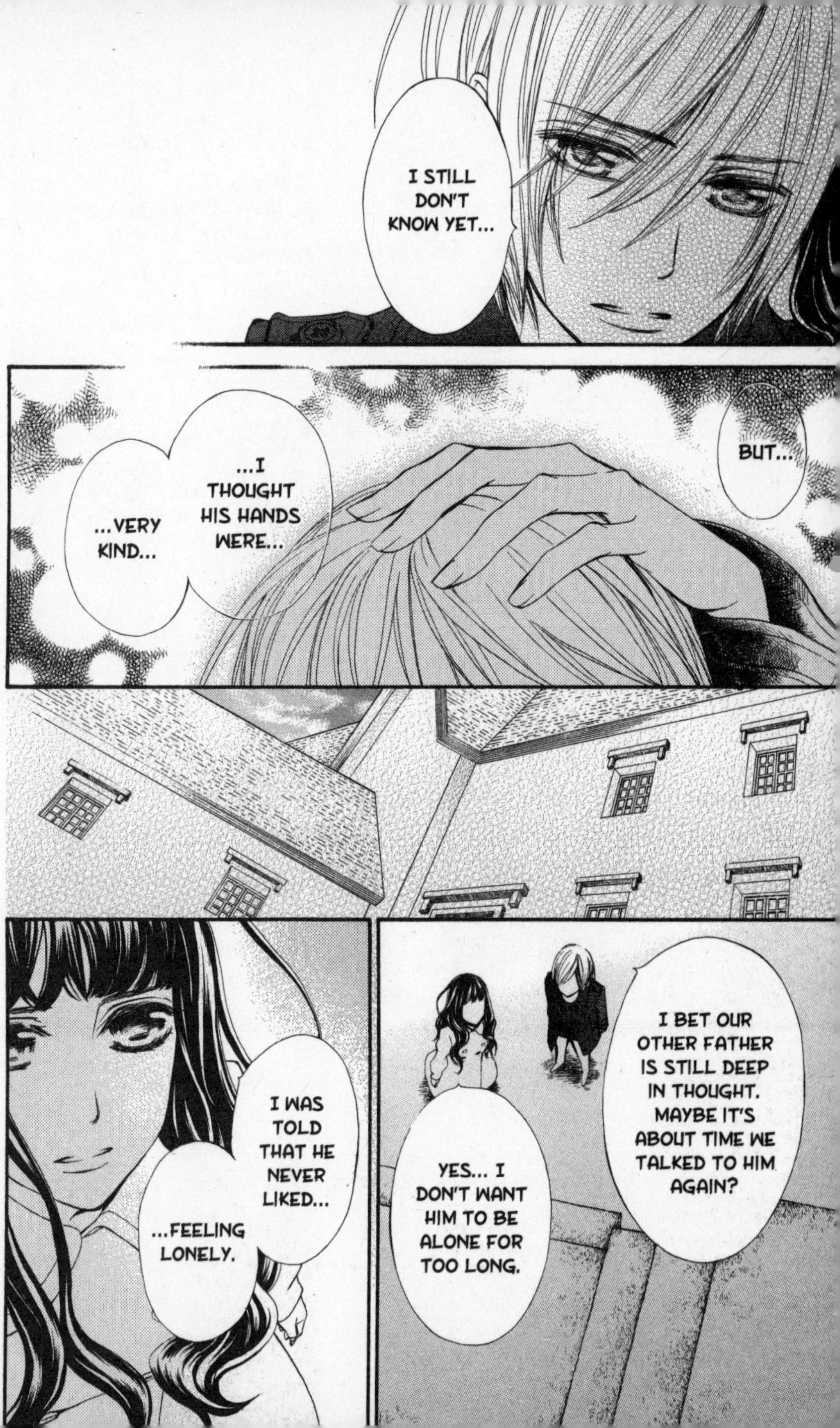
I STILL DON'T KNOW YET...
BUT...
...I THOUGHT HIS HANDS WERE...
...VERY KIND...
I BET OUR OTHER FATHER IS STILL DEEP IN THOUGHT. MAYBE IT'S ABOUT TIME WE TALKED TO HIM AGAIN?
YES... I DON'T WANT HIM TO BE ALONE FOR TOO LONG.
I WAS TOLD THAT HE NEVER LIKED...
...FEELING LONELY.

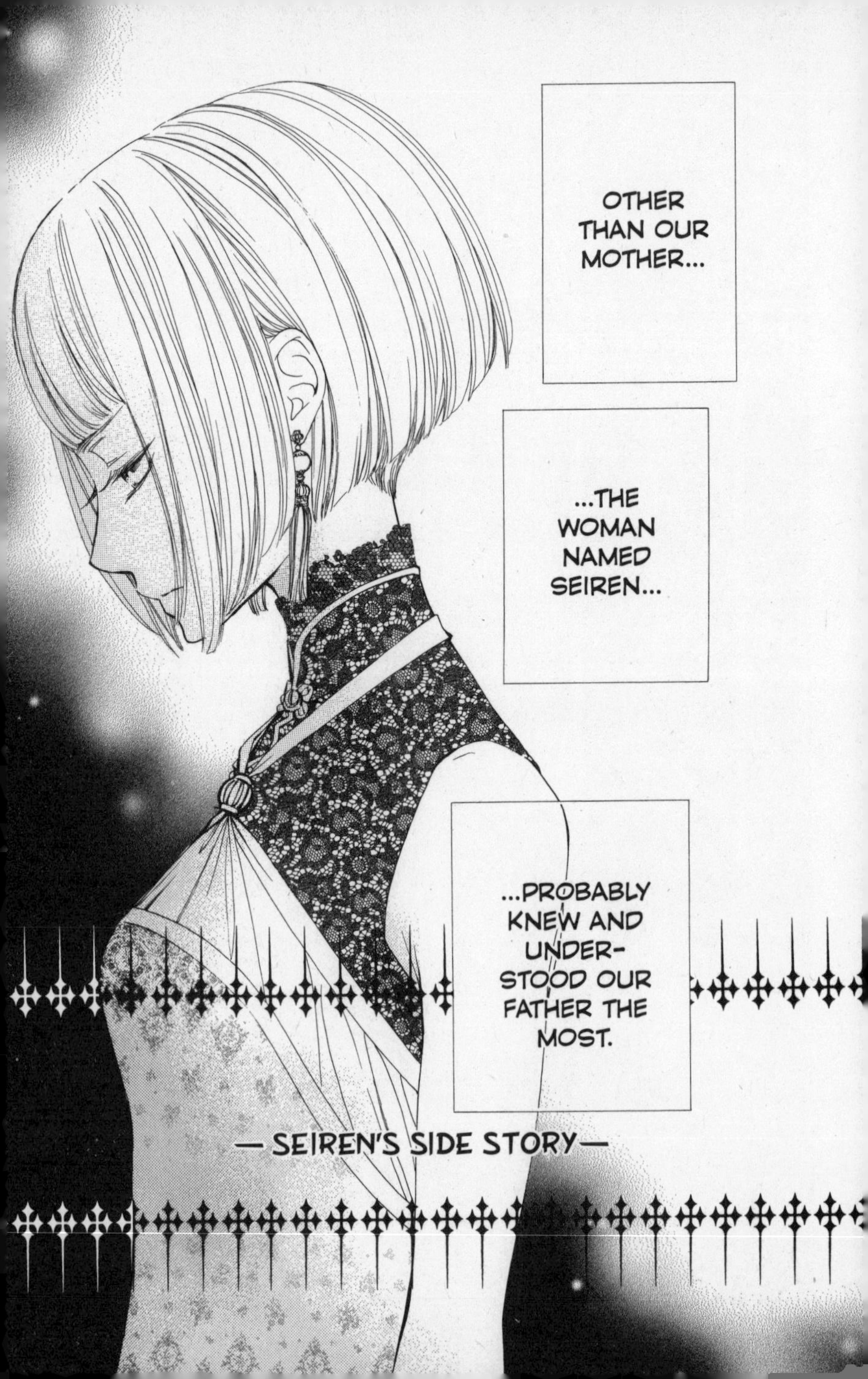
OTHER THAN OUR MOTHER...
...THE WOMAN NAMED SEIREN...
...PROBABLY KNEW AND UNDER-STOOD OUR FATHER THE MOST.
—SEIREN'S SIDE STORY—

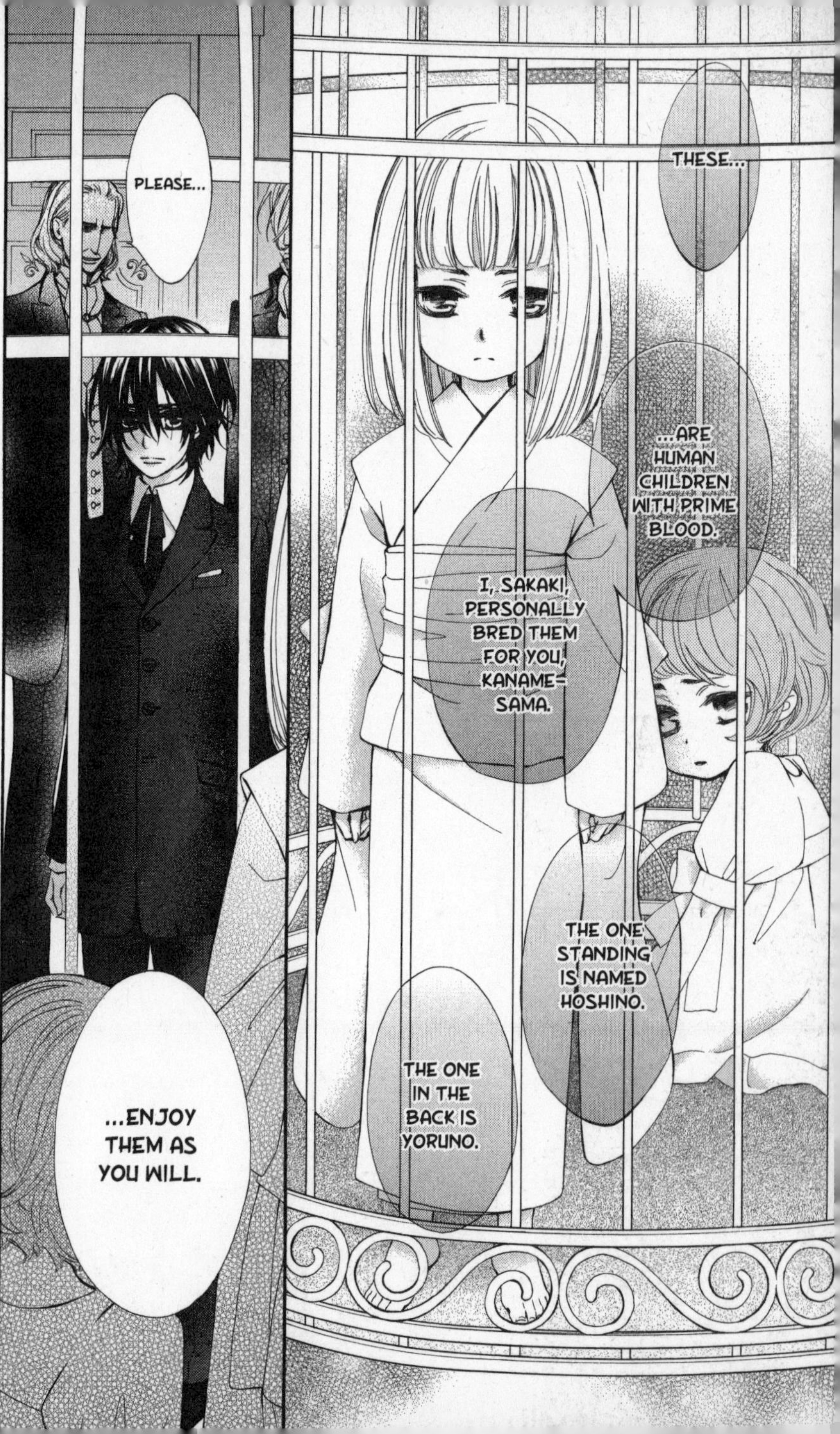
THESE...
...ARE HUMAN CHILDREN WITH PRIME BLOOD.
I, SAKAKI, PERSONALLY BRED THEM FOR YOU, KANAME-SAMA.
THE ONE STANDING IS NAMED HOSHINO.
THE ONE IN THE BACK IS YORUNO.
PLEASE...
...ENJOY THEM AS YOU WILL.

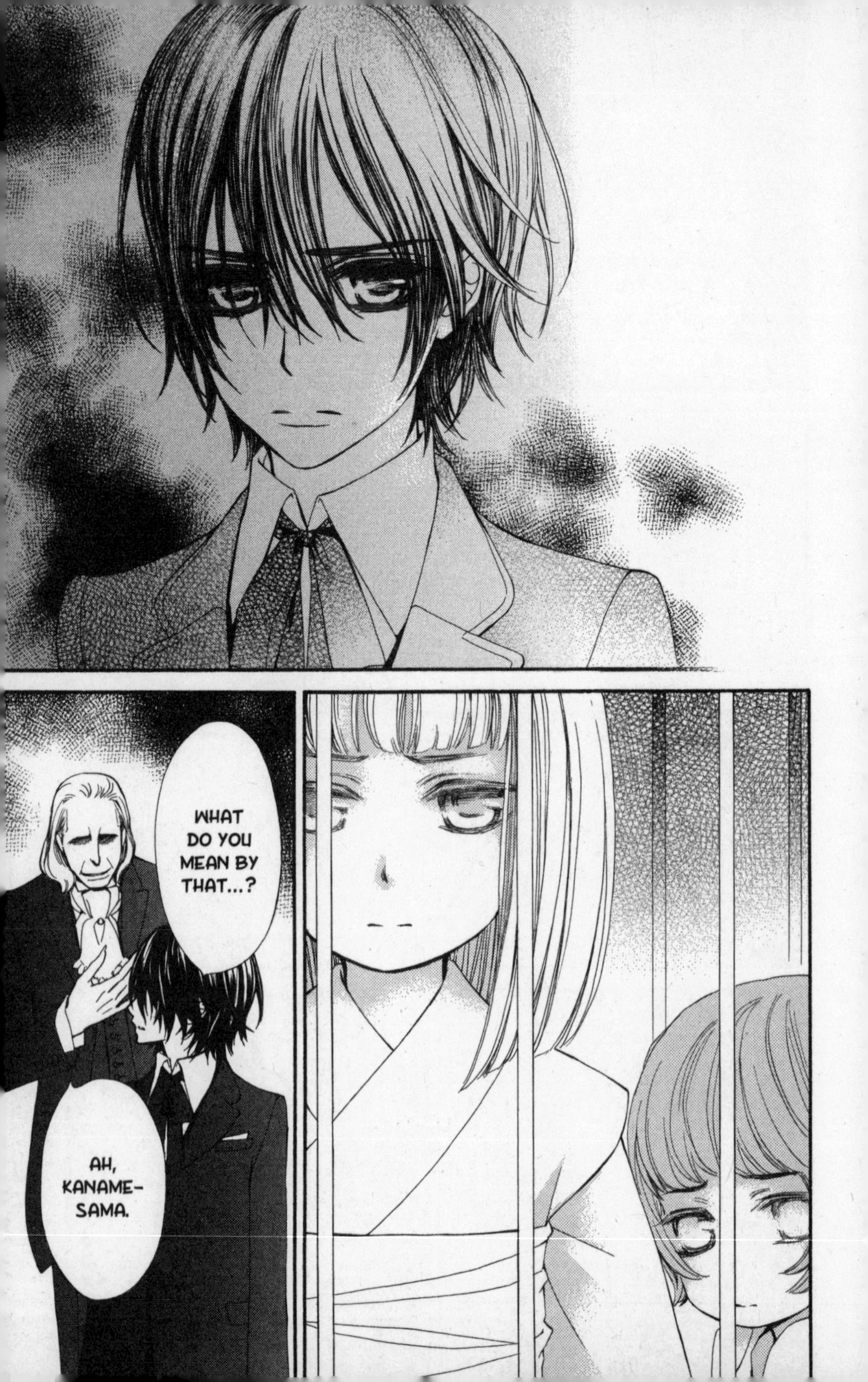
WHAT DO YOU MEAN BY THAT...?
AH, KANAME-SAMA.

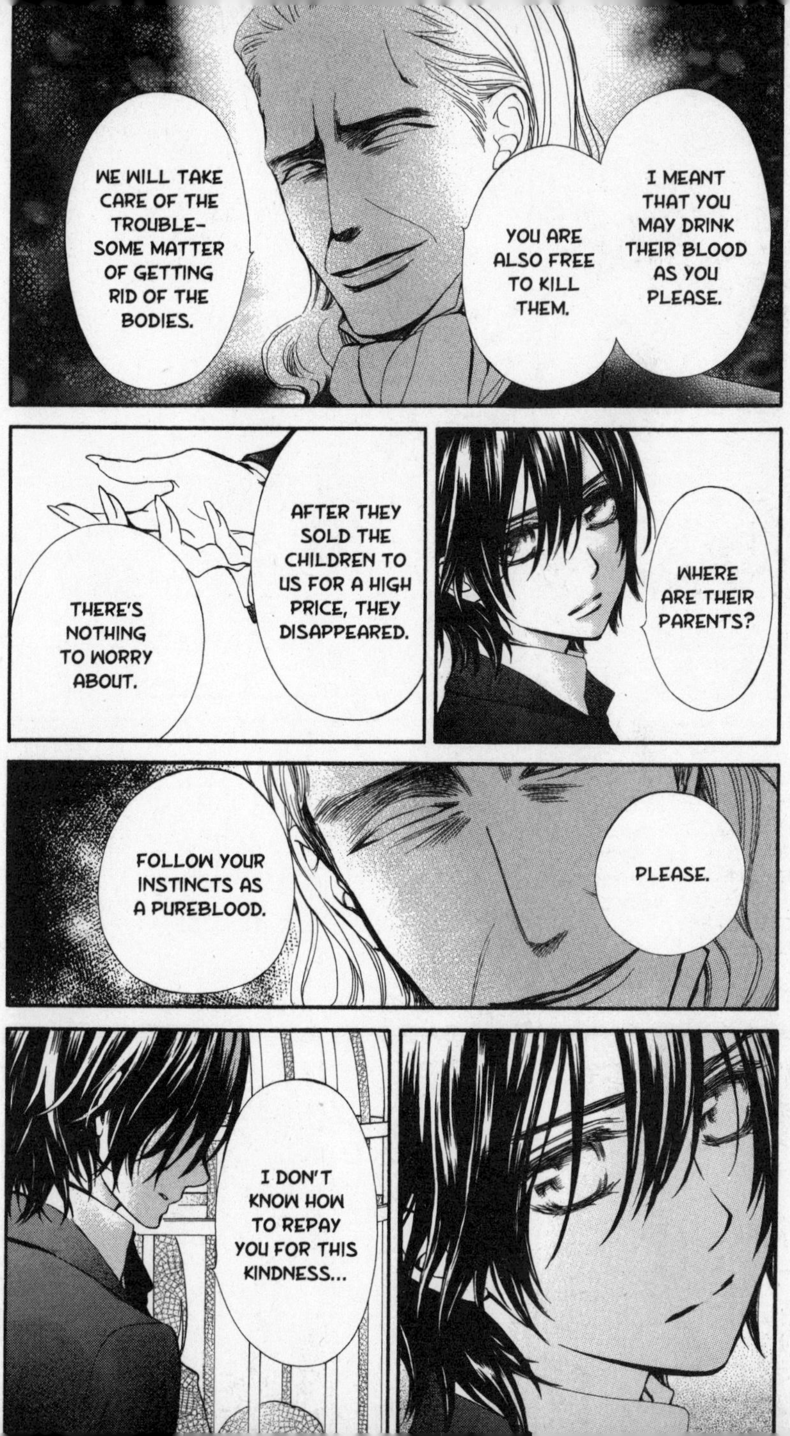
I MEANT THAT YOU MAY DRINK THEIR BLOOD AS YOU PLEASE.
YOU ARE ALSO FREE TO KILL THEM.
WE WILL TAKE CARE OF THE TROUBLE-SOME MATTER OF GETTING RID OF THE BODIES.
WHERE ARE THEIR PARENTS?
AFTER THEY SOLD THE CHILDREN TO US FOR A HIGH PRICE, THEY DISAPPEARED.
THERE'S NOTHING TO WORRY ABOUT.
PLEASE.
FOLLOW YOUR INSTINCTS AS A PUREBLOOD.
I DON'T KNOW HOW TO REPAY YOU FOR THIS KINDNESS...

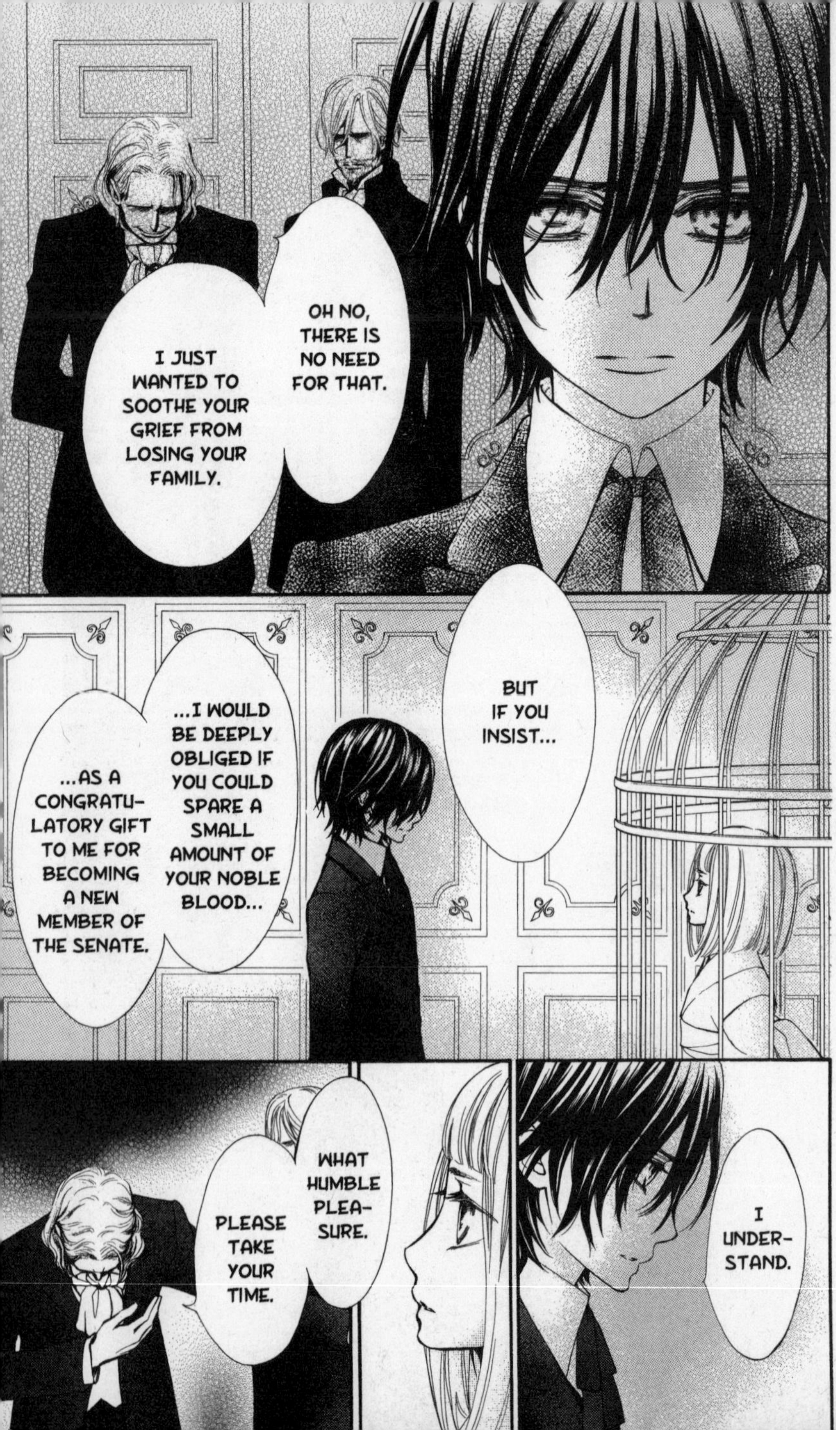
OH NO, THERE IS NO NEED FOR THAT.
I JUST WANTED TO SOOTHE YOUR GRIEF FROM LOSING YOUR FAMILY.
BUT IF YOU INSIST...
...I WOULD BE DEEPLY OBLIGED IF YOU COULD SPARE A SMALL AMOUNT OF YOUR NOBLE BLOOD...
...AS A CONGRATU-LATORY GIFT TO ME FOR BECOMING A NEW MEMBER OF THE SENATE.
I UNDER-STAND.
WHAT HUMBLE PLEA-SURE.
PLEASE TAKE YOUR TIME.

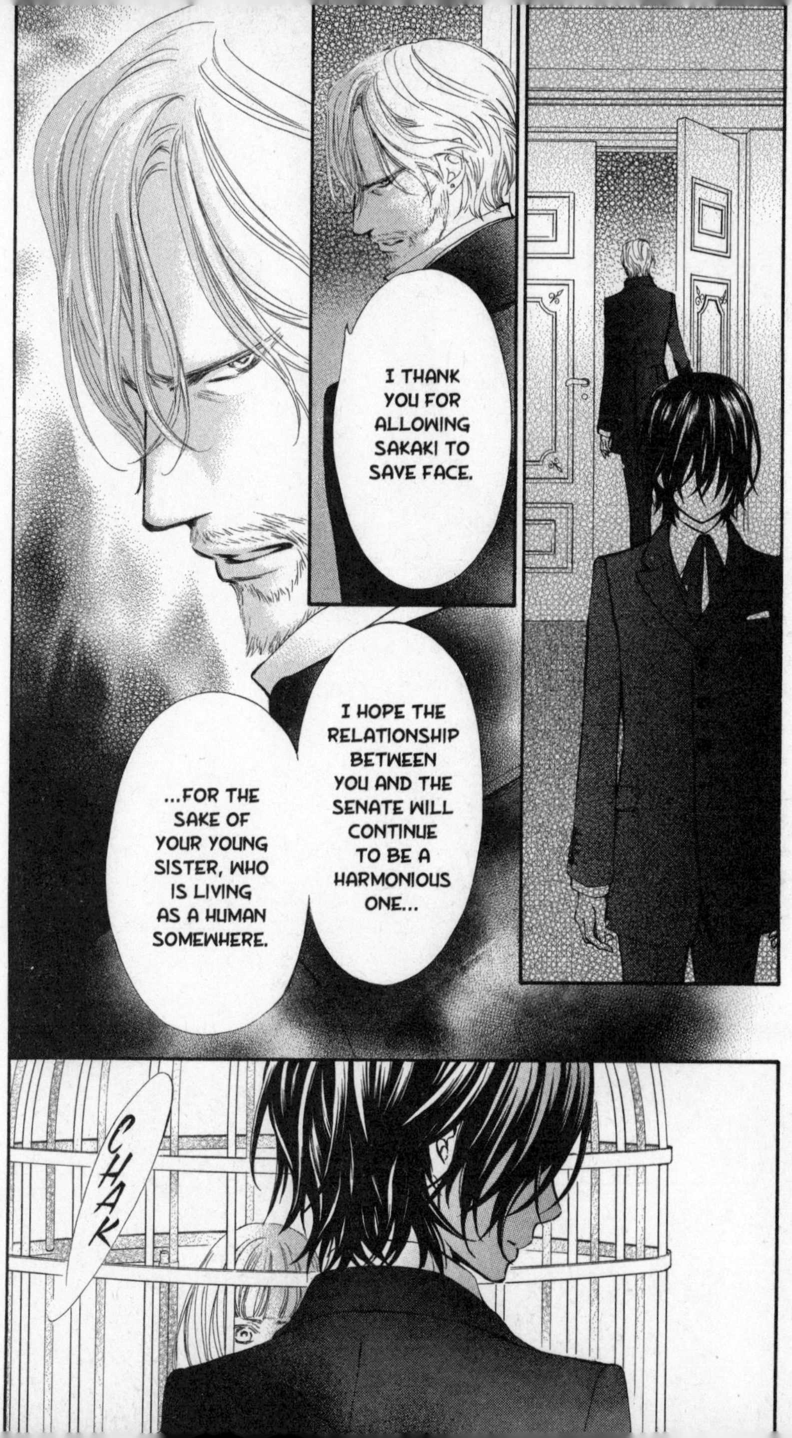
I THANK YOU FOR ALLOWING SAKAKI TO SAVE FACE.
I HOPE THE RELATIONSHIP BETWEEN YOU AND THE SENATE WILL CONTINUE TO BE A HARMONIOUS ONE...
...FOR THE SAKE OF YOUR YOUNG SISTER, WHO IS LIVING AS A HUMAN SOMEWHERE.
CHAK

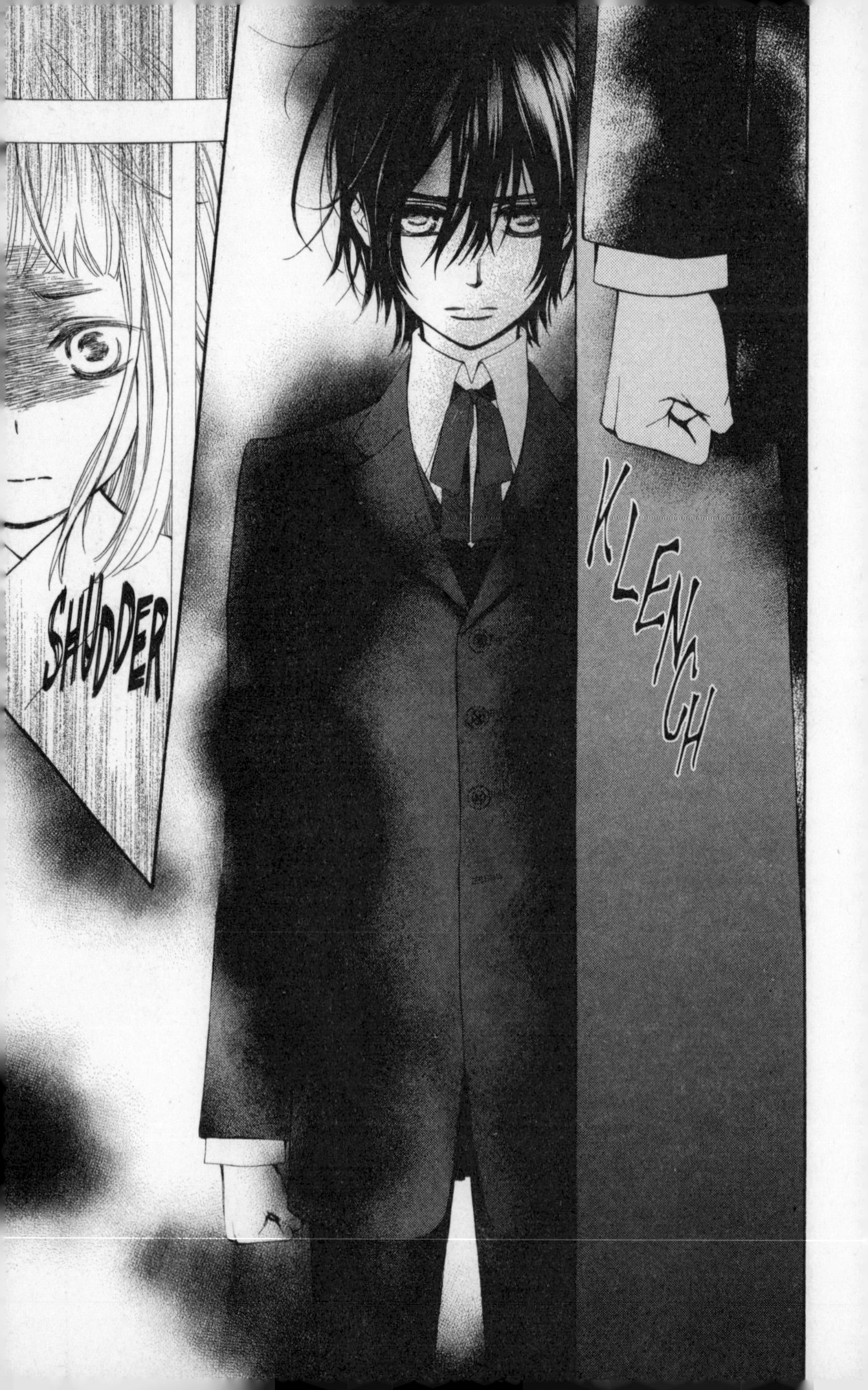
KLENCH
SHUDDER

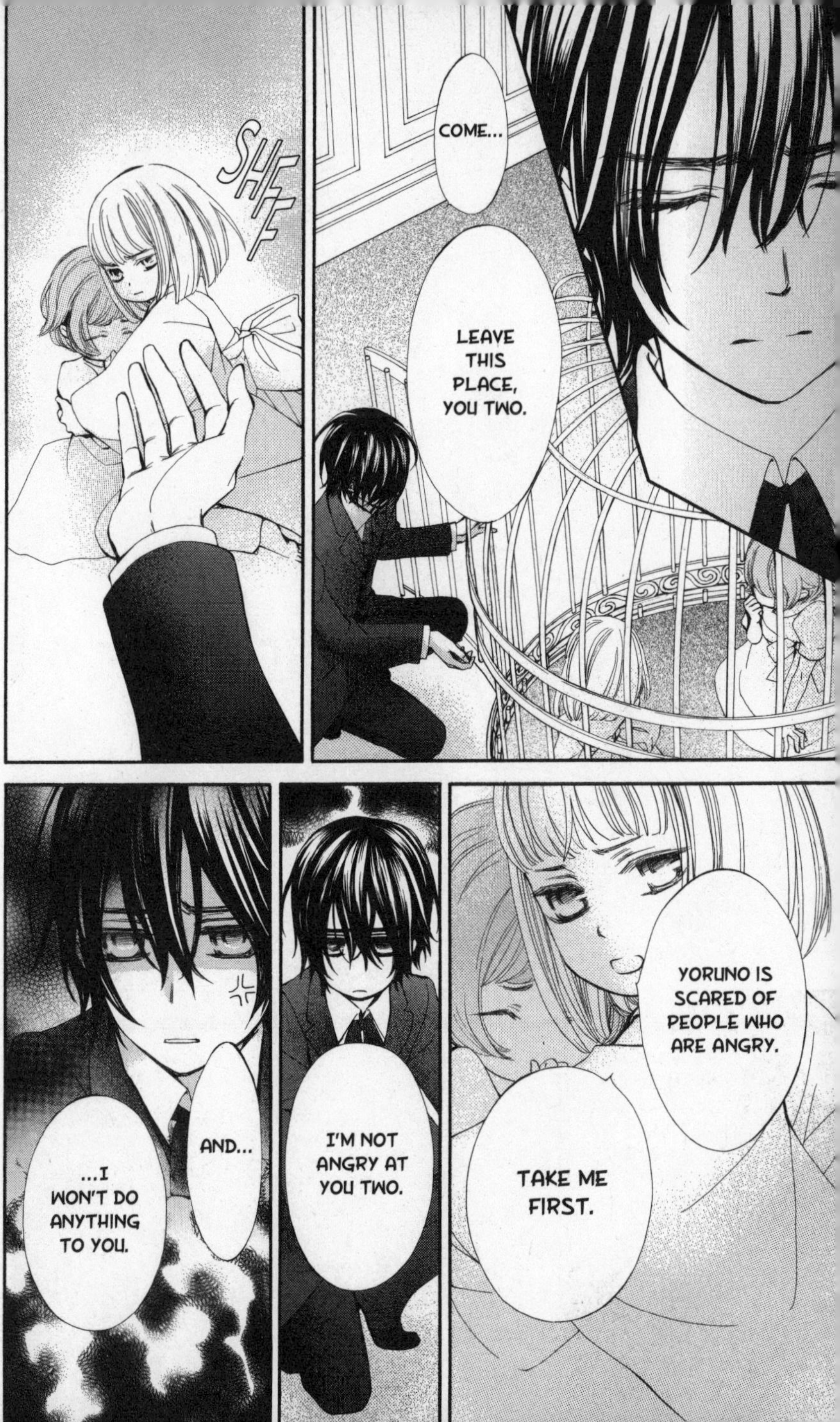
COME...
LEAVE THIS PLACE, YOU TWO.
SHFF
YORUNO IS SCARED OF PEOPLE WHO ARE ANGRY.
TAKE ME FIRST.
I'M NOT ANGRY AT YOU TWO.
AND...
...I WON'T DO ANYTHING TO YOU.

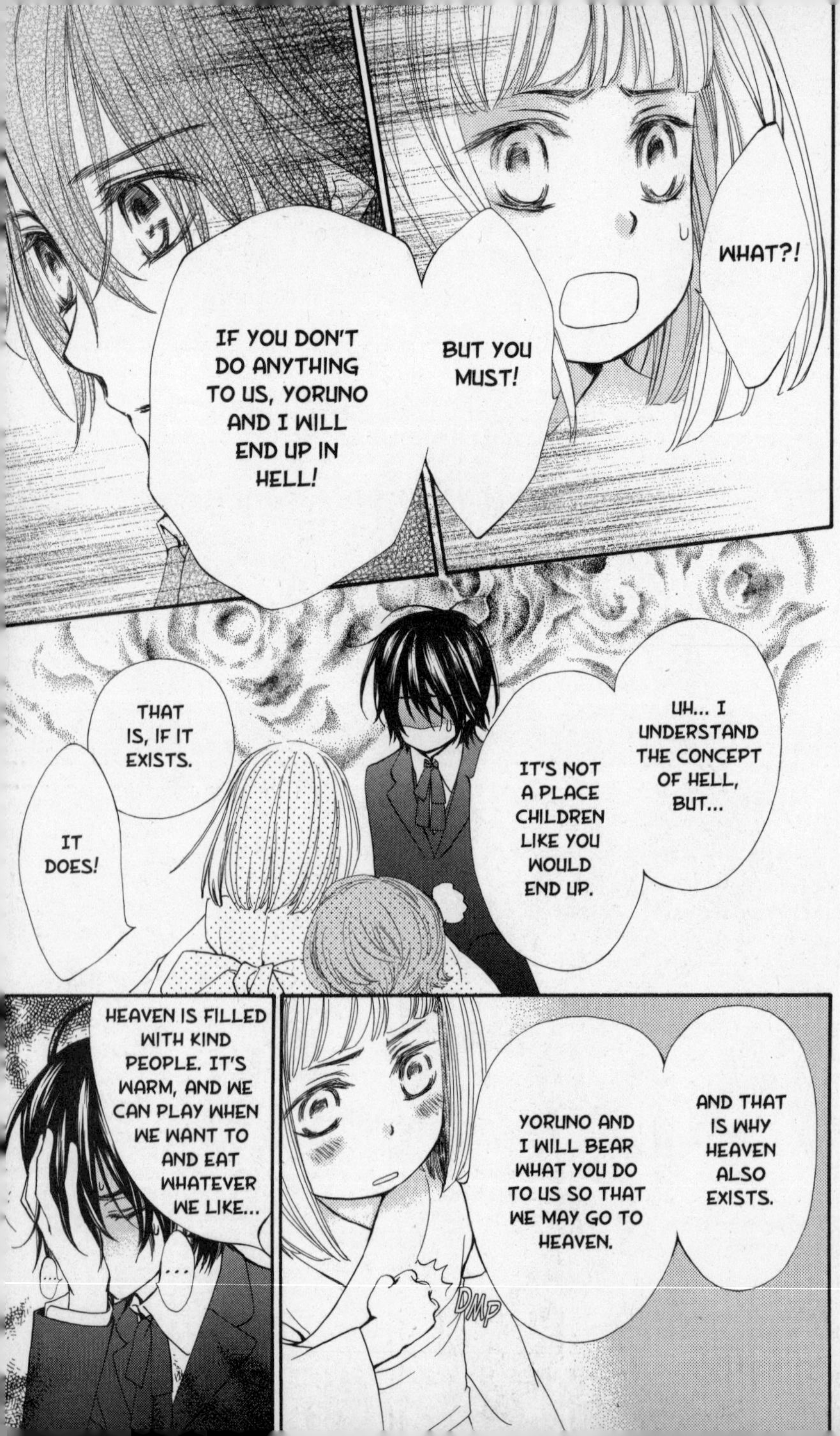
WHAT?!
BUT YOU MUST!
IF YOU DON'T DO ANYTHING TO US, YORUNO AND I WILL END UP IN HELL!
UH... I UNDERSTAND THE CONCEPT OF HELL, BUT...
IT'S NOT A PLACE CHILDREN LIKE YOU WOULD END UP.
THAT IS, IF IT EXISTS.
IT DOES!
AND THAT IS WHY HEAVEN ALSO EXISTS.
YORUNO AND I WILL BEAR WHAT YOU DO TO US SO THAT WE MAY GO TO HEAVEN.
DMP
HEAVEN IS FILLED WITH KIND PEOPLE. IT'S WARM, AND WE CAN PLAY WHEN WE WANT TO AND EAT WHATEVER WE LIKE...
...
...

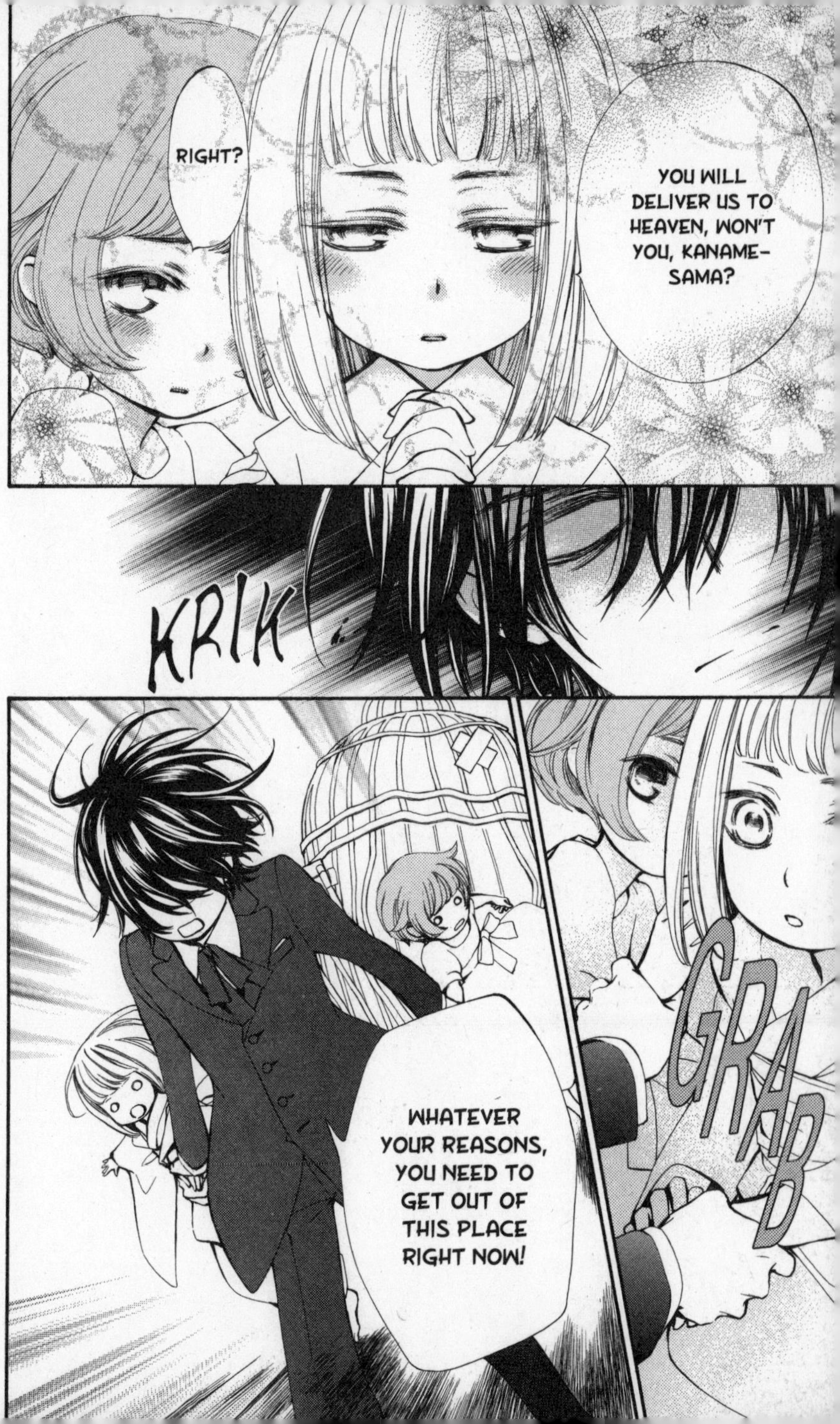
YOU WILL DELIVER US TO HEAVEN, WON'T YOU, KANAME-SAMA?
RIGHT?
KRIK
GRAB
WHATEVER YOUR REASONS, YOU NEED TO GET OUT OF THIS PLACE RIGHT NOW!

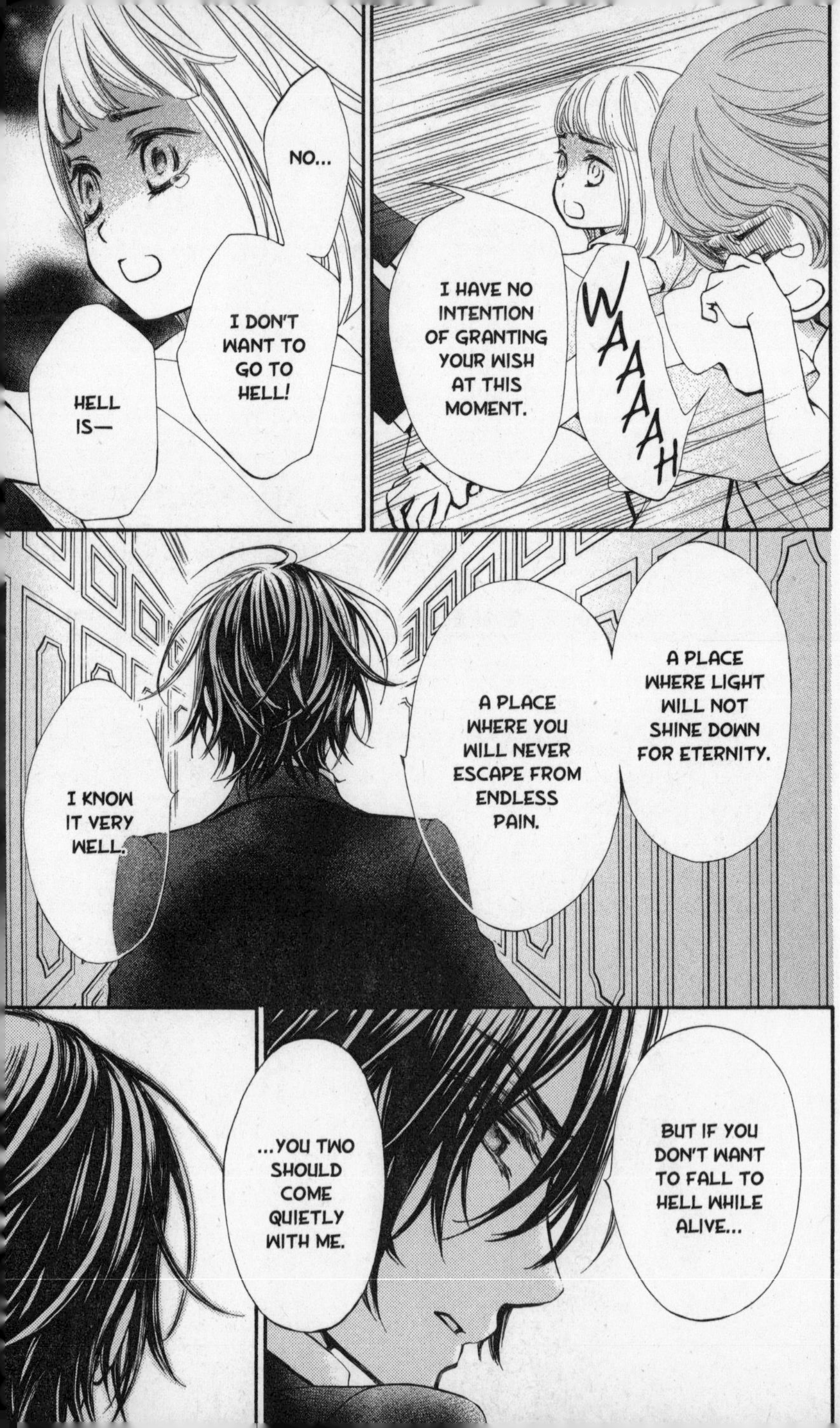
WAAAAH
I HAVE NO INTENTION OF GRANTING YOUR WISH AT THIS MOMENT.
NO...
I DON'T WANT TO GO TO HELL!
HELL IS—
A PLACE WHERE LIGHT WILL NOT SHINE DOWN FOR ETERNITY.
A PLACE WHERE YOU WILL NEVER ESCAPE FROM ENDLESS PAIN.
I KNOW IT VERY WELL.
BUT IF YOU DON'T WANT TO FALL TO HELL WHILE ALIVE...
...YOU TWO SHOULD COME QUIETLY WITH ME.

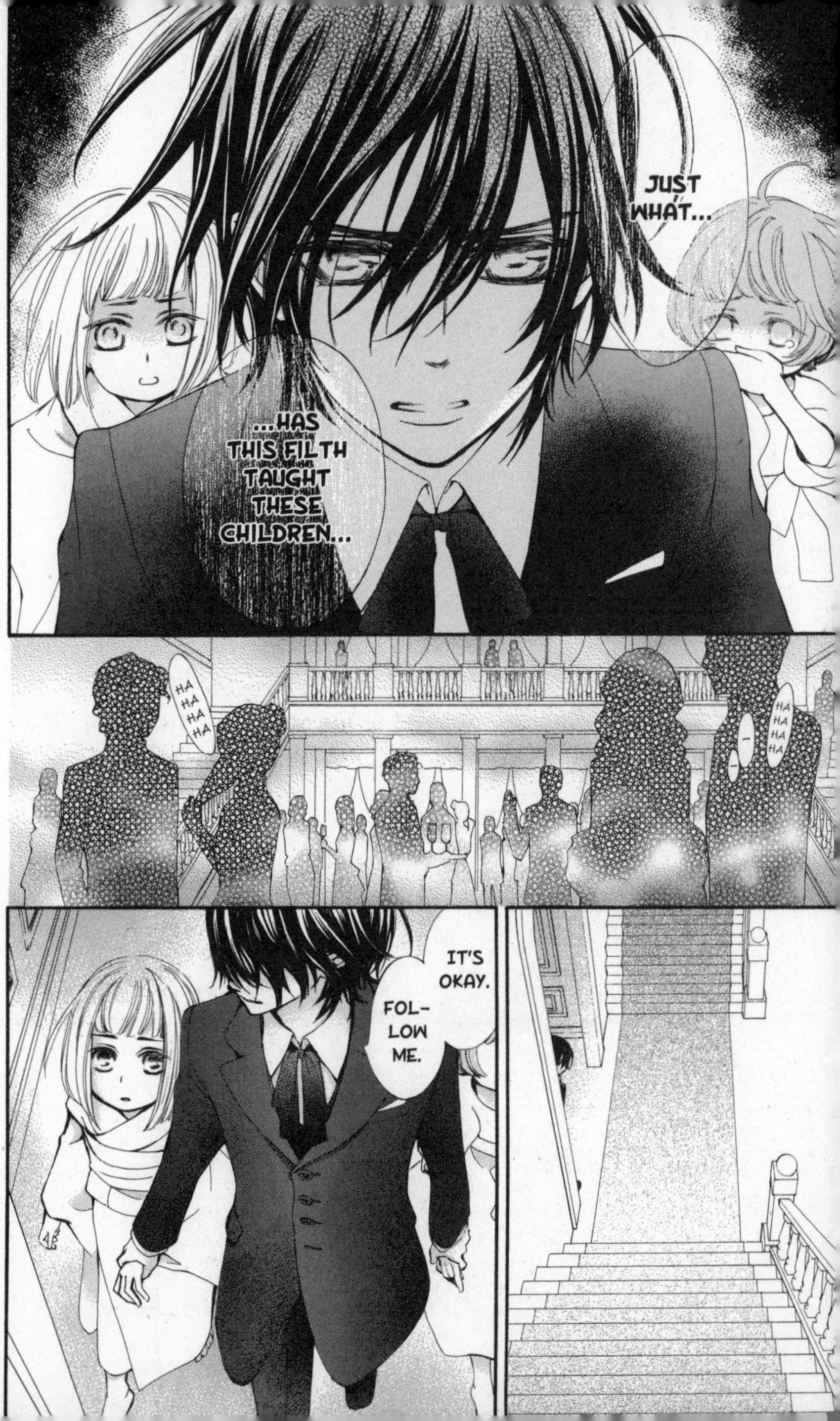
JUST WHAT...
...HAS THIS FILTH TAUGHT THESE CHILDREN...
HA HA HA HA
HA HA HA HA
IT'S OKAY.
FOL- LOW ME.

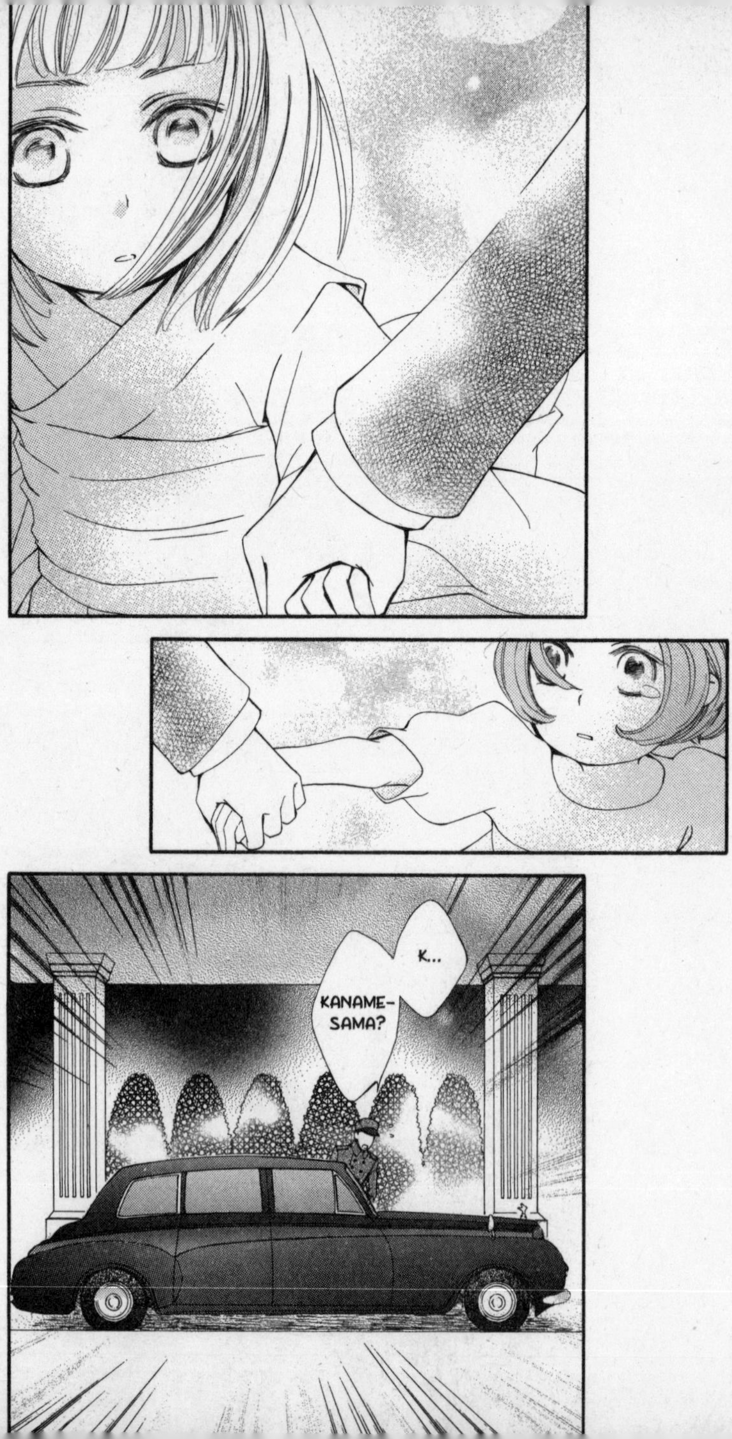
K... KANAME-SAMA?

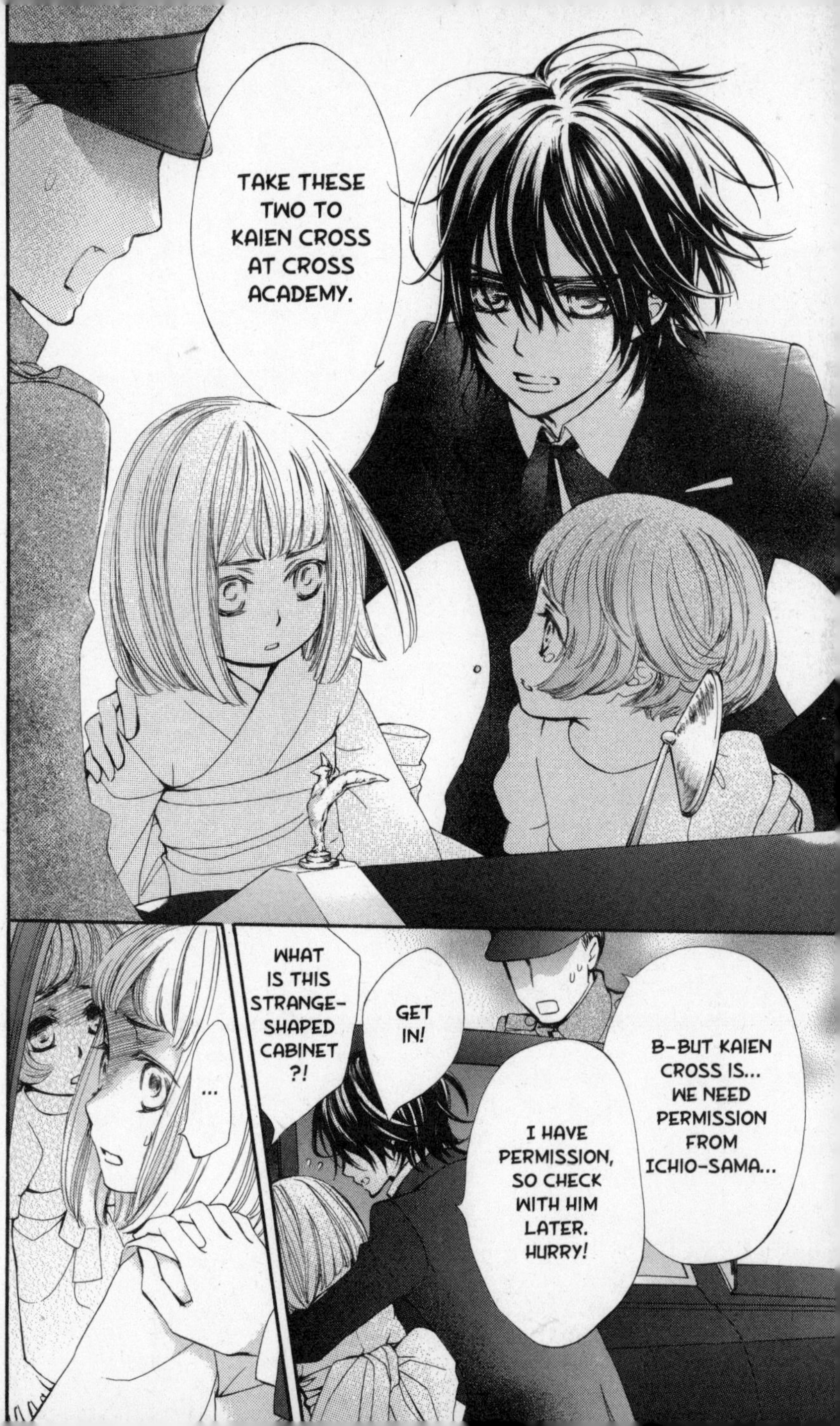
TAKE THESE TWO TO KAIEN CROSS AT CROSS ACADEMY.
B-BUT KAIEN CROSS IS... WE NEED PERMISSION FROM ICHIO-SAMA...
I HAVE PERMISSION, SO CHECK WITH HIM LATER. HURRY!
GET IN!
WHAT IS THIS STRANGE-SHAPED CABINET?!
...

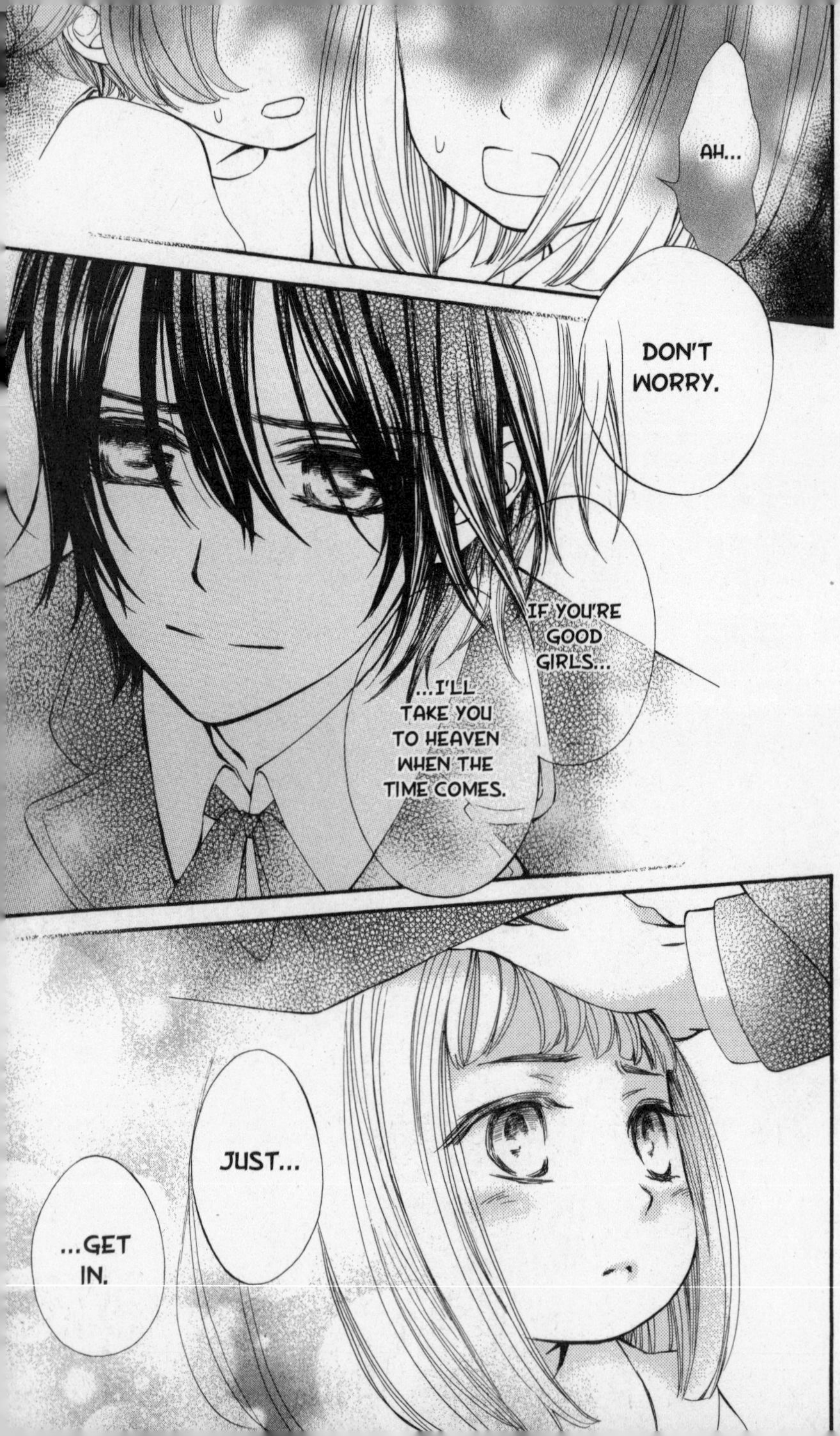
AH...
DON'T WORRY.
IF YOU'RE GOOD GIRLS...
...I'LL TAKE YOU TO HEAVEN WHEN THE TIME COMES.
JUST...
...GET IN.

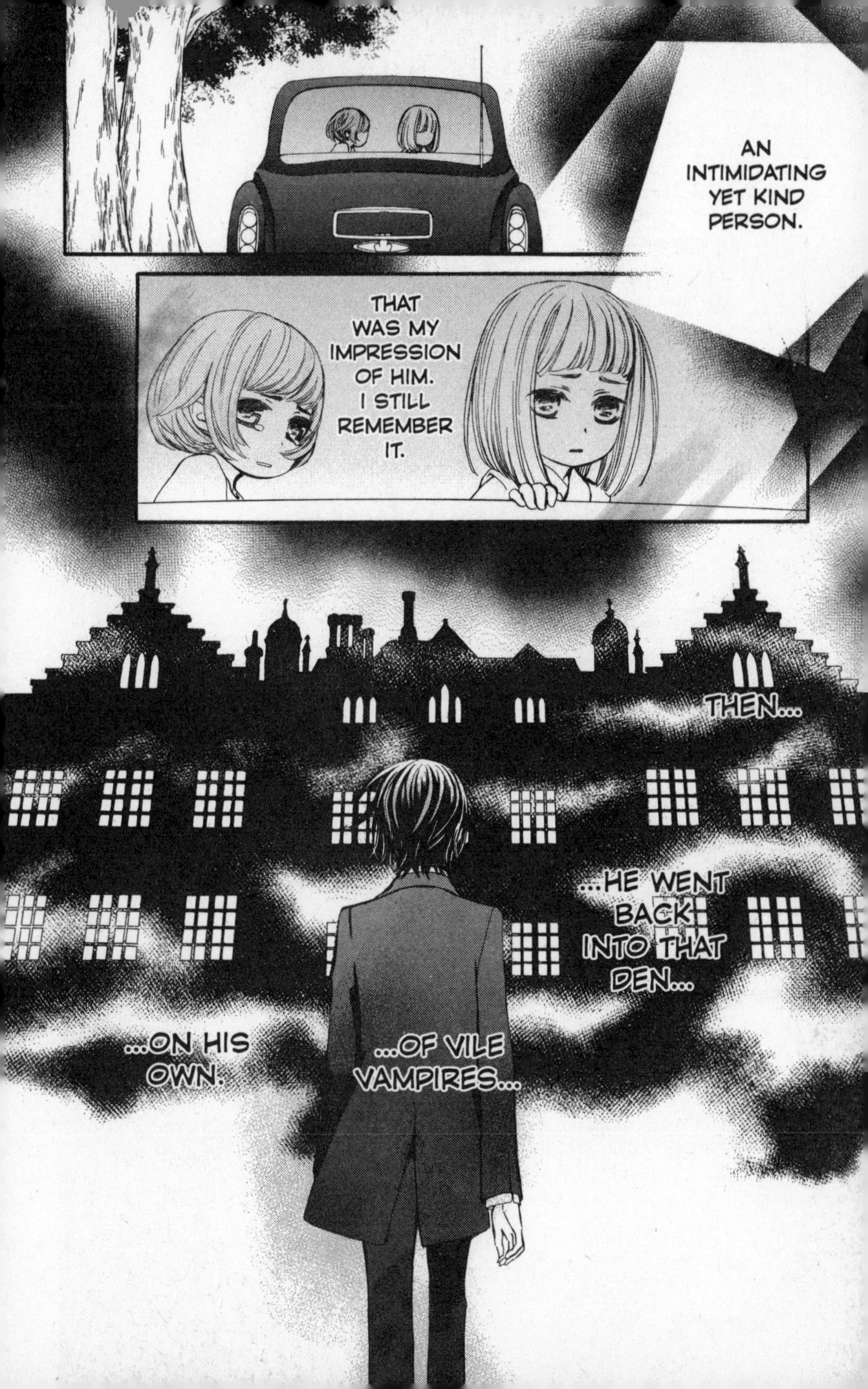
AN INTIMIDATING YET KIND PERSON.
THAT WAS MY IMPRESSION OF HIM. I STILL REMEMBER IT.
THEN...
...HE WENT BACK INTO THAT DEN...
...OF VILE VAMPIRES...
...ON HIS OWN.

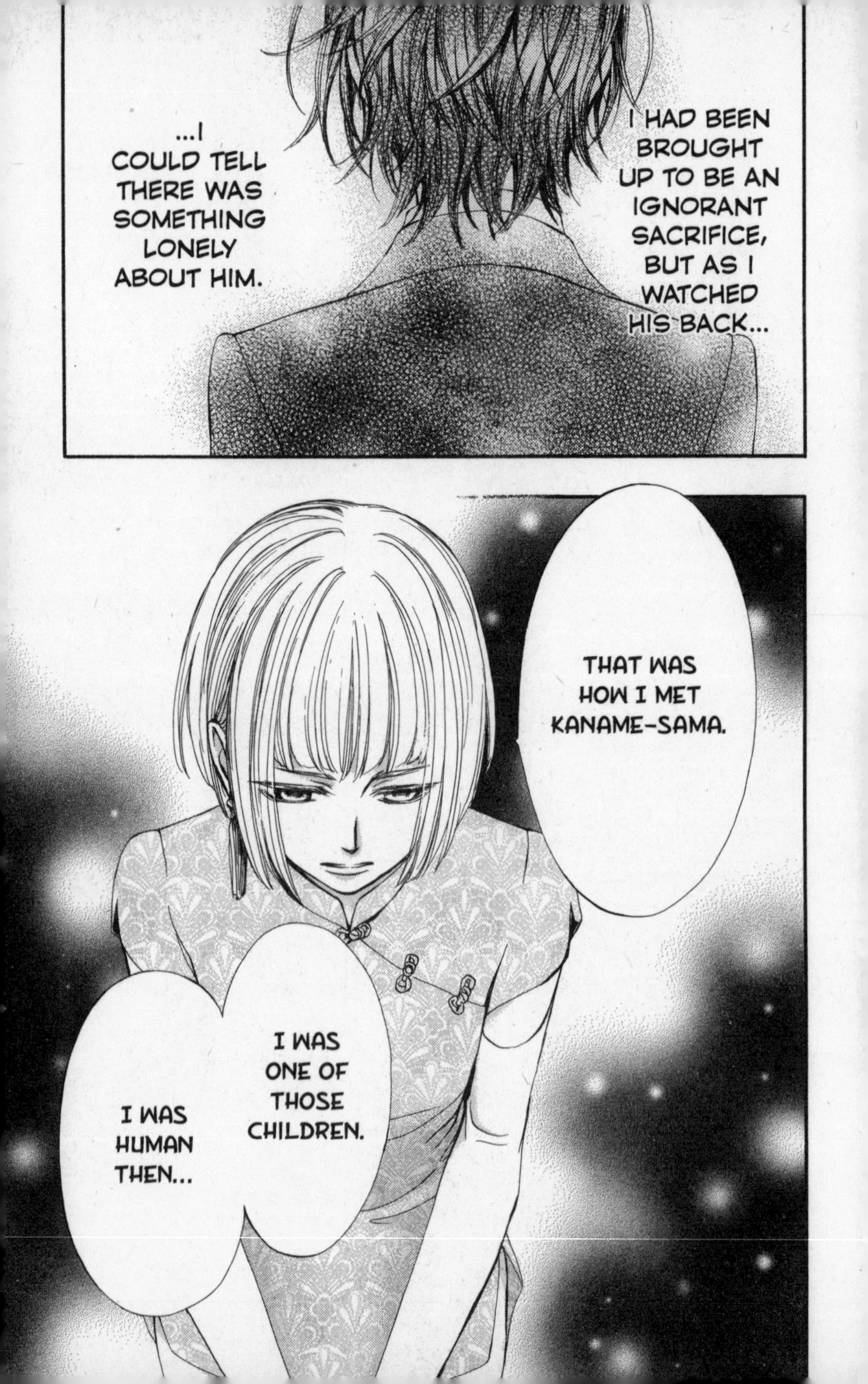
I HAD BEEN BROUGHT UP TO BE AN IGNORANT SACRIFICE, BUT AS I WATCHED HIS BACK...
...I COULD TELL THERE WAS SOMETHING LONELY ABOUT HIM.
THAT WAS HOW I MET KANAME-SAMA.
I WAS ONE OF THOSE CHILDREN.
I WAS HUMAN THEN...

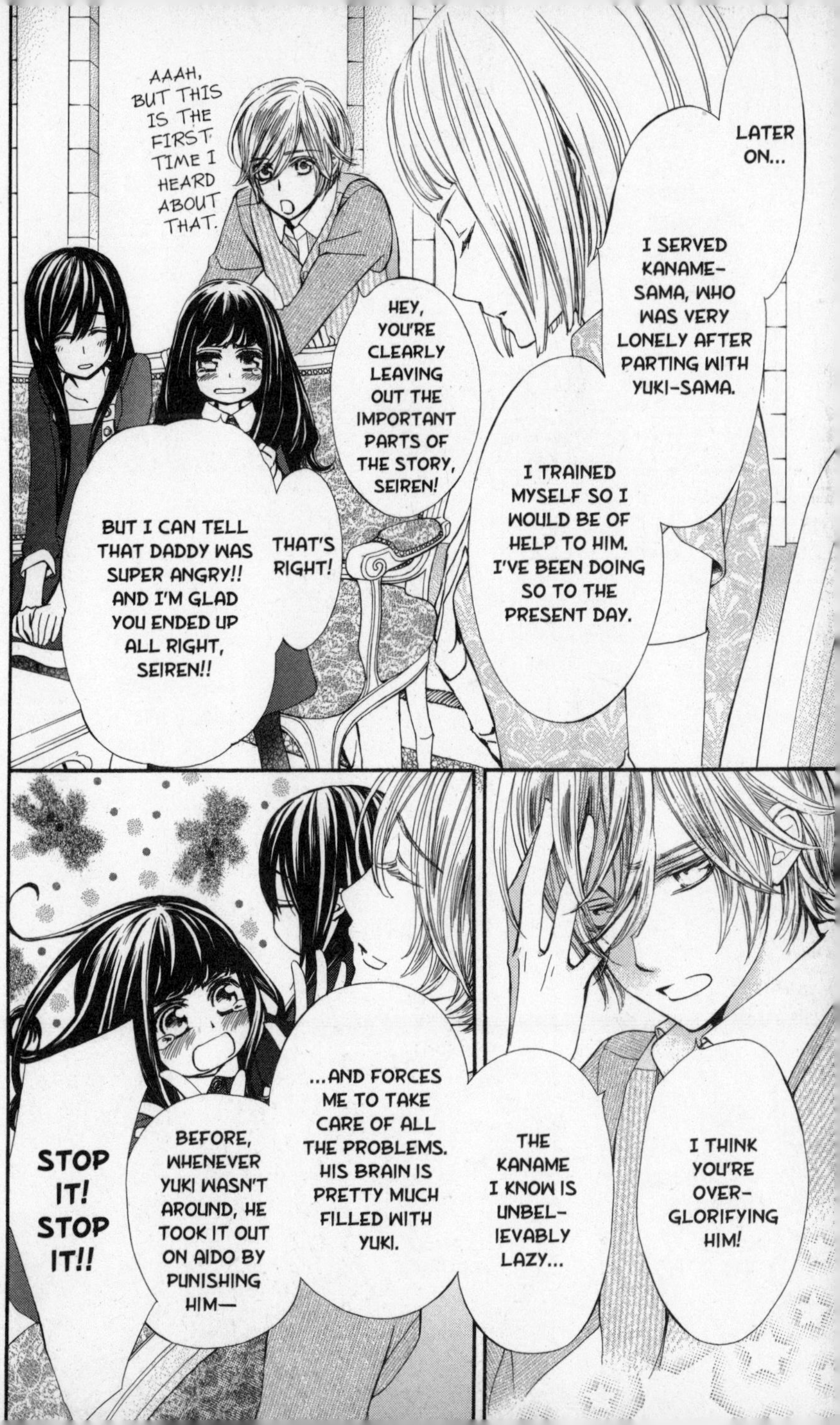
LATER ON...
I SERVED KANAME-SAMA, WHO WAS VERY LONELY AFTER PARTING WITH YUKI-SAMA.
I TRAINED MYSELF SO I WOULD BE OF HELP TO HIM. I'VE BEEN DOING SO TO THE PRESENT DAY.
HEY, YOU'RE CLEARLY LEAVING OUT THE IMPORTANT PARTS OF THE STORY, SEIREN!
AAAH, BUT THIS IS THE FIRST TIME I HEARD ABOUT THAT.
THAT'S RIGHT!
BUT I CAN TELL THAT DADDY WAS SUPER ANGRY!! AND I'M GLAD YOU ENDED UP ALL RIGHT, SEIREN!!
I THINK YOU'RE OVER-GLORIFYING HIM!
THE KANAME I KNOW IS UNBEL-IEVABLY LAZY...
...AND FORCES ME TO TAKE CARE OF ALL THE PROBLEMS. HIS BRAIN IS PRETTY MUCH FILLED WITH YUKI.
BEFORE, WHENEVER YUKI WASN'T AROUND, HE TOOK IT OUT ON AIDO BY PUNISHING HIM—
STOP IT! STOP IT!!

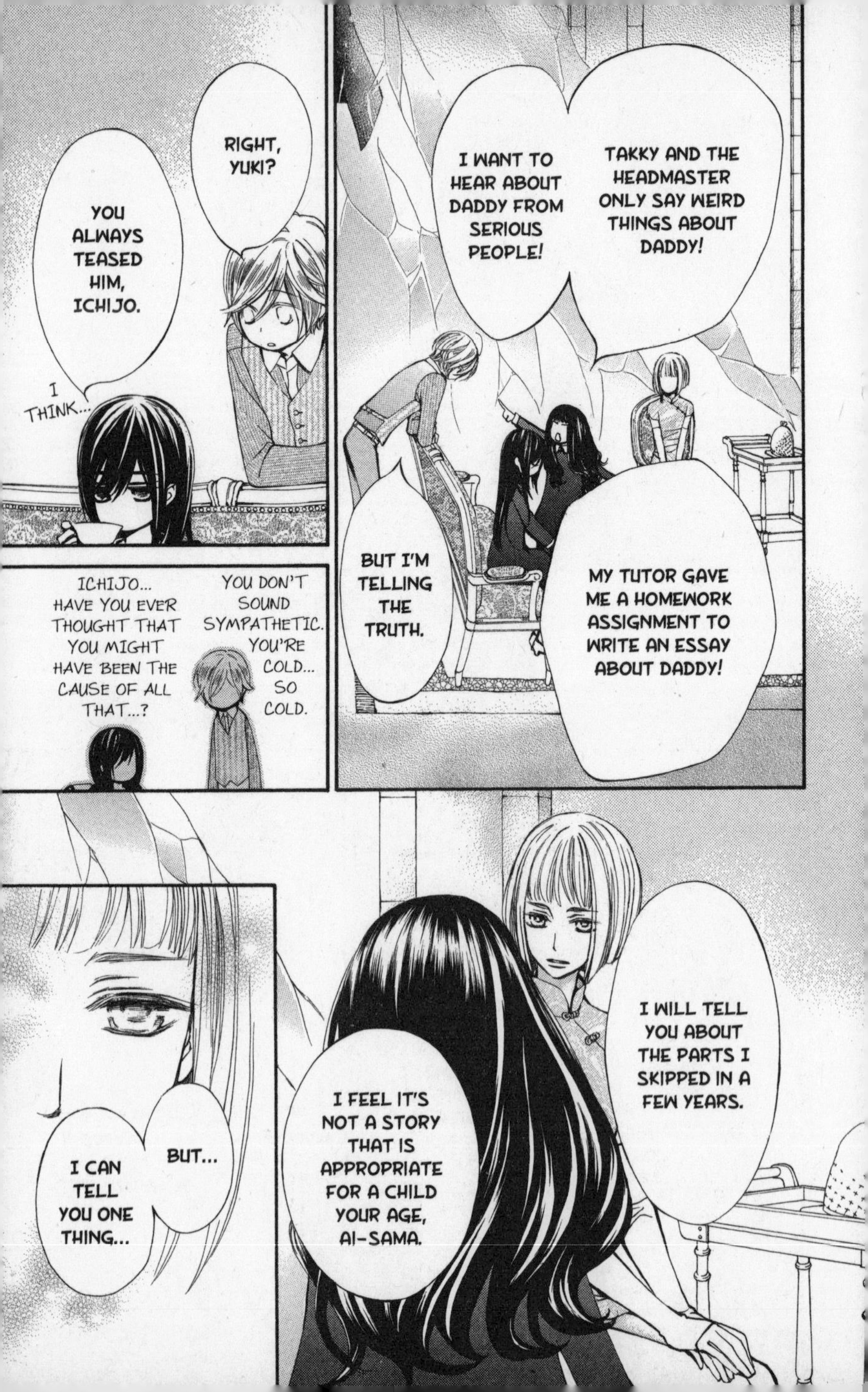
TAKKY AND THE HEADMASTER ONLY SAY WEIRD THINGS ABOUT DADDY!
I WANT TO HEAR ABOUT DADDY FROM SERIOUS PEOPLE!
MY TUTOR GAVE ME A HOMEWORK ASSIGNMENT TO WRITE AN ESSAY ABOUT DADDY!
BUT I'M TELLING THE TRUTH.
RIGHT, YUKI?
YOU ALWAYS TEASED HIM, ICHIJO.
I THINK...
YOU DON'T SOUND SYMPATHETIC. YOU'RE COLD... SO COLD.
ICHIJO... HAVE YOU EVER THOUGHT THAT YOU MIGHT HAVE BEEN THE CAUSE OF ALL THAT...?
I WILL TELL YOU ABOUT THE PARTS I SKIPPED IN A FEW YEARS.
I FEEL IT'S NOT A STORY THAT IS APPROPRIATE FOR A CHILD YOUR AGE, AI-SAMA.
BUT...
I CAN TELL YOU ONE THING...

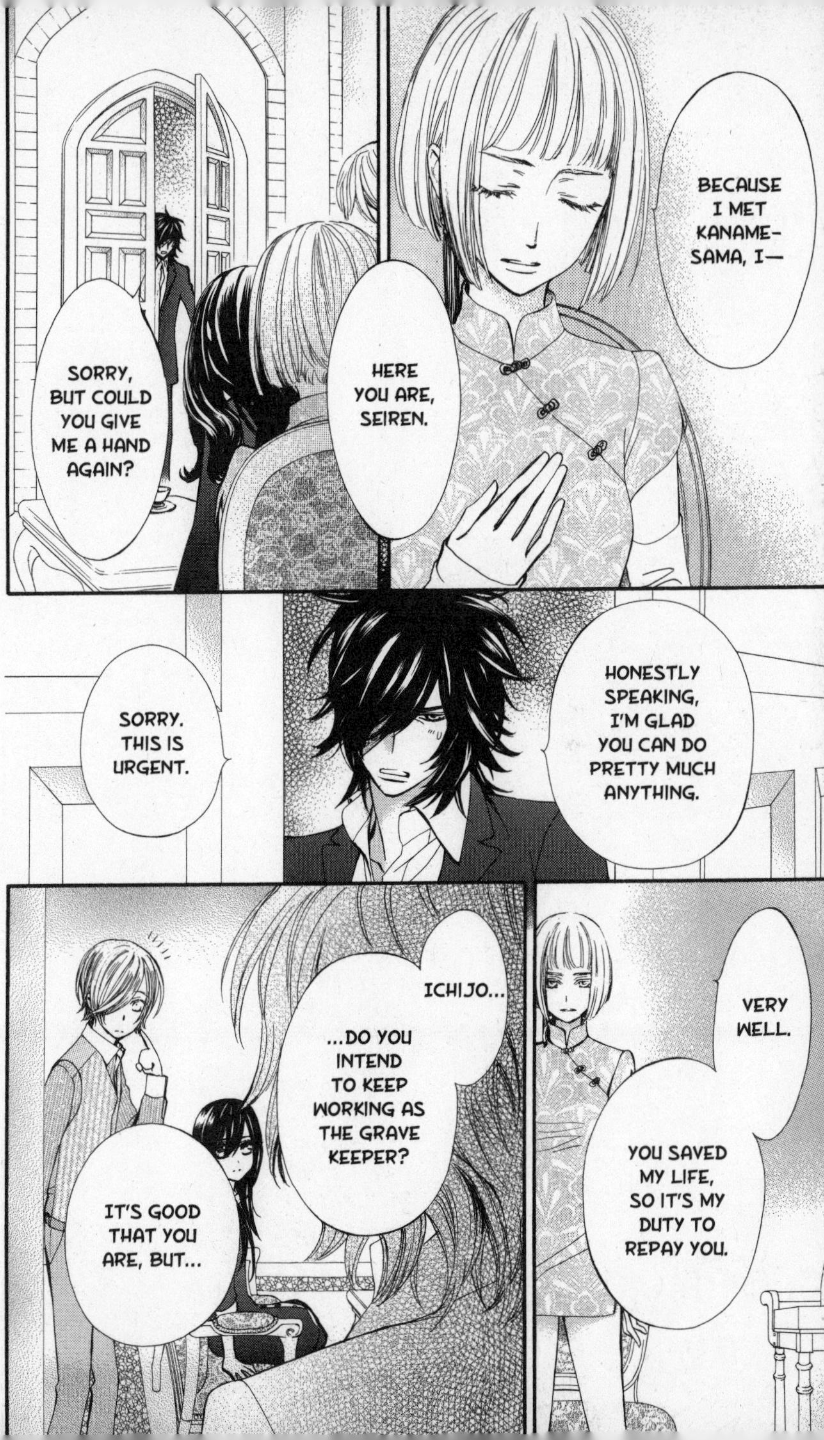
BECAUSE I MET KANAME-SAMA, I—
HERE YOU ARE, SEIREN.
SORRY, BUT COULD YOU GIVE ME A HAND AGAIN?
HONESTLY SPEAKING, I'M GLAD YOU CAN DO PRETTY MUCH ANYTHING.
SORRY. THIS IS URGENT.
VERY WELL.
YOU SAVED MY LIFE, SO IT'S MY DUTY TO REPAY YOU.
ICHIJO...
...DO YOU INTEND TO KEEP WORKING AS THE GRAVE KEEPER?
IT'S GOOD THAT YOU ARE, BUT...

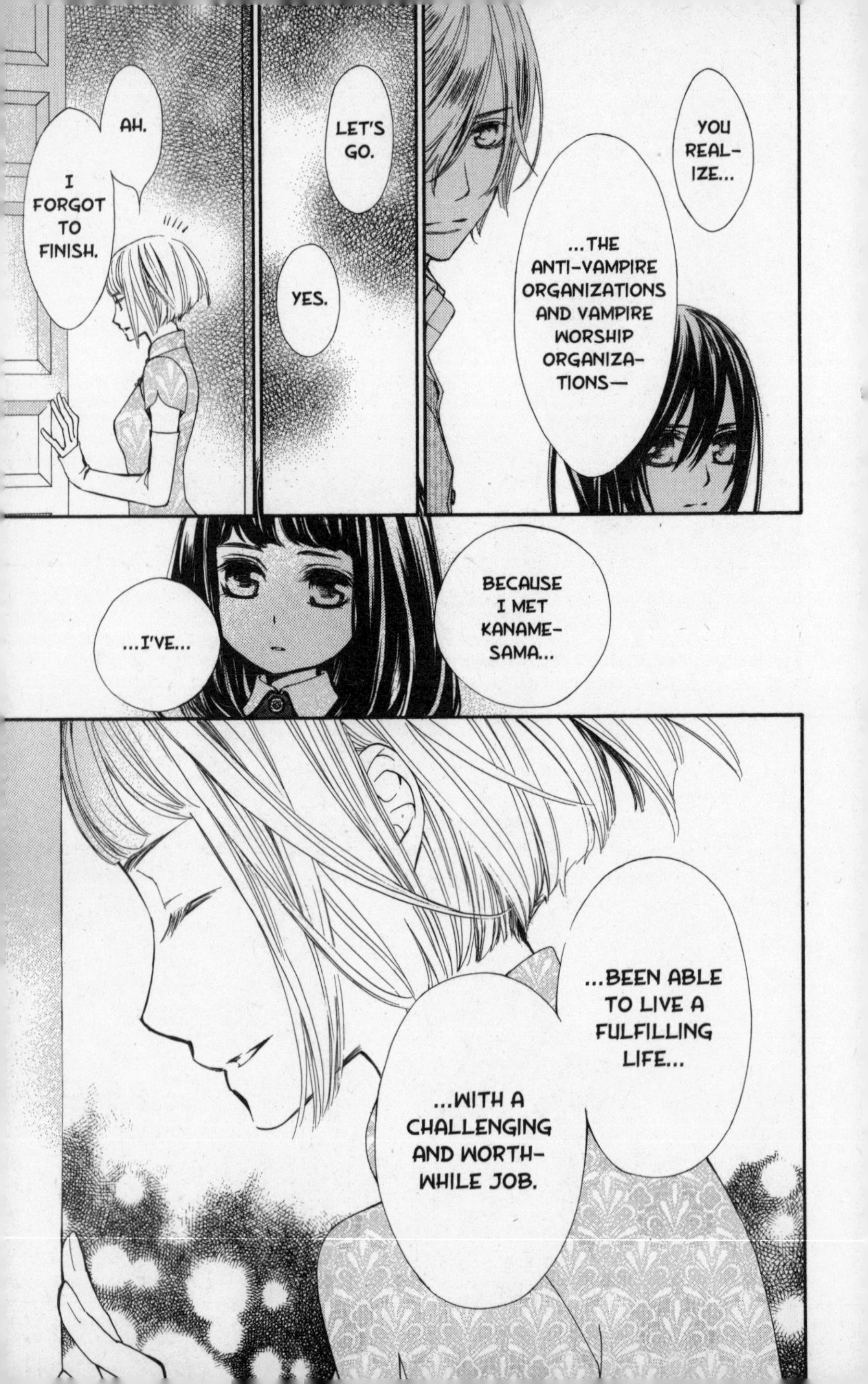
YOU REAL-IZE...
...THE ANTI-VAMPIRE ORGANIZATIONS AND VAMPIRE WORSHIP ORGANIZA-TIONS—
LET'S GO.
YES.
AH.
I FORGOT TO FINISH.
BECAUSE I MET KANAME-SAMA...
...I'VE...
...BEEN ABLE TO LIVE A FULFILLING LIFE...
...WITH A CHALLENGING AND WORTH-WHILE JOB.

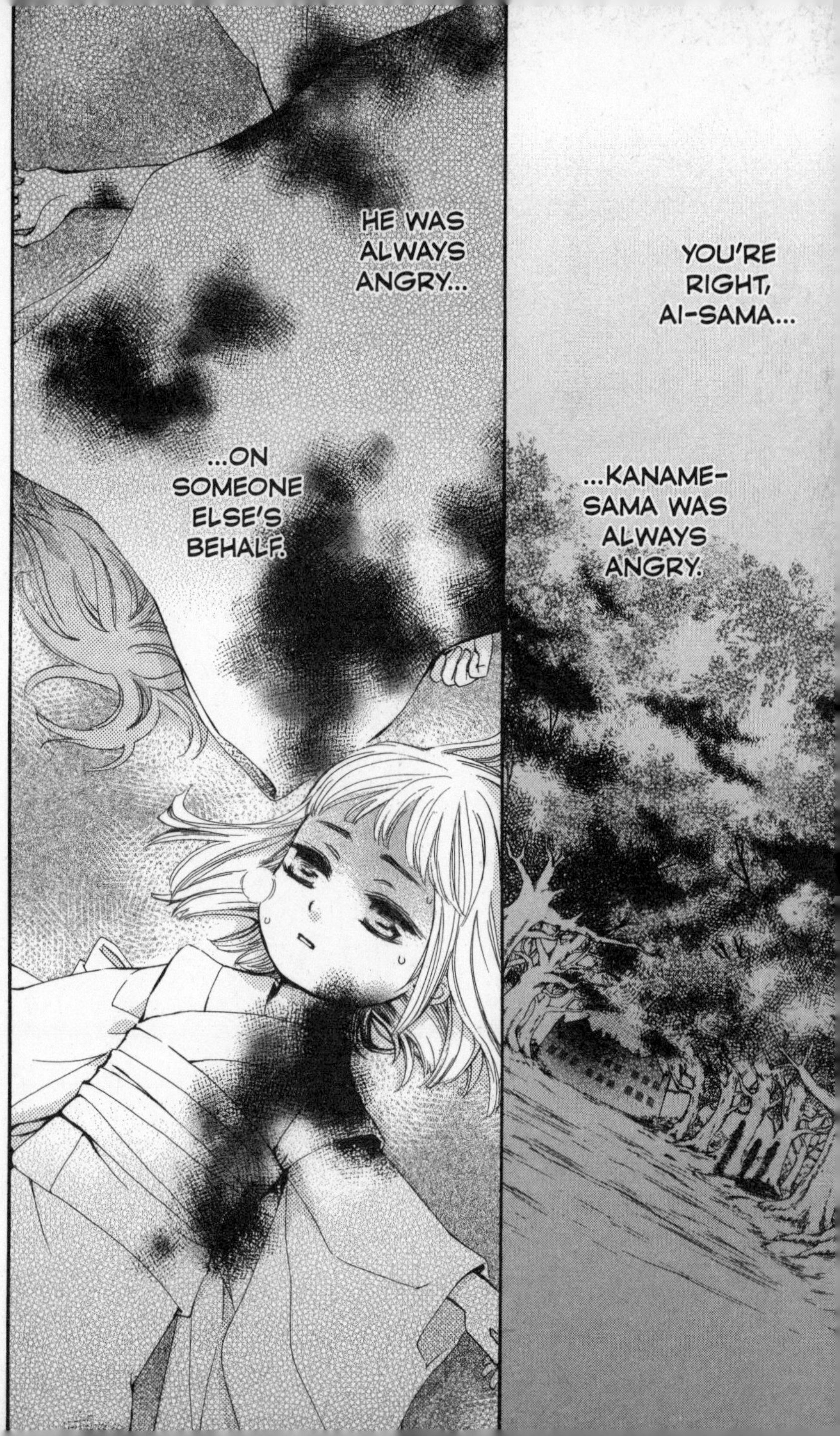
YOU'RE RIGHT, AI-SAMA...
...KANAME-SAMA WAS ALWAYS ANGRY.
HE WAS ALWAYS ANGRY...
...ON SOMEONE ELSE'S BEHALF.

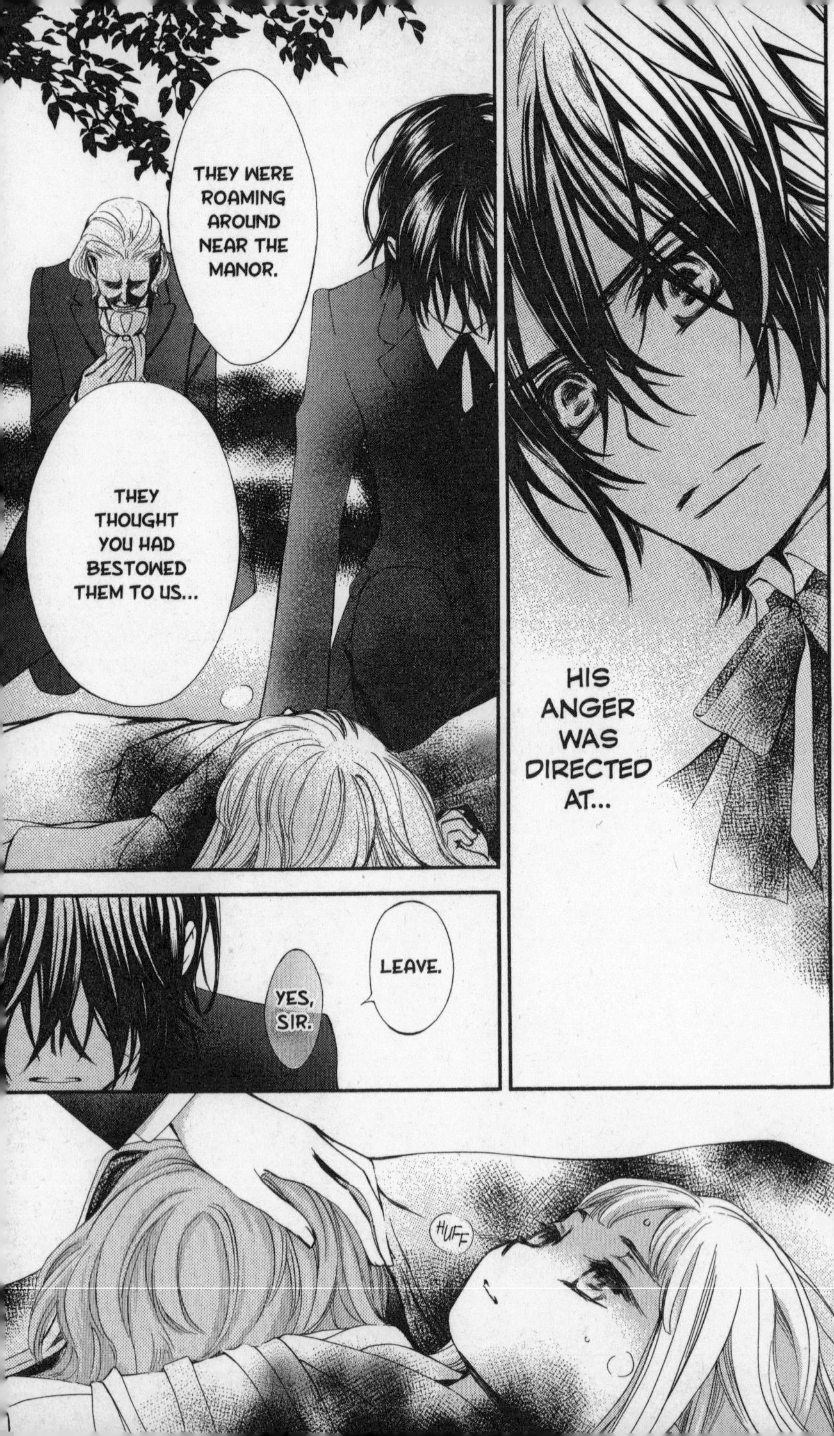

HIS ANGER WAS DIRECTED AT...
THEY WERE ROAMING AROUND NEAR THE MANOR.
THEY THOUGHT YOU HAD BESTOWED THEM TO US...
LEAVE.
YES, SIR.
HUFF

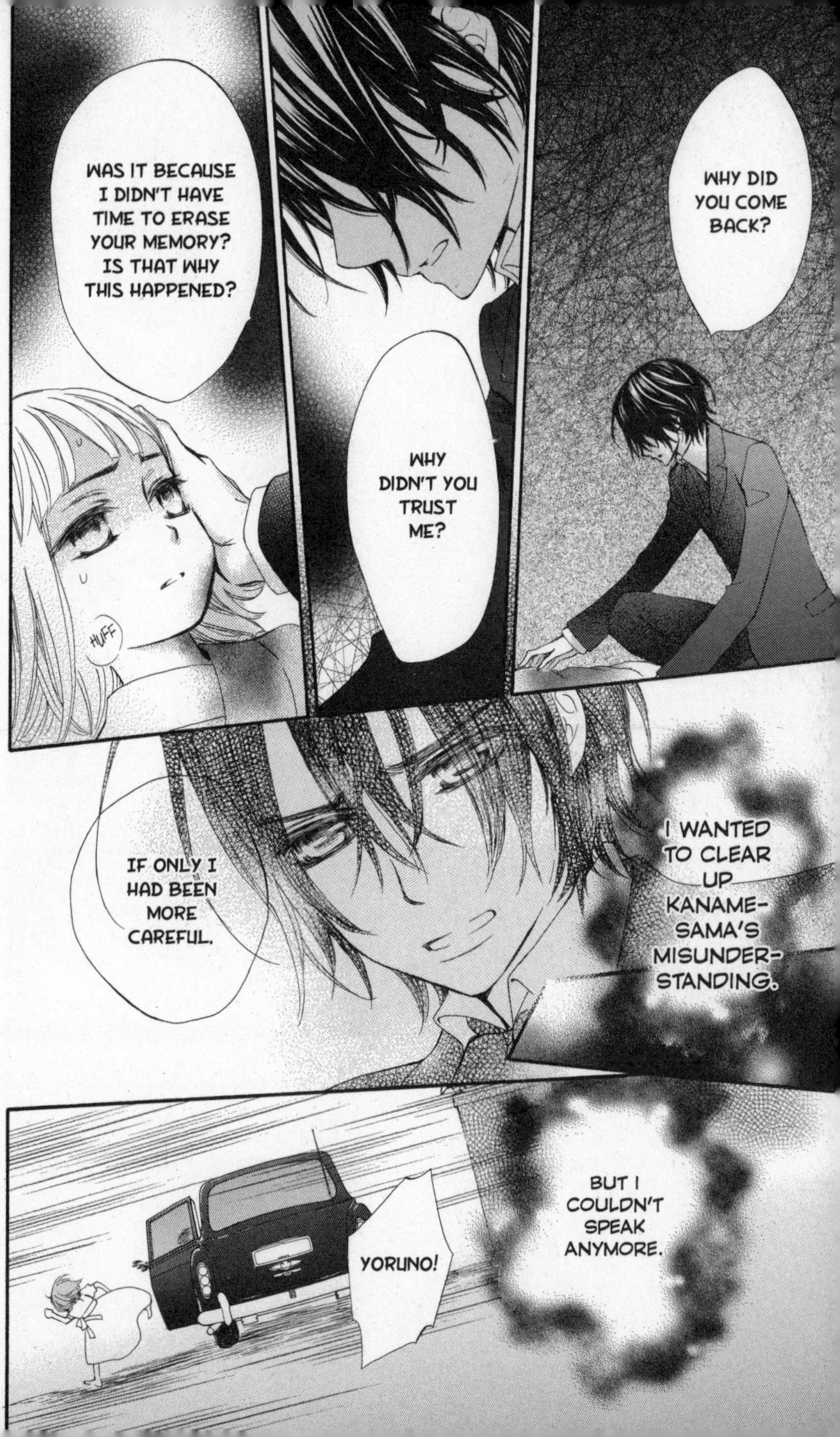
WHY DID YOU COME BACK?
WHY DIDN'T YOU TRUST ME?
WAS IT BECAUSE I DIDN'T HAVE TIME TO ERASE YOUR MEMORY? IS THAT WHY THIS HAPPENED?
HUFF
I WANTED TO CLEAR UP KANAME-SAMA'S MISUNDER-STANDING.
IF ONLY I HAD BEEN MORE CAREFUL.
BUT I COULDN'T SPEAK ANYMORE.
YORUNO!

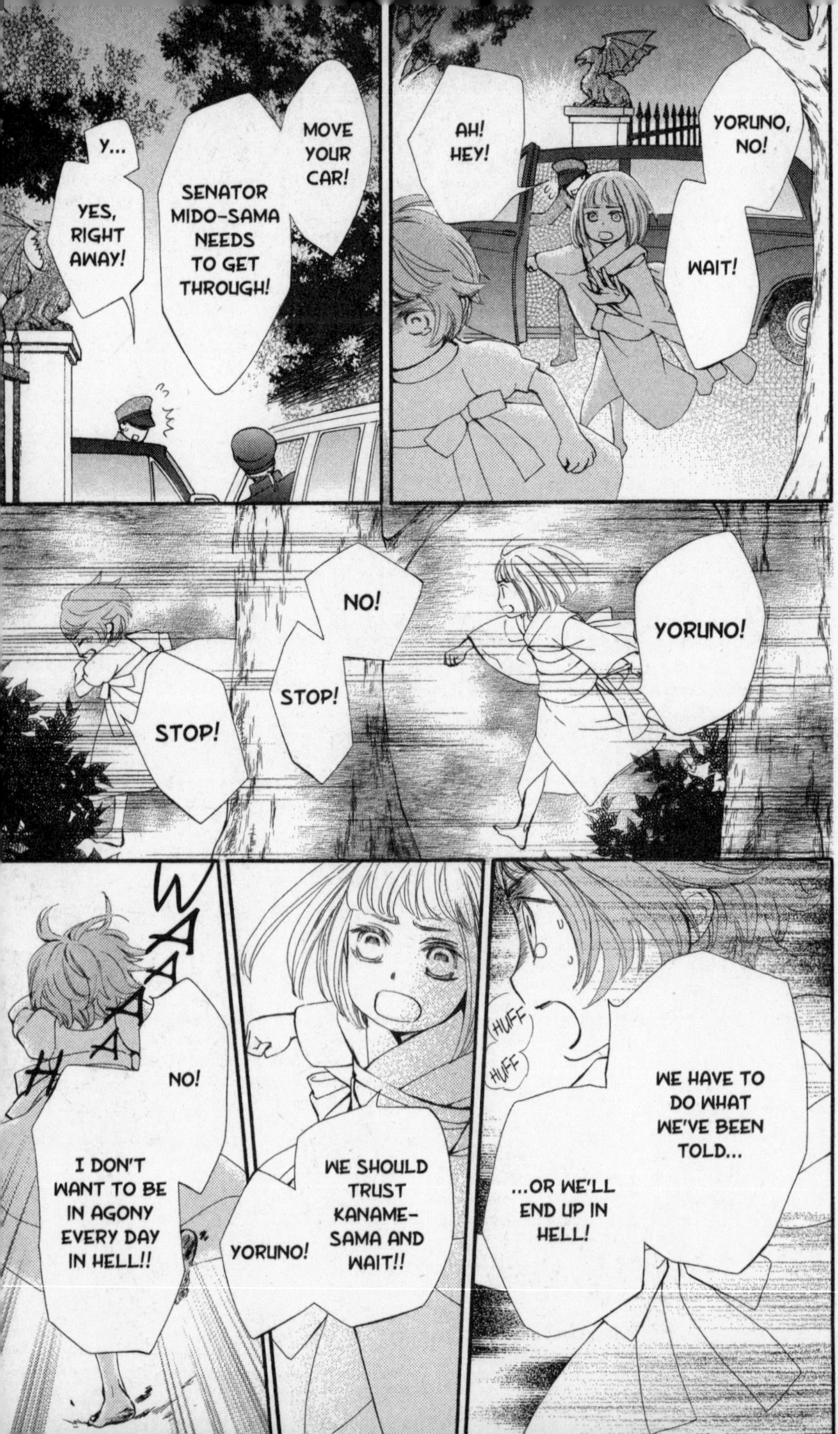
YORUNO, NO!
WAIT!
AH! HEY!
MOVE YOUR CAR!
SENATOR MIDO-SAMA NEEDS TO GET THROUGH!
Y...
YES, RIGHT AWAY!
YORUNO!
NO!
STOP!
STOP!
WE HAVE TO DO WHAT WE'VE BEEN TOLD...
HUFF
HUFF
...OR WE'LL END UP IN HELL!
WE SHOULD TRUST KANAME-SAMA AND WAIT!!
YORUNO!
WAAAAH
NO!
I DON'T WANT TO BE IN AGONY EVERY DAY IN HELL!!

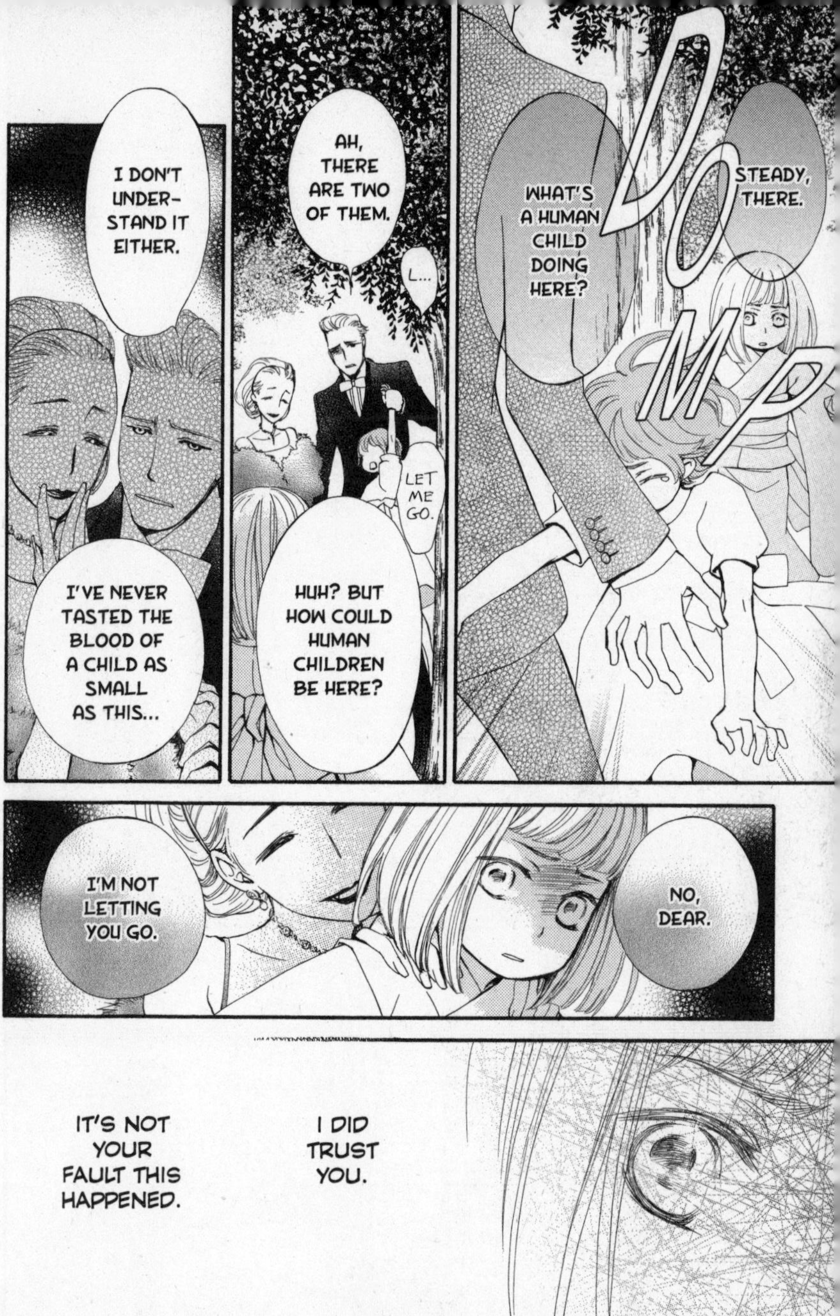
STEADY, THERE.
DOMP
WHAT'S A HUMAN CHILD DOING HERE?
AH, THERE ARE TWO OF THEM.
L...
LET ME GO.
HUH? BUT HOW COULD HUMAN CHILDREN BE HERE?
I DON'T UNDERSTAND IT EITHER.
I'VE NEVER TASTED THE BLOOD OF A CHILD AS SMALL AS THIS...
NO, DEAR.
I'M NOT LETTING YOU GO.
I DID TRUST YOU.
IT'S NOT YOUR FAULT THIS HAPPENED.

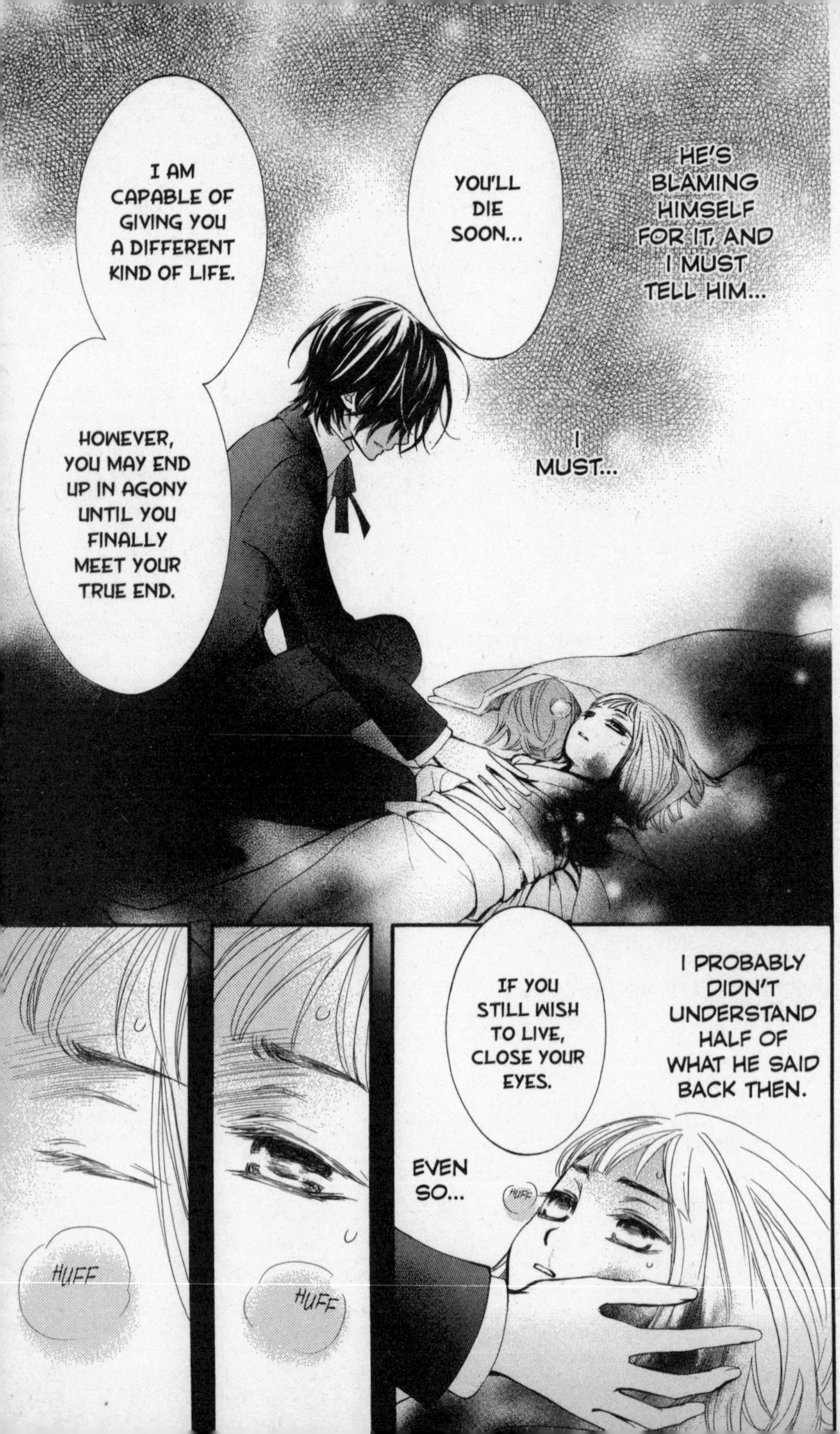
HE'S BLAMING HIMSELF FOR IT, AND I MUST TELL HIM...
I MUST...
YOU'LL DIE SOON...
I AM CAPABLE OF GIVING YOU A DIFFERENT KIND OF LIFE.
HOWEVER, YOU MAY END UP IN AGONY UNTIL YOU FINALLY MEET YOUR TRUE END.
I PROBABLY DIDN'T UNDERSTAND HALF OF WHAT HE SAID BACK THEN.
IF YOU STILL WISH TO LIVE, CLOSE YOUR EYES.
EVEN SO...
HUFF
HUFF
HUFF

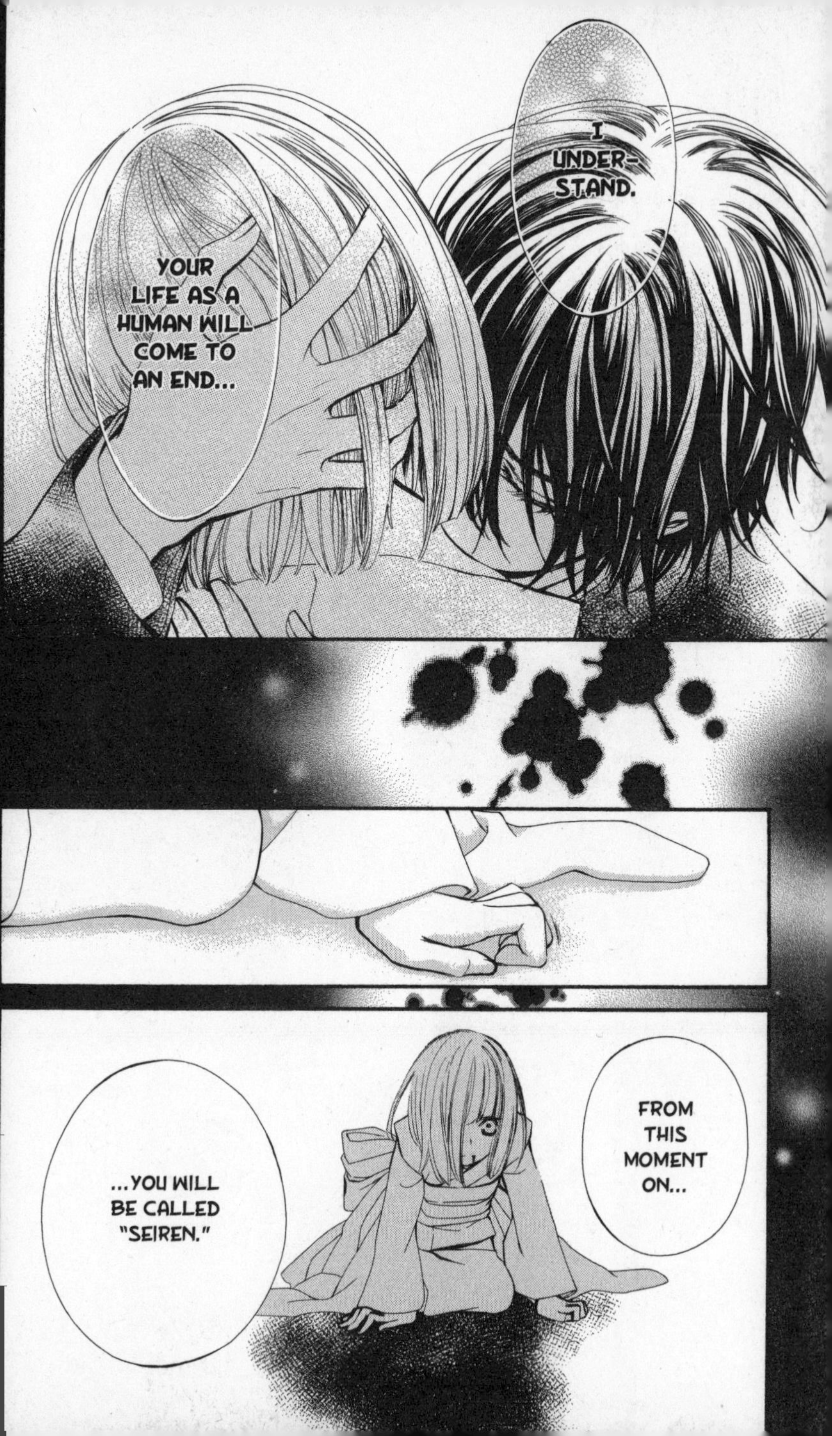
I UNDER-STAND.
YOUR LIFE AS A HUMAN WILL COME TO AN END...
FROM THIS MOMENT ON...
...YOU WILL BE CALLED "SEIREN."

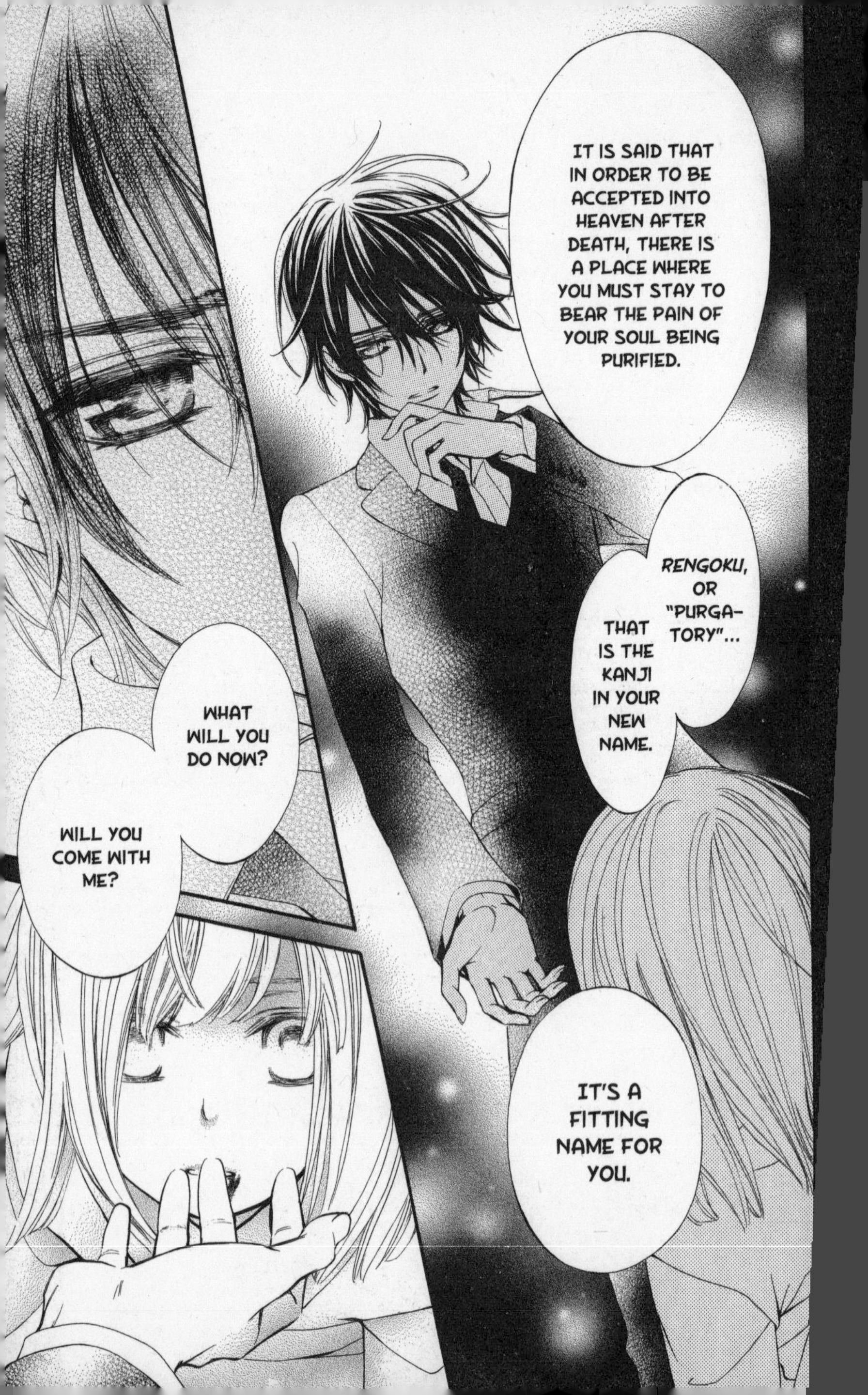
IT IS SAID THAT IN ORDER TO BE ACCEPTED INTO HEAVEN AFTER DEATH, THERE IS A PLACE WHERE YOU MUST STAY TO BEAR THE PAIN OF YOUR SOUL BEING PURIFIED.
RENGOKU, OR "PURGA-TORY"...
THAT IS THE KANJI IN YOUR NEW NAME.
IT'S A FITTING NAME FOR YOU.
WHAT WILL YOU DO NOW?
WILL YOU COME WITH ME?

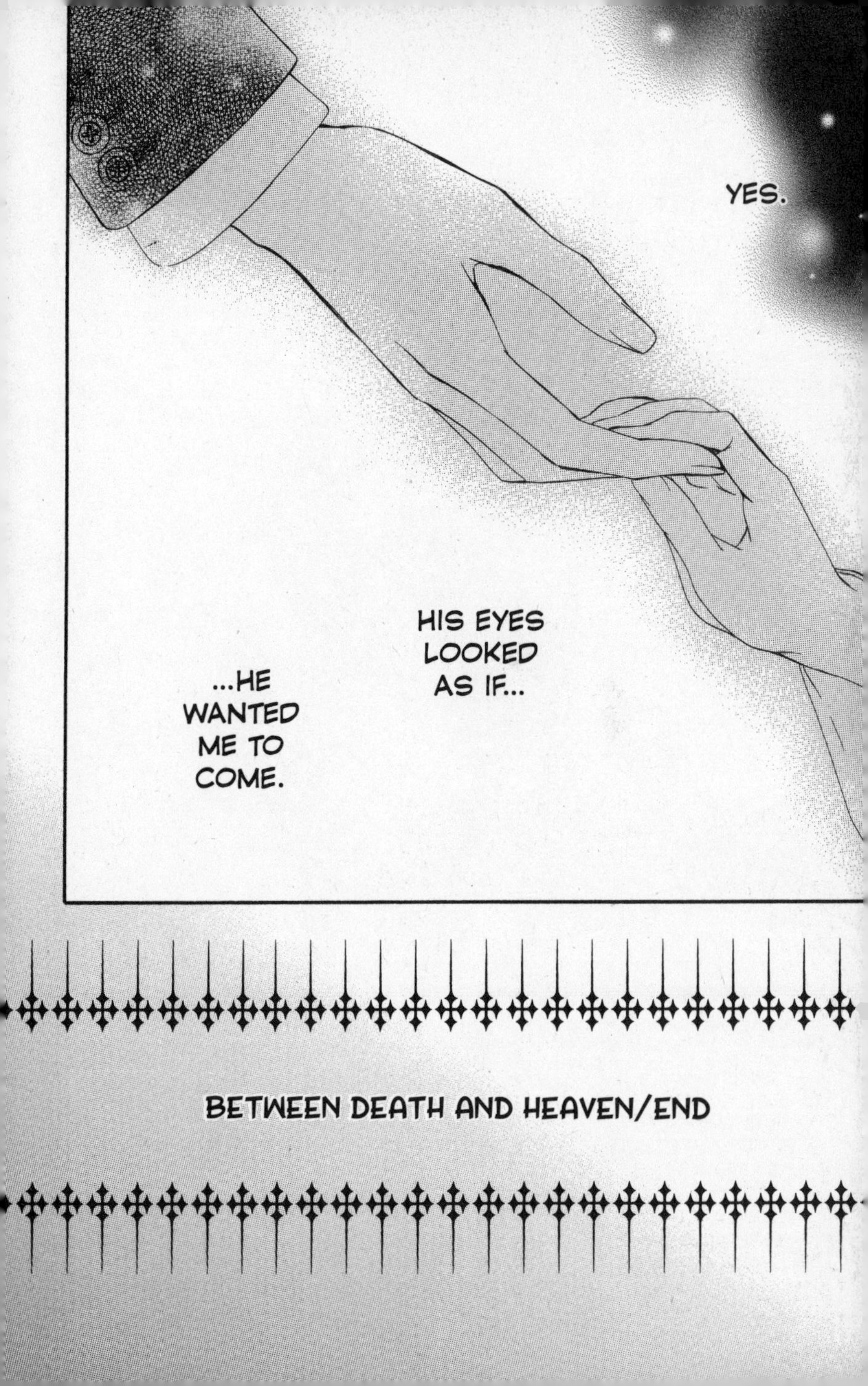
YES.
HIS EYES LOOKED AS IF...
...HE WANTED ME TO COME.

BETWEEN DEATH AND HEAVEN/END

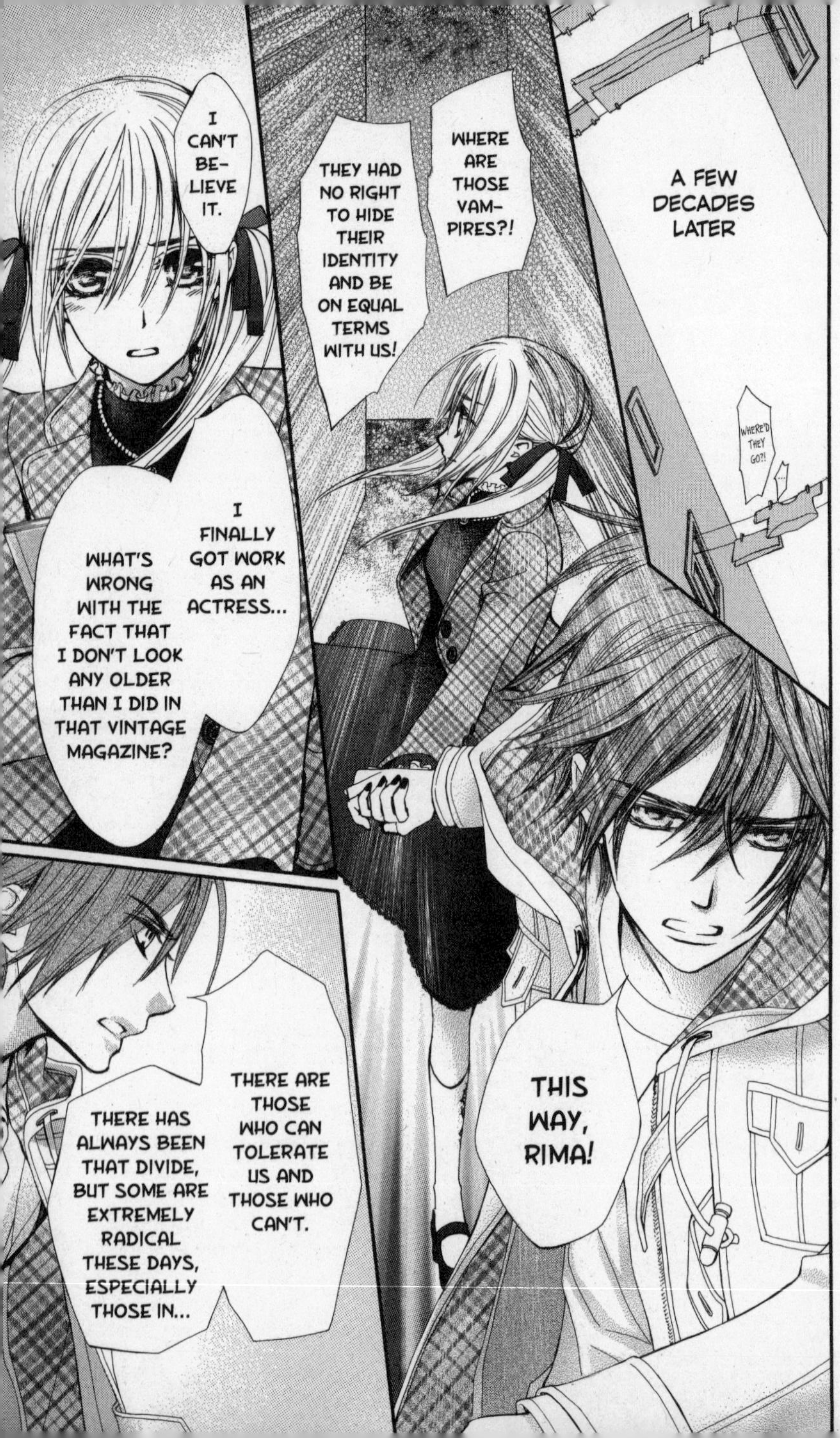
A FEW DECADES LATER
WHERE'D THEY GO?!
...
WHERE ARE THOSE VAM-PIRES?!
THEY HAD NO RIGHT TO HIDE THEIR IDENTITY AND BE ON EQUAL TERMS WITH US!
I CAN'T BE-LIEVE IT.
I FINALLY GOT WORK AS AN ACTRESS...
WHAT'S WRONG WITH THE FACT THAT I DON'T LOOK ANY OLDER THAN I DID IN THAT VINTAGE MAGAZINE?
THIS WAY, RIMA!
THERE ARE THOSE WHO CAN TOLERATE US AND THOSE WHO CAN'T.
THERE HAS ALWAYS BEEN THAT DIVIDE, BUT SOME ARE EXTREMELY RADICAL THESE DAYS, ESPECIALLY THOSE IN...

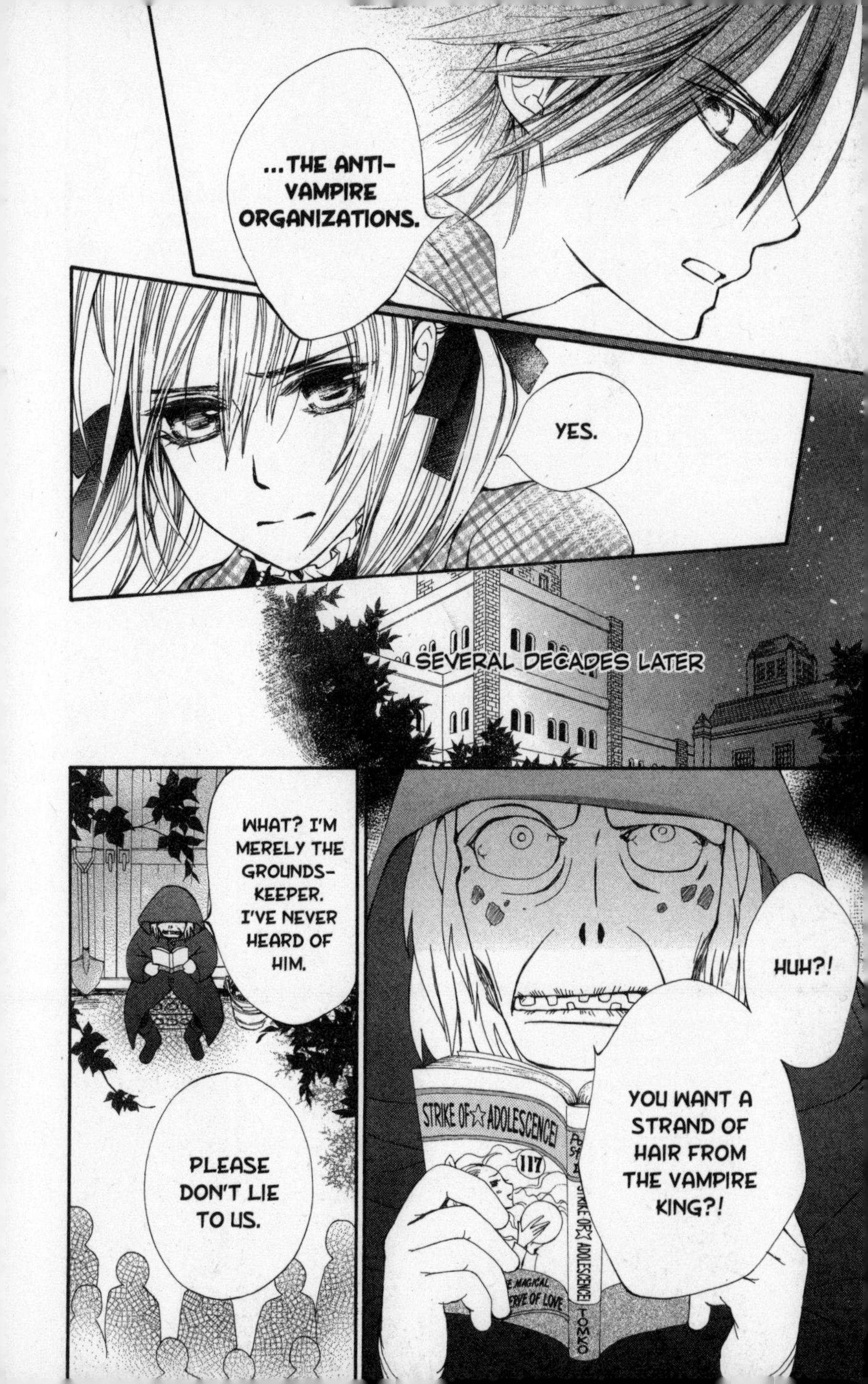
...THE ANTI-VAMPIRE ORGANIZATIONS.
YES.
SEVERAL DECADES LATER
HUH?!
YOU WANT A STRAND OF HAIR FROM THE VAMPIRE KING?!
STRIKE OF☆ADOLESCENCE!
117
STRIKE OF☆ADOLESCENCE!
WHAT? I'M MERELY THE GROUNDS-KEEPER. I'VE NEVER HEARD OF HIM.
PLEASE DON'T LIE TO US.

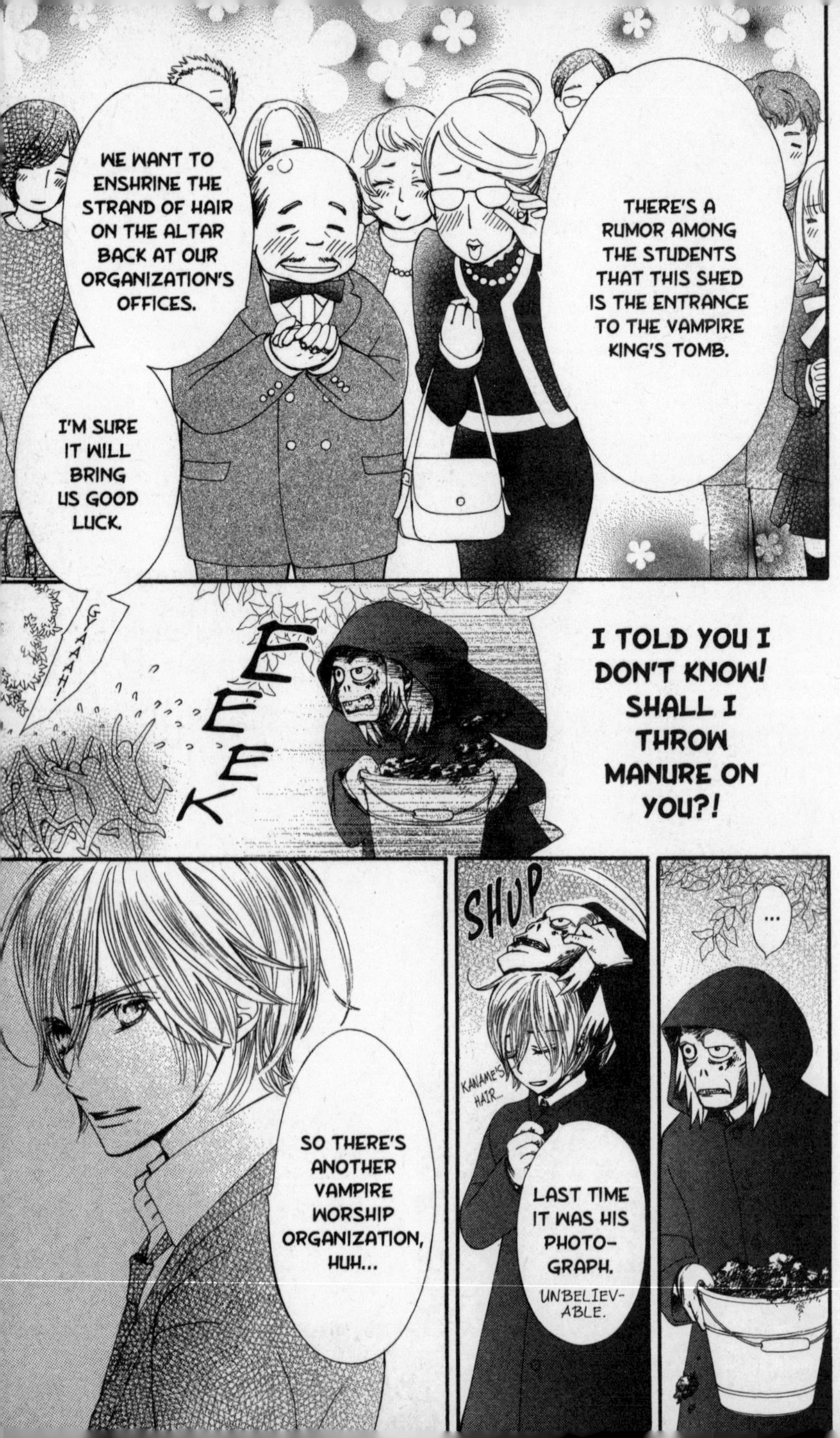
THERE'S A RUMOR AMONG THE STUDENTS THAT THIS SHED IS THE ENTRANCE TO THE VAMPIRE KING'S TOMB.
WE WANT TO ENSHRINE THE STRAND OF HAIR ON THE ALTAR BACK AT OUR ORGANIZATION'S OFFICES.
I'M SURE IT WILL BRING US GOOD LUCK.
I TOLD YOU I DON'T KNOW! SHALL I THROW MANURE ON YOU?!
EEEK
GYAAAH!
...
SHUP
KANAME'S HAIR...
LAST TIME IT WAS HIS PHOTOGRAPH.
UNBELIEVABLE.
SO THERE'S ANOTHER VAMPIRE WORSHIP ORGANIZATION, HUH...

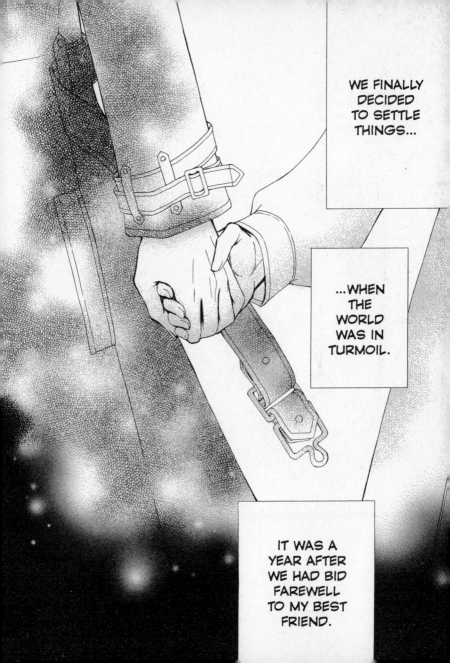

WE FINALLY DECIDED TO SETTLE THINGS...

...WHEN THE WORLD WAS IN TURMOIL.

IT WAS A YEAR AFTER WE HAD BID FAREWELL TO MY BEST FRIEND.

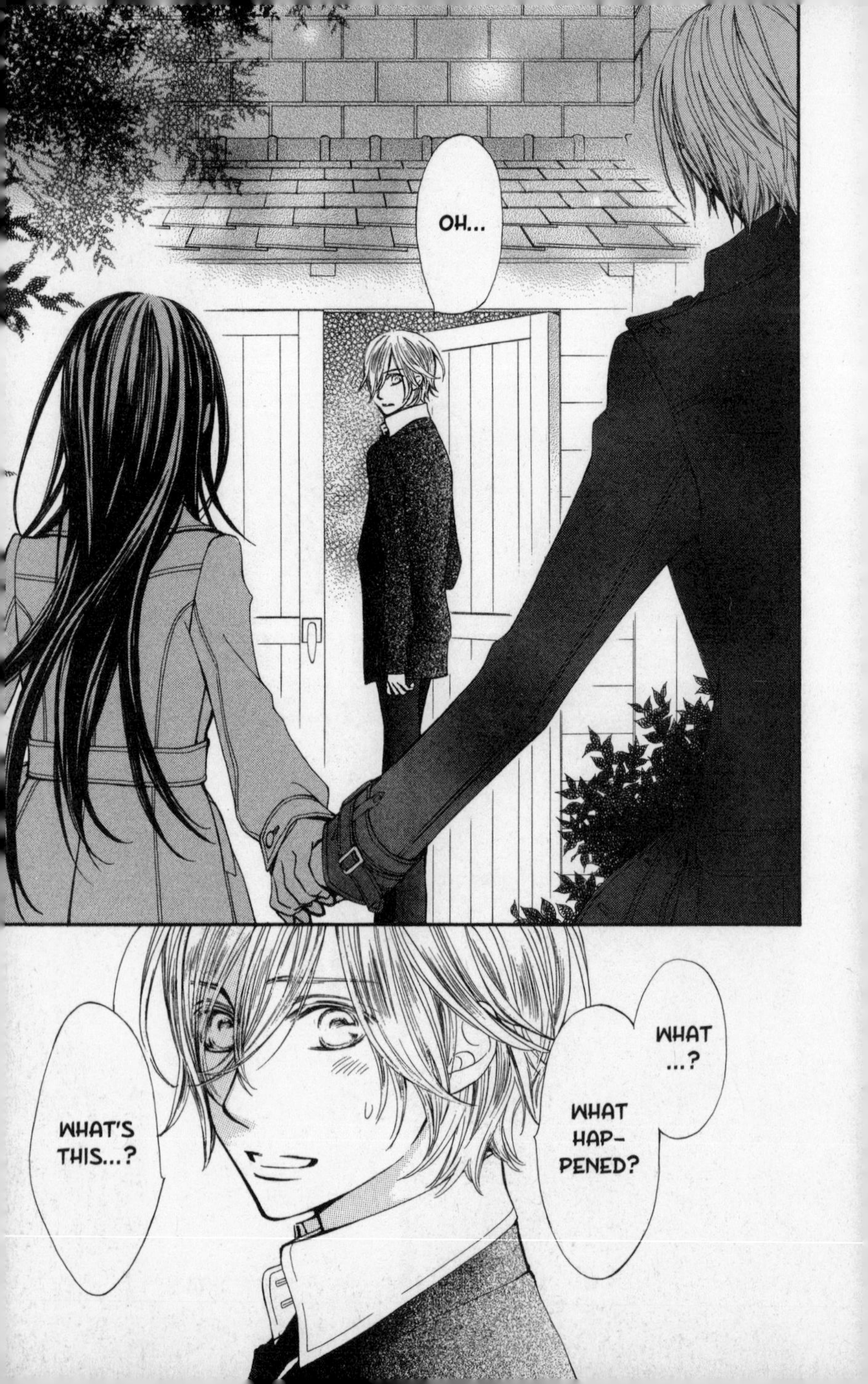
OH...
WHAT ...?
WHAT HAP-PENED?
WHAT'S THIS...?

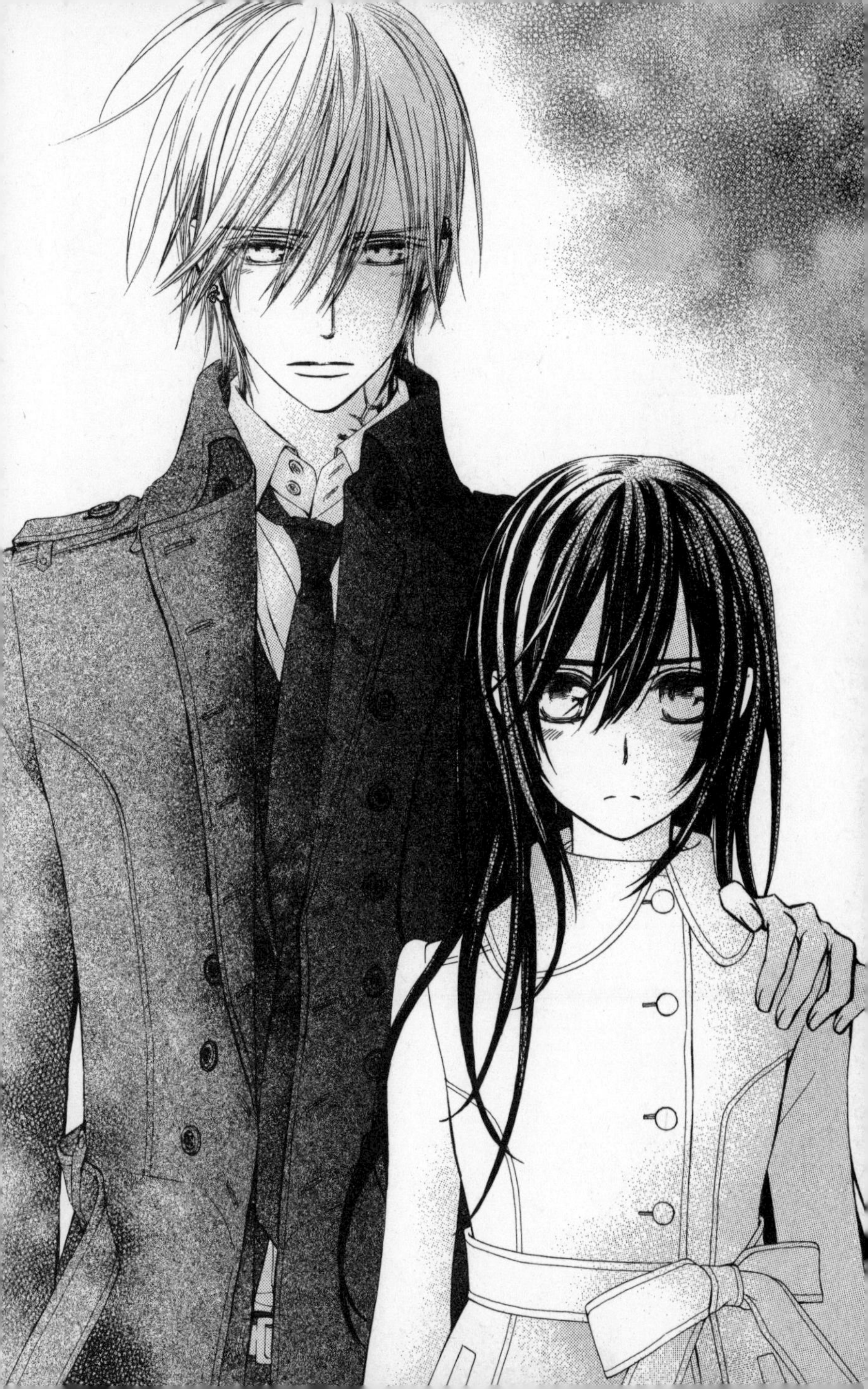

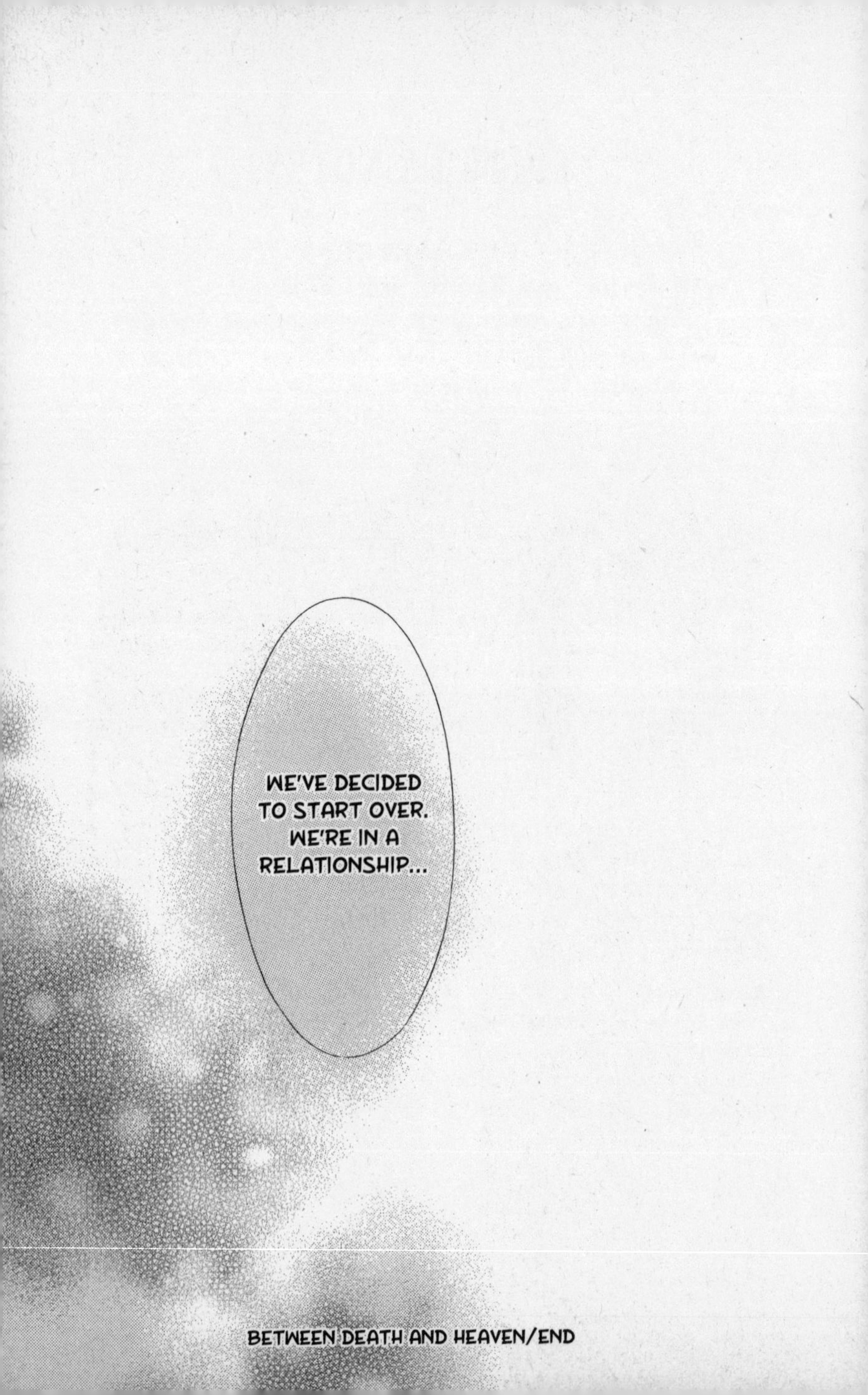
WE'VE DECIDED TO START OVER. WE'RE IN A RELATIONSHIP...
BETWEEN DEATH AND HEAVEN/END

# ❧ EDITOR'S NOTES ❧

## CHARACTERS

Matsuri Hino puts careful thought into the names of her characters in *Vampire Knight*. Below is the collection of characters throughout the manga. Each character's name is presented family name first, per the kanji reading.

黒主優姫

**Cross Yuki**
Yuki's last name, *Kurosu*, is the Japanese pronunciation of the English word "cross." However, the kanji has a different meaning—*kuro* means "black" and *su* means "master." Her first name is a combination of *yuu*, meaning "tender" or "kind," and *ki*, meaning "princess."

錐生零

**Kiryu Zero**
Zero's first name is the kanji for *rei*, meaning "zero." In his last name, *Kiryu*, the *ki* means "auger" or "drill" and the *ryu* means "life."

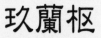

**Kuran Kaname**

*Kaname* means "hinge" or "door." The kanji for his last name is a combination of the old-fashioned way of writing *ku*, meaning "nine," and *ran*, meaning "orchid": "nine orchids."

# 藍堂英

**Aido Hanabusa**

*Hanabusa* means "petals of a flower." *Aido* means "indigo temple." In Japanese, the pronunciation of *Aido* is very close to the pronunciation of the English word *idol*.

# 架院暁

**Kain Akatsuki**

*Akatsuki* means "dawn" or "day-break." In *Kain*, *ka* is a base or support, while *in* denotes a building that has high fences around it, such as a temple or school.

# 早園瑠佳

**Souen Ruka**

In *Ruka*, the *ru* means "lapis lazuli" while the *ka* means "good-looking" or "beautiful." The *sou* in Ruka's surname, *Souen*, means "early," but this kanji also has an obscure meaning of "strong fragrance." The *en* means "garden."

# 一条拓麻

**Ichijo Takuma**

*Ichijo* can mean a "ray" or "streak." The kanji for *Takuma* is a combination of *taku*, meaning "to cultivate," and *ma*, which is the kanji for *asa*, meaning "hemp" or "flax," a plant with blue flowers.

# 支葵千里

**Shiki Senri**

Shiki's last name is a combination of *shi*, meaning "to support" and *ki*, meaning "mallow"—a flowering plant with pink or white blossoms. The *ri* in *Senri* is a traditional Japanese unit of measure for distance, and one *ri* is about 2.44 miles. *Senri* means "1,000 *ri*."

# 夜刈十牙

**Yagari Toga**

*Yagari* is a combination of *ya*, meaning "night," and *gari*, meaning "to harvest." *Toga* means "ten fangs."

# 一条麻遠, 一翁

**Ichijo Asato, a.k.a. "Ichio"**

*Ichijo* can mean a "ray" or "streak." Asato's first name is comprised of *asa*, meaning "hemp" or "flax," and *tou*, meaning "far-off." His nickname is *ichi*, or "one," combined with *ou*, which can be used as an honorific when referring to an older man.

# 若葉沙頼

**Wakaba Sayori**

Yori's full name is Sayori Wakaba. *Wakaba* means "young leaves." Her given name, *Sayori*, is a combination of *sa*, meaning "sand," and *yori*, meaning "trust."

# 星煉

**Seiren**

*Sei* means "star" and *ren* means
"to smelt" or "to refine." *Ren* is also
the same kanji used in *rengoku*, or
"purgatory." Her previous name,
*Hoshino*, uses the same kanji for
"star" (*hoshi*) and *no*, which can mean
"from" and is often used at the end of
traditional female names.

# 遠矢莉磨

**Toya Rima**

*Toya* means a "far-reaching arrow."
Rima's first name is a combination
of *ri*, or "jasmine," and *ma*, which
signifies enhancement by wearing
away, such as by polishing
or scouring.

# 紅まり亜

**Kurenai Maria**

*Kurenai* means "crimson." The kanji
for the last *a* in Maria's first name is
the same that is used in "Asia."

# 錐生壱縷

**Kiryu Ichiru**

*Ichi* is the old-fashioned way of writing "one" and *ru* means "thread." In *Kiryu*, the *ki* means "auger" or "drill" and the *ryu* means "life."

# 緋桜閑, 狂咲姫

**Hio Shizuka, Kuruizaki-hime**

*Shizuka* means "calm and quiet." In Shizuka's family name, *hi* is "scarlet" and *ou* is "cherry blossoms." Shizuka Hio is also referred to as the "Kuruizaki-hime." *Kuruizaki* means "flowers blooming out of season" and *hime* means "princess."

# 藍堂月子

**Aido Tsukiko**

*Aido* means "indigo temple." *Tsukiko* means "moon child."

# 白蕗更

**Shirabuki Sara**

*Shira* is "white" and *buki* is "butterbur," a plant with white flowers. *Sara* means "to renew."

# 黒主灰闇

**Cross Kaien**

Cross, or *Kurosu*, means "black master." *Kaien* is a combination of *kai*, meaning "ashes," and *en*, meaning "village gate." The kanji for *en* is also used for Enma, the ruler of the underworld in Buddhist mythology.

# 玖蘭李土

**Kuran Rido**

*Kuran* means "nine orchids." In *Rido*, *ri* means "plum" and *do* means "earth."

# 玖蘭樹里

**Kuran Juri**

*Kuran* means "nine orchids." In her first name, *ju* means "tree" and a *ri* is a traditional Japanese unit of measure for distance. The kanji for *ri* is the same as in Senri's name.

# 玖蘭悠

**Kuran Haruka**

*Kuran* means "nine orchids." *Haruka* means "distant" or "remote."

# 鷹宮海斗

**Takamiya Kaito**

*Taka* means "hawk" and *miya* means "imperial palace" or "shrine." *Kai* is "sea" and *to* means "to measure" or "grid."

# 菖藤依砂也

**Shoto Isaya**

*Sho* means "Siberian iris" and *to* is "wisteria." The *I* in *Isaya* means "to rely on" while the *sa* means "sand." *Ya* is a suffix used for emphasis.

# 橙茉

**Toma**

In the family name *Toma*, *to* means "Seville orange" and *ma* means "jasmine flower."

# 藍堂永路

**Aido Nagamichi**

The name *Nagamichi* is a combination of *naga*, which means "long" or "eternal," and *michi*, which is the kanji for "road" or "path." *Aido* means "indigo temple."

# 縹木

**Hanadagi**

In this family name, *hanada* means "bright light blue" and *gi* means "tree."

# 影山霞

**Kageyama Kasumi**

In the Class Rep's family name, *kage* means "shadow" and *yama* means "mountain." His first name, *Kasumi*, means "haze" or "mist."

# 愛

**Ai**

*Ai* means "love." It is used in terms of unconditional, unending love and affection.

恋

**Ren**

*Ren* means "love." It is used in terms
of a romantic love or crush.

## Terms

**-sama**: The suffix *-sama* is used in formal address
for someone who ranks higher in the social hierarchy.
The vampires call their leader "Kaname-sama"
only when they are among their own kind.

**Renai:** The combination of Ren's and Ai's
names (恋愛) means "romantic love."

# Shuriken
## *and* Pleats

When the master she has sworn to protect is killed, Mikage Kirio, a skilled ninja, travels to Japan to start a new, peaceful life for herself. But as soon as she arrives, she finds herself fighting to protect the life of Mahito Wakashimatsu, a man who is under attack by a band of ninja. From that time on, Mikage is drawn deeper into the machinations of his powerful family.

**Shojo Beat**  **viz media**  RATED TEEN
www.viz.com  ratings.viz.com

Kyoko Mogami followed her true love Sho to Tokyo to support him while he made it big as an idol. But he's casting her out now that he's famous enough! Kyoko won't suffer in silence— she's going to get her sweet revenge by beating Sho in show biz!

Vol. 1 ISBN: 978-1-4215-4226-3

Vol. 2 ISBN: 978-1-4215-4227-0

Vol. 3 ISBN: 978-1-4215-4228-7

Show biz is sweet...but revenge is sweeter!

# Skip·Beat!

Story and Art by YOSHIKI NAKAMURA

In Stores Now!

Only **$14.99** for each volume! ($16.99 in Canada)

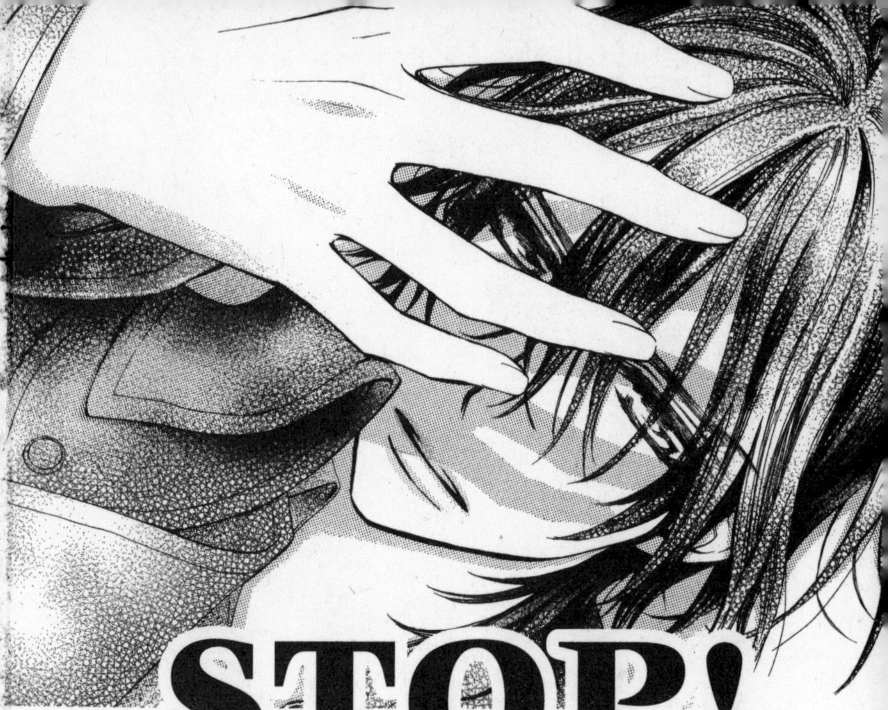

# STOP!

## You may be reading the wrong way!

In keeping with the original Japanese comic format, this book reads from right to left—so word balloons, action and sound effects and are reversed to preserve the orientation of the original artwork.

Check out the diagram shown here to get the hang of things, and then turn to the other side of the book to get started!

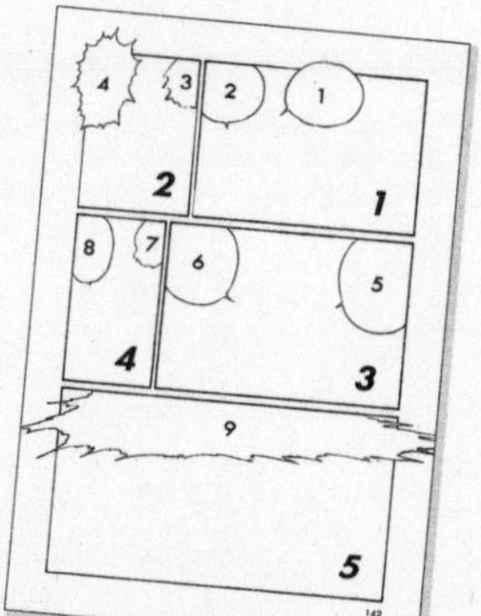